Dispensational Soteriology

James D. Quiggle

BOOKS BY JAMES D. QUIGGLE

DOCTRINAL SERIES

Biblical History
Adam and Eve, a Biography and Theology
Angelology, a True History of Angels

Essays
Biblical Essays
Biblical Essays II
Biblical Essays III
Biblical Essays IV

Marriage and Family
Marriage and Family: A Biblical Perspective
Biblical Homosexuality
A Biblical Response to Same-gender Marriage

Doctrinal and Practical Christianity
First Steps, Becoming a Follower of Jesus Christ
A Christian Catechism (with Christopher McCuin)
Why and How to do Bible Study
Thirty-Six Essentials of the Christian Faith
The Literal Hermeneutic, Explained and Illustrated
The Old Ten In the New Covenant
Christian Living and Doctrine
Spiritual Gifts
Why Christians Should Not Tithe

Dispensational Theology
A Primer On Dispensationalism
Understanding Dispensational Theology
Dispensational Soteriology
Dispensational Eschatology, An Explanation and Defense of the Doctrine
Covenants and Dispensations in the Scripture
Rapture: A Bible Study on the Rapture of the New Testament Church
Antichrist, His Genealogy, Kingdom, and Religion

God and Man
God's Choices, Doctrines of Foreordination, Election, Predestination
God Became Incarnate
Life, Death, Eternity
Did Jesus Go To Hell?

Against Physicalism, Annihilationism, and Conditionalism

Small Group Bible Studies
Elementary Bible Principles (with Linda M. Quiggle)
Counted Worthy (with Linda M. Quiggle)

COMMENTARY SERIES

The Old Testament
A Private Commentary on the Bible: Judges
A Private Commentary on the Book of Ruth
A Private Commentary on the Bible: Esther
A Private Commentary on the Bible: Song of Solomon
A Private Commentary on the Bible: Daniel
A Private Commentary on the Bible: Jonah
A Private Commentary on the Bible: Habakkuk
A Private Commentary on the Bible: Haggai

The New Testament

James Quiggle Translation (JQT) New Testament

The Gospels and Acts
A Private Commentary on the Bible: Matthew's Gospel
A Private Commentary on the Bible: Mark's Gospel
A Private Commentary on the Bible: Luke 1–12
A Private Commentary on the Bible: Luke 13–24
A Private Commentary on the Bible: John 1–12
A Private Commentary on the Bible: John 13–21
A Private Commentary on the Bible: Acts 1–14
A Private Commentary on the Bible: Acts 15–28
Four Voices, One Testimony (a Gospel harmony)
Jesus Said "I Am"
The Parables and Miracles of Jesus Christ
The Passion and Resurrection of Jesus the Christ
The Christmas Story, As Told By God
Christmas Card Theology and the Bible

Pauline Letters
A Private Commentary on the Bible: Galatians
A Private Commentary on the Bible: Ephesians

A Private Commentary on the Bible: Philippians
A Private Commentary on the Bible: Colossians
A Private Commentary on the Bible: Thessalonians
A Private Commentary on the Bible: Pastoral Letters
A Private Commentary on the Bible: Philemon

General Letters
A Private Commentary on the Book of Hebrews
A Private Commentary on the Bible: James
A Private Commentary on the Bible: 1 Peter
A Private Commentary on the Bible: 2 Peter
A Private Commentary on the Bible: John's Epistles
A Private Commentary on the Bible: Jude

Revelation
A Private Commentary on the Bible: Revelation 1–7
A Private Commentary on the Bible: Revelation 8–16
A Private Commentary on the Bible: Revelation 17–22

REFERENCE SERIES
James Quiggle Translation (JQT) New Testament
Dictionary of Doctrinal Words
Old and New Testament Chronology (With David Hollingsworth)
(Also in individual volumes: Old Testament Chronology; New Testament Chronology)

TRACTS
A Human Person: Is the Unborn Life a Person?
Biblical Marriage
How Can I Know I am A Christian?
Now That I am A Christian
Thirty-Six Essentials of the Christian Faith
What is a Pastor? / Why is My Pastor Eating the Sheep?
Principles and Precepts of the Literal Hermeneutic
(All tracts are in digital format and cost $0.99)

Formats
Print, Digital, Epub, PDF. Search "James D. Quiggle" or book title.

Dedication

Keith A. Sherlin
Friend, Dispensationalist, Theologian.
He began the conversation
that became this book.
We work toward the Kingdom together.

Table of Contents

Preface

How should we interpret the Scripture? Should we seek the plain and normal meaning of the language and words used by the biblical writers, also known as authorial intent? Or should we seek another meaning not present in the plain and normal meaning? Do we follow the rule a scripture text cannot mean what it never meant? Or do we create a meaning to make the Scripture mean what we want it to mean?

How did you interpret what I wrote above? How are you understanding what I am writing now? Are you investing my words with their plain and normal meaning according to the rules of English concerning vocabulary and syntax? Or did you just somehow decide what you think I should say?

Without much fear of contradiction I will say you are discovering my meaning, my "authorial intent," by seeking the plain and normal meaning of the language (American English) words (vocabulary, semantic range) and sentences (syntax) I have written. You are not seeking another meaning, you are not trying to make what I say to mean what it never meant. That is known as the Literal method of interpretation (the Literal hermeneutic).

Why then do some turn to the Bible and turn away from the method of interpretation and understanding used for every other form of written communication? The Bible was written by persons just like you and me. What they wrote was superintended by God (inspiration) so that what they wrote was what God wanted written. God used their own historical-cultural circumstances, their own education, their own language, their own vocabulary, their own understanding, and their own individual style of writing to create his communication to you and me. The Bible is a book written by God through humans and intended by God for humans to understand in the words written by their fellow human beings as superintended by God. No more, no less.

The way we read and interpret and understand written communication is at the heart of this book. Do we somehow decide what we think the author should say? Or should we understand the Bible the same way we understand every other form of written communication: apply the principles and rules of the Literal hermeneutic, in order to discover what the human author meant when

13

he wrote—when he used those words in that way according to his own particular historical-cultural circumstances? If we use the Literal hermeneutic, we will discover what the human author meant, which was exactly what the divine author, God the Holy Spirit, wanted written.

The question this book asks and answers is this.

> When the Holy Spirit helped the Old Testament peoples to understand what the Scripture meant, did he explain the plain and normal meaning of what was written, or did he give them unwritten revelation or illumination that changed the meaning of what was written?

In plainer words, did the Holy Spirit give the Old Testament people a New Testament understanding of their Old Testament Scripture? Some say yes. The person using the Literal hermeneutic always says no, because all any person in Old Testament times could know from Scripture is what was in the Scripture they had received prior to their time or during their time.

The subject this book will examine to answer those questions is the doctrine of soteriology, i.e., the biblical doctrine of salvation. The subject to be discussed is not the essential doctrine of salvation. That essential doctrine is "saved by God's grace through the sinner's faith without personal merit from the sinner but by Christ's merit alone." That is not an issue to be debated but a truth to be believed. The subject of this book is a second order doctrine: the means by which the Old Testament sinner knew how to be saved.

> Was an understanding of how to be saved communicated by the Holy Spirit giving to the sinner something in addition to the written Scriptures?

Or

> Was an understanding of how to be saved communicated by the Holy Spirit through the plain and normal meaning of the written Scriptures the sinner was given?

The first is the doctrine of Reformed soteriology and Dispensational Promise soteriology. The second is what I seek to prove from the Scripture as the genuine Dispensational soteriology.

Come and study the Scripture with me.

Introduction

This book is a Bible study, the kind of Bible study you might do sitting at your desk in your Bible study room. I have written this book, as with all my books, for the believer who is willing to study and consider the biblical evidence. Whether you agree or not, consider the arguments I present, and turn to the Scripture to work it out for yourself.

My Bible beliefs considered as a whole fall under the label Dispensational Calvinist. I subscribe to every historic orthodox doctrine of the Reformed faith, except where the Reformed faith has abandoned the Literal hermeneutic. From the earliest days of the New Testament church, the most significant characteristic of dispensationalism has been the literal hermeneutic. Not "all literalists in [the Nicene era] were 'dispensationalists' in exactly the way Dispensationalism is understood today, but all dispensational thinkers of the Nicene era were literalists" [Marsh, *Discovering*, 89, article by Mutie].

All dispensational beliefs, in every aspect of biblical doctrine, are the result of using the Literal hermeneutic to understand Scripture. So also the Reformed theology beginning in the 1500s, except for Reformed eschatology and ecclesiology. Unlike many Dispensationalists, I believe the Reformed faith has set aside some of the principles of the Literal hermeneutic in the doctrine of soteriology. This book explores that proposition.

(For eschatological and ecclesiological differences between Reformed and Dispensational, see my book, *Dispensational Eschatology, An Explanation and Defense of the Doctrine*. Because orthodoxy is critical to a discussion of differences, I have also included in an appendix my personal doctrinal statement.)

As I said, my theology might be labelled Dispensational Calvinist. Labels are incomplete without a list of ingredients. This book explores one of those ingredients, the doctrine of soteriology, and specifically one ingredient in soteriology, the content of Old Testament saving faith. If, as I propose, saving faith is always faith in God and God's revealed means or way of salvation, what was the way or means of salvation God revealed to the Old Testament sinner in the Old Testament revelation?

Put another way, in the historic progressive revelation of truth, did God use the Scripture as he had communicated it, progressively, a little here a little there, during the long history of redemption? Or did God give "something" in addition to that written Scripture, to give understanding of things he later, but had not yet, would reveal in written Scripture?

The historic progressive revelation of truth, also known as the doctrine of progressive revelation, is the simple observation God does not reveal all things at the same time, but over time God's revelation is completed. The completed revelation is both the Old Testament and New Testament, Genesis 1:1, through Revelation 22:21. From that point of view, the Old Testament revelation was not the completed revelation.

Did the Old Testament peoples understand the not-yet-completed revelation the Holy Spirit had given to them? Yes. Within each person's particular historical-cultural context it was to him or her a complete revelation. Therefore, the primary meaning of any Old Testament passage is found in that passage, or through written revelation given before that passage had been given.

The Holy Spirit gave the Old Testament peoples the necessary spiritual perception and illumination to understand what he had revealed to them in the written Scripture they had received from him prior to or during their particular historical-cultural circumstances.

Excursus: Extrabiblical Revelation

Did God save sinners through the written testimony of the Old Testament revelation they had received prior to or during their particular historical-cultural context? Or did God supplement that incomplete written revelation with extrabiblical revelation or illumination in order to save Old Testament sinners? Both Reformed and Promise soteriology say the Old Testament written revelation was supplemented with extrabiblical revelation in order to save sinners.

We should understand what "extrabiblical revelation" means in the context of the Old Testament revelation. Reformed and Dispensational Promise soteriology say Holy Spirit gave the Old Testament peoples a New Testament understanding of salvation. What Reformed and Dispensational Promise soteriology propose is extrabiblical, because the New Testament revelation was not yet given through the New Testament writers. Scripture is what the Holy Spirit had the Old Testament and New Testament writers write.

16

If it isn't written in the Scripture, it is extrabiblical. If it was not yet written, then to claim knowledge of it is extrabiblical.

Returning to the discussion

Concerning soteriology, the essential of the faith is the salvation principle found in Ephesians 2:8–9.

> Saved by God's grace through the sinner's faith without personal merit from the sinner but by Christ's merit alone.

That is the one and only way of salvation from the first word of Genesis 1:1 to the last word of Revelation 22:21.

The Reformation in the 16th century changed that essential doctrine, ever so slightly: "saved by grace alone, through faith alone, *in* Christ alone." That slight change from Ephesians 2:8–9 works well for the New Testament sinner, who has received the Good News of salvation by faith in the risen Jesus Christ alone. But the Old Testament sinner did not know Jesus Christ crucified and resurrected; unless you have a Reformed or Promise soteriology view of the Good News, which assumes the Old Testament sinner was given knowledge of a coming redeemer-messiah-christ that was not part of the written revelation the Holy Spirit delivered to the Old Testament peoples.

How the Good News of redemption from the penalty of sin was communicated through the Old Testament revelation to the Old Testament sinner is the subject of this book; although it would be more accurate to say this book discusses how the way of salvation was and was not communicated.

A genuine statement of soteriology that includes both Old Testament and New Testament revelation is this: "saved by grace alone through faith alone *by* Christ alone." Or as Ryrie stated, "The basis of salvation in every age is the death [propitiation] made by Christ" [Ryrie, *Dispensationalism*, 115]. The efficacy of the propitiation made by Christ is the one and only way to be saved. The way to access the merit of Christ's propitiation—through the content of faith as delivered in the progressive revelation of truth—changes, as Ryrie also said, "the content of faith changes in the various dispensations."

Excursus: In Christ

Dispensationalists are sometimes accused of saying the Old Testament saved were not in Christ—another way of accusing Dispensationalism of teaching more than one way of salvation. The term *én christós* occurs eighty-seven times in the New Testament. A corresponding Old Testament term might be *māshîah* (anointed) [thirty-seven times in the Old Testament beginning in Leviticus], and although in a few scriptures *māshîah* refers to saved Old Testament sinners in national ethnic Israel, e.g., Habakkuk, 3:13, there is no Hebrew term corresponding to *én christós* for all the Old Testament saved in every people group.

In Old Testament times the Holy Spirit came upon the saved but did not permanently indwell them. The New Testament saved are *én christós* because they are the first saved people group permanently indwelt by the Holy Spirit. [Jeremiah 31:31–33 seems to indicate the Spirit's permanent indwelling of the saved during the Davidic-Messianic Kingdom, when that covenant is in effect after the second advent.]

The term *én christós* indicates that through the Spirit's indwelling the New Testament church is uniquely and permanently joined to Christ as the body of Christ. But all saved in any people group from Genesis through Revelation are in Christ because saved "through faith alone *by* Christ alone," i.e., by the limitless merit of Christ's propitiation as the one and only basis for salvation. Colossians 1:20 is relevant here, "and [God, 1:19] through Christ to reconcile all things to him."

Returning to the discussion.

What the Old Testament sinner understood from God's historic progressive revelation of truth concerning redemption from the penalty due sin, and how that understanding was gained, are matters discussed in this book.

A clear and biblical understanding of salvation has been the goal of the New Testament church for almost two millennia. The principle of salvation is plain and simple: saved by God's grace through the sinner's faith without personal merit from the sinner but by Christ's merit alone, Ephesians 2:8–9. To this principle all biblical theological systems agree.

The differences between theological systems is in the details.

How is God's gift of grace-faith-salvation (Ephesians 2:8) applied? (aka: prevenient grace.)

How is a sinner is brought to saving knowledge of redemption?

How are sinners saved (the basis of salvation)

Who does one believe on in order to be saved (the object of saving faith)?

What does one believe in order to be saved (the content of

saving faith)?

The beliefs of the several theological systems concerning the application of the salvation principle may be divided into two broad groups: synergism and monergism.

Synergism: God is the origin and source of salvation, both God and the sinner make significant contributions to the sinner's salvation.

Monergism: God is the origin and source of salvation, the salvation of a sinner is exclusively the work of God.

Synergism's motto might be expressed as "Your contribution to your salvation is your faith plus something (neutral free will or good works). Monergism's motto is well known, "You contribute nothing to your salvation except the sin that made it necessary."

How synergism and monergism work out to effect the salvation of a sinner has resulted in five views. It must be stressed that each of these five views proclaims they believe in "saved by grace through faith." Each believes the application of God's grace is necessary to begin the processes (prevenient grace, testimony of Scripture, conviction of sin, exercise of saving faith) leading to the salvation of the sinner.

The two synergistic views are Roman Catholic soteriology and Arminian soteriology.

Roman Catholic soteriology. The Council of Trent, AD 1563, facing the Protestant rebellion, defined salvation as a mix of God's grace and man's works. Council of Trent, Session 6, Canon 1, Canon 9 [Source: Schaff, *Creeds*, 2:110, 112].

The Roman Catholic Church will stress that salvation is by grace alone, but they also stress the grace that saves is only effective for salvation through good works. Roman Catholic Church soteriology has an intrinsic contradiction: grace alone saves, but grace saves by making the sinner's works effective to save. "Hence, when a Roman Catholic thinks of being saved by grace, he is thinking of God giving him the ability to do things necessary for salvation, i.e., attend sacraments, do good works, keep from serious sin." [Source: Reverend Bill Jackson, *The Christian's Guide to Roman Catholicism*, unpublished manuscript, 1978.] Because the soteriology of the Roman Catholic Church violates the biblical principle, "not from works so that no one should boast,"

Ephesians 2:9, this book will not discuss Roman Catholic soteriology.

Why is Arminian soteriology synergism?

> Arminian soteriology. God gives his prevenient grace to every sinner, thereby removing the dominance of the sin attribute, allowing the sinner to freely choose to be saved, or choose not to be saved (a neutral free will), upon hearing the proclamation of the Good News of salvation by faith in the risen Jesus Christ.

Arminian soteriology is universal ability to believe or not believe, through God's prevenient grace. Although Arminian soteriology is synergism, in that it makes a neutral human free will the determining factor in salvation, it does hold to the "saved by grace not works" principle, and the necessity of prevenient grace. This book will discuss Arminian soteriology and whether Arminianism as a theology is heretical.

Also discussed in this book is the error of a neutral free will. The human will always functions within boundaries, as influenced by internal and external motivations and consequences, freely making choices within those boundaries, motivations, and consequences. See chapter, "What is Free Will?"

There are three monergism views: Reformed, Promise, Dispensational.

> Reformed soteriology says, "saved by grace alone through faith alone *in* Christ alone."

In Reformed soteriology the sinner's understanding of redemption depends on revelation and illumination given by the Holy Spirit that saving faith is in Christ, whether Old Testament times (Christ coming) or New Testament times (Christ arrived). Thus, Reformed Old Testament soteriology depends on the extrabiblical revelation of a New Testament revelation not yet given as Scripture. Scripture is what is written, the New Testament was not yet written in Old Testament times.

In Reformed soteriology Christ is both the object and the content of saving faith in both the Old Testament and the New Testament.

Reformed soteriology believes the Holy Spirit gave the Old Testament sinner extrabiblical (not in the Bible) revelation or illumination not contained in the written Old Testament scriptures. The extrabiblical revelation (or illumination) began in Genesis 3:15, and then more was slowly added by the Holy Spirit as the Holy Spirit delivered the written Old Testament revelation "here a little, there a little" in historical progressive revelation of truth. The outcome of this extrabiblical revelation/illumination theology is Reformed soteriology says the object and content of Old Testament saving faith is in a coming redeemer-messiah-christ, or faith in the specific person Jesus Christ (Reformed opinions vary on the content of this extrabiblical revelation or illumination).

Any doctrine built on extrabiblical revelation or illumination is false doctrine, even if it contains truth. Every cult depends on extrabiblical revelation or illumination. That is why it is so dangerous to truth. Reformed extrabiblical revelation or illumination is the truth of the New Testament revelation delivered to the Old Testament peoples before it was delivered in the written Scripture to the New Testament peoples.

In simpler terms, Reformed soteriology makes the Old Testament scripture mean what it does not say. That out-of-its-historical-context delivery is what makes it extrabiblical: the New Testament revelation is not in the Old Testament written scripture.

There is a relatively new Dispensational soteriology known as Promise soteriology.

Promise soteriology believes the Holy Spirit gave the Old Testament sinner extrabiblical revelation or illumination beginning with Genesis 3:15 ("promised seed"), and then as delivered "here a little, there a little" in the historic progressive revelation of truth, to the extent Promise soteriology says the object and content of Old Testament saving faith is in the continuing development of the promise of a coming Redeemer, as progressively understood from Genesis 3:15 to the end of Old Testament times.

> Promise soteriology is faith in a saviour [*sic*] promised by God. The revelation increased as time went on, and the requirement for salvation was faith in this deliverer as He was revealed at any given time. So, they could have faith in a "seed" that was promised, faith in a Messiah, faith in Yeshua [Jesus], and yet not believe in Jesus specifically, for Jesus had not yet been revealed. [James Meyers, quoted in Miles, *Current Issues in Soteriology*, 110.]

21

Many Dispensationalists subscribe to either the Reformed view or the Promise view. Those Dispensationalists claiming either view as "dispensational" or a "form of dispensationalism," must submit their claims to the Scripture for validation.

My view of Dispensational soteriology is summed in this statement.

> In every dispensation, in every age of humankind, in the entire history of redemption, a sinner is always saved by God's grace and the merit of Christ's propitiation, through the sinner's faith in God and God's historically current testimony as to the means of salvation, as given by the Holy Spirit in the written progressive revelation of truth. [Quiggle, *Dictionary.*]

My view must also be submitted to the Scripture for validation. All three monergism views will be examined in this book by seeking the plain and normal meaning of the scriptures.

Seeking the plain and normal meaning of the Scripture is another way of saying a person is using the grammatical-historical or Literal, hermeneutic, which always seeks the biblical author's intent through the plain and normal meaning of the biblical author's written text.

My view supposes there was no extrabiblical revelation or illumination from the Holy Spirit given to the Old Testament sinner to understand a coming Christ, or understand a promise of a coming redeemer, within the historic progressive revelation of truth, as found in the Old Testament Scripture, but only the Holy Spirit's normal illumination of the plain and normal meaning of the Scripture.

That statement of my view is complex, and it needs to be complex because the issue is complex. But I can restate it in a simpler form: "the Holy Spirit did not say in the Old Testament revelation what he had chosen to later say in the New Testament revelation." Nor did the Holy Spirit give the Old Testament sinner supplementary information to make a scripture, any scripture, mean what it does not say.

Therefore the Old Testament sinner did not and could not understand for salvation what the New Testament sinner can and does understand for salvation. More plainly, the method of salvation was the same (saved by God's grace through the sinner's faith without personal merit from the sinner but by Christ's merit alone), but the content of saving faith, the knowledge of "how to be saved," changed as the progressive revelation of truth accumulated.

Excursus: Authorial Intent

The Ethiopian eunuch, Acts 8:27, knew what Isaiah knew, because he was reading the prophet Isaiah, *but* he did not understand Isaiah 53 spoke about a coming redeemer from sin, Acts 8:30–34, until someone who did know, Philip, revealed it to him, Acts 8:35. Philip knew because the key to understanding Isaiah 53 had come, and lived, and spoken, and died, and resurrected. Philip knew because God had given Philip more information than he had given to the Old Testament people. Jesus the Christ incarnate, living, crucified, dead, resurrected, and ascended was the additional information.

We can explain an Old Testament passage in the light given by later revelation (as Philip did with the Ethiopian eunuch), but that explanation may not be allowed to change the within context interpretation of an Old Testament passage. As superintended by the Holy Spirit (inspiration), the New Testament writers applied the Old Testament revelation to create (parts of) the New Testament revelation. An application does not change the interpretation.

What we know now cannot be used to give the Old Testament people more knowledge than was communicated by the revelation given before or during their particular historical time. The Old Testament revelation had meaning for the Old Testament peoples within their particular Old Testament historical-cultural context.

In other words, Isaiah also did not know his chapter 53 spoke of Jesus Christ the Redeemer from sin. "A scripture cannot mean what it never said." Isaiah 53 never speaks about the messiah: the Hebrew word is not in the passage. Isaiah could not know what Philip knew. The Holy Spirit knew, but he did not reveal to Isaiah what he revealed to Philip, the Ethiopian, and Luke as he wrote the event in the Book of Acts.

The Holy Spirit's authorial intent in the revelation given to Isaiah was the same as Isaiah's authorial intent as he wrote that revelation under the superintendence of the Holy Spirit. The Holy Spirit's authorial intent in the revelation given to Philip and the Ethiopian was the same Philip's intent when he spoke the revelation, and Luke's authorial intent when he wrote that revelation under the superintendence of the Holy Spirit. The Old Testament revelation has a meaning independent of the New Testament revelation, and the application of the Old Testament revelation to create the New Testament revelation did not change that Old Testament meaning.

Summarizing: what Adam believed was not the same as what Abraham believed; what Abraham believed was not the same as what Moses believed. Each had been given more revelation than had been previously given. The progressive nature of revelation added to and built upon the previous revelation, such that the content of saving faith for each within his own historical-cultural context, was not the same as previous. The New Testament believer instinctively understands this concept: no New Testament believer brings a lamb to church to be sacrificed on the pulpit platform as atonement for his or her sins. Instead of following Leviticus, he follows 1 John 1:9 because of 1 John 2:2.

Returning to the discussion.

The intrinsic limitations of the progressive nature of revelation in Old Testament times means that no matter the content of that revelation at any particular time, or the spiritual perception given by the Holy Spirit to understand that revelation at any particular time, that Old Testament revelation was not and could not be the same as the New Testament revelation, either as a whole, or in bits and pieces here and there. The Holy Spirit did not give the Old Testament peoples extrabiblical revelation or illumination to change the plain and normal meaning of the written Old Testament text.

My proposition is this, the revelation and illumination each Old Testament sinner received from the Holy Spirit in the written Old Testament Scripture was sufficient for salvation within their own particular historical circumstances, without extrabiblical revelation or illumination of New Testament truths from the Holy Spirit.

What was the written revelation prior to Moses? The revelation received from God prior to the beginning of the written text, which was written beginning ca. 1445 BC, is documented in the written text, beginning with Genesis 1:1. We know what God said because God had Moses write what God said. We know what others said because God had Moses write what others said. We may use our imaginations and create unwritten revelation prior to Moses, or we can accept God had Moses write it under inspiration. Because written by Moses under the superintendence of the Holy Spirit, what is in the Book of Genesis is the inspired, inerrant written Scripture record of what was said and what was done, and anything else one might imagine during the time from Adam to Moses is not Scripture.

What was the written revelation prior to the New Testament being written? There was the Old Testament written Scripture, Genesis through Malachi. Then there was the verbal revelation given by Jesus Christ of himself during his earthly ministry, which is exactly the same as was later written by Matthew, Mark, Luke, and John. What Jesus said became the inspired, inerrant written New Testament Scripture under the superintendence of the Holy Spirit, which is why we know how 120 persons were redeemed, Acts 1:15. Because written by Matthew, Mark, Luke, and John under the superintendence of the Holy Spirit, what Jesus and others said prior to it being written is inspirated written Scripture.

An end date or event for the effectiveness of the Old Testament revelation to redeem must be selected. Several dates or events are available. Jesus' first public message, AD 30, was the prophesied Davidic-Messianic Kingdom and himself as its King, in agreement with 2 Samuel 7:13–16; Psalm 2. Then late in his public ministry, AD 32, Jesus began training his apostles for their coming ministry proclaiming the message of reconciliation (2 Corinthians 5:18–20), after his death and resurrection, culminating in their salvation and the indwelling of the Holy Spirit after his resurrection, John 20:22. They had previously believed Jesus was the Messiah-King. After his resurrection, they were brought to the faith Jesus is the Messiah-Redeemer, through his testimony and the illumination give to them at that time by the Holy Spirit.

What about others, those who did not follow Jesus as disciples through the crucifixion-resurrection event? The historical setting of the gospels is Old Testament times, and they are transitional Old Testament historical narratives bridging the gap from the Old to the New. As such, they reveal the limitations of the Old Testament revelation, in that most during those times in Israel lacked the understanding to accept Jesus of Nazareth as either Messiah-King or Messiah-Redeemer, despite his revelation to them that he was both. In this regard, what Jesus said concerning himself is of less importance than what those hearing believed.

Therefore the end date or event for the effectiveness of the Old Testament revelation is the AD 33 resurrection, and forty days after for some, and the AD 33 Day of Pentecost/Acts 2 event for all others.

Returning now to the question, what was the content of Old Testament faith for salvation?

Looking ahead to later chapters, the choices are:

1. Should we change the authorial intent of the Old Testament writers (and the Holy Spirit) by reading the New Testament

revelation into the Old Testament revelation, thereby giving the Old Testament sinner understanding he could not gain from the plain and normal meaning of the Scripture revelation he had received within his own historical-cultural circumstances?

Or.

2. Should we suppose the Old Testament sinner was saved the same way as the New Testament sinner: from the plain and normal meaning of the written Scripture revelation each group (Old and New Testament) of sinners was given within their own particular historical-cultural circumstances?

Choice one assumes the Holy Spirit gave the Old Testament sinner unwritten revelation or illumination and thus it was extrabiblical (not in the written scripture) revelation at the time it was given.

Contrary to choice one, the Holy Spirit works only through his written revelation, and he never exceeds the plain and normal meaning of the language he had the writers use and the words he had the writers write. Giving Old Testament peoples New Testament understanding before the New Testament was written makes that understanding extrabiblical. Therefore the Reformed and Promise soteriology that the Old Testament people saw a coming redeemer-messiah-christ in Genesis 3:15 is false doctrine. There is no mention of a coming redeemer-messiah-christ in Genesis 3:15 using the plain and normal meaning—the Literal hermeneutic—of the words within their particular historical-grammatical context.

Choice two assumes the Holy Spirit gave the Old Testament sinner illumination of the plain and normal meaning of the written revelation he had previously given in writing to each generation during the history of redemption.

Which choice is the correct choice depends on how one understands and applies the Literal hermeneutic. My choice is number two. Here is why.

The use of the Literal hermeneutic in interpreting the Old Testament revelation may be summed in three principles of interpretation everyone agrees with, but not everyone consistently applies. These three principles reflect the fact of the progressive revelation of truth.

Hermeneutic principle one.

1. Analogy of Scripture. This principle asks, "How does a passage fit into the total pattern of God's revelation that was revealed prior to its writing?"

More simply, the Old Testament people could only know what was revealed to them in the revelation delivered before or during their particular historical time.

Hermeneutic principle two.

2. Analogy of Faith. This principle asks, "How does a passage fit into the total pattern of God's revelation that has been revealed at any time?"

This principle means those receiving later revelation can understand previous revelation in the light given by that later revelation. If there was later revelation saying there was a coming redeemer-messiah-christ in Genesis 3:15, then we could understand that verse in that way—but we could not have the Old Testament people understand it in that way. However, there is no such revelation. There are only three scriptures that make reference to Genesis 3:15. Those scriptures are Genesis 4:25; Romans 16:20; Revelation 12:9.

Any understanding made possible by later revelation may not be allowed to change the within context interpretation of an Old Testament passage in earlier revelation. What we know now cannot be used to give the Old Testament people more knowledge than was communicated by the revelation given before or during their particular historical time.

Hermeneutic principle three.

3. "The primary meaning of any Bible passage is found in that passage. The New Testament does not reinterpret or transcend Old Testament passages in a way that overrides or cancels the original authorial intent of the Old Testament writers" [Vlach, *Dispensationalism*, 31].

What I am calling the Vlach principle, means don't read the New Testament revelation into the Old Testament revelation and then reinterpret what the Old Testament people understood by using the New Testament revelation. Don't make a scripture say what it never said.

The Analogy of Scripture and the Analogy of Faith predates the Reformation, having been adopted by the Reformers, and handed down to their spiritual descendants. Vlach's principle is a reasonable application of the Analogy of Scripture and Analogy of Faith

These three common sense principles of interpretation are part of the grammatical-historical, i.e., Literal hermeneutic (method of interpreting the Bible). If you use the Literal hermeneutic, then those three principles must be applied to the interpretation of every passage, Old Testament and New Testament.

The primary purpose of this book is to demonstrate Scripture validates as the genuine Dispensational soteriology the view I defined above as my view, through consistent use of the principles and rules of the Literal hermeneutic. The book will examine each view (excluding the works-based Roman Catholic Church view) for consistency with the Literal hermeneutic, which is the hermeneutic claimed by Reformed, Dispensational, and Arminian theological systems, though practiced and applied differently by each.

A secondary purpose of this book is to deny and defeat the commonly held misperception that Dispensationalists and Dispensational theology teaches more than one way of salvation. To oppose that misperception, I have written several chapters on important ingredients of biblical soteriology held by both Reformed and Dispensational theologies. There is simply no excuse to libel Dispensationalism and Dispensationalists by claiming they teach different ways of salvation. I have already expressed the most critical element: saved by God's grace through the sinner's faith not by any personal merit from the sinner but by Christ's merit alone.

I am aware there are some naming themselves as Dispensationalists, who do teach a different way of salvation in the Old Testament from the New Testament. I have two comments.

> A genuine Dispensationalist teaches salvation in every age or dispensation is one way only: by God's grace through the sinner's faith apart from any merit of the sinner but by Christ's limitless merit alone.

> You can paint strips on a cow and call it a zebra, but it is still a cow. Even so a person might paint himself with dispensational stripes, but unless he adheres to the historic orthodox essential

doctrines of the New Testament church, he is not a Dispensationalist.

I have a discussion of orthodox doctrines in my book, *Thirty-Six Essentials of the Christian Faith*.

The book in your hands (or on your monitor) includes chapters presenting an overview of the essential details of biblical soteriology: election, propitiation, salvation, justification, sanctification, perseverance, and eschatology as it relates to soteriology. The purpose is to present a whole picture of Dispensational soteriology through its doctrines. I want to stress again that the means by which salvation from the penalty of sin has been communicated to the Old and New Testament peoples is not an essential doctrine, but a second order doctrine.

In this book, I make reference to first order (essential) and second order doctrines. This is the concept of theological triage. The Precepts of Theological Triage:

First-order doctrines represent the most fundamental truths of the Christian faith, and a denial of these doctrines represents nothing less than an eventual denial of Christianity itself.

Second-order doctrines is distinguished from the first-order set by the fact that believing Christians may disagree on the second-order issues, though this disagreement will create significant boundaries between believers.

Third-order issues are doctrines over which Christians may disagree and remain in close fellowship, even within local congregations.

The essential, first order, soteriological doctrine of the faith is the salvation principle, Ephesians 2:8–9, "saved by God's grace through the sinner's faith without personal merit from the sinner but by Christ's merit alone." The subject of this book, the means by which the Good News of salvation was communicated to the Old Testament sinner, is not a first order doctrine, but something about which "Christians may disagree and remain in close fellowship, even within local congregations."

The heart of the debate about the Old Testament object and content of saving faith, is the hermeneutical failure to consistently apply the principles and rules of the Literal hermeneutic. There is also a consistent failure to hermeneutically recognize two related but independently developed streams of Old Testament messianic prophecy, a Messiah-King and a Messiah-Redeemer.

There is indeed a promise of a coming Messiah-King, a promise that may be followed from earlier to later Old Testament scriptures using only the Old Testament revelation. This king was to bring national redemption to Israel. Not individual redemption from the penalty due the crime of sin, but national redemption from gentile oppression. I will show that promise was clear to the Old Testament peoples.

The promise of a Messiah-Redeemer from sin is less clear in the Old Testament revelation, fully revealed in the New Testament revelation. Consistent application of the Literal hermeneutic makes this difference clear. The hermeneutic tendency to give Old Testament people New Testament understanding obscures this difference.

Throughout this book I will show the Messiah-Redeemer line of messianic prophecy did not begin at Genesis 3:15. The Messiah-Redeemer line began with the Abrahamic promise, Genesis 12:3, blessing to all families of the earth—a fact we know from the later revelation in Galatians 3:8—through Abraham's heir Isaac, Genesis 21:12, "in Isaac your offspring will be named," cf. Romans 9:7; Galatians 3:6–16; Hebrews 11:18. The offspring of the promise, Isaac, through his descendants, culminated in the offspring who would inherit all the promises, Jesus of Nazareth, Matthew 1:2–16; Luke 3:23–34.

This line of prophecy was fulfilled at the first advent through the crucifixion and resurrection.

The Messiah-King line of prophecy will be fulfilled at the second advent through the Davidic-Messianic Kingdom. This line of prophecy began at Genesis 49:10, and was further revealed in the promise to David at 2 Samuel 7:13–16, which he wrote about and under inspiration expanded in Psalm 2. Matthew 16:15–21 shows the moment when Jesus Christ changed the focus of his message to Israel from Messiah-King to Messiah-Redeemer.

The Holy Spirit never confuses or conflates those two lines of prophecy into one during Old Testament times. Neither should we. Those lines of prophecy meet in Jesus Christ, which means they are distinct in the Old Testament revelation. They do not directly include

Genesis 3:15. Which is to say, by a consistent and proper application of the principles and rules of the Literal hermeneutic, you cannot get to the Messiah-Redeemer line of prophecy from Genesis 3:15.

A Thought Occurs

I was working on my commentary on Acts 15–28 (Acts 1–14 having already been published) when I began writing this book. When I began work on Acts 17 in the commentary, a question occurred.

If the Old Testament people knew from Genesis 3:15 and other Old Testament scriptures, that salvation from the penalty due sin was by faith in a coming redeemer-messiah-christ, then why did the Bereans decide to check the Old Testament Scripture to see if Paul's message, that salvation from the penalty due sin was by faith in Jesus the Christ, was true to the Scripture?

Indeed, that question may be asked of every synagogue, of every Jew, during the times of Jesus of Nazareth and after, who rejected or questioned the Good News. If they already knew there was a coming redeemer-messiah-christ, beginning at Genesis 3:15, then why was the gospel message of "The Redeemer-Messiah-Christ Has Arrived" so soundly rejected by the Jews, from then to now? I will develop the answer to that question at the end of the chapter, "Reformed Soteriology."

Soteriology

Introduction

Soteriology is the label used by theologians to identify the biblical doctrine of salvation. The English word comes from the Greek word *sōtér*, a savior. The suffix "ology" denotes a field of study or a branch of knowledge. Soteriology is the branch of knowledge and field of study of the rescue of sinful human beings from the penalty due sin, aka: salvation, as effected by God through Jesus Christ.

The inspired, inerrant Scripture, which is to say the sixty-six canonical books of the Judeo-Christian Bible, is the primary source of knowledge used in the study of salvation and to develop a genuine understanding of the doctrine.

Although there are many details in the doctrine—election, propitiation, salvation, justification, sanctification, perseverance—the doctrine may be described in a few words.

> Soteriology (the doctrine of salvation). For human beings to be saved God must convict the sinner of his/her sin and give the sinner his gift of grace-faith-salvation, Ephesians 2:8. For a person to be saved he/she must respond to God-given conviction of sin and believe in God and God's testimony as the means by which God's grace in salvation is to be accessed. Every salvation is by grace through faith, without personal merit (works) but by Christ's merit alone, Eph. 2:8–9.

The description above is from my personal statement of faith as a Dispensational Calvinist.

I will repeat what I said in the Introduction. There is one salvation principle, only one way to be saved: saved by God's grace through the sinner's faith without personal merit from the sinner but by Christ's merit alone. The object and content of faith are respectively God and God's testimony: YHWH in the Old Testament, Christ in the New Testament, and the content of the progressive revelation of truth as was revealed in the Old and New Testaments. The basis of salvation is the same in the Old Testament and New Testament: the limitless merit of Christ's propitiation of God for human sin.

Sin, The Savior, Salvation

The essential message of the Good News is summed in the three terms sin, savior, salvation. By God's grace the sinner is permanently and endlessly saved from the penalty due sin, through the sinner's faith in God the Savior and God's testimony in his Word of truth, which grace and faith accesses the limitless merit of Christ's propitiation of God for human sin, thereby saving the sinner.

In Old Testament times the Savior was the ever-present YHWH, and the Word of truth is the written Scripture. In New Testament times the Savior is the risen, ever-present, Jesus Christ, and the Word of truth is the written Scripture. I will discuss those three elements of the Good News: sin, savior, salvation.

Let us begin with a definition of grace. Although there are many aspects to grace, the basic definition on which all aspects depend and are sourced from is this.

> Grace. God choosing to bless because he wants to bless, although blessing is undeserved.

Anything added to grace is not God's grace.

In the history of the New Testament church, there have always been Christians who add to the simple message of God's grace working through conviction of sin, the ever-present Savior, and salvation by God's grace through the sinner's faith. Some, such as the Roman Catholic Church added works: sin, the Savior, works, salvation.

Some, such as Arminianism, add a neutral will, that is, a will free from both the influence of sin and that efficacious aspect of grace that efficiently inclines the will to exercise saving faith. Arminian salvation is sin, the Savior, and the choice to deny or accept salvation.

Ohers add doctrine: sin, the Savior, a particular doctrine, and salvation. Water Baptism has been a popular addition (e.g., Roman Catholic Church baptismal regeneration). In the last hundred years or so a "baptism of the Spirit," became popular (the speaking in tongues phenomenon). The most recently popular doctrines added to the Good News by some Reformed and Dispensational are belief in the deity of the Savior, or obedience to the lordship of the Savior, as prerequisites for salvation.

Works or neutral free will are proposed as helps to salvation. Works, it will be said, are empowered by God's grace to give value to your faith so God will by his grace accept you. A neutral free will, it is said, was given to you by God's grace, who then waits for your choice to believe on God the Savior and be saved. Both are outside the biblical salvation principle, and therefore wrong, but they supplement that principle, they depend on God giving grace, they do not change the salvation principle by grace through faith, as does added doctrine.

The addition of doctrine is particularly pernicious. Adding doctrine creates a different gospel: believe in God and God's testimony, including this specific doctrine, and you will be saved. Adding doctrine sets a condition, a prerequisite, for salvation other than the simple condition of volitional faith, which is the duty to believe the message of the judicial guilt of your sin that brings condemnation, God (OT: YHWH; NT: the risen Christ) the only Savior from the penalty due your sin, and faith in God the Savior that by his grace delivers you from the penalty of sin into eternal life.

Adding doctrine is a different gospel. Adding doctrine says you *must* believe this doctrine in order to be saved.

You *must* believe in Christ's deity or you *cannot* be saved.

You *must* make a prior commitment to be obedient to the Lord or you *cannot* be saved.

The issue of added doctrine during these New Testament times was settled in AD 50 by the first church council. The addition was this.

You *must* be circumcised or you *cannot* be saved.

Or as the faith-plus-doctrine believers of the times said, "If you are not circumcised according to the custom of Moses you are not able to be saved," Acts 15:1. Those New Testament believers were reading Old Testament revelation into the New Testament revelation in order to achieve what they believed was the proper doctrine of salvation.

Am I exaggerating? No. The two modern additions may be easily discovered in various writings of their proponents in books or on social media.

If you do not believe in the deity of Christ according to the custom of the church you cannot be saved.

If you do not commit to obedience to Christ according to the custom of the church you cannot be saved.

But of course, such things are learned by discipleship after salvation. One must not add to the Good News things that may only be learned after salvation by discipleship.

No proclamation or description of the Good News in the Old or New Testament Scripture adds baptism of any kind, good works of any kind, a neutral free will, Christ's deity, or the sinner's obedience, *or anything else* to the simple Good News message of your sin, God the only Savior, and salvation through simple volitional faith in the Savior. That Good News is communicated through God's written Scripture.

The recorded Good News messages in the Book of Acts never requires belief in the deity of the Christ. Nor do those same messages require a commitment to any obedience other than obeying the command to believe and be saved. Read the Book of Acts, see for yourself.

The apostles knew Christ was God incarnate, but they never required that doctrine as a prerequisite for salvation. The apostles knew obedience was part of living the Christian life, but they never required that commitment in order to be saved. Matters beyond the simple message of the Good News of salvation are matters for the saved, not those being saved: discipleship, spiritual maturity, growing in grace and knowledge and understanding.

The only doctrines Scripture makes a vital part of the New Testament Good News are hamartiology (your sin), a satisfactory payment for the judicial debt for sin (propitiation through an acceptable sacrifice), and faith in God the only Savior.

Lest I be accused of proclaiming another gospel in the Old Testament age, the written Scripture is clear.

> The sin that makes salvation necessary, faith in YHWH the ever-present Savior, and an acceptable sacrifice to propitiate God for the judicial guilt for sin, results in forgiveness of sin and eternal life with YHWH the Savior. The written scripture communicates sin, the Savior, and salvation.

Lest I be accused of proclaiming another gospel in this New Testament age, the written Scripture is clear.

> The sin that makes salvation necessary, faith in God the ever-present Savior, and an acceptable sacrifice to propitiate God for the judicial guilt for sin, results in forgiveness of sin and eternal life with God the Savior. The written scripture communicates

36

sin, the Savior, and salvation.

What never changes is the necessity of an acceptable sacrifice to propitiate God for the judicial guilt of sin: it is always the propitiation Jesus Christ made to God for the judicial guilt of sin by suffering sin's penalty on the cross.

What does change is the expression of saving faith, as given to the sinner in the progressive revelation of truth. In the Old Testament saving faith in YHWH was expressed in many ways. Enoch, Noah, Abraham, Moses, and every other person saved in the Old Testament expressed faith in in YHWH as their Savior as required by the revelation they had received. Read the Scripture, Genesis 5:22–24; 6:8–9; 7:5; 15:6.

In whom did Moses believe? YHWH was his Savior, Exodus 3:6–7, 3:14. How did YHWH tell Moses and Israel to express their saving faith? Through an appropriate animal sacrifice. The sacrifice did not save, it was simply the proper expression of faith in YHWH and YHWH's testimony.

What *never* changes is the basis of salvation: by the limitless merit of Christ's propitiation of God on the cross. The unchanging salvation principle is *always* by God's grace, through the sinner's faith in God and God's testimony as received in the written progressive revelation of truth, not by personal merit, but by the limitless merit of Christ's propitiation of God on the cross.

What is the expression of saving faith in New Testament times? Every proclamation of the Good News in the New Testament revelation requires faith in the resurrected Savior, e.g., 1 Corinthians 15:4; Acts 2:24; 15:37; Romans 10:9. He is the appropriate sacrifice the sinner must bring to God as the proper expression of saving faith.

God's part in salvation never changes: a propitiation for sin; the Word of testimony. The sinner's part in salvation experiences change: the object of faith, OT: YHWH God; NT: the risen Jesus Christ the God-man; the content of faith: informed by the progressive revelation of truth.

The Doctrine of Sin

What is sin? The following is from my book, *Dictionary of Doctrinal Words*.

Sin is the moral violation of God's holiness by failure to conform to the image and likeness in which he created human nature, and sin is the legal violation of God's laws by disobedience.

At its most basic, sin is the failure to conform fully to God's image and likeness. In the final analysis, sin is any thought or action that does not conform to the essence, personality, character, attributes, or purpose of God.

Scripture uses the word "sin" in two ways,

The evil life principle, or attribute, of rebellion, usually displayed in disobedience. This is the sin attribute in human nature, 1 John 1:8.

Human nature as influenced by the sin attribute, i.e., choosing to commit acts of sinning, 1 John 1:10.

Sin is the principle of rebellion that results in acts of rebellion and disobedience.

God acts toward sin in one of three ways:

Retribution (punishment) in judicial vengeance for the crime with no view toward redemption or restoration.

Redemptive (salvific) to save the sinner from the penalty due his or her sin.

Remedial (chastisement) to discipline and correct his saved children in order to restore them to righteousness and fellowship.

The focus of this section on sin is to explore the nature of sin requiring God's redemptive action.

The principle of rebellion was added to human nature by Adam's choice to disobey God. God made sinless Adam the legal and seminal head of the human race. This was a reasonable decision, because by God's design Adam is the one and only original human being. All other human beings, including the Woman (Eve) are derived from Adam's body and soul—not copies, but Adam individualized in discrete individuals and two distinct genders. That is why Paul can say "in Adam all die," 1 Corinthians 15:22, because legally all, including Eve, are represented by Adam in God's judicial system, and seminally, by propagation, all but Eve are in Adam (she is in Adam by formation, Genesis 2:22).

When Eve and then Adam disobeyed God, that principle of rebellion was permanently added to their human nature: a sin attribute. God's Law of Biological Reproduction is "each kind of being reproduces its own kind of being and no other kind of being," Genesis 1:11–12, 21–22, 24–25, 28. The effect of that biological law is stated in the procreation of Seth, Genesis 5:3, Adam fathered a son in his own likeness, after his own image. Adam and Eve propagated their sinful likeness and rebellious image in Cain, Abel, Seth, and "sons and daughters." So also their children and their descendants were propagated in Adam's sinful likeness and image. So also you and me and your children and my children.

Adam was appointed by God the legal representative of his descendants. That is Paul's argument in Romans 5:12–14. Paul validates his argument with one irrefutable proof: death. "Just as through one person sin came into the world, and through sin the death, also in this manner the death came upon all persons, in that all sinned." Death is the irrefutable proof of sin. Because all are susceptible to death from the moment of conception, all are sinners.

All are sinners: legally, because represented by Adam.

All are sinners: by nature, the indwelling sin attribute.

All are sinners: by choice, in acts of sinning.

The sin attribute, as one attribute among many in human nature, through constructive interaction with other attributes in human nature, sin influences a person to self-determine his or her course in the world in opposition to God's holy character and revealed will, whether that will of God is discovered in Scripture, or in that revelation of himself God has made in human conscience. Sin is accomplished in acts of rebellion against God and disobedience to his commandments.

The effect of sin is every moral and spiritual aspect of the unsaved person's human nature has been affected in some greater or lesser degree by the sin attribute, such that the boundaries of his freely made choices (the will) are wholly determined by the influence of the sin attribute. See the chapter "What is Free Will."

The influence of sin is so pervasive, affecting every aspect of human nature, sin is said to have dominion. Sin has authority over the sinner, not as some invincible overlord, but as an innate part of human nature constructively working with all the other attributes of human nature, to persuasively incline the will to choose an act of sinning. The evil attribute sin influences every other attribute with the inclination to sin, and in that sense sin can be said to dominate the will. The sinner freely chooses sinning because his will is of itself always inclined to choose sinning, and as being rebellious and disobedient toward God, the sinner never desires to change his or her inclination to choose sinning to rebel against God, disobey his commandments, and seek a path in life apart from God.

Sin is not some evil force existing in the universe attacking innocent human beings. Sin is an attribute innate to human nature, added to the human nature common to all human beings by Adam's act of sinning. Only Jesus of Nazareth was excepted, for reasons beyond the scope of this book, see my book *God Became Incarnate*.

The result of sin is its demerit. The demerit of sin is its judicial guilt. The demerit of sin is finite. Because the sinner is a finite being, then the demerit of his sin is finite. The finite demerit of the sinner can be overcome by the application of a greater merit. In every age of man, from Adam forward, God's grace has caused a greater merit to be available. That greater merit is applied to a sinner seeking forgiveness and salvation by means of faith in God and God's historically revealed means (way) of salvation. That greater merit is the limitless merit of Christ's propitiation of God for human sin, which though taking place in a moment in time, was and is effective for all time past, present, and yet future. That greater merit is the one and only way of salvation.

It is because the demerit of sin is an innate part of the sinner that an external greater merit must be personally applied to overcome the sinner's judicial guilt-demerit. The means by which the greater merit is applied to save the soul from sin's demerit is by faith in God and God's testimony. The historical means by which the greater merit was applied is simple volitional faith in the content of faith revealed during any particular period in the history of redemption. In every age of man from Adam forward, faith in God and God's revealed content of faith was saving faith.

God imposes a penalty in the here and now of mortal life on those living persons who have not exercised saving faith in Jesus Christ. In the here and now of mortal life, the penalty of sin is separation from the spiritual life of God, which is to say, spiritually "dead." The result is the spiritual perception of the unsaved person is grossly dulled, resulting in their human nature being "dead" in trespasses and sins, Ephesians 2:1, i.e., unable to discern the things the Holy Spirit teaches, 1 Corinthians 2:12–14, because sin makes spiritual things seem absurd. This condition of spiritually dead can be resolved only though the application of God's gift, Ephesians 2:8.

Why do I say the sinner's spiritual perception is grossly dulled, when the Scripture says dead? Because I have not been led astray by popular representations, but I understand the Scripture.

What is "dead in trespasses and sins?" Not the corpse modern theology uses as an illustration of the unsaved sinner. Paul is describing spiritually dead not physically dead. The corpse analogy could not be more wrong if you tried.

The sinner always responds to spiritual things: he or she rejects God and God's salvation, and thinks of spiritual things as absurd. That is why I say the sinner's spiritual perception is grossly dulled, not dead. If dead there would be disinterested apathy, not active rejection.

"Dead in trespasses and sins" is a rabid dog attacking its master, not a corpse lying passively in a grave. Sinners are in active rebellion against God, not passively ignoring God. Sinner's hear spiritual things and then reject spiritual things because their automatic reaction toward spiritual things is spiritual things are absurd.

> 1 Corinthians 2:14, But a natural person does not accept things of the Spirit of God, for they are absurd to him, and he is not able to know them, because they are discerned spiritually.

When God throws a drowning sinner the life preserver of the Good News, the "dead in trespasses and sins" sinner doesn't ignore it and passively drown. The sinner grabs the life preserver and violently throws it back, all the while yelling curses at the one who tried to save him, because he is sure he can save himself.

Not every sinner may act so violently, but every sinner will act in rebellion and rejection.

That active rebellion and rejection is the result of dead in trespasses and sins: it is a negative spiritual response to spiritual things. That is why only God alone by his grace is able to change the sinner's nature so he or she does have a positive spiritual response to spiritual things, and does grab the life preserver of the Good News of salvation.

God imposes a permanent and endless penalty of separation from the spiritual life of God (endless spiritual death) on the unsaved person after physical death, as well as physical separation from the active presence of God. In Revelation 20:6, 14 this permanent endless separation is defined as the "second death." When the unsaved person physically dies, the first death, his/her unsaved spiritual state is permanently and endlessly confirmed, the second death. The endless penalty of spiritual death cannot be resolved after physical death.

The finite demerit of sin raises a valid question. If sin's demerit is finite, then why is the judgment of the unforgiven sinner endless? Among several reasons, the unforgiven sinner never stops being a sinner, and never stops committing acts of sinning. The power of physical death is to seal the unforgiven sinner in his or her spiritual state. Therefore, even in the lake of fire the sinner never stops sinning. One reason the punishment is endless because the sin that causes the judicial guilt is never ending.

The Savior

That in the Old Testament YHWH was known as the Savior seems sufficiently apparent from the testimony of Scripture, and therefore I will not make many comments in this chapter on Old Testament saving faith. The object of Old Testament saving faith was not a *coming* redeemer-messiah-christ but an *ever-present* YHWH. In this section I will focus on the basis for salvation, Jesus Christ and the limitless value of his propitiation of God for human sin. (For an in depth discussion of Christ's propitiation see the chapter, "Propitiation.")

Properly, the subject of Jesus Christ the risen Savior begins with the doctrine of Christology, a vast land whose extant has been explored by many. I have made my own contributions with commentaries on the four gospels, a harmony of the four gospels, and a doctrinal book *God Became Incarnate.* Below is my personal doctrinal statement on Christ.

Christology (the doctrine of Christ). God the Son is a genuine Person in unity with God the Father and God the Holy Spirit, being of the same one essence/substance with them, consubstantial, coequal, and coeternal with God the Father and God the Holy Spirit.

God the Son became the Christ, Psalm 2:2, when he joined in union with himself a human nature and a human body—the incarnation—by a super-natural, non-sexual act which procreated a genuine male human being—Jesus of Nazareth—through the virgin Mariam, in whom Jesus was conceived by the omnipotent power of God and from whom he was birthed, Psalm 2:7; Luke 1:35.

Jesus the Christ is one Person with two natures: genuine deity and a genuine rational sinless human soul and human body. He is immaterial deity essence and immaterial sinless human soul united with a genuine material sinless human body. In the Person Jesus the Christ, the attributes of deity were communicated to the humanity in such a way that, without adding to the humanity or subtracting from the deity, the humanity became an instrument through which the deity could exercise its power. The deity perfected the humanity, without elevating it to deity, so that his humanity possessed all things perfectly.

The symbol of Chalcedon, AD 451 (aka Chalcedon Creed, Chalcedon Definition), exactly describes my doctrine of the incarnation.

In relation to this chapter, my doctrinal statement concerning Jesus Christ the Savior.

Jesus the Christ in his first advent was the messianic-redeemer of Daniel 9:26, as further explained in Isaiah 52:13–53:12; Acts 8:35, and other relevant scriptures, fulfilling the promise first made to Abraham, Genesis 12:3 (a fact we know from Galatians 3:8).

Yes, I gave a New Testament explanation to Old Testament scriptures. That is rule two, the Analogy of Faith. The message of this book is not that we should ignore the New Testament revelation, but that the Old Testament peoples did not have the New Testament revelation. Their faith rested in what God had revealed both previous to their time and during their time.

But make no mistake and do not distort my doctrine: Jesus the Christ was and is always the Savior, because the basis of salvation was and always is the limitless merit of his propitiation of God for human sin. God the Son came at his first advent to accomplish the propitiation of God for human sin, a propitiaiton that God had decreed before God created the universe. Jesus Christ was, and is, and always will be the

Savior. Why? The basis of salvation in every age is the propitiation of God for human sin made by Jesus Christ on the cross.

My doctrinal statement continues.

> Jesus the Christ willingly took upon himself the sins of the world (2 Corinthians 5:21) and propitiated God (Isaiah 53:6, 10; Ephesians 5:2; Hebrews 9:14) for the crime of human sin (1 John 2:2; 4:10; Romans 3:25; Hebrews 2:17), dying spiritually (Matthew 27:46) and physically (Luke 23:46) to satisfy the judicial penalty for human sin.

I will take a closer look at Christ's act of propitiation in a later chapter. A preview.

> Propitiation. The satisfaction Christ made to God for sin by dying on the cross as the sin-bearer (2 Corinthians 5:21; Romans 3:25; Hebrews 2:17; 1 John 2:2; 4:10), for the crime of sin committed by human beings, suffering in their place and on their behalf. Christ's propitiation fully satisfied God's holiness and justice for the crime of sin.

> Christ's propitiation was of infinite merit, because his Person is of infinite worth. The application of that merit is personally made by each sinner to his or her sin through faith in God's testimony of Christ as the only Savior. Christ accomplished the propitiation of God for sin by enduring spiritual and physical death on the cross. Christ endured spiritual death when he was separated from fellowship with God ("My God, my God, why have you forsaken me?"), and physical death when he separated his soul from his body ("bowing his head, he gave up his spirit.")

Continuing with my doctrinal statement.

> Jesus the Christ was buried (John 19:40–42), was conscious and in heaven during his death (2 Corinthians 5:8), and three days later was resurrected by the power of God (Romans 6:4; John 10:17; Romans 8:11), being seen on the day of his resurrection (Luke 24:13–21; John 20:11–29), and for forty days after (John 21:4 ff.; Acts 1:3), by the Twelve and 500 other persons (1 Corinthians 15:5–6).

The death and burial of Jesus the Christ was a necessary part of his propitiation. He really and truly must die for the penalty of sin. That he was truly dead was revealed at the cross. From my book, *God Became Incarnate*.

> Skeptics doubt Jesus' physical death, stating that he merely fainted on the cross and revived in the coolness of the tomb. Such opinions show a gross ignorance of the facts.
>
> The Roman soldiers were masters of death. As in any military unit they had dealt death on the battlefield—not long distance as is done today, but face to face with a sword or spear. Each member of the Jerusalem unit was experienced at recognizing death. As in any military unit the crucifixion detail would have been a rotating duty performed by every member of the unit, so each was experienced at recognizing death by crucifixion. One of the soldiers, seeing that Jesus was dead, John 19:33 (compare Matthew 27:54; Mark 15:44–45; Luke 23:47), stabbed the body through the heart with a spear. Why did he do this if he knew Jesus was dead? In the Roman military the soldiers responsible for the execution would suffer the penalty of the condemned if they allowed the condemned to escape. The soldier wanted to make sure there was no mistake. Out of a strong sense of self-preservation he stabbed Jesus through the heart to make sure his initial evaluation was correct: Jesus was dead.

Jesus' burial showed he was really and truly dead. From my book, *God Became Incarnate*.

> Jesus' dead body was wrapped in linen cloth, spices, and aromatic gums, Matthew 27:59; Mark 15:46; Luke 23:53. John 19:39–40 says he was wrapped in strips of linen cloth with about seventy-five pounds (100 *litras*) of myrrh and aloes, with spices. He wasn't wrapped in a shroud, he was wrapped in strips of cloth "as the custom of the Jews is to bury" (NKJV). Myrrh was an exuded gum from a tree which could be dried to a solid resin and, among other uses, was used for embalming. The body was wrapped in multiple layers of linen strips of cloth. Each layer was coated with the myrrh, aloes, and spices. As these dried the cloth was hardened by the dried resin of the myrrh. No one so embalmed could have wriggled out of the

hardened cloths, compare John 11:44.

Consider the testimony of the two men who embalmed Jesus. Nicodemus and Joseph knew Jesus was dead, John 19:38–42. Death was a constant presence in the ancient world. There were no hospices, no hospitals, no funeral homes, no cremation societies. Family, relatives, and friends buried their dead. They knew a dead body when they saw one. Jesus died about 3:00 p.m. Sunset was about 6:00 p.m. Washing the body (the Jewish custom) and then embalming the body with layer upon layer of linen strips and myrrh and aloes and spices would have taken more than an hour. If Jesus had merely fainted, then the constant handling required to wash and wrap the body would have revived him. Jesus was physically dead. The soldiers knew he was dead, his enemies knew he was dead, and his friends knew he was dead.

Scripture states the death of Jesus in the plainest terms. Matthew 27:50, Jesus yielded up his spirit. Mark 15:37, Jesus breathed his last. Luke 23:46, Jesus breathed his last. John 19:30, Jesus gave up his spirit. He died physically, fully satisfying the physical penalty for sin.

Continuing with my doctrinal statement.

Jesus the Christ ascended into heaven (Acts 1:9) and is returning to earth at a yet-future date (Acts 1:11; Revelation 19:11–16), to judge his enemies (Revelation 19:17–21) and rule the world as the messianic-king (2 Sam 7:13, 16; Psalm 2; Zechariah 14:16–21; Revelation 20:4–6), after which he will judged the unsaved (Revelation 20:11–15), and reign on a new heaven and earth (Revelation 20:11; 21:1, 22–23).

Why did Jesus ascend into heaven? The first thing to notice about the ascension into heaven is the physically dead Jesus Christ resurrected to newness of life. The Savior of Christianity is unique among all the so-called "saviors" of the world: Jesus Christ is alive after having suffered death. He ascended because:

Hebrews 10:11–12, truly every priest stands every day serving and frequently offering the same sacrifices which are never able to completely take away sins. 12 But this one, having offered one sacrifice for sins in perpetuity, sat down at the right hand of God.

Hebrews 7:25, Wherefor also, he is able to save unto the completion of all those drawing near to God through him, always living to intercede for them.

Hebrews 9:24–26, For Christ has not entered into holies made by hands, illustrations of the true, but into heaven itself, to appear in the presence of God for us, 25 nor that many times he should offer himself, just as the high priest enters into the holy places every year with blood of another. 26 Otherwise it was necessary for him to have suffered many times from the foundation of the world. But now, once in the culmination of the age, he has been revealed for putting away sin by the sacrifice of himself.

Jesus the Christ is, therefore, the God-man, who will for eternity be Jesus the Christ, the Son of God, God the Son, the Savior. (John 1:1; 1 John 5:20; Hebrews 2:14, 16–17; Luke 1:27, 31, 35.) His propitiation of God for all human sin, 1 John 2:2, is the only basis for salvation in any age of humankind.

Did the human soul of Jesus Christ immediately enter heaven at the moment of his physical death? Yes, 2 Corinthians 5:8, "Now we are full of confidence and are pleased, rather, to be absent away from the body and to be at home with the Lord." The principle applies to every believer, Old and New Testament. Jesus was a believer; believers go to heaven immediately upon physical death.

Some say that faith in Christ's deity is necessary to add value to Christ's propitiation to save sinners. They do not frame their belief that baldly, but that is what they mean. Those persons ask, how can a person believe Christ is able to save unless he or she believes Christ is God? However, the apostles never required faith in Christ as God, but that God would save through faith in the risen Jesus Christ.

Acts 2:32–33, This Jesus God has raised up, whereof all we are witnesses. 33 Therefore, having been exalted to the right hand of God, and having received the promise of the Holy Spirit from the Father, he has poured out this which you are both seeing and hearing.

Acts 2:38–39, Then Peter to them: "Convert, and be immersed, every one of you, in the name of Jesus Christ, for the forgiveness of your sins, and you will receive the gift of the Holy Spirit. 39 For to you is the promise, and to your children, and to all those far away, as many as shall call to oneself our Lord and God [in context, the YHWH who had raised "this Jesus].

Acts 13:32–33, 38 And to you we proclaim the Good News, the promise made to the fathers, 33 this that God has fulfilled to their children, to us, having raised up Jesus .... 38 Therefore be it known to you, men, brethren, that through this one, to you forgiveness of sins is proclaimed.

Those who add the deity of Christ to the Good News of salvation confuse the content of saving faith with the basis of salvation. The basis of salvation is the limitless merit of Christ's propitiation. The Christ must be mortal to die to propitiate God, and must be deity to give limitless merit to his death. But the Holy Spirit has never required that knowledge of the Christ's deity in order to be saved.

Are some given that knowledge in a gospel presentation? Yes, some are. But others are not. I was one of those others, and my experience is validated by the Scripture, some of which I quoted above.

Did the Holy Spirit later given me that understanding? I believe that is obvious from my doctrinal statement. But for the doubters: Yes, the Holy Spirit did give me that understanding, about 1.5 years after my salvation; it has been 48 years and I still vividly remember the exact place and time, Wednesday night prayer and Bible study, in the basement of the church building in Oneida NY, November 1975, as vividly as I remember the exact place, time, and date of my salvation, Wednesday evening service, in the church building, Indian Springs, NV, May 19, 1974.

The simple fact is the Holy Spirit never adds faith in Jesus Christ as God to the content of faith necessary to salvation, but rather faith in the Jesus Christ whom God has raised out of the dead.

Salvation

What is salvation?

Salvation is the remission of sin's penalty by the application of the merit of Christ's propitiation of God on the cross to the sinner's spiritual need. The merit of the propitiation is applied to the sinner's spiritual need by God's grace through the means of the sinner's personal faith in God and God's testimony as to the way of salvation.

In salvation, God rescues a sinner out of the state of spiritual death and delivers him/her into a permanent state of spiritual life. Salvation is obtained by God's grace through the sinner's faith, not works, and is maintained by God's grace and the limitless merit of Christ's propitiation, not at all by works.

In this New Testament age of the church, we proclaim salvation occurs when a sinner repents of his or her sins and believes on the risen Christ as their Savior, Acts 2:38; 3:19–20; 11:18; Romans 3:22–26; 10:9–10, 13; Galatians 3:22; 1 Peter 1:21; 1 John 3:23.

But in times past, before the New Testament revelation of Jesus the Christ, salvation occurred when a sinner repented of his or her sins and believed on God and God's historically current testimony as to the means of salvation, as given by the Holy Spirit in the progressive revelation of truth, and illuminated by the Holy Spirit through the plain and normal meaning of the language and words.

The way today is not different, only the content of saving faith is different. Today's sinner must repent of his or her sins and believe on God and God's historically current testimony as to the means of salvation, as given by the Holy Spirit in the progressive revelation of truth, and illuminated by the Holy Spirit through the plain and normal meaning of the language and words.

Salvation is always the same: the believer's faith in the content of faith (given in God's historically current progressive revelation of truth) as the way of salvation; God's gift of grace-faith-salvation (Ephesians 2:8) efficaciously convicting the sinner to accept that content of faith as the way of salvation; God by grace applying the limitless merit of Christ's propitiation to save the believing sinner.

Make no mistake and do not distort my doctrine. The means of salvation is always God's gift of grace-faith-salvation, the believing sinner's faith, and the application of Christ's limitless merit. Therefore I and other Dispensationalists believe in one way to be saved, not many ways.

What Does It Mean To Be Born-Again

Although not strictly within the subject of this book, the

regeneration of human nature in salvation is part of soteriology.

Jesus did not say Nicodemus might fall short of the kingdom if he did not experience a new birth from above. Jesus said Nicodemus could not be a part of the kingdom without the new birth. The expectation of the kingdom was the hope of every Old Testament believer, Daniel 12:2, who had received and believed the revelation of redemption from sin.

Is there salvation without regeneration? No. As Charnock said [*Works,* 3:22], "No age, no time, no administration excludes it ... For being by nature spiritually dead, there must be a restoration to a spiritual life ... How can any, in any age, enjoy an infinite holy God, without being changed from their impurity?"

The concept of spiritual regeneration is present in the Old Testament, e.g., Ezekiel 11:19; 36:26. The Spirit positively assisted and supported the faith of the Old Testament saints, for no one comes to faith unless God draws him or her, and no one remains faithful unless kept by God. The Old Testament believers experienced spiritual regeneration, because without it there is no spiritual perception. (But the Spirit's indwelling, John 14:16–17, waited for the death and resurrection of Christ, by which the New Covenant for the New Testament church was inaugurated.)

What is the regeneration of the saved human nature. The following explanation is drawn from my book, *Dictionary of Doctrinal Words*.

Salvation is an instantaneous act with several results, which may be separated for the purpose of discussion. The unbeliever is unable to understand the things of the Spirit of God (1 Corinthians 2:14), because his/her faculty of spiritual perception is "dead," which is to say, grossly dulled, unable to perceive spiritual things (Ephesians 2:1, 5), rejecting spiritual things as absurd. The first part of "born-again" is the believer's faculty of spiritual perception is brought to life, thus enabling the spiritual understanding required to be convicted of sin, the Savior, and salvation. This is accomplished through God's gift of grace-faith-salvation (Ephesians 2:8) by the work of the Holy Spirit to accomplish the salvation decreed by God (Ephesians 1:4; 2 Thessalonians 2:13; 1 Peter 1:2).

Upon the exercise of saving faith by the sinner, God imparts to him/her eternal life, John 10:27–29; 17:2–3; Romans 6:23b; 1 John

2:25, which is God sharing (in a participatory way) the communicable aspects of his eternal life, creating communion with God and spiritual understanding. To be born-again, or regeneration, is the result of God sharing the communicable aspects of his eternal life. The attributes of human nature, which were jumbled and wrongly prioritized by the sin attribute, are normalized, which is to say, godliness is restored to human nature through the godly attributes of holiness, righteousness, love, mercy, etc. The believer is given new wants and new desires. His or her human nature is re-prioritized toward God.

Upon the exercise of saving faith, God imputes the righteousness of Christ to the now-believing sinner, freeing him or her from the judicial guilt and penalty of sin (justification) because Christ has satisfied God's law on behalf of the sinner, Romans 6:23. The now-saved sinner has been reconciled to God, 2 Corinthians 5:18–19. This brings peace with God, Romans 5:1, because with sin forgiven (Ephesians 1:7), and the judicial penalty satisfied through Christ's propitiation (1 John 2:2), there is no more enmity between God and the believer.

Upon the exercise of saving faith, the Holy Spirit accomplishes the sanctification of the believer, which is to set the believer apart from the defilement caused by sin and dedicate him to God, Ephesians 1:4; 1 Corinthians 1:30; 1 Peter 1:2. In the act of sanctification sin loses its dominating power, Romans 6:14–23, and a new principle of life, holiness, is added to the believer, Ephesians 4:24, becoming the dominating principle in his human nature, 1 Thessalonians 4:7; 1 Corinthians 3:17b; Colossians 3:12; 1 Peter 1:15.

The believer now stands before God in Christ as forgiven, justified, sanctified, regenerated, filled with eternal life. He is freed from the penalty, power, and pleasure of sin, with absolute assurance of the future transformation and glorification of his/her human nature and body, so that he/she will be freed eternally from the presence of sin. The believer is empowered to resist sin's temptations, live a holy life, understand the Scripture, worship, obey, fellowship with, and serve God. God hears and answers his prayers, and he (or she) perseveres in the faith to lead a holy life, looking toward resurrection and an eternal life in God's presence.

Every Old Testament sinner who was saved was born again,

because there is no salvation without regeneration.

The Practical Working Of God's Gift

I have spoken of God's gift of grace-faith-salvation, Ephesians 2:8, (and will speak of it again in the chapter "Election"). A primary question in salvation is, how does this gift work in the sinner? There are two competing views: the gift gives faith; the gift enables faith. The first view denies the Scripture's clear testimony the sinner is commanded to believe and be saved. The second places the efficacy of the gift within the sinner's choices.

Let me suggest something more reasonable. In the unsaved soul, the sin attribute has rendered spiritual perception grossly insensitive, such that the unsaved person does not have the spiritual discernment to receive or understand the things of the Spirit of God, 1 Corinthians 2:14, because their sin makes spiritual things absurd to them. In the sinful soul whom God is bringing to understanding leading to salvation, that understanding begins with the gift of God, Ephesians 2:8, applied by the Holy Spirit, which gift enlivens the soul's faculty of spiritual perception to perceive and understand the spiritual issues of sin and salvation.

God initiates salvation by his gift of grace-faith-salvation, Ephesians 2:8, given to those whom God has chosen to salvation, Ephesians 1:4, 2 Thessalonians 2:13. That gift of God changes human nature by removing the dominance of sin, and by opening the person's spiritual eyes to spiritual truths, so that by God's efficacious grace the person becomes willing to be saved, and desires to be saved, and willingly exercises his or her free will, now freed from the dominion of sin, to obey God's command to believe and be saved. God's gift efficaciously makes the unwilling sinner willing to believe and be saved. Salvation is the inevitable result of receiving God's gift.

Then, at the moment of salvation, the entire human nature is regenerated. That process—God's gift, spiritual discernment, saving faith, regeneration of human nature—was the same in Old Testament times as it is in New Testament times.

The Eternal Efficacy of Christ's Propitiation

Ryrie stated [*Dispensationalism*, 115], "the basis of salvation in every age is the death made by Christ." By "death" Ryrie meant propitiation. Christ's death accomplished the propitiation of God for human sin.

Some teach Christ's propitiation was not applied to fully save sinners until the historical act was completed at the cross. The Scripture teaches otherwise. So does the orthodox doctrine of the New Testament church.

How could Christ's propitiation on the cross be applied before Christ died on the cross? I answered that question in my book, *Did Jesus Go To Hell?*, which refutes the notion the Old Testament saved went to a "good" side of hades to wait for Christ's propitiation on the cross to take place, so their salvation would be completed and they could go to heaven.

Christ's propitiation, accomplished at a specific moment in time, was and is efficient to completely and fully and comprehensively save any sinner at any time since the creation of the world, according to God's eternal decree.

In eternity past before God created the universe, he decreed the propitiation to be made by his Son would provide the only merit to save sinners, Ephesians 1:4. That merit is always effective to save, Romans 4:17, God being "the one giving life to the dead and calling the thing not existing into existence." God acted in historical time to save by Christ's limitless merit *before* the propitiation was made in historical time on the cross—for it is certain all saved in the Old Testament were saved by Christ's limitless merit, decreed "before the creation of the universe" as the only merit by which sinners must be saved (Eph. 1:4; 2:8; Rom. 3:24–25; 8:28).

What God decrees in eternity is in effect from the beginning of time, even though some things, such as separating Abraham from the nations to create the nation Israel, took place at a moment in time. But unless we want to propose a different basis for salvation other than Christ's propitiation (e.g., the Reformed Covenant of Works), then the limitless merit of that propitiation accomplished at a moment in time, was made effective by God's decree for all time, from the beginning.

Perhaps more simply, there is no such thing as a partial salvation. One either is, or is not, saved. Either the Old Testament saved were fully saved and the principle of 2 Corinthians 5:8 applies to them, or they were not saved and went to hades upon physical death, and not to an imaginary "good side."

Was what God decreed in eternity past—that only Christ's propitiation had the merit to save the soul—efficient to fully and completely save the believing sinner before the historical moment in time when Christ made his propitiation of God for sin on the cross?

Let us ask that question another way. Is God limited by time? Time is a mechanism God created to manage the universe he created. There was no time before God created the universe. God is never limited by his creation. Deity is not limited by time, because God not only exists independent of the universe he created, God also exists omnipresently throughout all the time and space of the universe he created. Deity chose to create time and create creatures limited by time. Therefore Deity has chosen to work within the temporal limits of his creatures. The universe was created in a moment of time, the incarnation was a moment in time, the Christ's propitiation, death, and resurrection were moments in time.

But the decree of salvation, which was made *before* time was created, is not bound by time. God's decree of salvation is applied to a sinner to save (by grace through faith) at any moment during their particular time from conception to physical death, as per God's decrees respecting the salvation of individual sinners. As noted above, God calls those things which do not exist as though they did exist. When God decreed Christ's propitiation was the only merit for salvation, that act of propitiation was set for a particular moment in time. But having been decreed before time, it was efficient to completely save throughout all time. I am not teaching something new, this is the doctrine of all biblically based soteriology.

Dispensational soteriology teaches the basis of salvation is the same for everyone, beginning with Adam: saved by God's grace through the sinner's faith, not by personal merit but by the merit of Christ's propitiation (no Reformed Covenant of Works for Adam). The basis of salvation is always and only Christ's propitiation of God for human sin.

Dispensational soteriology recognizes that salvation is always accessed by faith. Dispensational soteriology believes God is the proper object for saving faith, because it is God who has given testimony in his Word as to the content of that faith. The content of faith changes in the various dispensations. The content of faith in this New Testament church age is, "Believe that Jesus the Christ propitiated God for your sins." This is stated in several ways, e.g., Acts 16:31; Romans 10:9; Acts 3:36–39; 4:12.

The church fathers support the propitiation as eternally effective, not bound by time.

> Justin Martyr (AD 100–165). "Their [believers'] souls, when they die, are taken to heaven." [Roberts and Donaldson, ANF, 1:239, *Dialogue with Trypho*, 80.] "The souls of the pious remain in a better place, while those of the unjust and wicked are in a worse, waiting for the time of judgment" [1:197 (*Dialogue*, 5)].

> Cyril of Alexandria (AD 378–444). "He [Cyril] presupposes the immediate entry of the souls of the righteous into heaven and the immediate chastisement of those of the wicked."[J.N.D. Kelly, *Early Christian Doctrines*, 482.]

> Gregory Nazianzen (AD 329–390). "I believe the words of the wise that every fair and God-beloved soul, when, set free from the bonds of the body . . . goes rejoicing to meet its Lord . . .. Then, a little later, it receives its kindred flesh [resurrection]" [Schaff, NPNF, 7:236 (Panegyric on His Brother S. Caesarius, 21).] Gregory believed "Abraham's Bosom" was the same as heaven. [Same reference.]

The Reformed of times past support my conclusion.

> The Westminster Confession of Faith (1646). Chapter 32.1. "The bodies of men, after death, return to dust, and see corruption: but their souls, which neither die nor sleep, having an immortal subsistence, immediately return to God who gave them: the souls of the righteous, being then made perfect in holiness, are received into the highest heavens, where they behold the face of God, in light and glory, waiting for the full redemption of their bodies. And the souls of the wicked are cast into hell, where they remain in torments and utter darkness, reserved to the judgment of the great day. Beside these two places, for souls separated from their bodies, the Scripture acknowledges none."

As do more recent Reformed.

> Haldane, *Romans*, 151. Jesus Christ hath been set forth by God

to be a propitiatory sacrifice, and by which it is now publicly manifested. On account, then, of this righteousness, even before it was introduced, God pardoned or remitted the sins of His people under the Old Testament dispensation.

C. Hodge, *Systematic Theology*, 2:619, 621. First Peter 3:18, 19 . . . afford no ground for the doctrine that Christ after death went into hell. The Romanists teach that the department of Hades to which Christ descended, was not the abode of evil spirits, but that in which dwelt the souls of believers who died before the advent of the Redeemer, and that the object of his descent was . . . to deliver the pious dead from the intermediate state in which they were and introduce them into heaven. (Hodge is opposed to the "Romish doctrine.")

W.G.T. Shedd, *Endless Punishment*, 59–60, summarizes the Reformed doctrine. "The substance of the Reformed view, then, is, that the intermediate [between death and resurrection] state for the saved is Heaven without the body, and the final state for the saved is Heaven with the body; that the intermediate state for the lost is Hell [*hádēs*] without the body, and the final state for the lost is Hell [*géenna*] with the body."

Louis Berkhof, *Systematic Theology*, 342. [Addressing the Apostolic Creed] The Catholic Church takes it to mean that, after death, Christ went into the Limbus Patrum, where the Old Testament saints were awaiting the revelation and application of his redemption, preached the gospel to them, and brought them out to heaven . . .. Calvin [*Institutes*, 2.16.8] interprets the phrase metaphorically, as referring to the penal sufferings of Christ on the cross, where he really suffered the pangs of hell . . .. Scripture certainly does not teach a literal descent of Christ into hell.

Wayne Grudem, *Systematic Theology*, 281, 586, 590. Not many Scripture references talk about the state of the Old Testament believers after they had died, but those that give us any indication of their state all point in the direction of immediate conscious enjoyment in the presence of God, not of a time of waiting away from God's presence. An examination of the biblical evidence indicates Christ did not descend into hell.

Scripture gives us no clear evidence to make us think that full access to the blessings of being in God's presence in heaven were withheld from Old Testament believers when they died—indeed, several passages suggest that believers who died before Christ's death did enter into the presence of God at once because their sins were forgiven by trusting in the Messiah who was to come (Genesis 5:24; 2 Samuel 12:23; Psalm 16:11; 17:15; 23:6; Ecclesiastes 12:7; Matthew 22:31–32; Luke 16:22; Romans 4:1–8; Hebrews 11:5).

There is no place in Reformed or Dispensational theologies for the view the saved Old Testament person went to hades until Christ resurrected.

Christ's propitiation, accomplished at a specific moment in time, was and is efficient to save any sinner at any time since the creation of the world, according to God's eternal decree. There is no such thing as a partial salvation. Either the Old Testament sinner was completely saved and went to heaven upon his or her physical death, 2 Corinthians 5:8, or was unsaved and went to hades—not to a non-existent "good side."

Summary

In this chapter I have demonstrated that my doctrine of salvation conforms to the historic orthodox doctrine of the Christian church. You may disagree that the content of saving faith is always faith in God and God's historically current progressive revelation of truth. You also may disagree the object of saving faith is God. But we agree that the basis of salvation in every age is the propitiation made by Christ, and the requirement for salvation in every age is faith.

I believe and teach as you believe and teach, that there is one way of salvation. Some teach that one way is a specific content of faith: faith in Jesus Christ coming, the Old Testament, or arrived, the New Testament. The Scripture teaches the one way to be saved is not the believer's content of faith, but by God's grace through the sinner's faith without personal merit from the sinner but by Christ's merit alone. That way is the one and only way of salvation.

The Literal Hermeneutic

The grammatical-historical hermeneutic, aka: the Literal hermeneutic, is the hermeneutic of all biblically based theologies. The application differs among the theological systems. At any point in the interpretation of Scripture, if the Literal hermeneutic is abandoned, that system of theology ceases to be biblical at that point of departure. Why? Because the plain and normal meaning is the only certain way to discover the writer's intent in his writing.

That conviction is born out of almost five decades of studying Scripture. I have written and published commentaries on twenty-three New Testament books; the remaining four are in progress or planned, if the Lord gives me strength and time. I have also written commentaries on eight Old Testament books. I have written and published thirty books on Bible doctrines, requiring extensive study of both Old and New Testament Scripture. Never in any of the sixty-six books of the Bible have I discovered a need to abandon the Literal hermeneutic. Nor have I found either the human authors, or the Holy Spirit, or Jesus used any other method of interpretation.

One of those doctrinal books is on soteriology: *God's Choices, the Doctrines of Foreordination, Election, and Predestination*. Another of my doctrinal books is *The Literal Hermeneutic, Explained and Illustrated*. I have a sound basis for understanding the Scripture, and an understanding of the issues I discuss in this book.

I do not say these things to boast, but to say my understanding of these things is a matter of public record which anyone may verify.

The Literal Hermeneutic: Basic Rules and Principles

A "hermeneutic" is a method of interpretation. What is the Literal hermeneutic?

> 1. To discern the plain and normal meaning of what the author wrote, through the normal conventions of the language and words used by the author, in order to discern the author's intent in writing. The phrase "normal conventions of the language and words" means understanding the uses of language, the vocabulary, the rules of grammar, and the rules of syntax for the language used by the author to communicate his intent in writing.

2. To seek no other meaning in what the author wrote than what may legitimately be discerned in the plain and normal meaning of the language and words used by the author.

That definition fits how you read any news item, blog, book, article, or label on the can of food you bought. It is the normal way people interpret whatever they read from fiction to non-fiction, from poetry to fantasy, from secular to biblical.

That definition is the way every word of the Bible should be read. "Hermeneutics" is the science of interpretation. Interpretation is the search for the meaning in communication. Biblical hermeneutics is the science of interpreting the Bible. The Literal hermeneutic understands the biblical text in the plain and normal sense of words and their meanings as used in the language of the human author.

In greater detail.

The Literal hermeneutic understands the words and language used by the human authors of the Bible in the normal and plain sense of words and language as used in everyday conversation and writing.

Understanding words in their plain and normal sense means all words in all languages have a semantic content and range that reflects the historical-cultural background of the original writer and reader.

Understanding words in their plain and normal sense means that languages also communicate meaning through well-defined rules of vocabulary, grammar, and syntax.

Understanding words in their plain and normal sense means recognizing all language includes idioms, slang, figures of speech, and symbols specific to that language and the historical-cultural circumstances of original writer and reader, and that these must be interpreted for the modern reader in terms of his or her language.

Understanding idioms, slang, figures of speech, and symbols in the plain and normal sense of language means an idiom, slang, figure of speech, or symbol is based on something literal and is intended by the writer or speaker to communicate something literal. And the corollary: A symbol is not intended to communicate the literal thing on which it is based.

Understanding the biblical use of words, figures of speech, idioms, slang, and symbols means recognizing the biblical authors sometimes used and invested these parts of language with specific theological or spiritual meanings, and that the Holy Spirit maintained the consistency of those meanings among the several human authors.

If an interpretation invests an author's words, figures of speech, idioms, slang, or symbols with a meaning other than the plain and normal meaning of their use in the language in which he is communicating, then it is not a literal interpretation, but is an allegorical or spiritual interpretation: an abstract distortion of the meaning of the text dependent on the interpreter's imagination, not the biblical writer's truth-intention.

A "literal" hermeneutic determines the biblical author's intended meaning (his truth-intention) through the normal and plain sense of the words and language he used. To discover the author's truth-intention the Literal method applies historical, cultural, contextual, grammatical, lexical, syntactical, theological, genre, and doctrinal analysis to the author's text.

The Methods of Analysis

What are the historical, cultural, contextual, grammatical, lexical, syntactical, theological, genre, and doctrinal analysis of the Literal hermeneutic.

The Literal hermeneutic is really the application of seven methods of analysis to the biblical text: historical-cultural, contextual, lexical-syntactical, theological, literary (genre), and doctrinal aspects of Scripture, and comparison with other interpreters using the same methods. The interpreter synthesizes the facts discovered through judicious application of these analyses to arrive at an understanding of the biblical text [Virkler, 76]. These analyses are described as follows:

Historical-Cultural analysis: considers the historical-cultural milieu in which the author wrote. The facts of the historical-cultural background involve the task of reconstructing or comprehending the historical and cultural features of the specific passage. This requires an understanding of:

The situation of the writer, especially anything that helps explain why he or she wrote the passage.

The situation of the people involved in the text and/or the recipients of the book that can help explain why the writer penned this material to them.

The relationship between the writer and audience or the people involved in the text.

The cultural or historical features mentioned in the text.

Contextual analysis: considers the relationship of a given passage to the whole body of an author's writing.

Lexical-Syntactical analysis: develops an understanding of the definitions of words (lexicology) and their relationships to one another (syntax).

Theological analysis: studies the level of theological understanding at the time the revelation was given in order to ascertain the meaning of the text for its original readers. It takes into account related Scriptures, whether given before or after the passage being studied.

Literary (Genre) analysis: identifies the literary form or method used in a given passage: historical narrative, letters, doctrinal exposition, poetry, wisdom, prophetic.

Doctrinal analysis: the harmonization of doctrine in a specific passage with the full teaching of Scripture on that doctrine.

After the analyses are performed, one should compare his or her tentative interpretation with the work of other interpreters who also use the Literal hermeneutic. This step will substantiate a valid interpretation or alert the interpreter to a novel or aberrant interpretation, perhaps one already considered and discarded in the past history of interpretation. Certainly a novel or new interpretation should be re-examined and validated by careful exegesis if it is to be retained.

The "Literal" hermeneutic is in reality the "grammatical-historical-contextual-lexical-syntactical-theological-genre-doctrinal analysis of the Bible" hermeneutic, judiciously applied to the various literary genres in Scripture, the results of which are compared with other competent interpreters of past and present, and used to understand just what it is the Bible is teaching, whether in a particular verse or passage, or in relation to doctrine.

The Importance of Context

Context is the relationship of one part to other parts. In hermeneutics, context is the words before and after, the subject of the passage, the historical-cultural setting, the literary genre, and the doctrines and theology within the text.

Context considers: why did this happen; what is the stated purpose or reason? Why is this word, term, information, incident, event, circumstance placed here? These questions are answered in relation to the immediate subject and in relationship to the larger theme/purpose or context. The importance of asking the Scripture questions and listening to (seeking out) the answers cannot be overstated. Questions propel your mind in directions that would otherwise have been left untraveled. There are six basic questions to ask and answer to understand the context.

> Who: was the writer, the listener, the intended audience? The actor; the one acted upon?
>
> What: was said, what happened, what ideas were expressed, what was expected, what was the result?
>
> Where: does the event, happening, circumstance, situation take place: geographically, physically, mentally? Is there a journey during which the events take place?
>
> When: does the event, happening, circumstance, situation take place: historically, culturally, temporally? Is there a sequence in which the events take place?
>
> Why: did this happen; what is the stated purpose or reason? Why is this word, term, information, incident, event, circumstance placed here; in relation to the immediate subject or context; in relationship to the larger theme/purpose or context?

How: did this happen? How are things accomplished? How well were they accomplished? How quickly? By what means?

There are four basic contexts for any Scripture passage

1. The literary units immediately before it and immediately after it.

2. The particular book the passage is in.

3. The Testament the passage is in.

4. Compare Scripture with Scripture

There are four internal contexts that must be considered.

1. The subject of the passage.

2. The theme of the larger literary paragraph or section.

3. The genre of the book.

4. The style of the author.

There are four external or social contexts

1. Culture and cultural conflicts

2. History past and present

3. Language: word meanings and grammar. Grammar affects meaning.

4. The immediate reason for the writing (the external context).

There are four theological contexts to be remembered

1. The human author's original meaning and intent.

2. The divine author's universal meaning and intent.

3. The principles and precepts must harmonize with the entire Scripture.

4. The doctrines must harmonize with the entire Scripture.

To these may be added a fifth, the literary style of the biblical author. Literary style is the way an author combines words and grammar and kinds of expressions to form sentences and paragraphs. A literary style is often called the author's "voice," the way in which an author tells a story. One of the principles of divine inspiration is the Holy Spirit let each writer express himself in his own style of writing. When that style or voice is removed, it is kind of like removing the cream from the milk. Yes, skim milk is still milk, but the flavor is missing. Paying attention to a biblical writer's style helps the reader and interpreter gain a better understanding of the Scripture. Translators also create style, so read more than one translation.

The Literal Hermeneutic Is The Biblical Hermeneutic

The Literal hermeneutic is the hermeneutic of the Bible from the beginning. A few examples. Moses understood the universe and the world he inhabited was literally created and formed in seven sunset-to-sunset days. Abraham understood God to say he, Abraham, would literally procreate an heir to the promises. Abraham also understood literally God's command to sacrifice Isaac, and was stopped by God as he picked up the knife to kill his son.

Another example from Abraham's willingness to sacrifice Isaac will more fully illustrate the importance of the Literal hermeneutic. As Isaac and Abraham were walking up the mountain, Isaac asked Abraham a question. Isac was not a child, but an older adolescent or young adult. His question was an adult question, requiring an adult answer. (Scripture from Brenton LXX.)

> Genesis 22:7, And Isaac said to Abraam his father, "Father." And he said, "What is it, son?" And he said, "Behold the fire and the wood, where is the sheep for a whole-burnt-offering?"

> Genesis 22:8, And Abraam said, God will provide himself a sheep for a whole-burnt-offering, my son.

A non-literal hermeneutic, such as that used by Reformed soteriology and Promise soteriology, will say Abraham was pointing to a coming redeemer-messiah-christ. A non-literal hermeneutic will say Abraham's faith was in an unknown yet-future redeemer-messiah-christ that no Scripture, no Word from God then existing in the world, had ever mentioned. A non-literal hermeneutic gives no reason why Abraham bound Isaac and laid him on the altar and raised the knife to kill his son Isaac. A non-literal hermeneutic denies the later revelation of Hebrews 11:19, that Abraham believed God was able to raise Isaac out from the dead after Abraham killed him. A non-literal hermeneutic takes away Abraham's faith in YHWH and places it in an unknown, redeemer-messiah-christ.

A literal hermeneutic says either Aabraham expected God to step in and provide a sheep for sacrifice, or God intended Isacc to be the sheep. Certainly Abraham and Isaac understood the later interpretation as the literal interpretation, because:

> Genesis 22:8b–9, And both having gone together, came to the place which God spoke of to him; and there Abraam built the altar, and laid the wood on it, and having bound the feet of Isaac his son together, he laid him on the altar upon the wood. And Abraam stretched forth his hand to take the knife to slay his son.

Isaac allowed Abraham to bind his feet and put him on the altar and lay there as Abraham raised the knife over his body, all without a word of protest. The Literal hermeneutic prevails.

Jesus understood the historical narratives of creation and Jonah through the Literal hermeneutic. His every application of Scripture, e.g., his parables and illustrations, were based on a Literal understanding the Scripture, given with the expectation his followers would apply those principles to understand those parables and illustrations. So also the Twelve apostles and the apostle to the gentiles, Paul of Tarsus. This was the hermeneutic used by most of the church fathers. The Reformers picked up this hermeneutic from Augustine, who learned it from the Bible. Two Reformed examples.

> Thou shalt therefore understand that the Scripture hath but one sense which is the Literal sense. And that Literal sense is the root and ground of all, and the anchor that never faileth whereunto if thou cleave thou canst never err or go out of the way. And if thou leave the Literal sense thou canst not but go out of the way. [William Tyndale, *The Obedience of a Christian Man*, AD 1528. Accessed October 2018 at https://reformedreader.wordpress.com/2012/02/13/tyndale-on-biblical-interpretation/.]

> Let the plain text be thy guide, and the spirit of God (which is the author thereof) shall lead thee in all truth.[Miles Coverdale, *Coverdale Bible*, 1535 AD, "Translator to the Reader."]

A modern voice is Bernard Ramm [241].

> The word *Literal* may mean to somebody like Luther or Calvin the general philological approach to the Old Testament in contrast to the allegorical interpretation of the Church Fathers. But to a Dispensationalist *Literal* not only means a philological

approach but that the things predicted will be literally fulfilled.

How odd then that the Reformers did not also reform Augustine's eventual allegorical approach to eschatology (he began with the Literal hermeneutic), and also (the Reformers) applied a non-Literal exegesis to Old Testament soteriology, as I will show in the chapters Reformed Soteriology and Promise Soteriology.

A Good Bad Example

One of the sine qua non [Latin: without which nothing] characteristics of genuine Dispensational theology is the consistent application of the Literal hermeneutic to every scripture, every doctrine. "Consistently literal, or plain, interpretation indicates a dispensational approach to the interpretation of Scripture" [Ryrie, *Dispensationalism*, 40]. That some Dispensationalists have abandoned the Literal hermeneutic in soteriology is disheartening and confusing. Do I exaggerate?

In an otherwise excellent book, *What is Dispensationalism*, which I recommend, the author of the chapter, "How Were People Saved Before Jesus Came?" wrote this bit of Reformed soteriology as an explanation of Dispensational soteriology.

> Abraham, Job, and Moses illustrate that before Jesus came, people were saved by believing in the Christ who was yet to come [p. 168].

Now anyone who has read the Old Testament stories of Abraham, Job, and Moses—even casually—knows in those stories there is no mention that Abraham, Job, and Moses were saved by believing in the Christ who was yet to come; there is no mention of the Christ who is yet to come. As illustrations go, that is a meaningless illustration.

That writer then adds by way of explanation, "The [Old Testament] writers," he means the writers of the historical, wisdom, and prophetical books, thereby summarizing the entire written revelation in those terms, "assume that the readers [of the Old Testament] already know the way of salvation through the verbal revelation given by the prophets [p. 172].

By "verbal revelation" he meant "not written" revelation; he meant the Holy Spirit did not have the Old Testament authors write as Scripture the way of salvation (in his view) "believing in the Christ who was yet to come," but instead the Holy Spirit supposedly told the writers to become speakers and tell people to "believe in the Christ who is yet to come," without writing what they were saying. That verbal revelation to give the people knowledge not in their written Scripture, is not biblical soteriology.

My friends, that "verbal revelation" explanation is extrabiblical (not in the Bible) revelation. If it wasn't in the written Scripture given to the Old Testament peoples, it was not biblical revelation. That is exactly how cult leaders start cults, with revelation they received verbally, just like this fellow in that book said the Old Testament people received verbal revelation about Christ.

Depending on verbal revelation is not biblical hermeneutics; neither is it proper Dispensational hermeneutics. That explanation is the same as the Roman Catholic Church's "Deposit of Faith" concept, which (supposedly) includes unwritten, verbal tradition left to the New Testament church by Christ and passed down in the Roman Catholic Church verbally from one priest to another. Verbal tradition is not Scripture; neither is verbal revelation. To be Scripture it must be *written* revelation that is available to be read.

That particular writer's contribution to *What is Dispensationalism* mars an otherwise excellent book. Sadly, many who are dispensational in other doctrines adopt his non-dispensational soteriology, which may be why (?) the book's Editor selected that person to write the chapter. The writer summarily dismisses what I believe Scripture validates as a genuine dispensational view of soteriology. He wrote [165],

> How were people saved before Jesus came? Some suggest that people were saved by sincerely responding to what God had revealed to them at that time. They assert that this revelation did not include the need to believe in Christ.

Why does the writer deny a Literal hermeneutic and suggest extrabiblical revelation delivered verbally? He wrote [171].

> It would have been exceedingly difficult for someone to find the way of salvation [he means faith in the person Christ] in the unfinished OT since it is exceedingly difficult to find the way of salvation [faith in the person Christ] in the completed OT.

If I could, I would remind this author that the means by which he expects readers to understand what he meant is the Literal hermeneutic applied to his written word. Why then does he deny the Holy Spirit illuminated for the Old Testament peoples the plain and normal meaning of that Old Testament Scripture he gave to the Old Testament people for their salvation? The influence of Reformed soteriology, that willingness to abandon the Literal hermeneutic to meet doctrinal presuppositions, runs deep.

The means by which redemption was made known and grace was accessed in the Old Testament is exactly what that author rejected: faith in what God had revealed to them and explained to them in the Scripture God gave to them during their particular time in the history of redemption. That chapter in that book is what happens when a Dispensationalist abandons the Literal hermeneutic.

The Christocentric Hermeneutic

The Christocentric hermeneutic may be defined as "scripture should be interpreted primarily from the perspective of either of Jesus' character, values, principles, and priorities as revealed directly or indirectly by the biblical revelation of what he said and did." Another definition says, "The Christocentric principle advocates that we interpret all scripture in the light of the full and final revelation of God in Christ."

The focus of this hermeneutic is to see all of Scripture as a revelation of Christ, and therefore interpret all Scripture "in the light of the full and final revelation of God in Christ." That is how the Reformed find Christ in the Old Testament. When a Christocentric interpretation is applied to the Old Testament revelation, it means seeking another meaning than the plain and normal meaning.

Am I exaggerating? A proponent of the Christocentric hermeneutic said one of the recurring problems with this hermeneutic is the tendency of expositors to "impose a distorted picture of Christ upon other biblical texts" [Smith, 1].

My analysis of this hermeneutic, as I have seen it practiced, notices expositors using the Christocentric hermeneutic do three wrong things.

1. Discovering Christ in every Old Testament passage, or at least putting Christ in Old Testament passages where no reasonable exegesis can find him.

2. Reinterpreting Old Testament passages to speak about Christ

when no reasonable exegesis can find him in that passage.

3. Saying the Old Testament sinner was saved by believing on Christ as the object and content of faith—some using a Christocentric hermeneutic will even say Old Testament saving faith was belief in the specific person Jesus Christ.

This is what one would expect from a hermeneutic whose basis is to see all of Scripture as a revelation of Christ, and therefore interpret all Scripture in the light of the full and final revelation of God in Christ.

Am I exaggerating? One person said he saw Christ on the cross in Moses outstretched arms, Exodus 17:11–12, in the battle against Amalek.

A non-Dispensational friend (he describes himself as non-dispensational) told me how he applies the Christocentric hermeneutic. He stated his use of the Christocentric hermeneutic asks these questions.

1. What did the original audience understand and what is the original meaning of the text.

2. What revelation have we received since the transmission of this particular text, and what is the impact that it would have in the extent of what we understand this text to be teaching.

3. Further revelation does not CHANGE the original meaning, rather, it adds to, qualifies, or clarifies the meaning of an original text...if it has any impact on the original text at all.

I appreciated his honesty, and knowing something about him, I have confidence he is careful in applying those three questions to his scripture exegesis and his pastoral ministry. I did not tell him he had restated the three basic principles of the Literal hermeneutic.

1. Analogy of Scripture. This principle asks, "How does a passage fit into the total pattern of God's revelation that was revealed prior to its writing?

2. Analogy of Faith. This principle asks, "How does a passage fit into the total pattern of God's revelation that has been revealed at any time?

3. "The primary meaning of any Bible passage is found in that passage. The New Testament does not reinterpret or transcend Old Testament passages in a way that overrides or cancels the

original authorial intent of the Old Testament writers" [Vlach, *Dispensationalism*, 31].

The Christocentric hermeneutic errs in practice, if not in principle. The Old Testament revelation, because of the limitations imposed by the nature of the Holy Spirit's progressive revelation—here a little, there a little—is like many steps on a long stairway. Each successive step builds upwards to the landing at the top, and when we reach the landing, after taking each successive step, we can look back and see the entire stairway. But as we climb the steps our vision is necessarily limited to the step we are on, and the ones below us. So the Old Testament peoples only knew what came before, and what was told to them during their particular time in history. They could not see further ahead than the step they were on. To discover a coming Messiah-Christ in Old Testament scriptures where the Hebrew *māshîah* is not used of a coming messiah, or where a coming messiah is not legitimately within in the normal and plain meaning of the text, is the consistent hermeneutical error of Reformed and Dispensational Promise soteriology.

Today we have the completed New Testament revelation. Therefore we understand, as my non-Dispensational friend said, "the impact that it [a particular text] would have in the extent of what we understand this text to be teaching." But the Old Testament peoples did not and could not have that perspective, because they did not have the New Testament revelation.

Again because we have the completed New Testament revelation, we also understand, as my non-Dispensational friend said, how the completed revelation "adds to, qualifies, or clarifies the meaning of an original text ... if it has any impact on the original text at all." But the Old Testament peoples did not and could not have that perspective, because they did not have the New Testament revelation.

If we keep those limitations in mind, then we will without fail seek the biblical author's meaning through application of the Literal hermeneutic. My experience with many of those using a Christocentric hermeneutic does not justify confidence those limitations of the Old Testament peoples will be kept in mind.

The Old Testament text must be interpreted within its own context. The New Testament writers applied the Old Testament revelation, under the superintending influence of the Holy Spirit, to create the New Testament revelation, without changing the meaning of Old Testament revelation had fer the Old Testament peoples.

Therefore, we must understand how the application of the Old in the New is able to deeply enrich our faith, without changing the Old. For example, the Old Testament people understood Psalm 2:7, Isaiah 7:14; 9:6–7; 52:13–53:12 much differently than we are able to understand those verses through the lens of completed New Testament revelation. That fuller understanding is important. The exegete must apply *both* the Analogy of Faith and the Analogy of Scripture equally to respect the integrity of the message, but must never conflate the two, thus rule three.

Excursus: Hermeneutics and Scripture

I am of the school that believes examples and illustrations are the best teachers.

One of the tools of the Literal hermeneutic is Lexical-Syntactical analysis. Lexical is a two-bit word for vocabulary: denotation, connotation, semantic range.

Denotation: the literal or primary meaning of a word.

Connotation: an idea or feeling that a word invokes in addition to its literal or primary meaning.

Semantic Range: meaning created by the use of a word in context and culture.

Semantic range is not as difficult as it sounds. The word "ran" as an example. I ran a mile; I ran a business; I ran my mouth; and many more. Synonyms and antonyms are part of semantic range. Synonyms: I ran, trotted, jogged, sprinted a mile. Antonym: I walked a mile.

Syntactical, or "syntax" is how words and grammar are used to put together meaningful sentences. Did the cat eat the rat? Did the rat eat the cat? How one uses words and grammar to put that sentence together in English makes a difference.

Just as there are rules for words there are rules for grammar. The most commonly known are verb tenses: past, present, future; perfect, pluperfect, and imperfect; etc. In the Greek language verb tenses often result in strange English translations. For example, Ephesians 2:8 should be translated, "For by grace you are having been saved," to express the combination of the Greek present and perfect tenses. The combination indicates the present continuing result of a past completed action. God saved the believer by his grace in the past, and by his grace God maintains the believer's salvation in the present. How much confusion over the eternal security of salvation might have been avoided with a proper translation?

Another rule of grammar concerns conjunctions: and, or, but, also, since, because, when, however, therefore. The conjunction "and" is a coordinating conjunction. When used it means the subjects connected by the conjunction are in some way equal; or the action performed by the subjects is in some way equal.

For example, Galatians 6:16. The two parties on either side of the "and" are in some way equal. The "Israel of God" is a subset of the larger group of believers, "those who walk according to this rule." The rule is faith in Christ as Savior is what matters, not circumcision or uncircumcision. 6:12–15. The New Testament church is not Israel, the "Israel of God" are Hebrew believers in the New Testament church conforming to the rule.

Genesis 3:15 is another place where grammar is important. "He [Woman's offspring] shall *shup* your [serpent's offspring] head and you [serpent's offspring] shall *shup* his [Woman's offspring] heel." The word *shup* means bruise, strike, or crush. The coordinating conjunction "and" means 1) both offspring are in some way equal, and 2) both offspring perform equal actions.

In the usual interpretation of this scripture, Satan shall *shup* Christ, and Christ shall *shup* Satan. The problem with that usual interpretation is it ignores the grammatical value of the coordinating conjunction "and." To say that more clearly, both parties are equal in that they are both doing the same action. Following the usual interpretation, if Satan does significant physical harm to Christ, then Christ must do significant physical harm to Satan. Satan killed Christ. What physical harm did Satan suffer from Christ? Nothing. The usual interpretation breaks down when the Lexical-Syntactical analysis of the Literal hermeneutic is applied.

The better interpretation is the Woman's *unbelieving* offspring do physical harm to the Woman's *believing* offspring, and vice versa. That has been the experience of the ages: the continuing conflict between those of faith with those of no faith. In this interpretation the grammatical value of "and" plays an interpretive role. Both parties are the same, and both actions are the same. Looking to the Analogy of Faith, the only references to Genesis 3:15 in the entire Scripture are Genesis 4:25; Romans 16:20; Revelation 12:9. Genesis 4:25 supports the continuing conflict interpretation, as does Romans 16:20 if we understand Satan as the one motivating the conflict between human beings of faith and no-faith.

When interpreting Scripture one must always consider all the rules of the Literal hermeneutic before arriving at a conclusion. One of those rules, based on the Analogy of Faith, is don't read later revelation into earlier revelation. I have a quite simple rule for exegesis.

> The foundation of the New Testament revelation is the Old Testament revelation, but the Old Testament revelation, being the foundation, exists without the structure built upon it, which is the New Testament revelation. Therefore, one is able to understand the Old Testament revelation without resorting to the New Testament revelation for understanding. An interpretation of the Old Testament revelation that consists of New Testament truths is eisegesis, not exegesis. An interpretation of the New Testament revelation that does not include Old Testament truth is incomplete exegesis.

I have included an Appendix: Principles and Precepts of the Literal Hermeneutic.

The Content of Faith Concept

Content of Faith. A term in Dispensational theology that describes God's testimony in history, as the means by which God's grace in salvation is accessed. The sinner is always saved by God's grace through the sinner's faith in God, through God's historically current testimony as given in the progressive revelation of truth. That "historically current testimony" is the content of faith.

The content of faith changes as God progressively gives new revelation and changes the economies (dispensations) through which he administers his affairs in the world. As faith is the means by which God's grace in salvation is accessed, the content of faith (God's testimony), was the historical means whereby God's grace was accessed in the various dispensations. [Quiggle, *Dictionary.*]

The "content of faith" concept says the sinner is always saved by God's grace through the sinner's faith in God, through God's historically current testimony as given in the progressive revelation of truth.

What is the progressive revelation of truth?

> Progressive Revelation. The doctrine of progressive revelation is the simple observation God does not reveal all things at the same time, but over time God's revelation is completed. As God said through Isaiah 28:10 (ESV), "For it is precept upon precept, precept upon precept, line upon line, line upon line, here a little, there a little." The concept recognizes "the identity of the germ contained in the earliest mention of a theme continues in the buildup of that theme as the same seminal idea takes on a more developed form in later revelation" [Kaiser and Silva.] [Quiggle, *Dictionary.*]

Noah did not know what Abraham knew. Abraham did not know what Moses knew. Moses did not know what King David knew, and King David did not know what Isaiah knew. Each man successively in the progress of history had received additional revelation in the progressive revelation of truth as history progressed.

How does this relate to Dispensational soteriology? Whether the content of faith is, e.g., believe in the judgment to come and get in the ark (Noah's dispensation), or bring the proper sacrifice in repentance and confession (Moses' dispensation) the salvific elements are:

The believer's faith in the content of faith given to them in Scripture as the way of salvation.

God's gift of grace-faith-salvation infallibly convicting the sinner to accept that content as the way of salvation.

God by grace applying the merit of Christ's propitiation to save the believing sinner.

The Reformed accuse the Dispensational of teaching more than one way of salvation, because in Reformed soteriology the one way of salvation is a particular content of faith: faith in Christ. However, in Scripture the one way of salvation is the third item on the above list: the propitiation made by Christ. Substituting the means, the content of faith, by which salvation is made known and accessed, for the actual act of salvation—by Christ's merit alone—is the great error of Reformed soteriology.

Ryrie's explanation of salvation is relevant [*Dispensationalism*, 115].

The basis of salvation in every age is the death [propitiation] made by Christ; the requirement for salvation in every age is faith; the object of faith in every age is God; the content of faith changes in the various dispensations.

In every dispensation, in every age of humankind, in the entire history of redemption, a sinner is always saved by God's grace and the merit of Christ's propitiation, through the sinner's faith in God and God's historically current testimony as to the means of salvation, as given by the Holy Spirit in the written progressive revelation of truth.

The Holy Spirit did with the Old Testament revelation for the Old Testament believer, exactly what he does with the Old and New Testament revelation for the New Testament believer: he illuminated (gave spiritual perception for understanding) the plain and normal meaning of the Old Testament revelation for the Old Testament believer, within the grammatical-historical-cultural-lexical-syntactical context of that Old Testament revelation, as given to each Old Testament believer within his or her receipt of the historical progressive revelation of truth.

Adam was given understanding of the revelation he had been given. Noah was given understanding of the revelation he had been given.

Abraham was given understanding of the revelation he had been given. Moses was given understanding of the revelation he had been given. And so on to the end of the Old Testament revelation, Malachi, ca, 435-400 BC. In the intertestamental period those Old Testament believers were given understanding of the Old Testament revelation: Genesis through Malachi. But no one in the Old Testament was given a New Testament understanding of the Old Testament revelation they had received.

Examples of Content of Faith During The Old Testament

What saved Enoch? When Enoch "walked with God," he had faith in God and God's testimony, as given from Adam's time to his time, and ordered his behavior to conform to that faith and testimony.

(We must consider that in this early time in both human history and the progressive revelation of truth, God may have used the natural revelation (Paul speaks of natural revelation in Romans 1:20), as part of the content of saving faith. Can natural revelation be sufficient testimony to save? Only if God has given the sinner his gift of grace-faith-salvation, Ephesians 2:8, to make that natural testimony efficacious to save. The possibility of natural revelation to be salvific during the time from Adam to Noah must be considered, whether actual or not. However, the more likely salvific source from Adam to Noah was the testimony of salvation through Adam and his believing descendants. God's historically current testimony, however delivered, is always the content of saving faith.)

What saved Noah? Perhaps the beginning question should be, was Noah saved from the penalty of sin, regenerated, and given eternal life? The Writer of Hebrews said (11:7), Noah "became heir of the righteousness which is according to faith." Noah was saved in the same sense that word is used of New Testament believers: from the penalty of sin, regenerated, and given eternal life; as were all the Old Testament persons who were saved.

So, by what means was Noah saved? Noah "found grace in the eyes of YHWH." That grace was the same given to Enoch, because Noah was part of that dispensation. Then God said (paraphrasing), "Build an ark; I will destroy the earth with a flood; I will make my covenant with you; you and your family will go into the ark with the animals (take food for you and them)." And "Thus Noah did; according to all that God commanded him, so he did," Genesis 6:13–21.

What saved Noah's soul? He believed God and God's testimony given to Adam, as did Enoch The demonstration of his salvation is he believed God and God's further testimony of coming judgment and deliverance. There is no mention of a coming redeemer or messiah in Genesis chapters 1:1–9:29. The object of Noah's faith was God. The content of Noah's faith was God's testimony before YHWH's announcement of the Flood, and faith in God's testimony concerning the flood and the means of deliverance from the flood. Noah, like Abraham 400 years later, believed God and God's testimony. His faith was accounted to him for righteousness.

(It is worth noting here that anyone could have believed God's testimony as given through Noah and entered the ark, until God closed the door, Genesis 7:16. Those who did enter the ark had received God's gift of grace-faith-salvation. However, any might have entered, because God does not prevent any sinner from coming in faith and being saved; that is what sin does.)

What saved Moses? The Old Testament sinner bringing a lamb to sacrifice for his or her sins did not save anyone during the time of the Law. What saved was their faith was in God and God's testimony that their sin would be forgiven if they brought a sacrificial lamb by faith with repentance and confession for their sin. How did they know to do that? That was what God's testimony told them to do as the expression of their faith in God's forgiveness. Just bringing a sacrifice didn't save them.

What saved the believer under the Law of Moses was God's grace accepting their faith in God and God's testimony that the proper sacrifice offered with faith and repentance resulted in the forgiveness of sin. Is it different today? What saves the sinner today is God's grace accepting the sinner's faith in God and God's testimony that the proper sacrifice—Jesus the Christ—offered with repentance from sin and faith in God and his testimony, results in the forgiveness of every past, present, and future sin.

I must add that the testimony by which God's saving grace was accessed during the times of the Law of Moses, and the testimony by which God's saving grace is accessed during the times of the New Testament church, are not two ways of salvation. There is one way of salvation: God's grace through the sinner's faith apart from any personal merit by the sinner but by Christ's merit only. The different testimonies given by God to different people groups in the natural course of God's progressive revelation are the expression of saving faith for those people groups. In a word, the "content" of faith.

According to Dispensational soteriology, Abel believed God's testimony and sacrificed. Enoch believed God's testimony and walked with God. Noah believed God's testimony and built an ark. Abraham believed God's testimony and moved to the land and had an heir. Joseph believed in the covenant God made with his great-grandfather Abraham, and faith caused him to give instructions concerning his body. Moses believed God's testimony, that God would accept his faith through sacrifice and confession and repentance, and by grace would forgive his sin. In these New Testament times, the sinner believes God's testimony that salvation is by grace through faith in the risen Jesus Christ.

What saves—what has always saved the sinner—is Christ's merit, God's grace, and the sinner's faith in God and his testimony, through the scriptures that God gave to them within their historical-cultural context, in order to the salvation of their souls.

An Objection

Reformed theology's approach to Dispensational soteriology is to try to kill the doctrine with a thousand meaningless objections. Yet, every objection falls to the consistent application of the Literal hermeneutic. I will answer one objection as an example of all.

John 8:56 reads, "Abraham your father rejoiced in that he should see my day, and he saw and rejoiced." The main problem in interpreting this verse is that it is deliberately misread as, "Abraham saw Me." No, Abraham did not see Christ, he saw Christ's "day." Did Abraham see the day of the Messiah? That would be difficult from the promises given to him, as no messiah was mentioned. There is no Old Testament scripture that states or implies Abraham saw the advent of Messiah. (That he did see the Messiah is a Jewish interpretation, originating in the intertestamental period, that has seeped into Reformed soteriology.)

Abraham's faith was in God's promise of an "offspring" to fulfill the covenant. Abraham need not understand that the offspring in the promise of an heir was a coming redeemer-messiah-christ, because Abraham believed in the promise of fulfillment through an offspring from his own body. God gave Abraham certain promises concerning his posterity, and it was Abraham's faith in these promises to which Jesus referred. Abraham perceived by faith that through his descendant all the families of the earth would be blessed. Later revelation, the Analogy of Faith, confirms that interpretation. Abraham believed and sought a heavenly country; Hebrews 11:14, 16, Abraham believed and looked for a city whose builder and maker is God; Hebrews 11:10. Abraham believed God would fulfill the promise through Isaac, even if he killed Isaac, Hebrews 11:17–19, because God had told Abraham twenty years earlier he, YHWH, would establish his covenant with Abraham through Isaac, Genesis 17:19, 21.

If we will just let the Scripture speak—if we do the hard work of interpreting by the Literal hermeneutic—instead of telling the Scripture what to say, the Holy Spirit will reward our faith with understanding. Abraham need not understand messianic fulfillment to have faith in and rejoice in the promises which later New Testament revelation said was fulfilled by the Messiah.

Is it not the same for the New Testament believer? The Christian by faith perceives the day in which he or she will be delivered from the presence of sin; and the day of resurrection; and the day of the Kingdom on earth. Even the same, by faith Abraham perceived there would be a time in which an heir from his body—every descendant of Isaac was from Abraham's body—would receive the promises.

A Consistent View

A genuine Dispensationalism practicing the rules and principles of the Literal hermeneutic has a consistent view of salvation: a consistent, biblical way of salvation applicable to every sinner beginning with Cain and Abel. In every dispensation, sinners access God's grace through their faith in God and his historical testimony, not by belief in some as yet unknown future person or event discovered through extrabiblical revelation or illumination.

What do Dispensationalists believe?

> Salvation is God by grace forgiving a sinner's judicial guilt and remitting sin's penalty through the application of Christ's limitless merit.

Salvation is gained by receiving God's gift of grace-faith-salvation and applying that gift by means of personal faith in the content of faith God has revealed in any particular age or dispensation.

The basis of salvation in every age is the propitiation made by Christ; the requirement for salvation in every age is faith; the object of faith in every age is God; the content of faith changes in the various dispensations.

Whether the content of faith is, e.g., believe in the judgment to come and get in the ark (Noah's dispensation), or bring the proper sacrifice in repentance and confession (Moses' dispensation) the salvific elements are: the believer's faith in the content of faith as the way of salvation; God's gift of grace-faith-salvation infallibly convicting the sinner to accept that content as the way of salvation; God by grace applying Christ's merit to save the believing sinner.

Salvation is obtained only by grace through faith, not by works, and is maintained by grace through faith, not by works.

The means by which any sinner knows how to be saved, is in Dispensational soteriology the rational consequence of what Ryrie named "the content of faith." The changing "content of faith" is always based in God and his historical testimony—what God had revealed to them at that time.

Salvation has always been accessed by God's grace through the sinner's faith. The content of that faith has changed throughout the history of redemption. Salvation in the New Testament Church dispensation occurs when a sinner repents of his or her sins and believes on Christ as their Savior, Acts 2:38; 3:19–20; 11:18; Romans 3:22–26; 10:9–10, 13; Galatians 3:22; 1 Peter 1:21; 1 John 3:23.

In the chapter "Dispensational Soteriology" I will state the content of faith, as I understand it from the Scripture, for each dispensation during the history of redemption.

What Is Free Will

Before discussing Arminian soteriology, there is a need to understand how the Scripture defines free will. The Scripture is not a dictionary, but by observing the whole teaching of Scripture, throughout the Old Testament and New Testament, definitions of doctrinal concepts may be developed. The following is an extract from my book, *Dictionary of Doctrinal Words*.

Free Will, Or Freely Made Choices.

The will is the decision-making faculty of human nature. Free will may be defined as the moral authority God designed into his sentient creatures to make choices within the physical, moral, and spiritual boundaries of their nature, as further influenced by internal and external motivations and consequences.

The two important aspects of that definition are the "physical, moral, and spiritual boundaries," and "internal and external motivations and consequences."

Free will is not a license to think or do anything I want. Free will is limited by the attributes and characteristics of human nature. These form the boundaries in which free will may be exercised. If it helps, think of those attributes and characteristics of human nature as a fence beyond which one cannot go, whether physically, morally, or spiritually. Any decision may be made that the fence allows, including decisions to commit acts of sinning, and the decision to reject God and his salvation. The latter, in fact, that decision to reject God and his salvation, is the only decision regarding God and his salvation that the fence formed by the sinful unsaved human nature will allow.

The other important aspect to the exercise of free will is the influence of internal and external motivations and consequences. The internal motivations of the person, the external motivations applied to the person by influences outside the person, and the consequences arising from a person's freely made choices—all influence the exercise of free will, but do not change the fact the will freely makes decisions.

Right now, you are deciding to continue reading or stop. No one is making that decision for you. Your decision will be influenced by various internal motivations, such as your spiritual state (saved or unsaved), curiosity, the desire to learn, or perhaps the desire to respond to this "bloated windbag of a theologian" (as some have said). You are also experiencing various external motivations, including prior teaching you have received on the subject, and your own investigations of relevant scriptures. Whatever you decision, you exercised your free will.

As sinful human beings we try to hide, or even deny, our free will behind motivations and consequences. If the motivations and consequences are good we claim the choices we made. If the motivations and consequences are bad we say we were forced or coerced to make those choices. No, the choice is always yours, you alone are responsible for your choices.

Even the slave—even a slave to sin—makes a decision to obey or not to obey, as influenced by motivations and by the consequences of his choices. Even the slave is not prevented from exercising his free will because of the consequences of those choices.

So free will, like liberty or freedom, isn't a license to think or do anything I want. Just as a physical fence limits choices to "this far, no further," even so the fence formed by the physical, moral, and spiritual aspects of human nature say "this far, no further"; and these are fences one cannot climb over. One cannot freely choose to flap his arms and fly to the store because of the physical boundaries of human nature. Even so, the moral and spiritual boundaries limit the exercise of free will.

Free will is limited by the attributes and characteristics of human nature. Looking at the spiritual boundaries, the will is not neutrally suspended between good and evil, but is inclined toward one or the other by its spiritual attributes as created by God, corrupted by sin, and in the case of the saved, regenerated by salvation. The spiritual boundary does not allow the sinner to initiate salvation, nor believe and be saved unaided by the efficacious influence of God's gift of grace-faith-salvation (Ephesians 2:8).

In the case of unsaved human beings, the will is inclined toward sin because of the principle of rebellion (the sin attribute) that became part of human nature following Adam's sin and propagation. The inclination of sin is to rebel against God and disobey his commandments, thereby effectively persuading human beings to choose their path in life apart from God. The sinner freely chooses to commit acts of sinning, including the sin to reject God and his salvation. The unsaved human being is unable to overcome the spiritual boundary of the sin attribute without God's gift of grace-faith-salvation.

The sinner freely chooses to sin, his choice conditioned by the moral and spiritual boundaries set by the sin attribute in his or her human nature. Without that freely made choice there is no responsibility, accountability, or liability. When we deny that free exercise of the will, we have denied God made humankind with the power to choose, the moral authority to exercise choice, the responsibility to choose rightly, and equally as important to God's justice, the accountability and liability for every freely made choice. When we deny the free exercise of will, we have proclaimed God made human beings programmed automatons who dance on the string of God's sovereignty.

God changes the spiritual boundary of the sinner through his gift, Ephesians 2:8, thereby changing the kind of choices that may be made. Staying with the same illustration, God moves the fence to a different spiritual boundary, so different choices may be made. God by his gift initiates salvation in the sinner by changing the spiritual boundary (1 Corinthians 2:14; Romans 6:14) in which free will operates. The gift enlivens the person's spiritual perception, whereby the sinner is able to understand the spiritual issues of his sin, Christ the only Savior, salvation by faith alone, and thereby the sinner willingly obeys God's command to believe and be saved, whereupon God completes that salvation through the regeneration of the human nature from unsaved to saved.

The saved, born-again believer freely chooses to deny temptation because those choices are within the spiritual boundary of the born-again human nature.

All decisions made by every human being are made within the limits imposed by the boundaries of the human nature of sinner or saint, as further influenced by internal and external motivations and consequences. That is free will.

Arminian soteriology originates in two philosophical principles.

Divine sovereignty is not compatible with human freedom, and therefore not compatible with human responsibility.

Ability limits obligation.

Therefore, says Arminian soteriology, faith cannot originate in God, but is a free and responsible human act exercised independent of God, and since the Bible regards faith as obligatory, then the ability to believe must be universal.

To understand the error of Arminian soteriology, one must understand the exercise of free will is not the error, but rather the error is making free will the determining factor between saved or unsaved. Faith is freely exercised, but the determining factors are God's foreordination, Ephesians 1:4, God's gift of grace-faith-salvation, Ephesians 2:8, and Christ's propitiation, Romans 3:21–26; Hebrews 2:17; 1 John 2:2; 4:10.

The salvation principle, at its most basic, is by God's grace through the sinner's faith by Christ's propitiation. God's grace does not enable a sinner choose between No or Yes. The sinner's faith is the consequence of God's grace, and is the God-ordained means by which the sinner accesses the unlimited merit of Christ's propitiation. Without God's grace there is no faith; without Christ's propitiation there is no merit to overcome the demerit of sin. The faith expressed by the sinner as a consequence of God's gift (Ephesians 2:8) is the empty hand of the soul reaching out to receive God-given salvation.

Divine Sovereignty And Human Freedom

Divine sovereignty is compatible with human freedom. This is not the place to discuss foreordination (see my book, *God's Choices*), but succinctly, before God created anything, God omnisciently knew within himself all the possible consequences that could arise from his decision to create. That omniscient knowledge included all possible freely made choices that might be made by the sentient creatures he would create. God foreordained certain possible freely made choices from possible to actual, such as fit his purpose in creating, and his plans and processes to fulfill that purpose. God's choice of which to effectuate from possible to actual was not based on prescience (foresight) but his omniscient wisdom as to which freely made choices fit his purpose in creating.

> Omniscience is what God knows within himself without input from any source outside himself. Omniscience is that attribute of God which is the perfection of his knowledge and wisdom. His knowledge and wisdom are without limitation. God knows all things, including himself and everything actual or potential in his creation.

Therefore all freely made choices are certain, because foreordained, but not necessary, because freely made by the person within his or her circumstances.

The orthodox doctrine is this. What God knew in himself is that he chose (foreordination) to effectuate Adam's freely made choice to sin: permission to sin, not a decree mandating sin. Whether or not there were other possible choices is hypothetical and irrelevant. Perhaps all of Adam's possible choices led to his act of disobedience? We may be certain at least one of Adam's possible choices was to disobey God's command. That is the freely made choice God chose to effectuate from possible to actual.

Adam, not God, is culpable (criminally responsible) for his sin, because in the historical moment Adam's choice was freely made. In relation to human freedom and responsibility, the choice to sin originated in Adam, both in relation to God's foreordaining decree, and in the historical moment. God did not decree Adam would sin (contra supralapsarianism), God effectuated Adam's freely made choice to sin. Therefore, Adam's choice was not necessary, because freely made, but it was certain, because foreordained.

By God's foreordaining decree Adam was appointed the legal representative of all his descendants. By God's Law of Biological Reproduction Adam was made the seminal head of the human race. By Adam's freely made choice to sin, and by Adam's propagation after he sinned, all in Adam, the entire human race, became sinners, 1 Corinthians 15:22.

God therefore, by his sovereign choices, in the timelessness before God created anything, knew that all human beings who would exist in the universe God would create, would be sinners by reason of Adam's freely made choice to sin. That meant without God's intervention none would be saved. On the basis of his internal knowledge, God chose (foreordination) to give some sinners his gift of grace-faith-salvation, thereby changing the boundary of sin's rebellion to willingness, so the sinner receiving the gift would freely and willingly choose to believe and be saved. God's electing choices does not prevent faith, that is what sin does. God's grace in salvation is so completely and perfectly efficacious the sinner's human nature will be changed, the sinner will inevitably freely choose to believe, and thereby will be saved.

Therefore, God's act of foreordination of human freely made choices is compatible with human freedom and responsibility, having been sovereignly designed to be compatible in the timelessness of eternity before God's act of creating the universe. Out of all possible freely made choices, God chose to effectuate some freely made choices from possible to certain, because those freely made choices were agreeable to his purpose in creating.

Obligation And Ability

The second Arminian principle is, "ability limits obligation." This was a response to the Reformed doctrine that sin renders human beings unable to freely respond to the obligation to believe and be saved. However, Reformed theology overstates the case for inability, and Arminian theology misunderstands inability.

There are two effects of inability caused by the indwelling sin attribute. The first is stated in 1 Corinthians 2:14, "But a natural person does not accept things of the Spirit of God, for they are absurd to him, and he is not able to know them, because they are discerned spiritually." The unsaved person lacks spiritual perception. What is spiritual perception?

> Spiritual perception. A faculty of the human soul that allows man to perceive, understand, and communicate with God. The ability of the soul to receive and understand spiritual things. A faculty of the soul through which man has communion with God. The ability of the soul to receive, understand, and appropriately apply biblical knowledge to live godly in this present world. In the unsaved soul the sin attribute has rendered spiritual perception grossly insensitive, such that the unsaved person does not have the spiritual discernment to receive or understand the things of the Spirit of God, 1 Corinthians 2:14. [Quiggle, *Dictionary.*]

The unsaved sinner's inability to perceive spiritual things leads to a second effect of inability. Ephesians 2:1, "... dead in your trespasses and your sins." Some (too many) of Reformed theology compare "dead" to physically dead. Such is not the case. The unsaved person is spiritually dead. The practical implications of spiritually dead and lacking spiritual perception are simple: constant, willing, freely made choices to act in unremitting rebellion against and rejection of God and his salvation. The fact that rebellion is freely chosen means sin does not create inability, but gives the wrong kind of ability: to freely choose to reject God and God's salvation.

The unsaved sinner is spiritual dead in relation to God, spiritually active in relation to his freely made choices to commit acts of sinning.

The sinner's inability to receive spiritual things generates a freely chosen response of rebellion and disobedience to the obligation to positively respond to God's call to believe and be saved. Therefore, inability does not limit obligation, because the sinner does respond, by acting in obligation to his sinful human nature. A negative response reflects the ability to respond as much as a positive response. And whether or not we agree that God's sovereignty is compatible with human freedom, the human freedom to choose rebellion versus belief is compatible with human responsibility.

Let us return to the definition of free will (previous chapter). "Free will is the moral authority God designed into his sentient creatures to make choices within the physical, moral, and spiritual boundaries of their nature, as further influenced by internal and external motivations and consequences." The sinner is making choices. The internal motivation is the "fence" set by the sin attribute allowing negative choices, but not positive choices, in relation to the obligation to believe.

When the sinner is confronted by the obligation to believe, God is not preventing the sinner from choosing a positive response. The sinner's sinful human nature chooses to make a negative response. Because the negative response is a freely made choice, the sinner is culpable for his or her wrong choice. The issue is not inability but culpability. Ignorance of the law is a legal principle holding that a person who is unaware of a law may not escape liability for violating that law merely by being unaware of its content. So also God and his laws.

However, the sinner is without the excuse of ignorance, because God designed into the human conscience God's moral principles of right and wrong. The sinner knows the right choice concerning faith and salvation, but rejects that choice because it is absurd to him. Through God's design of human nature the sinner knows the right choice. Because the sinner knows the right choice, the sinner is culpable for his or her freely made wrong choice.

How do I know a sinner is aware of right and wrong? Because God designed a conscious into human nature, informed by God's moral laws.

> Romans 1:18–21, For the wrath of God from heaven is revealed upon all ungodliness and unrighteousness of humankind, by unrighteousness suppressing the truth, 19 because the known of God is revealed in them, for God has revealed it to them. 20 For that which cannot be seen visibly of him are perceived, being understood from the creation of the world by the things made, both his eternal power and deity, for them to be without excuse. 21 For having known God, they did not glorify him as God, or were thankful, but were without real wisdom in their reasonings, and their foolish heart was darkened.

> Romans 2:12–16, For as many as sinned without Law also without Law will perish. And as many as with Law sinned according to Law will be judged. 13 For not the hearers of Law are righteous with God, but doers of Law will be justified. 14 For when gentiles not having Law by nature do the things of the Law, these not having Law are to themselves a law, 15 who show the work of the Law written in their hearts, their conscience testifying, and between one another the reckoning accusing or else defending, 16 in that day when God will judge the secrets of men, according to my Good News, by Christ Jesus.

Ability does not limit obligation, because all know, and all are culpable. No one sins unwillingly, every act of sinning is a freely made choice.

Arminian Soteriology

Biblically, free will is the empty hand of the soul reaching out to receive salvation from God. The soul freely extends its hand—willingly exercises saving faith—because the gift of God has changed human nature so efficiently (efficacious grace) that the former rebel against

God now willingly desires salvation.

The main issue in Arminian soteriology, seldom identified by others, is prevenient grace. The word "prevenient' means goes before. Prevenient grace means grace goes before salvation. Every soteriology, including Arminian, believes in the prevenient grace of Ephesians 2:8. The difference among the competing soteriologies is when and how prevenient grace is applied.

Reformed and Dispensational soteriology view prevenient grace as applied individually by God through his foreordained gift of grace-faith-salvation, Ephesians 2:8, thereby electing certain individuals to receive the gift. That gift is individually efficacious in changing the spiritual boundaries of the person receiving the gift, so the person freely, willingly, and inevitably chooses to exercise saving faith.

Arminian soteriology believes prevenient grace is applied universally by God to every human being through his gift of grace-faith-salvation, Ephesians 2:8. Arminian soteriology views prevenient grace as God giving every sinner the grace needed to freely decide for him or herself whether or not to believe the gospel and be saved: a neutral free will neither disinclined by sin nor inclined by God's efficacious grace. In Arminian soteriology, the way in which prevenient grace is efficacious is to enable any sinner to choose to believe and be saved, or chose to remain a sinner. God gives this prevenient grace to all because of Christ's work on the cross, so that all people are capable of hearing and responding gospel as they may choose. (A few Dispensationalists accept Arminian soteriology.)

The history of the Arminian view is instructive.

> In the original Arminian view, the sinner is in bondage to sin until he/she hears the gospel, and the hearing of the gospel is itself the application of prevenient grace, by which the sinner is enabled to exercise saving faith, or not, as he/she may choose.

> In the second Arminian view, the sinner is in partial bondage to sin, but God is always indiscriminately drawing sinners to Christ, and this act of drawing is the prevenient grace which, as the gospel is heard, makes the sinner capable of hearing and responding gospel as he or she may choose to believe and be saved, or not.

The third, and modern, Arminian view (developed by Charles Wesley) is that because of the first coming and atoning work of Christ, God has dispensed a universal prevenient grace that fully negates the depravity of every person. This prevenient grace places sinners in a neutral spiritual state, so when the gospel is presented they may freely choose to believe unto salvation, or not. Wesleyan prevenient grace is universal in its scope (every human being) and effect (completely freed from the effects of sin).

Reformed and Dispensational soteriology say God's gift of prevenient grace is the consequence of God's foreordaining action to give the gift of grace-faith-salvation to select persons, thereby electing those persons to salvation by reason of the efficacious action of God's gift to change the unwilling and unable to able and willing.

Arminian soteriology separates election from prevenient grace. Arminianism says everyone gets God's prevenient grace. But Arminian soteriology says election to salvation is by prescience, i.e., by foresight. The Arminian doctrine of foresight election God says looked outside himself into the history of the universe he would create, saw who would believe and who would not believe after receiving prevenient grace, and elected to salvation those he foresaw would believe. God acted because of what he learned.

How could God look outside himself throughout all of time and space? That is the doctrine of God's omnipresence. Arminian foresight election is based on God's omnipresence: God knows and decides because he looked outside himself and learned. Calvinistic election is based on God's omniscience: God knows within himself and decides based on what he knows without looking outside himself.

(One of the more serious problems with the prescient (foresight) election view is God learns by consulting persons and events outside himself. Biblically, either God knows by looking within himself, the attribute of omniscience, or God is not omniscient and must learn from others.)

Reformed and Dispensational soteriology say election to salvation is by foreordination. God looked inside himself and decided to whom of those he knew would create he would give prevenient grace for salvation. Those individuals to whom God decided to give prevenient grace are identified as elected to salvation, because of the infallible efficacy of the gift.

In both Reformed, Arminian, and Dispensational soteriology, salvation is "saved by God's grace through the sinner's faith without personal merit from the sinner but by Christ's merit alone." The choice to exercise saving faith is not meritorious whether viewed from the Reformed, Dispensational, or Arminian perspectives of prevenient grace. For Arminianism prevenient grace makes the exercise of saving faith possible. For Reformed and Dispensational prevenient grace makes the exercise of saving faith certain. Election is a second order doctrine because election is not an essential doctrine of the faith. (How God knows is an essential doctrine of the faith.)

Arminian soteriology does not concern itself, as do Reformed and Dispensational soteriology, with how the Old Testament sinner understood the means to salvation. That is because in the Arminian system, universal prevenient grace resolves that issue. Whatever the Good News might be at any time in the history of the world, however the sinner might gain understanding of the means to salvation, the Arminian view of prevenient grace places the sinner in a neutral spiritual state, so when the Good News is presented any sinner may freely choose to believe unto salvation, or not. Because Wesley came out of a Reformed background, I suspect his use of the word "gospel" focused solely on faith in Christ, and therefore he probably believed with Reformed soteriology that Christ was both the object and content of saving faith for the Old Testament sinner.

Is Arminian Soteriology Heretical?

The remainder of this chapter will focus on the question, are those professing Arminian soteriology heretics?

All the statements below reflect my understanding of Arminian theology, and my understanding of Scripture as a Dispensational Calvinist. (There are some Dispensationalists, a minority, who have an Arminian theology and soteriology.)

> Arminian: I am elected to salvation because God foresaw my faith.
> Scripture: I was elected to salvation because God foreordained my salvation.

Arminian: Christ gained the possibility of my salvation at Calvary.

Scripture: Christ's propitiation of God at Calvary is the only basis for my salvation.

Arminian: God's gift of grace efficaciously set me free from the dominion of sin to exercise my free will in salvation to believe or not believe, as I might choose.

Scripture: God's gift of grace efficaciously transformed me from unable and unwilling to willing and able to believe and be saved.

Arminian God's gift of grace freed my will from the effects of sin, so that I alone decided for Christ, I alone made up my mind to believe and become saved.

Scripture: God alone is the Savior. God's gift of grace enlivened my spiritual perception, giving me understanding of the spiritual issues of my sin, God the only Savior, and salvation by faith, so that through the efficacious action of God's grace I was made willing and thereby willingly believed.

Arminian: God by his prevenient grace given to all has freed human beings from sin's corruption of human nature, so that any sinner is able to choose to savingly believe the gospel when he hears it, or chose to reject the gospel when he hears it.

Scripture: Sinful man in his natural state of corruption by sin is unable and unwilling to believe the gospel despite all external incentives that may be extended to him. Only God is able to make the unable and unwilling to be willing and able.

Arminian: Man is never so completely controlled by God that he cannot freely accept or reject the gospel.

Scripture: The sinner is not forced but is made able and willing by the efficacious action of God's grace, with the inevitable result he or she will exercise saving faith.

Arminian: God elects those whom he foresees will voluntarily and without intervention by God (apart from prevenient grace given to all) choose to believe.

Scripture: God's election of those who will be saved is a result of his foreordaining choice to give that individual his gift of grace-faith-salvation, thereby guaranteeing their salvation.

Arminian: Christ's death did not ensure the salvation of anyone, for it did not secure the gift of faith to anyone (there is no such gift); what it did was secure the possibility of salvation for anyone who chooses to believe.

Scripture: God's foreordaining choices 1) saw all human beings as unrepentant sinners, 2) secured the salvation of certain human beings, 3) without denying salvation to any human being. The primary purpose of Christ's propitiation of God for all human sin was the legal satisfaction of God's holiness and justice for the crime of human sin. That legal satisfaction means God can justly act in mercy with temporal benefits toward all, and eternal benefits toward his elect, in agreement with his eternal decrees concerning such matters. Election guarantees salvation, nothing more, nothing less.

Arminian: The only work of the Holy Spirit is to give understanding of the gospel.

Scripture: The work of the Holy Spirit is to apply God's gift of grace-faith-salvation to those foreordained to receive God's gift, and through the spiritual perception given by the gift, 1) convict the sinner of his or her sin; 2) convict the sinner that God is the only Savior; 3) convict the sinner of the necessity of salvation through faith alone; 4) thereby making the unable and unwilling sinner both willing and able to exercise saving faith in God and God's testimony of the way of salvation; 5) regenerate the believing sinner's human nature immediately upon the exercise of saving faith; and 6) in these New Testament times to permanently take up residence in the saved person's soul.

Arminian: It rests with believers to keep themselves in a state of grace by choosing to maintain their faith; those who choose otherwise fall away and are lost (some Arminians believe salvation lost may regained by choice).

Scripture: Believers are endlessly kept in faith and grace by the unlimited merit of Christ's propitiation both in this mortal life and in the immortal life to come.

Arminian: Makes man, not God, the sovereign decider. In the Arminian view man's salvation depends on man himself, because saving faith is man's work, not God's work in man.

Scripture: Teaches God is the sole origin and source of salvation.

The following comparison is sourced from Schaff, *Creeds of Christendom*. The doctrine of the Arminian Remonstrants (AD 1610) is from *Creeds* at 3:545–549. The Calvinistic doctrines promulgated by the Synod of Dort (AD 1619) is from *Creeds* at 3:595.

Arminian: Article II, "Jesus Christ, the Savior of the world, died for all men and for every man, so that he has obtained for them all, by his death on the cross, redemption and the forgiveness of sins."

Synod: Second Head of Doctrine, Article III, "The death of the Son of God . . . is of infinite worth and value, abundantly sufficient to expiate the sins of the whole world ... its saving efficacy is limited to the elect."

The Arminian doctrine is that Christ, through his propitiation on the cross, died with the intention to, and actually did, procure salvation for every human being from Adam forward. The outcome of the Arminian doctrine is that redemption is waiting for every human being to come and claim it, or reject it, through the exercise of a free will rendered neutral by universal prevenient grace.

The doctrine promulgated by the Synod is that because the merit of Christ's propitiation on the cross is of limitless worth, that propitiation is more than sufficient to pay for the sins of the whole world. There is, however, a difference between the sufficiency of the propitiation and the efficiency of the propitiation. The Reformed doctrine is that Christ did not procure salvation for all human beings, but only for those human beings who access that propitiation by personal faith through the means of God's grace according to God's foreordaining decree concerning the bestowal of that gift of grace-faith-salvation (sufficient for all, efficient to salvation for the elect).

What does Arminian theology have in common with Reformed and Dispensational theology.

God is a Trinity of persons. The Father is God, the Son is God, the Holy Spirit is God.

Jesus the Christ is the incarnation of God the Son with Jesus of Nazareth.

Grace is God choosing to bless because he wants to bless.

Salvation is God forgiving a sinner's sin-guilt and remitting sin's penalty.

Jesus Christ alone propitiated God for the crime of human sin.

The gospel message in the age of the New Testament church is believe on the risen Lord Jesus Christ and you will be saved

The Scripture is inspired, accurate, credible, and authentic in everything it reports.

There is an endless heaven for the saved and an endless hell for the unsaved.

What does Arminian soteriology have in common with Reformed and Dispensational soteriology?

Saved by God's prevenient grace through the sinner's faith in God, through God's testimony as to the means of salvation.

All human beings are sinners from the moment of their conception and judicially culpable for their sin; hence the need for prevenient grace.

God must give prevenient grace for salvation to occur.

All those who are saved have been elected to salvation.

Whosoever calls upon the name of the Lord will be saved.

Believe on the Lord Jesus Christ and you will be saved.

What does Arminian soteriology not have in common with Reformed and Dispensational soteriology?

Arminian: Election to salvation by foresight.
Scripture: Election to salvation by foreordination.

Arminian: Prevenient grace given to all human beings.
Scripture: Prevenient grace given only to individuals chosen to salvation.

Arminian: Prevenient grace changes human nature so as to enable a person to freely choose or freely not choose salvation.
Scripture: Prevenient grace is efficacious to change human nature, inevitably leading to a desire for salvation and the freely made choice to act on that desire and exercise saving faith.

Arminian: Some Arminians believe salvation once gained can be lost and then regained.

Scripture: God gives to his saved people the grace of perseverance in the faith by means of faith; salvation once gained cannot be lost.

Arminianism has much more in common with Reformed and Dispensational theology than many want to believe. The differences are not in the proclamation and message of the gospel. The differences are secondary doctrines: how sinners are chosen to salvation; how prevenient grace is distributed; how prevenient grace acts in the sinner's soul.

Christians can and should courteously and respectfully discuss the differences in secondary issues, but let us go out hand in hand to proclaim the Good News of salvation in the risen Jesus Christ. Hating one another is not a Christian virtue. How a person is able to decide for faith or no faith does not affect the proclamation of the Good News to all.

Many Arminian doctrines are in error, but Arminians hold to the essential doctrine of biblical soteriology: saved by God's grace through the sinner's faith without personal merit but by Christ's merit alone. In that respect Arminians are not heretical.

An Essential Criticism Of Arminian Soteriology

Above I concluded Arminian soteriology is not heretical because it holds to the essential of the faith regarding salvation, differing only in second and third order doctrines. But opposing that conclusion is a troubling aspect of Arminian soteriology, mentioned briefly above.

Earlier in this chapter I stated, "before God created anything God omnisciently knew within himself all the possible consequences that could arise from his decision to create." The key words are "within himself." If God is omniscient, then the source of all knowledge is himself, he does not need to look outside himself to know anything.

Arminian soteriology says election to salvation is by prescience, that is, by foresight. That means God looked outside himself into the history of the universe he would create, from its beginning (Genesis 1:1) to its end (2 Peter 3:10; Revelation 20:11), and learned who would believe and who would not believe after receiving prevenient grace, and then he elected to salvation those he learned through foresight would believe. In Arminian soteriology God elected because of what he learned by viewing all of history. (To be able to view all of human history is affirmation of God's omnipresence.)

I am not sure those holding Arminian soteriology understand, or are aware of, the consequences of this "God learning" aspect of their doctrine of election: it means God is not omniscient. The technical name for this belief is Open Theism. Open Theism is based on an oxymoron: though God is omniscient, God does not know what human beings will freely do in the future, God must learn what human beings will do through his experience with human beings.

No. Either God is omniscient and thereby knows within himself all the consequences arising from his decision to create, or he is not omniscient and does not know but must learn.

Now, election to salvation is not in itself a first order doctrine (not an essential belief of the faith). Election from a Reformed and Dispensational point of view (I believe it is the biblical point of view) is God's foreordination of whom he will give his gift of grace-faith-salvation, Ephesians 2:8; or in terms used in this chapter, to whom God will give prevenient grace. If Arminian soteriology had eschewed election and let the rest of their soteriology stand, then it would be a simple matter of Reformed-Dispensational monergism versus Arminian synergism. They could have said God chose to give every human being prevenient grace and then God chose to let each human being decide his or her salvific fate: no election doctrine but a synergistic salvation.

But needing to respond to the undeniable fact God does elect to salvation, Ephesians 1:4; 2 Thessalonians 2:13, Arminian soteriology felt impelled to develop an election doctrine. That brings us to this: the prescient election view requires God to learn by consulting persons and events outside himself. That makes God less than omniscient. Biblically, either God knows without looking outside himself, the attribute of omniscience, or God is not omniscient and must learn from others.

An omniscient God knows from within himself who will believe, because he has foreordained the gift of God, his prevenient grace, to selected individuals, guaranteeing they will believe unto salvation, by means of his efficacious grace.

From the point of view of means, the prescient view of election has a troubling, first order issue, that pursued to its logical, rational conclusion, is the heresy of Open Theism.

On the one hand, Arminian soteriology proclaims the right gospel: saved by God's grace through the sinner's faith without any personal merit by the sinner but by Christ's merit alone. On the other hand, Arminian soteriology says God must learn who will choose to believe so he can elect those persons to salvation. It is easy to see why some condemn Arminian soteriology as heretical.

Reformed and Dispensational soteriology says election to salvation is by foreordination. God looked inside himself and decided which of those he knew he would create he would give prevenient grace for salvation. Those individuals whom God chose to give prevenient grace are identified as elected to salvation, because of the infallible efficacy of God's gift. Omniscience is clearly the basis for this view.

Introduction

Genesis 3:15 is the key verse for Reformed soteriology's claim the Old Testament sinner was saved by belief in a coming redeemer, a coming Messiah, a coming Christ, or the person Jesus the Christ (Reformed opinions vary). Genesis 3:15 is also the key scripture for Dispensational Promise soteriology's claim the Old Testament sinner was saved by belief in a promised "seed," i.e., a coming redeemer.

Because this is the key verse for two systems of soteriology, upon which all their Old Testament soteriology rests, I will present a lengthy exegesis and discussion of Genesis 3:15 before discussing Reformed and Promise Old Testament soteriology. A small part of this discussion is from my book *Adam and Eve, A Biography and Theology*, lightly edited the present purpose.

In this discussion I will refer to two principles of the Literal hermeneutic.

1. Analogy of Scripture. This principle asks, "How does a passage fit into the total pattern of God's revelation that was revealed prior to its writing?"

2. Analogy of Faith. This principle asks, "How does a passage fit into the total pattern of God's revelation that has been revealed at any time?"

The Scripture

Genesis 3:15 reads (ESV), "I will put enmity between you and the woman, and between your offspring and her offspring; he shall bruise your head, and you shall bruise his heel."

The Analogy of Scripture: Genesis 1:1–3:19 is the totality of God's revelation Adam and Eve knew and had available to understand Genesis 3:15 at the time that Scripture was given.

The Analogy of Faith asks us to include any additional revelation that might have helped Adam to understand 3:15. Adam lived 930 years, which means he died when Lamech, Genesis 5:28, was 56 years old. The additional revelation given from Genesis 3:15 to Adam's death was Genesis 3:16–5:28. The only relevant scripture in that additional revelation is Genesis 4:25, which gives Eve's understanding of Genesis 3:15. According to the written Scripture nothing else was said about Genesis 3:15 during the days of Adam and Eve.

The Analogy of Faith also asks us to include any additional revelation that might have helped Adam's descendants (in the Old Testament revelation) to understand Genesis 3:15. Except for the aforementioned Genesis 4:25, nothing is said concerning Genesis 3:15 from Genesis 3:16 to Malachi 4:6.

The Exegesis

The woman's offspring shall bruise the serpent's offspring, and the serpent's offspring shall bruise the woman's offspring. The Hebrew word the ESV correctly translates "offspring" is *zera*', semen, plant seed, or offspring [Harris et al., s. v. 582a]. The word is always in the singular number, whether it refers to one offspring, or a group of offspring (descendants). The fact it is in the singular form in 3:15 is not significant. The fact the pronouns associated with *zera*' are singular is a matter of grammar. The interpretation of *zera*' as one or many is significant.

The English "enmity" translates a Hebrew word (*'êbâ*) meaning "enmity, hatred," which in most occurrences implies the hatred which underlies a hostile act [Harris et al., s. v. 78a].

Is God's curse prescriptive or descriptive? In a prescriptive sense, God's curse states the cause and effect relationship between his laws and sin, between his saved people and the unsaved. God's laws are hostile to sin, and therefore establish enmity between saved and sinner.

Descriptively, God's curse identifies a continuing state of hostility between the serpent's offspring, those of no faith, and the Woman's offspring, those of faith: each will be the natural enemy of the other.

I said above the Hebrew word *zera*', can mean semen or offspring. Here *zera*' does not refer to semen but to offspring of both the serpent and the Woman. The Woman understood *zera*' to mean her offspring, see Genesis 4:25, "God has appointed for me another offspring [*zera*'] instead of Abel, for Cain killed him" (ESV). The Woman understood her *zera*' in a collective sense: Abel and Seth. So does later scripture.

Genesis 5:3–4 (ESV), When Adam had lived 130 years, he fathered a son in his own likeness, after his image, and named him Seth. The days of Adam after he fathered Seth were 800 years; and he had other sons and daughters.

Without Adam's participation, there would not be offspring from the Woman.

Compare Genesis 21:12, 13. The singular form of *zera'* is used in a collective sense, e.g., the large group of descendants of Abraham, Genesis 12:7; 13:16; 17:7–10. Although translators translate *zera'* in the plural when the reference is to a large group of descendants, in the Hebrew text the word is always in the singular [Hamilton, 199]. Therefore, *zera'* can bear the meaning of a single offspring, e.g. Seth in Genesis 4:25, or many descendants, Genesis 3:15; 4:25; 17:7–10.

Note also in Genesis 4:25 Cain is a single offspring, though not accepted by the Woman as her offspring in the same way Abel and Seth were her offspring. In fact, in no scripture is Cain recognized as the Woman's offspring, although he is physically her offspring. Looking to the Analogy of Faith, 1 John 3:12 tells us Cain was the serpent's offspring. This interaction between Genesis 3:15 and 4:25 gives us a clue to the identity of the two kinds of offspring in Genesis 3:15.

The enmity, then, between the *zera'* of the serpent, and the *zera'* of the Woman, does not exclusively refer to enmity between one specific serpent and one specific human being, but to enmity between the offspring of the serpent and the offspring of the Woman, whether all or one. If all are at enmity, then each is at enmity, so again the singular is not significant.

Genesis 3:15 says "you" shall strike at his heel." Who is the person identified as "his?" In context it is the Woman and her offspring. The personal pronouns look back to the nouns.

> And I, God, will put enmity between you, serpent, and the woman, and between your, serpent's offspring, and her, woman's offspring. He, the woman and her offspring, shall strike at your, the serpent and his offspring's, head, and you, the serpent and his offspring, shall strike at his, the woman and her offspring's, heel.

The use of a singular masculine pronoun to collectively include both male and female descendants is not unusual in Hebrew or English. Whether *zera'* is used in Genesis 3:15 in a singular sense or a collective sense is a matter of context—or presuppositions as to how the verse should be interpreted.

The Woman's descendants will have continuing conflict with sinners. Why do I say, "with sinners?" The reason given for the continuing conflict is continuing opposition by the serpent and his offspring. We have already seen using the Analogy of Faith, Genesis 4:25; 1 John 3:12, that Cain is one of the serpent's offspring, validating the interpretation.

> Cain killed Abel.

> Not by Eve or at any place in the Old or New Testaments is Cain identified the Woman's offspring.

> Cain is of the evildoer.

> Cain is one of the serpent's offspring.

Therefore, the serpent's *zera'* is not one or more supra-natural beings, but human beings, who like the serpent are men and women characterized as of no faith.

Summary

The within context interpretation of Genesis 3:15 using the Literal hermeneutic is continuing conflict between those of faith and those of no faith.

In this interpretation through the Literal hermeneutic, I used lexical analysis: the words; syntactical analysis: the grammar; the Analogy of Scripture: Genesis 1:1–3:19; the Analogy of Faith: Genesis 4:25; 1 John 3:12. I also used genre analysis: 3:15 is prophecy; literary analysis: Genesis is historical narrative; theological analysis: conflict with sinners because of sin.

I did not consider Moses' relationship to this history (historical and contextual analysis): Moses wrote Genesis to explain to the nation of Israel their origin, providing a solid foundation for the people and their faith as a nation created by God and chosen by God. Genesis 3:15 supports the Law and history: conflict between the people of God and those persons not the people of God.

Discussion

In Genesis 4:25, the Woman makes clear that she now believes Abel and Seth to be her offspring in fulfillment of the promise, implying that she now believes Cain was the offspring of the serpent. As will be discussed below, the Woman's offspring refers to the believing descendants of Adam and Eve, and the serpent's offspring refers to the unbelieving descendants of Adam and Eve. How do we know this? There were no other offspring available to fulfill the prophecy except the descendants of Adam and Eve. Those of no faith are constantly attacking those of faith, and those of faith constantly respond.

Do I stand alone in representing the Woman's offspring as her literal posterity throughout the ages of humankind? Let us briefly consult the Christian whose works systematized biblical doctrine to form the beginning of what is today known as Reformed theology. John Calvin said, "I explain, therefore, the seed to mean the posterity of the woman generally." [*Commentaries on the First Book of Moses called Genesis.* In the edition I am using (see Sources), the quote is on p. 170.] I will address Calvin's complete view on Genesis 3:15 in the next chapter.

Most Bible students using the Literal hermeneutic believe when God is speaking to the serpent he is speaking to a powerful entity who empowered the serpent to speak. That powerful entity is millennia later discovered to be Satan, Revelation 12:9. But here Adam and Eve understood the serpent to be the snake, and must have wondered about his *zera'*, his offspring. By the time of Genesis 4:25 Eve had stopped wondering; she knew.

Eventually, Scripture identifies the serpent as Satan, Revelation 12:9; 20:2. Moses' original readers could not have known that, but when he published the Pentateuch they would not have had difficulty identifying the tempting serpent as empowered by an evil being. Serpents had been used as a symbol of evil for centuries before Moses, based on the oral and written history of the events in the Garden.

But here let us stick to what Adam and Eve knew. The curse in Genesis 3:15 is a divine decree of continuing hostility between the Woman's offspring and the serpent's offspring. Who were those offspring?

The term offspring can and does refer to either believers or unbelievers. Cain, Abel, and Seth were physically the Woman's offspring, but Cain was an unbeliever and Abel and Seth were believers. The conditions of the decree of enmity are that the Woman and her offspring will be repeatedly in conflict with the evil serpent and his offspring and vice versa. "The imperfect verb is iterative. It implies repeated attacks to both sides to injure the other. It declares lifelong mutual hostility between mankind and the serpent race" [Wenham, 80].

In deciding the identity of "offspring" we do not need to set aside all we know from later revelation (the Analogy of Faith), we just need to not allow that knowledge to influence a within context interpretation. As Vlach said, "The primary meaning of any Bible passage is found in that passage."

The biblical terms "offspring of," "sons of," or "daughters of," are, when speaking metaphorically, those persons whose characteristics are like the person of whom they are a "offspring of," "son of," or "daughter of." I have already noted there were no other offspring available to fulfill the prophecy except the descendants of Adam and Eve. Offspring possess the characteristics of the person or thing of whom they may be considered offspring. For example, John 8:44, "you are of your father the devil," not physically but by their character. Those persons were of the serpent's offspring.

Adam and Eve were believers. They also committed occasional acts of sinning—both Old and New Testament history as well as the Analogy of Faith informs us that believers commit acts of sinning, e.g., 1 John 1:8–10—which does not detract from their status as believers. Therefore it is reasonable to posit the Woman's offspring are those possessing her characteristic of faith.

The serpent is evil, a being of no faith, as amply demonstrated by his actions in Genesis 3:1–5. Therefore it is reasonable to interpret the serpent's offspring as those possessing his characteristic of no faith. Because there were no other offspring available to fulfill the prophecy except the descendants of Adam and Eve, then all the *zera'* are physically her offspring by procreation, but some of her *zera'* are of faith and others of her *zera'* are of no faith.

Therefore we know the serpent's offspring will have the characteristic of evil, but do not need to be literal serpents. The "sons of the prophets" (e.g., 1 Kings 20:35; 2 Kings 5:22; Acts 5:35) were not physically the offspring of this or that prophet, but persons who studied and taught the scriptures like the prophets, who had faith like the prophets. The serpent's offspring are those who were evil like the serpent. Again, there were no other offspring available to fulfill the prophecy except the descendants of Adam and Eve. Those of no faith were the serpent's offspring, those of faith were the Woman's offspring.

I know I am repeating, but more than one theologian holding to Promise soteriology proposes the serpent's offspring were fallen angels. I will discuss that view below.

Adam and Eve would have thought of the serpent's offspring as evil, because the serpent had proven he was evil. Would Adam and Eve had thought their good offspring would have conflict with evil speaking serpents? Or would they have understood the conflict would be with an evil offspring comparable to their good offspring? Genesis 4:25 gives us an answer. "God has appointed for me another offspring [*zera*] instead of Abel, for Cain killed him." (ESV)

The Woman's literal offspring are, of course, every human being who has been born or ever will ever be born. However, in the context of the decree of continuing enmity the term, "the Woman's offspring," must refer to those who have her characteristic of a continuing relationship and fellowship with God. In the same context, the term, "the serpent's offspring," must refer to those who have the serpent's characteristic of a continuing enmity and no faith toward God. There is also a grammatical reason for that view, which I will discuss a little further below.

The relationship the Woman had with God was established at the moment of her formation body and soul from Adam: she was formed sinless and in a relationship with God. To use an Old Testament term, she was righteous; to (inaccurately) use a New Testament term, she was saved. She wasn't really saved (neither was Adam) because she was never lost. She was created in a relationship with God. Her sin did not cancel her relationship with God, it broke her fellowship with God, a fellowship that God restored. (Unless we want to propose an act of sinning breaks one's relationship with God, an idea opposed by the teaching of Scripture as a whole.)

So some of the Woman's offspring were those in a relationship with God—Abel and Seth are the examples—and some of the Woman's offspring were not in a relationship with God—Cain is the example. Eve confirms that view in Genesis 4:25 (the Analogy of Scripture), and the later revelation in 1 John 3:12, supports that view, Cain was "out of the evil one" (the Analogy of Faith).

Using the syntactical analysis function of the Literal hermeneutic, specifically the grammatical function of the conjunction "and," the term "serpent's offspring," is comparable to the "Woman's offspring," in that both are human and both engage in the same conflict with the other. Because the only persons producing offspring are Adam and Eve, the serpent's offspring must refer to the those of their offspring who have the serpent's evil characteristics. Again, Eve demonstrates she and Adam had this understanding, Genesis 4:25.

Five considerations reveal who are the Woman's offspring and who are the serpent's offspring.

One, there is a fundamental difference between each offspring that is the cause for continuing enmity. That difference is a relationship with God. Since the Woman's offspring partake of her characteristics, which is a continuing relationship and fellowship with God, then her offspring are those human beings who by faith have their sin forgiven and as a result are in a salvific relationship with continuing fellowship with God. Those who have no-faith are like the serpent (the evil the serpent represents): they are unforgiven human sinners who are not in a relationship with God. The difference between faith and no-faith, between a relationship and no relationship, is the cause of the enmity.

Two, the facts of history reveal that the evil opponents of the Woman's offspring are not serpents. Nor, looking at later revelation, are Satan's offspring the fallen angels, who might (in a figurative sense) be considered as Satan's offspring, because he successfully tempted them to choose sin over God. How do we know the serpent's offspring are human beings? Cain, not a fallen angel, killed Abel. Sinful humankind, not fallen angels, were the cause of the Noahic Flood, 6:5–7. The "spiritual things of evil in the heavenly realms," Ephesians 6:12, indirectly oppose those of faith by working through those human beings who are in direct opposition to those of faith: "the rulers, the authorities, the lords of the darkness of this world": persons of no faith.

Three, for the serpent's offspring to be fallen angels would mean all the Woman's offspring were believers, but this is not consistent with history, biblical or secular. Moreover, if such were the case, then man would have the ability to "bruise, strike at, crush" angelic beings, a biblical impossibility.

Four, for the serpent's offspring to be Satan's literal offspring would mean he must be procreating. However, nothing in Scripture suggests that angels procreate; in fact, the opposite is suggested, Matthew 22:30; Mark 12:25. (See my book *Angelology, A True History of Angels*, and my commentaries on Matthew's Gospel and Mark's Gospel.) The serpent's offspring are not literal snakes, nor literally the result of angels procreating. Metaphorically the serpent's offspring are those human beings who demonstrate the same sinful, lost, unbelieving character as the serpent/Satan/fallen angels, and the Analogy of Faith supports that conclusion, Genesis 4:25; Romans 16:20; John 8:44; Acts 13:10; 1 John 3:8, 10, 12; Revelation 12:9, and every Old and New Testament scripture passage that shows unbelievers persecuting believers.

Because Satan does not procreate, and because the kind or type of enmity most often experienced by believers is committed by other human beings (however motivated), and because the only offspring available are human beings, then the term "the serpent's offspring" must refer to the unbelieving offspring of the Woman who have the characteristics of evil: sin, rebellion, disobedience, and "every intent of the thoughts of his heart was only evil continually."

Five. Grammatically, the coordinating conjunction "and" connects two subjects that are performing the same action. "He [Woman's offspring] shall crush your [serpent's offspring] head and you [serpent's offspring] shall crush his [Woman's offspring] heel."

The Woman's offspring will cause physical injury or death to the serpent's offspring and the serpent's offspring will cause physical injury or death to the Woman's offspring. If, as is the case, both offspring are performing the same action, then both offspring must be equal in some manner, as grammatically required by the coordinating conjunction: "He will *shûp* you and you will *shûp* him."

The Hebrew word *shûp* in 3:15 may be translated bruise, strike at, or crush. Those soteriologies proposing Genesis 3:15 speaks of a coming redeemer, also believe *shûp* is Satan killing Christ. Christ was killed. Was Satan physically injured? No, he suffered no harm to his person in having others kill Christ. In the "coming redeemer" view of Genesis 3:15, neither the action nor the subjects meet the grammatical requirement of the coordinating conjunction. A hermeneutic that ignores the grammar is wrong.

To use a metaphor, you cannot switch horses midstream in an interpretation. Either *shûp* applies in the same way to both kinds of offspring in the same physical manner, or *shûp* applies in the same way to both offspring in a non-physical manner. Either both kinds are injured/dead or both kinds are not injured/dead.

The "coming redeemer" interpreters want it both ways: Christ was physically killed but Satan was only spiritually or metaphorically injured. Hermeneutically that is not possible. The grammar requires both offspring and their actions to be equal in some manner. The only interpretation that makes both offspring equal in some manner is both are the Woman's physical descendants in conflict with one another. Jesus Christ and his death on the cross are not in view in Genesis 3:15, unless one imports the idea into the verse.

Both serpent's and Woman's offspring must physically harm the other. The Literal interpretation does recognize what happens to one must happen to the other. The better translation of *shûp* is "strike," which incorporates injury or death. The Literal interpretation understands both kinds of offspring are the Woman's, one kind is of faith the other kind is of no faith. In the continuing conflict between those of faith and those of no faith, some will be hurt, some will die.

That has been the experience of those of faith for millennia. The Analogy of Faith supports that interpretation in that the only mentions of or allusions to Genesis 3:15 in all the Scripture (relevant to the grammatical condition), are Genesis 4:25; Romans 16:20. The later revelation in Romans 16:20 gives further information allowing the person with the New Testament revelation to see victory for those of faith in the conflict. One should notice Romans 16:20 does not speak of Jesus Christ, and puts the victory into the future, not the past.

Another effect of the traditional interpretation of Genesis 3:15 is that those believing Genesis 3:15 was a gospel message of salvation to the Old Testament sinner, must bring into that gospel the message the coming Redeemer will crush Satan as part of redemption. But the genuine gospel is God crushing the Redeemer for human sin, by allowing sinners to be sinners, Acts 2:23.

Satan has no part to play in the redemption of sinners. God imputed to the Redeemer the judicial guilt of human sin, the Redeemer voluntarily agreed to that imputation, and as a result the Redeemer willingly suffered the wrath of God against human sin, thereby being crushed by God's wrath: the Redeemer died as full payment for the judicial debt of human sin, a fact validated by his resurrection out from the state of physical death. The Redeemer's death was not caused by the cross, but by himself, by voluntarily and omnipotently separating his soul from his body in payment for the physical penalty due sin.

Whatever means God used to deliver the Good News of redemption from the penalty due sin to the Old Testament sinner (as we know opinions vary), the source of redemption is God crushing the redeemer for sin—in theology-speak, Christ propitiated (fully satisfied) God for the crime of human sin in his suffering and death on the cross.

Satan's part was to be used by God to arrange the circumstances of that death through his power of temptation to persuade human beings to murder the Redeemer, Acts 2:23.

Some Christians believe they were prisoners of Satan, and salvation is being freed from the power of Satan. Scripture teaches Redemption does not free sinners from Satan, but from God's just wrath as the penalty due sin. Sinners are not freed from Satan because never owned or imprisoned by Satan. His power is limited by God to tempt others to commit acts of sinning. He may use that power in many ways to tempt to sinning, e.g., see Job chapters 1, 2, but the authority over his life, who is the omnipotent and sovereign God, limits his use of his power to temptation.

Satan was not crushed, or killed, or injured, or rendered impotent, or ineffective by Christ's death. Did Satan stop tempting you when you were redeemed? No. He continues to use his power of temptation to cause death. Christ through his death destroyed Satan, Hebrews 2:14, not by crushing him, but by rescuing sinners and sinning believers from the power of death, which is caused by sinning. Satan tempts to sinning, human beings commit acts of sinning, the wages of sin is death, but Christ rescues sinners from death, Romans 6:23. Bottom line: Christ did not crush Satan to save sinners, God crushed Christ to save sinners. Redemption from sin has nothing to do with crushing Satan, but in satisfying God's justice for the crime of sin.

What is the true message of Genesis 3:15? In the context of continuing enmity between offspring, the serpent's offspring are the Woman's unbelieving, unsaved descendants who are in conflict with

113

her believing, saved descendants. Notice how the Woman, Moses, and the Holy Spirit carefully do not identify Cain as the Woman's offspring, but do so identify Abel and Seth. Cain was of the serpent's offspring, cf., 1 John 3:12, but Abel and Seth were of the Woman's offspring, Genesis 4:25; Hebrews 11:4.

The only reference, mentions, or allusions to Genesis 3:15 in both Old Testament and New Testament, are Genesis 4:25; Romans 16:20, both of which speak of conflict because of sin, and Revelation 12:9 which identifies Satan as "the serpent of the beginning." Romans 16:20 speaks of conflict and victory—not a past victory through Christ's crucifixion, because the tense is future, but continuing victory in the conflict (because of Christ's propitiation of God, which other New Testament revelation tells us). My within context interpretation of Genesis 3:15, using the Literal hermeneutic, is supported by later revelation, which is hermeneutic rule number two, the Analogy of Faith.

Not Adam, not Eve, not any of their Old Testament descendants, saw Christ or a yet-future coming redeemer-messiah-christ in Genesis 3:15. To say they saw what is not in the scripture is eisegesis using the as yet unwritten New Testament revelation, and therefore extrabiblical in an Old Testament context.

While it is true the basis of the believer's victory over his or her own sin, and victory over the opposition of those of no faith (however motivated), is the propitiation made by Christ, that is not the message of Genesis 3:15. Genesis 3:15 speaks of continuing conflict between those of faith and those of no faith, and continuing victory by those of faith.

Discussion: Is Genesis 3:15 The Protevangelium

In the understanding given by the application of the Literal hermeneutic to Genesis 3:15, we must ask, "Is Genesis 3:15 the first gospel proclamation?" That is what Reformed and Promise soteriology teach. Does Genesis 3:15 promise the defeat of Satan and the redemption of mankind through one specific offspring of the Woman?" That is what Reformed soteriology teaches, and what Promise soteriology has adopted from Reformed soteriology.

What was the origin of this interpretation? "The oldest Jewish interpretation found in the third century (ca. 250) BC Septuagint, the Palestinian targums (Ps.-J., Neof., Frg), and possibly the Onqelos targum [the Targums were 1st to 7th century AD translations of the Hebrew into Aramaic], takes the serpent as symbolic of Satan and looks for a victory over him in the days of King Messiah" [Wenham, 80]. Notice two things about this interpretation: 1) is *after* the closing of the Old Testament revelation, ca. 435–400 BC, the Book of Malachi; 2) it is an interpretation of Messiah-King, not Messiah-Redeemer. The persons originally receiving the Old Testament revelation did not develop that interpretation, but their descendants about 200 years after the Old Testament canon was closed.

That Jewish interpretation, first developed ca. 250 BC, was changed and then adopted by many in the New Testament church. Few actually understand it is a Jewish interpretation created after the Old Testament revelation was closed. But also notice this—it is important. The Jewish interpretation was the victory of Messiah-King, not the appearance of Messiah-Redeemer. As I will show in the next chapter, the Old Testament peoples were looking for national redemption from oppression by a king, not individual redemption from the penalty due sin by a redeemer. The change from king to redeemer was made by Reformed soteriology. (Promise soteriology adopts and repeats the error.)

A Messiah-Redeemer was not the expectation of the Jewish people at any time from Genesis 1:1 to Malachi 4:6, nor in the 400 plus years from Malachi to Christ's resurrection. There is no documented proof any person living prior to the New Testament revelation was waiting for a future coming promised redeemer, or placed their faith in a future coming promised redeemer.

What was saving faith during Old Testament times? The same as in New Testament times: faith in God and God's written Scripture as given during their historical time, in the progressive revelation of truth, as illuminated by the Holy Spirit through the plain and normal meaning of the written Scripture he had inspired. In the Old Testament the Savior's name is YHWH, not coming, but ever-present. In the New Testament his name is the Lord Jesus Christ.

The false interpretation of a (so-called) promised seed—a messiah-christ-redeemer—in Genesis 3:15, is sometimes called the protevangelium (or protoevangelium) meaning "the first Good News." Historically this term has been used in two senses.

The first use was the title of an apocryphal book, supposedly written by James the Less, but actually written about AD 150. This book is a work of religious fiction claiming to tell the story of the miraculous birth of Jesus' mother Mariam. In AD 1552 this book was given the title *The Protevangelium of James*. This first use reflects the Mariolotry of the Roman Catholic Church.

The second use is the Reformed soteriology view that refers to Genesis 3:15 as a prophecy of Christ (the offspring of the Woman) overcoming Satan through his birth, death and resurrection. This use, by Reformed theology, tends to restrict Genesis 3:15 to messianic prophecy, with the application that by faith in this one verse Old Testament sinners were saved.

Reformed soteriology, and some misguided Dispensationalists, call Genesis 3:15 the protevangelium, the first gospel, because Reformed theology is determined to support their soteriology by (supposedly) discovering Jesus in as many Old Testament passages as possible (a misuse of the Christocentric hermeneutic). Many base their soteriology in false history—that the church fathers identified Genesis 3:15 as the protevangelium.

I have done a digital search of the thirty-seven volumes of the writings of the Ante-Nicene, Nicene, and Post-Nicene church fathers, using the online resources at Christian Classics Ethereal Library, "Early Church Fathers" (CCEl.org). I searched for the terms "protevangelium" and "protoevangelium." I have those volumes in my personal library. I searched each index in those thirty-seven volumes, and each table of contents. What were the results?

The terms occur only in translator's prefaces, footnotes, or comments, never in the original writings. The terms were not used in the early church, at least not in the documents the Holy Spirit was pleased to leave to us from their writings. Two passages are used to buttress the argument [Wenham, 80–81]. (Below, the abbreviation "*ANF*" represents Roberts and Donaldson, *Ante-Nicene Fathers*.)

> Justin Martyr. *ANF*, 1:249, *Dialogue With Trypho*, 100. "And by her has He been born, to whom we have proved so many Scriptures refer, and by whom God destroys both the serpent and those angels and men who are like him; but works deliverance from death to those who repent of their wickedness

and believe upon Him."

ANF, 1:250, *Dialogue With Trypho*, 102. "As soon as He was born in Bethlehem, as I previously remarked, king Herod, having learned from the Arabian Magi about Him, made a plot to put Him to death and by God's command Joseph took Him with Mariam and departed into Egypt. For the Father had decreed that He whom He had begotten should be put to death, but not before He had grown to manhood, and proclaimed the word which proceeded from Him. But if any of you say to us, Could not God rather have put Herod to death? I return answer by anticipation: Could not God have cut off in the beginning the serpent, so that he exist not, rather than have said, "And I will put enmity between him and the woman, and between his seed and her seed?"

It is a stretch to say Justin regarded Genesis 3:15 as a protoevangelium. How did Irenaeus view the promise?

ANF, 1:457, *Against Heresies*, 3.23.7. "For this end did He put enmity between the serpent and the woman and her seed, they keeping it up mutually: he, the sole of whose foot should be bitten, having power also to tread upon the enemy's head; but the other biting, killing, and impeding the steps of man, until the seed did come appointed to tread down his head,—which was born of Mariam, of whom the prophet speaks: "Thou shalt tread upon the asp and the basilisk; thou shalt trample down the lion and the dragon;"—indicating that sin, which was set up and spread out against man, and which rendered him subject to death, should be deprived of its power, along with death, which rules [over men]."

ANF, 1:548, *Against Heresies*, 5.21.1. "He [Christ] has therefore, in His work of recapitulation, summed up all things, both waging war against our enemy, and crushing him who had at the beginning led us away captives in Adam, and trampled upon his head, as thou canst perceive in Genesis that God said to the serpent, 'And I will put enmity between thee and the woman, and between thy seed and her seed; He shall be on the watch for thy head, and thou on the watch for His heel.' For from that time, He who should be born of a women, from the

Virgin, after the likeness of Adam, was preached as keeping watch for the head of the serpent. This is the seed of which the apostle says in the Epistle to the Galatians, 'that the law of works was established until the seed should come to whom the promise was made.'"

Irenaeus viewed the promise as continuously accomplished through Adam and Eve's children, because he viewed the ultimate fulfillment to be accomplished in the Person and work of Christ. That ultimate fulfillment is a New Testament revelation not an Old Testament revelation.

Irenaeus words, "from that time, He who should be born of a women, from the Virgin, after the likeness of Adam, was preached" is overstatement by Irenaeus, it is homiletic hyperbole, because there is absolutely zero validation from the Old Testament and New Testament revelation that Genesis 3:15 was preached by any person, of the Christ "keeping watch for the head of the serpent." In fact, the only reference of any kind to Genesis 3:15 in the written revelation of both testaments is Genesis 4:25; Romans 16:20; Revelation 12:9.

(Irenaeus' "seed of which the apostle says in the Epistle to the Galatians," Galatians 3:16, is from Genesis 12:3; 15:6; 17:21, not Genesis 3:15. No one knew Christ was the offspring to fulfill Genesis 15:6 until Paul wrote Galatians 3:8–16.)

Neither Justin nor Irenaeus, nor any other church father, used the term "protevangelium" or the equivalent phrase "first gospel." Identifying Genesis 3:15 as the "first gospel" is an invention of Reformed theology, as I will show below.

In the New Testament, Paul seems to refer to Genesis 3:15 at Romans 16:20, "And the God of peace will crush Satan under your [the believers'] feet shortly." But there is no reference in this passage to Christ, his birth, or his crucifixion. In fact, this post-crucifixion verse looks to the future: Satan will shortly be crushed under the believers' feet, not Christ's feet.

Some imaginatively suggest the Old and New Testament writers may have had Genesis 3:15 in mind at 2 Samuel 7:12; Psalm 89:4, Hebrews 2:14; 1 Corinthians 15:25; Revelation 12:4, 11. However, no Old or New Testament passage quotes the verse, and no Old or New Testament passage refers to Genesis 3:15 as a messianic verse. A reference to the passage is significantly missing from any Bible text concerning the virgin birth, incarnation, crucifixion, or resurrection, and is missing from the four Gospels, every gospel proclamation in Acts, and every passage, e.g., Romans 10:1–13; Ephesians 2:1–10, explaining the way of salvation.

Genesis 3:15 as the protevangelium did not exist in Christianity for 1600 plus years, in any form. The earliest documented mention I know is in the works of Benjamin Keach (1640-1704), *The Metaphors*, and *Exposition of the Parables*, reprinted 1972 as *Preaching from the Types and Metaphors of the Bible* (from an 1855 edition, *Tropologia: A Key to Open Scripture Metaphors, together with Types of the Old Testament.*)

In the chapter "Allegory," p. 192, Keach specifically mentions Genesis 3:15 as "The first promise of the Gospel and the whole mystery of redemption to come, is proposed by God himself in this allegory." Keach does not pretend "the first promise of the Gospel" may be derived from Genesis 3:15 by any hermeneutic other than an allegorical hermeneutic. Would that all interpreters were as honest. By the way, the hermeneutical basis for allegory is the interpreter's imagination; unless inspired by the Holy Spirit, which happened only once in the Scripture, Galatians 4:25, and was not about Genesis 3:15.

The lack of antiquity does not make a Reformed protevangelium from Genesis 3:15 wrong, but neither does its newness make it right. The simple and inescapable fact that the Holy Spirit through the New Testament writers never used Genesis 3:15 as a protevangelium, and that for 1600 plus years no Christian saw Genesis 3:15 as a protevangelium, does render the Reformed interpretation suspicious, and in my view untenable.

Summary Of Genesis 3:15 Discussion

Neither Old or New Testament directly relates Christ to Genesis 3:15. The reason is the promise of victory over the serpent and his offspring by the Woman's offspring was applicable to every believer (the Woman's offspring) from Abel forward. We see in Able's death victory is not mere physical survival, but eternal life, and a continuing testimony, Hebrews 11:4.

Adam and his descendants are promised victory over evil-doers in their historic present. We must therefore conclude Genesis 3:15 was not understood by the Old Testament peoples as a promise of a coming

Redeemer, unless we want to follow the Reformed doctrine of extrabiblical revelation and illumination—but in this case it is imagination and eisegesis, because there is nothing in all of the Old Testament or the New Testament that teaches Genesis 3:15 is about Jesus Christ.

The supposed protevangelium is the product of Reformed imagination attempting to connect their soteriology to Genesis 3:15, to support their content of faith, "Christ coming (OT) or Christ arrived (NT)," as the only way of salvation in both testaments. The Bible teaches the one and only way of salvation is by God's grace through the sinner's faith, apart from any personal merit of the sinner, only by Christ's merit. The eternal, one and only one, basis for salvation is the full and complete satisfaction (propitiation) of God's justice and holiness for humankind's crimes of sin. Christ's propitiation is the one way of salvation. (The Reformed wrongly make the message of salvation as the one way.)

What is the message of Genesis 3:15? Continuing enmity between the Woman's believing offspring and the Woman's unbelieving offspring. Look at Genesis 4:25, the Woman makes clear that she now believes Abel and Seth to be her offspring in fulfillment of the promise, implying that she now believes Cain was the offspring of the serpent. What does the history of humankind tell you? Unsaved human beings, however motivated (by their own sin or supra-natural influence), persecute saved human beings. There are no offspring but human offspring to fulfill the prophecy: the *zera'*, descendants, of Adam and Eve.

Bottom line: no one in the Old Testament thought Genesis 3:15 was a prophecy of a coming messiah-christ-redeemer. No one in the times between the Old and New Testaments, thought Genesis 3:15 was a prophecy of a coming messiah-christ-redeemer. No one during the times when Jesus walked the earth thought Genesis 3:15 was a prophecy of a coming messiah-christ-redeemer. No one in the New Testament church for 1600 plus years thought Genesis 3:15 was a prophecy of a coming messiah-christ-redeemer.

Consider this. Perhaps Genesis 3:15 actually means what a plain and normal understanding of the words mean within the historical circumstances of the two people who received the prophecy, and their descendants who received it from them. Perhaps the prophecy does not need an injection of New Testament revelation. Perhaps it really is about continuing conflict between those of no faith versus those of faith, and continuing victory by those of faith over those of no faith. I find that within context interpretation validated by the only references to Genesis 3:15 in the Scripture, Genesis 4:25; Romans 16:20; Revelation 12:9.

Excursus: An Imaginary Conversation on Genesis 3:15

(Based on actual conversations.)

JQ. How do you interpret Genesis 3:15?
Reformed Friend. Christ destroys Satan, Satan kills Christ.

JQ. Does the verse says that?
RF. Yes. He shall bruise your head and you shall bruise his heel.

JQ. So "He" is Christ and the serpent is Satan?
RF. Yes.

JQ. How do you know the verse is talking about Christ and Satan?
RF. Because in the NT Satan kills Christ on the cross and by his death Christ destroys Satan.

JQ. Did Adam and Eve know the seed was Christ and the serpent Satan?
RF. Yes.

JQ. So the gospel is in Genesis 3:15?
RF. Yes, it is the first gospel.

JQ. How did Adam and Eve know the seed was Christ and the serpent was Satan?
RF. The Holy Spirit told them.

JQ. Can you show me in the verse that the seed is Christ.
RF. The words "seed" and "he" are singular. That means one male person. So that person must be Christ because the NT says Christ destroyed Satan by his death on the cross.

JQ. But can you show me in Genesis 3:15, or any OT scripture, that the seed is Christ?
RF. I did, the seed is one person and the NT says that person is Christ.

JQ. Can you show me where the NT says the seed in Genesis 3:15 is Christ?
RF. Hebrews 2:14 says Christ destroyed Satan. In Genesis 3:15 Satan bruises Christ's heel and Christ bruises the serpent's head.

JQ. Can you show me in Genesis 3:15 Adam and Eve could identify their seed as Christ?
RF. I told you, the Holy Spirit told them.

JQ. So, the verse does not say the seed is Christ, and no OT or NT scripture says the seed is Christ, but they knew because the Holy Spirit told them the seed is Christ.
RF. Yes.

JQ. So the Holy Spirit did not use the Scripture he gave them to tell them, he just told them?
RF. Yes.

JQ. Isn't that extrabiblical revelation and illumination?
RF. The Holy Spirit helped them understand the verse was speaking about Christ.

JQ. Did other OT people know Genesis 3:15 was about Christ? And how did they know?
RF. Yes, they knew. That is how they were saved. Adam and Eve told their children and their children told their children, and so on, or the Holy Spirit told them.

Conversation ends.

That is how things not in the Bible are transformed into Scripture.
My friends, either the Scripture is what has been written, or anyone can say they have had a revelation from God and we must accept it as

equal with the written Scripture. Either the Holy Spirit works through his written Scripture, or anyone can say the Holy Spirit told me and we must accept it as equal with the written Scripture.

Verbal revelation and illumination are how cults are started. The Roman Catholic Church calls it verbal tradition handed down from the apostles. The Mormons call it the Book of Mormon. Reformed soteriology calls it the way the Old Testament people were saved, by believing the "first gospel," in Genesis 3:15, not because it is in the written Scripture, but because the Holy Spirit gave them verbal revelation and illumination. They were told, it is claimed, but where is it written? How is this different from the Roman Catholic Church and Mormonism?

The Scripture teaches the Old Testament peoples were saved by God's grace through their faith in the written Scripture God gave them in their historical times. Isn't that how you were saved?

The imaginary conversation above is not fiction. After I explained the grammar, that what happened to one offspring must happen to the other, and had explained Christ crushing Satan is not in Genesis 3:15; that in fact God crushed Christ on the cross, I watched two friends, one Reformed one Dispensational, have this conversation (I am quoting).

> Dispensational friend. The way I understand it is that the promise [in Genesis 3:15] to crush the serpent (who symbolized Satan at that moment & often is the symbol for him) did occur at the cross.

> Reformed friend: me too.

What was my Dispensational friend's justification?

> The promise of Genesis 3 is that the woman's offspring will "strike the head" of the serpent. When did this occur? Well anytime godly offspring opposes the serpent (Satan) the offspring strikes his head. But Jesus Christ came from the woman's line & certainly is one of those offspring that struck Satan-Serpent in his death on the cross. He struck him so hard it disarmed Satan & his demons of their powers.

His justification is Christ was struck so hard he died, but Satan was struck so hard he lived but is now disarmed. My friend points to Colossians 2:15, "disarming the rulers (Satan & demons are in that category) & authorities, he has made a public disgrace of them, triumphing over them by the cross."

So, in the view of these two friends, one Reformed one Dispensational, each offspring strikes the other, but it is a literal outcome for Christ, a metaphorical outcome for Satan. All from Genesis 3:15, which never mentions Christ or Satan. If I could have a conversation with Satan, I would ask him how it feels to have been "disarmed of his powers" during the 1,990 years since the crucifixion. After his laughter subsided, what would he say?

What is the meaning of Colossians 2:15? From my commentary on Colossians.

> 15 He stripped away the power of the rulers and authorities, publicly shaming them, leading them in his triumph.

> EXPOSITION

> In v. 15 the phrase "publicly shaming them" is *deigmatízō parrēsía*, to make a public show or spectacle [Zodhiates, s. v. 1165]. The context is set by *thriambeúō*, which originally meant "celebrate a triumph" [Harris, *Colossians*, 99], which I have translated "leading them in his triumph." The cultural reference is the parade given Roman generals upon returning from a significant victory in battle. Selected numbers of his captives trailed behind him, chained to his chariot. Thus he led his captives in his triumph (*thriambeúō*), publicly displaying his greatness and their humiliation (*deigmatízō parrēsía*). For the only other use of *thriambeúō* see 2 Corinthians 2:14.

> Paul uses an act familiar to the Colossians to illustrate Christ's complete victory over sin, death, and the evil spiritual powers of the world, through the event, his crucifixion, that was supposed by others to have been his defeat. Through his crucifixion and resurrection Christ "stripped away the power" the world had over the believer (when he/she was a sinner) through temptation, sin, and death. In different terms, sin and death have no more dominion over the believer (Romans 6:9, 14), that he should fear death and obey sin.

> The Christian often triumphs over the world by accepting defeat from the world. The believer who refuses to participate in worldly actions may suffer persecution: the world believes

he/she has been defeated. But Christ rewards his servants for their righteous works and obedience. The believer triumphs when he/she remains steadfast to Christ, not regarding the evil of the worldling.

No appeal to Genesis 3:15 needed. The Literal hermeneutic triumphs.

A Question From Acts 17:11

In Acts 17, Paul has been forced to leave Thessalonica, and has come to Berea. Luke says this about the Bereans in 17:11. "Now these were more noble-minded than those in Thessalonica, who received the word with all readiness, every day examining the Scriptures, if these things were so."

Luke's comment raised a question in my mind. If the Old Testament people knew from Genesis 3:15 and other Old Testament Scripture that salvation from the penalty due sin was by faith in a coming redeemer-messiah-christ, then why did the Bereans decide to check Paul's message that salvation from the penalty due sin was by faith in Jesus the Christ? They certainly were not checking the Scripture—which was only the Old Testament revelation—to decide if Jesus of Nazareth was the messiah. That Jesus of Nazareth was the messiah is New Testament revelation, initially spoken by Paul, who received it directly from Christ, Galatians 1:11–12. So why were they searching the Old Testament scriptures to see "if these things were so," if they already knew and had saving faith in a coming messiah-christ-redeemer, per the Reformed and Promise soteriology of Genesis 3:15?

Indeed, that question may be asked of every synagogue, of every Jew, at any time during this New Testament age, who rejected or questioned the Good News, beginning with Christ's public ministry. If they already knew there was a coming redeemer-messiah-christ, beginning at Genesis 3:15, then why was the gospel message of "The Christ-Redeemer Has Arrived" so soundly rejected?

A passage from Matthew's Gospel gives us the answer.

> Matthew 12:22–23, Then was brought to him a person inhabited by a demon, blind and mute, and he healed him, so that the mute man spoke and saw. 23 And all the crowds were amazed, and said, "This is not the son of David, is he?"

They did not say, "This is not the seed of the Woman who strikes the serpent's head, is he?" They did not say, "This is not Abraham's seed who blesses all the families on the earth is he?" They did not say, "This is not the one who fulfills all the sacrifices of the Law, is he?" They did not say, "This is not the one Isaiah said God made his soul an offering for sin, is he?"

They questioned if he could be the "son of David." Which David? King David of 2 Samuel 7:13–16; Psalm 2. No Jew in the Gospels and Acts understood the Old Testament to speak of a coming redeemer to save from sin, but rather a coming King to save the nation from oppression and rule as king—until told by Christ and his apostles, and their disciples. Why were they not looking for a coming redeemer-messiah-christ? Because they did not have the New Testament revelation that identifies the coming redeemer-messiah-christ as the redeemer of individuals *from their sins*, until told by Christ and his apostles, and their disciples.

There was no extrabiblical revelation or illumination during Old Testament times identifying a coming redeemer-messiah-christ in Genesis 3:15, the Reformed view, and there was no progressive understanding from Old Testament scripture, beginning in Genesis 3:15, the Dispensational Promise view, whereby the Old Testament peoples identified a coming redeemer-messiah-christ in Genesis 3:15 and other Old Testament scriptures.

If there had been such knowledge, the people seeing and hearing Jesus, and later hearing the apostles, and still later hearing any believer, would have asked themselves if this Jesus of Nazareth could be that coming redeemer-messiah-christ of Genesis 3:15. That did not, and never has, happened.

Reformed Soteriology

Before I show my investigation into Reformed soteriology, I am going to anticipate the outcome in a quote from historian Emil Schurer (1844–1910). Mr. Schurer wrote the five volume *A History of the Jewish People in the Time of Jesus Christ*, a well-respected and credible history. My copy is reprinted from the 1890 T&T Clark edition.

In Division 2, 2:129–130, Mr. Schurer describes what he names the "older Messianic hope." By that term he means before the intertestamental period. The quote is long, but it should lay to rest any hopes the Old Testament peoples believed in a promised redeemer from the penalty due sin, as both Reformed and Promise soteriology claim. Emphasis is by Schurer.

> The older Messianic hope virtually moves within the boundary of the then present circumstances of the world, and is nothing else than the hope of a better future for the *nation*. That the nation should be morally purified from all bad elements, that it should exist unmolested and respected in the midst of the Gentile world, whilst its enemies were either destroyed or forced to acknowledge the nation and its God, that it should be governed by a just, wise, and powerful king of the house of David, and that therefore internal justice, peace and happiness would prevail, nay that all natural evils would be abolished and a state of unclouded prosperity would appear—this may be said to have formed the foundation of the future hope among the older prophets.

Mr. Schurer then speaks about "alterations" to this view "partly in the times of the later prophets, but especially in the post-canonical period." Did any of those alterations point to a Messiah-Redeemer from sin? No. The view expanded to include the world; the world would be judged; the king would rule over all humankind; belief in personal resurrection of the righteous (later defined by adherence the Mosaic Law) to share in that future Messianic Kingdom; possibly a resurrection for the wicked to face judgment.

There was in the Old Testament revelation a line of prophecy concerning a coming redeemer, Genesis 12:3; 21:12; Daniel 9:26, but the people did not understand it. They were not looking for a Redeemer but a King. They did not understand from Genesis 3:15 a promised-coming redeemer-messiah-christ, because that information is not in the verse.

Reformed Soteriology

Reformed theology's Old Testament soteriology may be summarized in two statements.

> The object of saving faith in every age is Christ.

> The content of saving faith is always Christ, either coming (OT), or arrived (NT).

That object and content of faith is what Reformed soteriology claims as the one and only way to salvation.

The goal of Reformed soteriology is to have the one way of salvation be faith in Jesus Christ. The Scripture teaches the one way of salvation is the unlimited efficacy of the propitiation made by Christ to save the soul from the penalty due sin. Reformed soteriology subtly changes salvation from what Christ has done to what man should do.

This is the question I asked three Reformed Systematic theologians, using their published work as the source.

> Using only the written Old Testament revelation, show me a scripture or scriptures given to the Old Testament peoples where they were told they must believe on a future redeemer, a future Messiah or future Christ, or a future person named Jesus, to be saved. Remember, only the written Old Testament revelation may be used, because that written Old Testament revelation was the only Word of God the Old Testament people had received from YHWH by which to be saved.

I consulted only three, because the answer never changes. I consulted three from different generations, to demonstrate the answer never changes.

Theologian Charles Hodge (1797–1878)

I recommend Hodge's *Systematic Theology* to any believer desiring a better understanding of the essentials of the faith. However, in explaining Old Testament soteriology (and eschatology and ecclesiology) he followed the traditions of his theological ancestors. In his work *Systematic Theology*, 2:371–372, published in the mid-1800s, Hodge explained the kind of Old Testament saving faith required by Reformed soteriology.

> As the same promise [of a personal Messiah who was to redeem the people of God] was made to those who lived before the [first] advent [of Christ], which is now made to us in the gospel, [and] as the same Redeemer was revealed to them who is presented as the object of faith to us, it of necessity follows that the condition, or terms of salvation, was the same then as now. It was not mere faith or trust in God, or simple piety, which was required, but faith in the promised Redeemer, or faith in the promise of redemption through the Messiah.

A close look at Hodge's statement reveals the faulty premise: "the same Redeemer was revealed to them who is presented as the object of faith to us." Hodge is unable to show any Old Testament scripture to satisfy that premise. Only by going to the New Testament revelation and reading it into the Old Testament Scripture to change the Old Testament revelation can Hodge demonstrate his premise. But that is not the Literal hermeneutic.

According to Hodge, during Old Testament times—in the Reformed covenant of grace the times that began after Adam's sin—the requirement for salvation was the understanding a Redeemer is coming in the future. According to Hodge, this personal Redeemer was "made known" to the Old Testament peoples; but Hodge never states how he was made known.

Hodge is not speaking of just any Redeemer, but "the same Redeemer was revealed to them [the Old Testament believers] who is presented as the object of faith to us [New Testament believers]. Now this Redeemer, Jesus Christ, is presented in New Testament times by the New Testament revelation. But Hodge cannot point to any scripture in the Old Testament revelation that clearly taught the Old Testament sinner to place his or her saving faith in a coming Redeemer. Hodge simply states, as though an irrefutable fact, that the Old Testament sinner had to have faith in a "promised Redeemer, or faith in the promise of redemption through the Messiah .. the same Redeemer ... who is presented as the object of faith to us" New Testament believers.

Theologian Louis Berkhof (1873–1957)

Louis Berkhof [262–300] has one of the best defenses of Reformed theology in his work, a defense I do not believe has been superseded. However, as did Hodge, Berkhof followed the theological presuppositions of his predecessors. Berkhof defined the Reformed Covenant of Grace as,

> That gracious agreement between the offended God and the offending but elect sinner, in which God promises salvation through faith in Christ, and the elect sinner accepts this believingly, promising a life of faith and obedience. [p. 277.]

Berkhof isn't speaking only of New Testament believers, but of the Old Testament believer also, claiming those Old Testament believers were saved, "through faith in Christ." Let us understand what Berkhoff is saying: in order for an Old Testament sinner to be saved, he/she must believe God's "promises [of] salvation through faith in Christ."

Berkhof stated, "in the covenant of grace, it is faith in Jesus Christ" [p. 272]. Let us remember that in Reformed theology the Covenant of Grace began with the fall of Adam. Berkhof was teaching that the saving faith of every person saved in the Old Testament was faith in Christ, even millennia before the first unambiguous Scripture mention of a coming Redeemer or a coming Christ. The first mention of a coming Christ is Psalm 2:2, the Messiah-King. The first mention of a coming Messiah-Redeemer is Daniel 9:26, which is never mentioned in the New Testament.

(Yes, because of the New Testament revelation you know of several earlier scriptures of a coming redeemer, but in the Old Testament none of those earlier scriptures were connected to the Hebrew word *māshîah*, the equivalent to the Greek *christós*.)

Berkhof also taught that human beings in the Old Testament responded to the promises of God in regard to, "the promise of justification unto the forgiveness of sins, the adoption as [God's] children, and eternal life, he [the elect sinner] responds by saving faith in Jesus Christ, by trust in Him for time and eternity, and by a life of obedience and consecration to God" [p. 277].

Theologian Wayne Grudem (1948–)

Wayne Grudem is a recent Reformed theologian. Grudem states [519, emphasis Grudem],

> The *condition* (or requirement) of participation in the covenant [of grace] is *faith* in the work of Christ the Redeemer (Rom. 1:17; 5:1, et al.). This requirement of faith in the redemptive

work of the Messiah was also the condition of obtaining the blessings of the covenant in the Old Testament, as Paul clearly demonstrates through the examples of Abraham and David (Rom 4:1–15). They, like other Old Testament believers, were saved by looking forward to the work of the Messiah who was to come and putting their faith in him.

Let us make certain we understand Grudem's soteriology. Grudem unequivocally states the Old Testament believers understood the redemptive work of a specific person yet-to-come and placed saving faith in him. Grudem believes he proves thesis by citing Paul in Romans 4:1–15, where Paul *never* mentions Jesus Christ, or faith in Jesus Christ, or faith in a promised Redeemer, or faith in the promise of redemption through the Messiah. Grudem defends his proposition by appealing to the New Testament revelation and reading it into the Old Testament Scripture. But that is not the Literal hermeneutic.

Grudem says, without any proof from the Old Testament revelation, that in order for an Old Testament sinner to gain participation in the Covenant of Grace—to be saved—he or she must place their faith in Christ the Redeemer—faith in the specific person Jesus the Christ, as he later makes clear. They must "look forward to the work of the Messiah," Jesus Christ. Again—I know I am being repetitious, but the point is important—in Romans 4:1–15, which Grudem cites as proof of his assertion, Paul *never* mentions Jesus Christ, or faith in Jesus Christ, or faith in a promised Redeemer, or faith in the promise of redemption through the Messiah.

How did the Old Testament sinner know to believe in a promised redeemer-messiah-christ (let alone the specific person Jesus)? Because these Reformed theologians cannot supply anything from the Old Testament revelation, their answer is extrabiblical revelation or illumination. They point to the New Testament, which in Old Testament times did not exist and therefore for the Old Testament person to know New Testament revelation is extrabiblical revelation during the Old Testament times.

Reformed Old Testament soteriology is built on a supposition that cannot be demonstrated from the Old Testament revelation. Reformed Old Testament soteriology is built on an incorrect premise: that every aspect of Old Testament salvation must be identical with every aspect of New Testament salvation, otherwise it is a different gospel.

Let me be clear (and again I admit to being repetitious), the one and only way of salvation in both testaments is not the same object of faith Old and New Testaments, and is not the same content of faith Old and New Testaments. The one and only way of salvation in both testaments is the salvation principle.

> Saved by God's grace through the sinner's faith in God and God's testimony, without any works by the sinner, but by the limitless merit of Christ's propitiation of God for the crime of human sin.

God's grace, the sinner's faith, Christ's merit. Those are the essentials of salvation. The object and content of faith are not the essentials, but must conform to the Scripture.

> God is the Savior: YHWH in the Old Testament; Jesus Christ in the New Testament.

> Faith in God's testimony, as given in the historical progressive revelation of truth, tells the sinner way of salvation.

> The limitless merit of Christ's propitiation powers salvation in both Old and New Testaments.

Is it scripturally reasonable that the object of faith and the content of faith should change as God gives the historical progressive revelation of truth to tell the sinner way of salvation? Yes. Even a casual examination of God's works throughout Scripture reveals God uses different means to accomplish the same end. One time Moses was to hit a rock to bring forth water, a second time he was to speak to the rock to accomplish the same end. When Elijah was hungry, did God rain manna down from the heavens? No, a raven brought Elijah food.

Even so, the means by which redemption may be made known to the sinner need not be a proclamation of Jesus Christ (Berkhof, Grudem), or a promised redeemer or a promised messiah (Hodge). Faith in God and God's testimony in the Scripture delivered within the current historical circumstances of the sinner is made sufficient by the Holy Spirit giving understanding of the plain and normal meaning of the words of Scripture, no extrabiblical revelation or illumination needed. The unchanging, *sine qua non* of salvation is not the object of faith or the content of faith but is this: saved by God's grace through the sinner's faith in God and God's testimony without personal merit from the sinner but by Christ's merit alone.

Theologian John Calvin (1509–1564)

I quote John Calvin as one of the original leaders of the Reformed faith; whose writings form the substance of Reformed doctrine, usually.

John Calvin is at the beginning of the era of Reformed theology. Having his opinion on Genesis 3:15 should prove valuable to this discussion. Did Calvin believe Christ was in Genesis 3:15?

The following is from Calvin's *Commentaries on the First Book of Moses called Genesis.* In the edition I am using (see Sources), the quote below is on p. 170. Emphasis is Calvin's.

> There is, indeed, no ambiguity in the *words* used here by Moses; but I do not agree with others respecting their *meaning*; for other interpreters take the seed for *Christ*, without controversy; as if it were said, that someone would arise from the seed of the woman who should wound the serpent's head. Gladly would I give my suffrage [assent] in support of their opinion, but that I regard the word *seed* as too violently distorted by them; for who will concede that a *collective* noun is to be understood of one man *only*? Further, as the perpetuity of the contest is noted, no victory is promised to the human race through a continual succession of ages. I explain, therefore, the *seed* to mean the posterity of the woman generally.

Having then interpreted the verse by the Literal hermeneutic, Calvin continues, with an understanding afforded by the New Testament revelation. "But since experience teaches that not all the sons of Adam by far, arise as conquerors of the devil [meaning that some do], we must necessarily come to one head, that we may find to whom the victory belongs. So Paul, from the seed of Abraham, leads us [those having received the New Testament revelation] to Christ."

Calvin recognized two critical things. One, Adam and Eve could not know what Paul knew, nor could Abraham, although having received additional revelation in his times, know what Paul knew. Two, Paul reveals Christ in Galatians 3:8, not from Genesis 3:15, but from the seed of Abraham, Genesis 12:3; 15:6; 17:19, 21, and leads those— "us"—having received the New Testament revelation to Christ.

Calvin clearly and neatly separates what Adam and Eve could know through the revelation given them, from what Christians can know through the revelation they have received. Would that all using Calvin as a source of their understanding, also adopt his understanding of the Scripture, and his hermeneutical methodology.

A Simple Example

There is a simple example of the unhappy effect Reformed Old Testament soteriology has on Christian theology, that comes in the most unlikely place: a Reformed title for the Christ. Notice, not a biblical title. That Reformed title is the "Preincarnate Christ." Of course, you say, an Old Testament appearance of God the Son is known as the preincarnate Christ. In Reformed soteriology and Christology, yes. But the term "Preincarnate Christ" is decidedly not biblical.

Reformed theology invented that term so they could say, "See, Christ is in the Old Testament." and thereby support their Old Testament soteriology that Old Testament sinners believed in a coming redeemer-messiah-christ for their salvation. Remember, Reformed soteriology says this.

The object of saving faith in every age is Christ.

The content of saving faith is always Christ, either coming (OT), or arrived (NT).

If Christ was present pre-incarnate in the Old Testament times, then obviously the Old Testament peoples knew of Christ and could believe on him for saving faith.

No.

The first mention of God's anointed, *māshîah*, in the context of the coming one, is Psalm 2:2, the coming *Māshîah*-King. And when would he come? Psalm 2:7, I have begotten you. There was no *māshîah-christós* until "I have begotten you" happened. When did "I have begotten you" happen? Luke 1:31–33, and specifically 1:38, "See the handmaid of the Lord. May it be to me according your word."

There is no such thing as a "pre-incarnate," Christ, because the *māshîah-christós*, the anointed, is an office of God the Son. It is a duty he entered into when he incarnated. Until "I have begotten you" happened there was no Christ. A "preincarnate" Christ is an oxymoron: a contradiction in terms. God the Son *was not* the Christ until the incarnation. We may speak of the preincarnate God the Son. He appears in the Christophany known as the Messenger of YHWH, aka; the Angel of YHWH. There are several "Angel of YHWH" appearances in the Old Testament, but only some are the preincarnate God the Son. See my book, *Angelology, A True History of Angels*, appendix 5.

In Contrast, The Dispensational View.

"We believe . . . that the principle of faith was prevalent in the lives of all the Old Testament saints. However, it was impossible that they should have had as the conscious object of their faith the incarnate, crucified Son, the Lamb of God (John 1:29), and it is evident that they did not comprehend as we do that the sacrifices depicted the person and work of Christ." (Dallas Seminary, Doctrinal Statement, Article V, quoted in Ryrie, *Dispensationalism,* 116.)

"The basis of salvation in every age is the death [i.e., propitiation] of Christ; the requirement of salvation in every age is faith; the object of faith in every age is God; the content of faith changes in the various dispensations." [Ryrie, *Dispensationalism,* 115.]

The Dallas' statement is one of the arguments of the Book of Hebrews. If the Old Testament believers had known their sacrifices pointed to Christ, they would have stopped offering those sacrifices and worshiped Christ. Is this not what he is saying to his readers who do know Christ? Because you do know Christ, why are you considering returning to the sacrificial system, which Christ has fulfilled and superseded?

The Old Testament believers did continue to offer those sacrifices, Hebrews 10:1, which have been superseded by the sacrifice of the Christ, Hebrews 10:12, 14. Therefore the Old Testament believers did not know of a coming redeemer-messiah-christ. They did not see a coming redeemer-messiah-christ in Genesis 3:15, nor in Noah's ark, nor in the promise of an heir to Abraham, nor in the Mosaic Law. To say they did is eisegesis of the Old Testament revelation; it is injecting not yet written New Testament revelation or illumination to create an understanding not possible from the plain and normal meaning of the revelation given to them. Reformed Old Testament soteriology knows that, for that is why they appeal only to the New Testament revelation for their Old Testament soteriology. But they deliberately do not acknowledge what they know to be true. They are deliberately and knowingly ignorant.

Just as Reformed soteriology and Dispensational Promise soteriology may be summarized in the two statements of Reformed soteriology (above), so also the genuine Dispensational soteriology may be summarized—has been summarized—in two statements, by Ryrie.

The object of saving faith in every age is God.

The content of saving faith changes in the various dispensations.

(I do not want to misrepresent Dr. Ryrie. He believed in and taught Promise soteriology. In Dr. Ryrie's view, the "changing content of faith" during each Old Testament dispensation was additional revelation given in the progressive revelation of truth that supported finding a redeemer-messiah-christ in Genesis 3:15.)

I discussed the content of faith concept in a previous chapter. In the long history of Old Testament redemption from Adam to Christ, the salvific content of faith changed according to the historically given progressive revelation of truth.

Reformed Objections To Dispensational Soteriology

Naturally it is impossible to discuss every objection. But here I will discuss a few key scriptures. I have previously discussed the primary Old Testament Scripture Reformed and Promise soteriology use as the keystone, Genesis 3:15, please see that chapter.

Genesis 15:6

Abraham believed God's promise of an heir from his own body and that faith was accounted to him for righteousness. Did Abraham see a coming Christ as his heir? No. By faith Abraham looked forward to an heir receiving the promises, not knowing if that heir would be Isaac or a descendant of Isaac, Genesis 17:21. Only when we get to the New Testament revelation are we given the knowledge of which heir of Abraham will receive all the promises made to Abraham. Abraham did not and could not know which heir from the scriptures he received (of which Moses has given us a written record).

Psalm 2

Psalm 2 is viewed by Reformed soteriology as teaching a coming Redeemer. Psalm 2:2 speaks of the "anointed" (*māshîah*), and 2:7 says this anointed is God's begotten son. But interpreting Psalm 2 as mentioning a coming Redeemer for sin ignores the context. The context of this Psalm is ruling not redeeming from sin. The coming one is anointed as King to redeem the nation from gentile oppression, not as the Redeemer of souls from the penalty of sin.

Identifying a believer as God's son was not unknown to the Jews. The Jews believed they were sons of God. David's heir, who would come out of David's body, 2 Samuel 7:12, was a son of God. In the light of New Testament revelation we know 2 Samuel 7:12 will be fulfilled in David's greater heir, the Christ, but the Jews thought of a human descendant of David, 1 Chronicles 22:7–11; 28:6, not God incarnate. In the context of Ezekiel 21:10, God's son is Israel, 21:11–12. And when Hosea 11:1, "When Israel was a child, I loved him, and out of Egypt I called My son," was written ca. 720 BC, it referred to the Israelites, not Christ. No one knew Hosea 11:1 referred to Christ until Matthew published his gospel, perhaps as early as ca. AD 42, Matthew 2:15.

The angel Gabriel told Mariam, Luke 1:32–33, that her son "will be called the son of the Most High," see Psalm 2:2, 7, "and the Lord God will give him the throne of David, his father," see 2 Samuel 7:13–16. "He will reign over the house of Jacob to the ages" see Genesis 49:10, "and of his kingdom there will not be an end." Mariam had no reason to understand her son would be God the Son incarnate, nor that he would be the redeemer of sinners. The key words in relation to her son are throne, David, reign, and kingdom. We see what kind of redeemer Mariam was looking for in Luke 1:51–52, a king.

Neither did Joseph understand Mariam's son as God incarnate, Matthew 1:18–25. The angel identified Joseph as a "son of David," thus referring to the 2 Samuel prophecy. He quoted Isaiah 7:14, which prophecies a birth—confirmed as a virgin birth in Luke 1:35; Matthew 1:20, but not the incarnation of a redeemer of souls. The announcement to the shepherds, Luke 2:8–14, gives no hint of a redeemer of souls, but only the fulfillment of 2 Samuel 7:12; Micah 4:8, 5:2.

So when, for example, Jesus answered the high priest, Mark 14:61–62, "Are you the Christ, the son of the Blessed?" and Jesus said, "I am," and no one present understood the title, "Christ" (the Greek translation of the Hebrew *māshîah*), nor the phrase, "son of the

Blessed," as indicating Jesus was God incarnate in Jesus of Nazareth, or that he was come to redeem them from sin.

When Jesus said "I am" they understood he was claiming to be the anointed one of Psalm 2:2, 7, a human being chosen by God to be their king and deliver them from the Gentiles. They never considered Isaiah 53 or Daniel 9:25–26 as referring to Messiah-King, because the Messiah-King cannot die and be king.

But when Jesus said, "Moreover, I say to you, from now you will see the Son of Man sitting at the right hand of the Power, and coming in the clouds of heaven," Matthew 26:64, then they realized he was claiming to be deity, and they condemned him to death. They crucified the Lord of glory because they did not understand God's redemptive purpose in the Christ, 1 Corinthians 2:8.

When interpreted with the Literal hermeneutic, Psalm 2 speaks of an Anointed King who will rule the earth, not a redeemer of men's souls from sin.

The First Mention Of A Coming Redeemer

The first unambiguous mention of a coming Redeemer is Daniel 9:26. The *māshîah* will die but not for himself. Today we know that Genesis 12:3, and Isaiah 53:5, and Psalm 22 refer to Messiah-Redeemer, a fact we know from Galatians 3:6–18, among other New Testament scriptures. How do we know that? The same as the Jew in Acts 8:35–35 found out: Philip gave him New Testament revelation.

Why did the Ethiopian, or any other Jew, not know, if the Jews knew Genesis 3:15 was about a coming messiah-christ-redeemer, and had received confirming information in later Old Testament revelation? Why did they not know? Three reasons.

Genesis 3:15 is not about a coming redeemer-messiah-christ.

There was no additional revelation confirming Genesis 3:15 was about a coming redeemer-messiah-christ.

The person described by Isaiah, ca. 700 BC, is not called *māshîah*, Messiah, so there was no biblical way for any Old Testament person reading Genesis 12:3, or Isaiah 53:5, or Psalm 22 to associate those scriptures with the *māshîah* of Psalm 2:2, written ca. 1000 BC.

We see from every testimony in the four gospels that although

138

some Jews thought of Jesus of Nazareth as their anointed (Messiah) king to redeem the nation from the gentiles, none thought of Jesus as a redeemer from sin. (There may have been exceptions, e.g., Mariam of Bethany, who was not at the crucifixion because she believed Jesus' testimony that he would resurrect, a belief based on the New Testament revelation given by Jesus.)

From Adam to Daniel 9:25, there was no scripture mention of a redeemer-messiah-christ who was promised to come and remit the penalty due sin. The very first chronological mention in Scripture of a coming *māshîah*, "anointed," is in Psalm 2, ca. 1000 BC, where the subject is the King, not the Redeemer. The next mention of a coming *māshîah*, "anointed," is Daniel 9:26, ca. 540 BC, where the subject is the Redeemer, not the King.

But Daniel 9:26 is not mentioned in the four gospels, and no one during Jesus' lifetime accused Jesus of claiming he was a redeemer from sin. In fact, just the opposite, Peter rebuked Jesus for saying he would die, which is what Daniel 9:26 teaches. Certainly Jesus' enemies gave no thought that they might be fulfilling Daniel 9:26. Compare Daniel with 1 Corinthians 2:7–8.

> Daniel 9:26, After sixty-two sevens Messiah will be cut off and have nothing for himself.
>
> 1 Corinthians 2:7–8, But we speak God's hidden wisdom, having been hidden, which God foreordained before the ages of the ages for our glory, 8 which not one of the rulers of this age has known. For if they had known, the Lord of glory they would not have crucified.

Let us look at other scriptures.

John 8:56

John 8:56 reads, "Abraham your father rejoiced in that he should see my day, and he saw and rejoiced." The main problem in interpreting this verse is that it is deliberately misread as, "Abraham saw Me." No, Abraham did not foresee a coming redeemer-messiah-christ. Abraham perceived by faith a time when a heir from his own body—that is what God had promised—would receive the promises.

Did Abraham see the day of the Messiah? This would be difficult from the promises given to him as no messiah was mentioned. There is no Old Testament or New Testament scripture that states or implies Abraham saw the advent of Messiah.

Abraham's faith was in God's promise of an "offspring" to fulfill the covenant God had initiated in Genesis 12:2–3, confirmed and supplemented by later revelation given to Abraham. Abraham need not understand that the offspring in the promise of an heir was a coming redeemer-messiah-christ, because Abraham believed in the promise of fulfillment through an offspring from his own body.

God gave Abraham certain promises concerning his posterity, and it was Abraham's faith in these promises to which Jesus referred. Abraham perceived by faith that through his descendant all the families of the earth would be blessed. Later revelation, the Analogy of Faith, confirms that interpretation. Abraham believed and sought a heavenly country; Hebrews 11:14, 16, Abraham believed and looked for a city whose builder and maker is God; Hebrews 11:10. Abraham believed God would fulfill the promise through Isaac, even if he killed Isaac, Hebrews 11:17–19, because God had told Abraham twenty years earlier he, YHWH, would establish his covenant with Abraham through Isaac, Genesis 17:19, 21.

Hebrews

Hebrews 11:13 reads, "These all died in faith, not having received the promises, but having seen them afar off were assured of them." Did the Old Testament believers see Jesus in the promises, as Reformed theology claims? Or were they able to persevere as strangers and pilgrims because they saw the fulfillment of the promises through the certainty of God-given faith, as Hebrews 11:1–2 states? They believe in things hoped for, not in things seen. As Hebrews 11:1 states, they believed through faith in the things promised by faith.

That expectation of fulfillment formed the core of their life. They embraced the promises and wove them into the fabric of their life as they practiced their faith, remaining strangers and pilgrims on the earth. They embraced the promises as sure and genuine, assured by faith of possession. They didn't understand the promise of "an heir from your own body," or a land to inherit, as a future Messiah who would be king, or as a promise of a coming personal Redeemer from sin. They simply believed those literal promises would someday be fulfilled.

The promise of a Redeemer, Isaiah 53, was so mysterious, that the Ethiopian Jew did not know if the passage referred to Isaiah or someone else, Acts 8:31–34, without New Testament revelation, Acts 8:35. So also other Jews of Jesus' time. No Jewish religious leader, and not one follower or disciple or apostle of Jesus of Nazareth, ever applies Isaiah 53 to Jesus in the four gospels. If Dispensational Promise soteriology is correct, they should have known; but it is not correct, because they did not know.

Hebrews 11:24–26 reads, "By faith Moses . . . esteemed the reproach of Christ greater riches than the treasures in Egypt; for he looked to the reward." Did Moses intuit Christ from the promises given to Abraham and Israel? The key word is "faith." Moses did not have to have direct knowledge of Christ—if he was given a divine revelation it is not revealed in the written Old Testament Scripture. But through his faith in God's promises Moses looked forward to receipt of the promises. Moses knew of and understood the reward of faith. The Hebrews Writer's point is that his New Testament readers, and we are included, should esteem the reproach of Christ greater riches than the treasures of the world, because just like Moses we look to the reward.

Luke 24:25–27

Jesus said, "Oh foolish and slow of heart to believe in all that the prophets have spoken. 26 Was it not necessary for the Christ to suffer and enter into his glory?" 27 And beginning from Moses and from all the prophets, he clearly and exactly explained to them in all the Scriptures the things concerning himself."

Some believe this verse means New Testament believers have been authorized by Jesus to discover him in *every* Old Testament Scripture. Of course, that is foolish. Through the additional information given in the New Testament revelation we understand some Old Testament scriptures speak of Jesus; most do not.

Others believe Jesus' statement allows us to reinterpret the meaning the Old Testament scriptures had for the Old Testament peoples. That view ignores that the Old Testament scriptures had a meaning for the Old Testament peoples that was not about Jesus. That view ignores the hermeneutical rule of authorial intent. That view denies the principle of the Analogy of Scripture, by distorting the principle of the Analogy of Faith.

Others believe the Old Testament people knew about the coming

Christ as Messiah-Redeemer. These believe Noah saw Christ in the ark. That Abraham saw Christ in the heir from his own body. That those under the Law saw Christ in the sacrifices and the elements of the temple. As I have said before, if they did have that understanding it is not communicated in the written Old Testament revelation. Therefore, to propose they somehow had that understanding is false doctrine built on extrabiblical revelation or illumination.

In Luke 24:25–26, those two believers could not perceive the spiritual truth until the Holy Spirit opened their spiritual perception and the New Testament revelation of the Christ was revealed. So too you and me. Without the New Testament revelation we could not know some of the Old Testament is about the Christ.

So, is Christ being unjust in criticizing their lack of understanding? After all, the New Testament revelation was not yet written. No, Christ was not being unjust. Jesus Christ himself, present and ministering on earth, was himself the New Testament revelation of Old Testament truth about himself. During the three years of his public ministry, all the Christ did and all the Christ said illuminated those Old Testament scriptures that concerned the Christ. On the road to Emmaus, Jesus revealed what the Old Testament said about him, and the Holy Spirit gave them understanding. That understanding was impossible until the Christ came and the New Testament revelation was revealed.

Chapter Summary

Summarizing Reformed soteriology: Old Testament salvation was by "faith in Jesus Christ" (Berkhof) or "faith in the promised Redeemer . . . the promise of redemption through the Messiah" (Hodge) or "those who were saved under the old covenant were also saved through trusting in Christ" (Grudem). In Reformed Old Testament soteriology, salvation is by faith in a coming redeemer-messiah-christ as both object and content of faith.

Because no, zero, absolutely no Old Testament scripture says place saving faith in a *coming* redeemer-messiah-christ, the only rational answer to explain the Reformed soteriology view is that the Holy Spirit worked personally with each elect person, to give each elect person extrabiblical revelation or illumination, showing them that the Old Testament revelation referred to a coming redeemer-messiah-christ (or the specific person Jesus of Nazareth according to some), in whom they must believe for salvation.

As Hodge put it, "it was not mere faith or trust in God" that saved them." Dispensational soteriology says it was faith in God's and God's testimony, as received in the historical progressive revelation of truth, that saved the Old Testament sinner. That is also what the Scripture says.

More to the point, if we rely on anything but the written Scripture to form our doctrine, then we will create false doctrine. That is what Reformed Old Testament soteriology has done.

Promise Soteriology

Introduction

Origin of Promise Soteriology in Dispensationalism

Dispensational Promise soteriology is the view "that the Old Testament believers believed a coming redeemer/deliverer that would crush the head of the serpent, a symbol of Satan [Genesis 3:15], but did not have all of the details then and only understood as much as was revealed progressively through eras of history until the full picture was revealed in the New Testament." [Dr. Sherlin, conversation with the author.]

What is the origin of this promise soteriology?

The introduction of "Promise Soteriology" into Dispensationalism seems to have been a historically recent development. C.I. Scofield may have been the first Dispensationalist to document Genesis 3:15 as prophecy of a promised redeemer. His correspondence course (of which I am a graduate), begun in 1890, in vol. 2:180, teaches the "chain of messianic promise," beginning with Genesis 3:15. I know now what I was too inexperienced in Scripture to notice then (in 1976): none of the ten scriptures in the chain (all in Genesis) mention, allude to, or imply a coming redeemer, nor crushing a serpent's head for any reason.

The concept appears in 1905 in *The Prophets and the Promise*, by Willis J. Beecher [Rydelnik, 18]. Beecher's view (as described by Rydelnik) was "the prophet's message pertained to the promise made to Abraham [Genesis 12:3] that would ultimately culminate in the Messiah." Beecher proposed that what was believed at any one time in history was the current prophetic development as given in the progressive revelation God gave to Israel concerning the promise made to Abraham.

Beecher believed the promise in Genesis 12:3 "would ultimately culminate in the Messiah" because of Galatians 3:8. Beecher was not saying the Old Testament peoples understood the promise would culminate in the Messiah, but that he understood the Old Testament promises would culminate in the Messiah.

As I do not have a copy of Beecher's book, I cannot with certainty say Beecher did not mention Genesis 3:15. However, Rydelnik's purpose in his book (see Rydelnik section below) is to show the Old Testament is a messianic book, and I assume if Beecher had said Genesis 3:15 was messianic, Rydelnik would have mentioned that.

The historical documentation of the "Promise" idea in Dispensationalism seems to have continued with Scofield through his 1909 *Scofield Reference Bible* (in continuous publication to the present times). In his notes in the *Reference Bible*, Scofield says (*in loco*) that Genesis 3:15 is "the first promise of a Redeemer." He names his list of supporting Old Testament references the "Highway of the Seed." None of those Old Testament scriptures mention, allude to, or imply a coming redeemer.

The Redeemer in the Old Testament was not coming, he was already there, in the person of the ever-present YHWH. Why would the Holy Spirit teach sinners to place their faith in a coming redeemer when there was an ever-present Redeemer, YHWH, on the scene, saving sinners?

The careful reader takes notice that the views of Scofield, Beecher and others did not single out either line of messianic prophecy—a king, Psalm 2; a redeemer, Daniel 9:26—but conflate the two lines into one. For example, Scofield references Genesis 12:3 and 49:10 as messianic promises of a coming redeemer. Genesis 12:3 is the Redeemer of individuals from sin, a fact known only from the later revelation of Galatians 3:8. Genesis 49:10 is the national redeemer, the Messiah-King, described in Psalm 2. Those are not one messianic promise but *two distinct lines* of messianic prophecy, that do not meet in the Old Testament.

That these are two distinct lines of messianic prophecy was fully revealed by the New Testament revelation of two advents of the Messiah. The first advent was Messiah-Redeemer; the second advent will be Messiah-King. These lines were given separate development in the Old Testament, but the Messiah-Redeemer prophecies were given less attention. As Schurer pointed out (emphasis Schurer, see previous chapter for full quote).

> The older Messianic hope ... is nothing else than the hope of a better future for the *nation* .... it should be governed by a just, wise, and powerful king of the house of David.

The modern proponents of Promise soteriology focus on the

Messiah-Redeemer line of prophecy. These Dispensationalists believe Old Testament salvation was by believing in the future fulfillment of a promised seed-redeemer, as supposedly revealed in Genesis 3:15, as (supposedly) supplemented by later revelation. These Dispensationalists believe the historic development of the Messiah-Redeemer prophecies, as given in the progressive revelation of truth, were understood with respect to Genesis 3:15. In practice, Promise soteriology is little different from Reformed soteriology. The names have been changed, but the concepts are the same.

The newness of Dispensational Promise soteriology does not make it novel, or wrong. Neither age nor youth make a doctrine right or wrong. Our understanding of Scripture, and our ability to explain Scripture, increases as we mature. Each generation of the New Testament church inherits what has come before, sometimes correcting, sometimes changing, sometimes adding to the accumulated knowledge and wisdom of the past. As someone somewhere has said, we see further because we stand on the shoulders of giants. Sometimes doctrines once anciently held pass out of view, and then are rediscovered by a later generation, giving them the appearance of new doctrines.

For example, looking at Reformed soteriology, the Reformation which grew out of Luther's 95 Thesis, AD 1517, against the sale of indulgences, rediscovered Augustinian doctrines of soteriology, from ca. AD 400, that had been set aside for centuries. To the Roman Catholic Church, Reformed soteriology was new and dangerous; to the Reformers their "new" soteriology was biblical; to anyone with the proper historical perspective Reformed soteriology was the revival of the ancient Augustinian soteriology. Anyone knowing Augustinian soteriology perceives it is based on what the Scripture teaches.

Did Augustine view Genesis 3:15 as a promise of a coming redeemer-messiah-christ. I searched all the "index of texts" in the eight volumes of Augustine's writings in the Nicene and Post-Nicene Fathers (*NPNF*, First Series) set of books.. Only in vol. 8, *Expositions on the Book of Psalms*, is Genesis 3:15 mentioned.

> *NPNF* 8:91, on Psalm 37, "Therefore, when the Lord would caution His Church, He said, 'it shall watch thy head, and thou shall watch his heel.' The serpent watcheth when the foot of

pride may come against thee, when thou mayest fall, that he may cast thee down. But watch thou his head: the beginning of all sin is pride.

NPNF 8:170, on Psalm 49, "What was said by God to the serpent? She shall mark thy head, and thou shalt mark her heel.' The devil marketh thy heel, in order that when thou slippest he may overthrow thee. He marketh thy heel, do thou mark his head. What is his head? The beginning of an evil suggestion."

(Why the translator decided to translate Augustine's Latin text into KJV English I do not know.)

At *NPNF* 8:346, on Psalm 74:13, the verse reads (ESV), "You [YHWH] divided the sea by your might; you broke the heads of the sea monsters on the waters." (Note: in the following comments, Augustine called the sea monsters "dragons." Comments in brackets are mine, for clarification.) Augustine said.

What with him [the chief dragon], hath He [YHWH, 74:12] done? 'Thou hast broken the head of the dragon.' That is, the beginning of sin. That head is the part which received the curse, to wit, the seed of Eve should mark the head of the serpent. For the Church was admonished to shun the beginning of sin. Which is that beginning of sin, like the head of a serpent? The beginning of all sin is pride.

In later comments on 74:13, Augustine makes clear he considered the Church to be the seed. Not Christ, but the Church is the seed of Genesis 3:15. For Augustine, the Church began with Adam and Eve. Augustine points to the believing descendants of Adam and Eve, as the seed that would "mark the head of the serpent."

Far from pointing to the seed in Genesis 3:15 as a redeemer-messiah-christ, Augustine says "the Son of God was to come out of the seed of Abraham" not the "seed" in Genesis 3:15. [*NPNF* 8:148, on Psalm 45.]

Augustine commented allegorically, but it is clear the Reformers did not get their allegorical interpretation of Genesis 3:15 from Augustine.

Origin Of This Chapter

One of my Dispensational friends kept talking about the Old

Testament sinner saved by belief in the "promise." This "promise" was to him not the same as Reformed soteriology.

His perception was not the same as my experience with the promised seed doctrine. I asked him to explain his perception; he recommended material I could research. He gave me the names of several theologians and their works, in addition to the resources I had already researched.

Below I will present the result of my research of Promise soteriology Dispensationalists. The theologians suggested by my friend confirmed the conclusions obtained from my previous research. Promise soteriology is Reformed extrabiblical revelation or illumination given a new name, with an added emphasis on progressive revelation.

Reformed soteriology says the Old Testament peoples believed in a coming Christ, or a coming Messiah, or a coming redeemer, or a coming Jesus (opinions vary) in order to be saved. This belief is based on the Reformed view of Genesis 3:15 as the "first gospel," aka: the protevangelium.

Promise soteriology says the Old Testament peoples believed in the promise of a coming Seed who would be the redeemer. As with Reformed soteriology, the key scripture is Genesis 3:15. The word "seed" is taken from an English translation of the Hebrew *zera'*, "semen, seed, offspring," which I discussed in a previous chapter. The "promise" doctrine is purely the Reformed soteriology view of Genesis 3:15, but instead of believing in a coming Christ they name him a coming Redeemer.

Reformed soteriology believes Genesis 3:15 teaches a coming Christ who will redeem individuals from sin. Promise soteriology believes Genesis 3:15 teaches a coming Redeemer who will redeem individuals from sin. Where is the difference? There is no difference. One names the coming Redeemer "Messiah" or "Christ"; the other names the coming Messiah-Christ the "Seed" or "Promise" or "Redeemer."

A point needs to be repeated from the Introduction. There is indeed a promise of a coming Messiah-King that may be followed from earlier to later Old Testament scriptures. This king is to bring national redemption to Israel. Not individual redemption from the penalty due the crime of sin, but national redemption from gentile oppression.

The promise of a Messiah-Redeemer from sin is less clear in the Old Testament revelation, fully revealed in the New Testament revelation. Consistent application of the Literal hermeneutic makes this difference clear. The hermeneutic tendency to give Old Testament people New Testament understanding obscures this difference. The hermeneutical failure is twofold.

Failure to use the Literal hermeneutic to properly exegete Genesis 3:15.

Failure to use the Literal hermeneutic to properly distinguish two streams of messianic prophecy, a king and a redeemer.

Promise soteriology is guilty of the first, less guilty of the second. For example, Promise soteriology adopts the New covenant given in Jeremiah 31:31–34 as partially fulfilled in the New Testament church. When is this New covenant given to national ethnic Israel to be fulfilled? At the second advent by the Messiah, who is both King and Redeemer in the Davidic-Messianic Kingdom.

(National ethnic Israel and the New Testament church share many similar eschatological promises with applications distinct to each people group. The New Testament church has a New covenant, made in the death of Christ for the New Testament church, with similarities and distinctions in relation to the New covenant for national ethnic Israel. See Hebrews 8–10. For a good discussion of the several views of the New covenant see Miles, *What is Dispensationalism?*)

In a previous chapter, I demonstrated through the Literal hermeneutic that Genesis 3:15 cannot be understood of a far future redeemer from sin, whether he is named Messiah, Christ, Jesus, Promise, Redemer, Seed, etc. There is no promised far future redeemer from sin in Genesis 3:15, unless one imports the New Testament revelation into Genesis 3:15; and even then it is a stretch of exegesis. In the Old Testament, YHWH is the ever-present Redeemer, who restored Adam and the Woman to fellowship from their sin, saved Abel and Seth, and a host of Adam's descendants, as exampled in the list in Genesis 5.

To complete this introduction, I will quote from a recently published book, digital edition.

What does the Old Testament itself say about salvation from sin? How were people saved in the Old Testament before Jesus

Christ came in the flesh? It has often been said that people in the Old Testament were saved by looking forward to the cross by faith while people after Christ are saved by looking back to the cross. But is this true? Remarkable as it may seem, there is no explicit gospel message to be found in the Old Testament [by "gospel message" the writer means there is no "believe in Jesus Christ" message]. There is no specific command to believe in a future Messiah for salvation, nor is there any mention of an Old Testament saint who put faith in a promised saviour [*sic*] for salvation. There are no clear salvation verses like John 3:16 or Acts 16:31 to be found in the Old Testament. [James Meyers, quoted in Miles, *Current Issues in Soteriology*, 106.]

Allow me to also quote a Dispensationalist previously mentioned

It would have been exceedingly difficult for someone to find the way of salvation [faith in the person Christ] in an unfinished Old Testament, since it is exceedingly difficult to find the way of salvation [faith in the person Christ] in the completed Old Testament, [Pastor Bob Bryant, in Miles, *What is Dispensationalism?*, 171].

Every Dispensational Promise theologian and exegete (and every Reformed theologian and exegete), recognizes the truth of those assertions. That is why both give a New Testament understanding of salvation to Adam and Eve and their descendants, beginning with Genesis 3:15, so the "One Way Of Salvation" will be faith in a coming Christ or coming Redeemer, instead of the substance which that faith depends on. That substance is what the Scripture teaches: "saved by God's grace through the sinner's faith in God and God's testimony in the progressive revelation of truth, apart from any personal merit of the sinner, but by Christ's merit only." I will show below God's testimony in the progressive revelation of truth did not begin with Christ in Genesis 3:15 (but it does end with Christ in the New Testament revelation).

Before moving on, a comment on the word "gospel" in the above quotes. The word most English versions (and perhaps other languages) translate as "gospel" is the Greek *euaggélion*, or *euangélion*. This word means "Good News." *Euangélion* did not mean "gospel" until ca. AD 950.

The etymology of "gospel" from the online *Oxford Languages* dictionary accessed through Google.

Old English *gōdspel*, from *gōd* 'good' + *spel* 'news, a story' (see spell2), translating ecclesiastical Latin *bona annuntiatio* or *bonus nuntius*, used to gloss ecclesiastical Latin *evangelium*, from Greek *euangélion* 'Good News' (see evangel); after the vowel was shortened in Old English, the first syllable was mistaken for *god* 'God'.

There is Good News concerning salvation from sin's penalty that is not the New Testament revelation's Good News of salvation through faith in the risen Jesus Christ. To misidentify the Old Testament Good News of salvation as "you must believe in a coming redeemer-messiah-christ to be saved" is the hermeneutical error of transcending the Old Testament revelation with the New Testament revelation. The one way of redemption from sin's penalty is the limitless merit of Christ's propitiation, not the content of faith that accesses that one way. How to apply that one way of redemption through faith is the "Good News," which has been stated in many ways during the history of redemption.

God is not limited to one way only to communicate his message of salvation. If he was limited he would have skipped the Old Testament revelation and given New Testament revelation from the beginning, instead of the "here a little, there a little" God the Holy Spirit has obviously used as his method of giving revelation. But giving the New Testament revelation in the beginning, in Genesis 3:15, is exactly what Reformed and Promise soteriologies teach as doctrine.

We see, then, how dependence on an English translation, "gospel," has restricted the "Good News" of redemption in the Scripture to one content of faith, through the influence of Reformed soteriology. Meyers, in the quote above, might have more accurately said, "there is no explicit Good News message of faith in Christ to be found in the Old Testament."

Below, I will look specifically at the claims of Promise soteriology, through eight Dispensational theologians.

This is what I was seeking of those eight Dispensational Promise soteriology authors as I researched their books.

Using only the written Old Testament revelation, show me a scripture or scriptures given to the Old Testament peoples where they were told they must believe on a promised future seed, or a promised future redeemer, to be saved. Remember, only the written Old Testament revelation may be used, because that written Old Testament revelation was the only Word of God the Old Testament people had received from YHWH to be saved.

Let us examine their writings.

Promised Seed Soteriology Research

Definition

Promise soteriology is faith in a saviour [*sic*] promised by God. The revelation increased as time went on, and the requirement for salvation was faith in this deliverer as He was revealed at any given time. So, they could have faith in a "seed" that was promised, faith in a Messiah, faith in Yeshua, and yet not believe in Jesus specifically, for Jesus had not yet been revealed. [James Meyers, quoted in Miles, *Current Issues in Soteriology*, 110.]

Promise soteriology says from the very beginning God had a plan for man's salvation which is centered in the Seed, the one promised in the protoevangelium. In describing this soteriology, one theologian wrote, "Most of the believers who came to faith before New Testament times are those who give evidence that their faith was based on the God who disclosed himself in the Seed of the Woman." [Kaiser, *Is it the Case?* Quoted in Miles, *Current Issues in Soteriology*, 111.]

Promise soteriology is "the view that the Old Testament believers believed a coming redeemer/deliverer that would crush the head of the serpent, a symbol of Satan [Genesis 3:15], but did not have all of the details then & only understood as much as was revealed progressively through eras of history until the full picture was revealed in the New Testament." [Dr. Sherlin in a conversation with the author, on the Facebook "Christicommunity" page.]

Notice again how Reformed soteriology has influenced others, re: Kaiser and the protoevangelium. Reformed soteriology named Genesis 3:15 the protoevangelium and Dispensational Promise soteriology has adopted the term. I have before explained Genesis 3:15 became known by that name after 1600 plus years of Christianity, in an allegorical interpretation, having never before been known as the protoevangelium. To refresh the reader's memory.

> No one in the Old Testament thought Genesis 3:15 was a prophecy of a coming redeemer. No one in the times between the Old and New Testaments, thought Genesis 3:15 was a prophecy of a coming redeemer. No one during the times when Jesus walked the earth thought Genesis 3:15 was a prophecy of a coming redeemer. No one in the New Testament church for 1600 plus years thought Genesis 3:15 was a prophecy of a coming redeemer.

See discussion, "Is Genesis 3:15 the Protoevangelium?" in the chapter "Genesis 3:15." The first documented mention of Genesis 3:15 as the "first promise of the Gospel" was by Keach in the late 1600s.

Notice also that even Kaiser, a proponent of Genesis 3:15 Promise soteriology, must admit (however inadvertent) that saving faith was in YHWH, not a promised coming redeemer. "their faith was based on the God [YHWH is the one speaking in Genesis 3:15] who disclosed himself in the Seed of the Woman." If, as is the case, YHWH presented himself as the ever-present Redeemer, what need was there for faith in a not-present-yet-to-come redeemer-messiah-christ?

Dr. Sherlin's definition (above) is carefully constructed to enforce the doctrine of progressive revelation, an important doctrine given proper recognition in Dispensationalism. Yet even this experienced Dispensationalist depends on a Reformed interpretation of Genesis 3:15 for his Old Testament soteriology. For it is certain the allegorical interpretation of Genesis 3:15 of a promised redeemer was not inherited from the dispensationalists of the early church, coming neither from Augustine nor others, but was an invention of Reformed theology.

The Old Testament peoples did not have faith in a coming redeemer from the penalty of sin disclosed in Genesis 3:15, because he is not there. There was salvation, but it was not by faith in a coming redeemer-messiah-christ, not by faith in the promise of a seed-redeemer. Saving faith in the Old Testament times was exactly the same as in these New Testament times: faith in God and God's testimony as to the way of salvation, as given in the historic progressive revelation of truth. In the Old Testament YHWH was the Savior: faith in YHWH and YHWH's testimony was the way of salvation

Dispensational Promise Soteriology As Defined By Certain Of Its Advocates.

Overview

> From Genesis 3:15 and throughout the Old Testament, the central character is the Messiah . . . . Everywhere he is to be traced in type, symbol, promise and prophecy. [Couch, 28.]

> [T]he promise of a redeemer to come (Genesis 3:15), set the context for the object of faith for all Old Testament saints. They placed their faith in the Lord [YHWH] and his promise to deliver. [Dr. Sherlin, manuscript, *The Calvinism of Dispensationalism.* I had access to this manuscript as its copyeditor. Soon to be published. Update, published, 2023. p. 285.]

> It seems appropriate to understand Genesis 3:15 as the first specific messianic prophecy of the Bible .... this text ... does promise that Messiah will descend from humanity and he will destroy the evil force that tempted Eve. [Rydelnik, 145.]

> It is always by God's grace through faith in the divine revelation about the Savior and his atoning work, whether promised (Genesis 3:15, 21; 15:5-6; Hebrews 11:41) or fulfilled (John 3:16). [Barackman, 365.]

The Promise Dispensationalists

Theologian Mal Couch (1938–2013)

Dr. Couch's book is *Messianic Systematic Theology of the Old Testament.* This book was only available in digital form. For this research I first went to chapter nine, "Doctrine of Salvation." Dr. Couch makes his soteriology clear.

> The Rabbis believe in the doctrine of salvation. There is no other way for men to find redemption except by faith, to trust in what God has said, specifically about salvation through the Lord Jesus Christ, the promised Messiah!

I respect Dr. Couch as a teacher and theologian, as I know of him through one of his former students (Dr. Sherlin), and this book. He is "spot on" with Dispensational issues and distinctives, and the essential doctrine of salvation, saved by grace through faith not works. But his statement (above) about the object and content of saving faith, is Reformed soteriology, not Dispensational soteriology.

One thing was clear from Dr. Couch's book: he must apply the New Testament revelation to the Old Testament revelation to prove his Promise proposition. Why? Every Old Testament scripture Dr. Couch uses in his book disproves his case. For example, the Rabbis' belief on Isaiah 53:11.

> The Jews say that the passage is about the nation of Israel being the Suffering Servant.

Dr. Couch does not tell us this statement is not about the beliefs of the Hebrews during Old Testament times (Genesis through Malachi), but Judaism—which was not the YHWH-ism of the Old Testament but developed after the New Testament canon was closed. If we want to know how the Hebrews viewed Isaiah 53, the Ethiopian eunuch gives unambiguous testimony. Acts 8:34, "I beseech you, concerning whom the prophet says this? Concerning himself, or concerning some other?"

Dr. Couch's response to the Jewish Rabbis? "But by all principles of interpretation this cannot be what Isaiah had in mind." What does Dr. Couch think Isaiah had in mind? Dr. Couch has something other than authorial intent—the object of the grammatical-historical (Literal) hermeneutic—in mind. He adds in some New Testament revelation to support his Promise soteriology view. Dr. Couch wrote.

> Isaiah 53 is prophecy of things that would happen some seven hundred years after they were recorded by the prophet.

Wait a moment. Isn't one of the principles of the Literal hermeneutic to seek authorial intent through the plain and normal meaning of the Scripture, by the application of the author's historical-cultural circumstances, and the lexical and syntactical aspects of the language and words? Yes, it is.

Why would Dr. Couch teach the prophet Isaiah had in mind an event "some seven hundred years" after Isaiah wrote chapter 53? Because when it comes to soteriology Dr. Couch follows the Reformed hermeneutic principle of transcending the Old Testament revelation with New Testament revelation.

When we apply the rules and principles of the Literal hermeneutic, we are not to use the New Testament revelation to discover the Old

Testament peoples' understanding of the passage. As I recently said to another.

> The foundation of the New Testament revelation is the Old Testament revelation, but the Old Testament revelation, being the foundation, exists without the structure built upon it, which is the New Testament revelation. Therefore, one is able to understand the Old Testament revelation without resorting to the New Testament revelation for understanding. An interpretation of the Old Testament revelation that consists of New Testament truths is eisegesis, not exegesis. An interpretation of the New Testament revelation that does not include Old Testament truth is incomplete exegesis.

Or as Vlach has said, "The primary meaning of any Bible passage is found in that passage."

Dr. Couch's comment is irrelevant. No one in Old Testament times, including the prophet Isaiah, understood Isaiah 53 was about "things that would happen some seven hundred years after they were recorded by the prophet."

When the four servant Songs are seen as a whole, within their literary and historical context (Isaiah 51–54) the prophecy is about the future of national ethnic Israel. The immediate context for Isaiah 53 is 52:13–15, nations and kings. Indeed, if chapter 54 is the consequence of the Suffering Servant, then an everlasting covenant with Israel that affects the world (saved and unsaved) is coming. The Jewish view the passage is about the nation Israel really is the interpretation within the Old Testament historical context.

In my understanding of the Isaiah 52:13–53:12 passage, the Holy Spirit is speaking about an individual and how his actions will affect national ethnic Israel in a distant future. The question then becomes, "concerning whom the prophet says this? Concerning himself, or concerning some other?" even as the Ethiopian eunuch said to Philip. The passage itself provides an answer: 53:3, a man of sorrows; 53:11, my righteous servant. Who that individual might be is unknown and unnamed in the Old Testament revelation. The careful Bible student will take note the prophecy does not direct saving faith be placed in the man of sorrows, in the righteous servant. Faith is to be placed in YHWH, 53:1, 10. In the Old Testament revelation, YHWH is the Savior, an ever-present Redeemer, not a coming redeemer.

Nor can this man of sorrows, this righteous servant in Isaiah 53 be connected to 2 Samiel 7:13–16 or Psalm 2, written about 300 years earlier. Why? 1) Nathan's prophecy to David is never referenced, and 2) the word *māshîah* is not used. Only the New Testament revelation connects the dots between David's *māshîah* and Isaiah's man of sorrows-righteous servant.

What Dr. Couch ignores in his zeal to prove his soteriology is the Old Testament Hebrews *did not and could not know* the events of Isaiah 53 would happen seven hundred years later, unless we transcend the Old Testament Scripture with extrabiblical revelation or illumination. Instead of interpreting that scripture according to the Literal hermeneutic—an interpretation within context, within the original historical-cultural setting, with an appropriate literary, lexical, and syntactical analysis—Dr. Couch bypassed biblical hermeneutics by using New Testament revelation to "discover" a New Testament meaning.

Dr. Couch also quoted a 1979 book to "show" the Rabbis believed the Isaiah passage was about the Messiah: *The Messiah Texts*, by Raphael Patai, published by Wayne State University, 1979. And what was the subject of that book? The publisher's description.

> Renowned scholar Raphael Patai has skillfully selected passages from a voluminous literature spanning three millennia. Using his own translations from Hebrew, Aramaic, Arabic, Latin, and other original texts, Patai excerpts delightful folk tales, apocalyptic fantasies, and parables of prophetic power.

So, there did exist Hebrew literature about a coming messiah, but a) it was not scripture, b) it was folk tales, fantasies, and parables, and c) it was not about a promised redeemer from sin.

In fact most, if not all sources of Jewish literature, other than the Old Testament Hebrew scriptures, are *after* the Old Testament revelation was completed, which was ca. 400 BC (Malachi). The apocrypha were written between 200 BC to AD 100 (some say to AD 400). The Targums, an Aramaic translation of the Hebrew scripture texts, were written (with some commentary) between AD 100–700. The Mishnah was compiled 200 BC to AD 200. The Jerusalem Talmud was compiled ca. AD 350; the Babylonian Talmud ca. AD 500. The

Kabbalah was created ca. the 12th century AD. The *Sifre* were legal commentaries (midrash halakhah) on Leviticus, Numbers, and Deuteronomy, written AD 300 and later. The Septuagint and commentaries associated with its translation was written ca. 250 BC.

So none of the writings left by the Rabbis actually tell us what the people living between Genesis 2:7 and 400 BC (Malachi) understood about the Old Testament. The Old Testament people living from Genesis through Malachi did not leave commentaries interpreting their Old Testament Scripture. Everything "renowned scholar Raphael Patai" translated and excerpted was 100 years or more—sometimes a 1,000 years more—*after* the Old Testament revelation was completed.

Dr. Couch is not alone in his belief some Rabbis thought Isaiah 53 was about the Messiah. David Baron (1855–1926) was a Jew who came to saving faith in Christ. All his works have value to the Bible student. In his work, *The Servant of Jehovah*, Chapter, "The Ancient Jewish Interpretation of Isaiah LIII" he also cannot demonstrate his thesis from the Old Testament revelation. He cites and quotes from the Babylonian Talmud, Targums, and Jewish Liturgy. All are products of the AD era not the BC era.

Dr. Couch is right that Old Testament salvation was based on faith, but he always applies a New Testament understanding to the Old Testament Scripture to define that content of that faith. He wrote.

> There is no question that salvation in the Old Testament is by faith and not by works. The key passage is Genesis 15:6. Abraham believed what God had told him about having an innumerable company of children. "Then [Abraham] believed in the LORD, and He reckoned it to him as righteousness." It is clear that the Suffering Servant, the Messiah, would be the one who could justify, legally acquit, or make righteous, those who trusted in Him.

My question is this, where in Genesis 15:6, does one find "the Suffering Servant, the Messiah, would be the one who could justify, legally acquit, or make righteous, those who trusted in Him." Where may one find those things in the Suffering Servant passages in Isaiah? How were those things made clear to Abraham, a thousand years before it was written in the Old Testament revelation? Where in Isaiah, or after Isaiah, does the Scripture say those between Abraham and

Isaiah, or even those after Isaiah, understood "the Suffering Servant," was the Messiah, who "would be the one who could justify, legally acquit, or make righteous, those who trusted in Him." Dr. Couch again gives the Old Testament people a New Testament understanding of the Old Testament revelation.

To be fair, the quote may be read in another way. Despite reading New Testament revelation into Isaiah, Dr. Couch may have meant the limitless merit of Christ's propitiation is what redeemed Abraham, and that is biblically correct soteriology. But how did God save Abraham? Dr. Couch knows the biblical answer: "Abraham believed what God had told him," Genesis 15:4–6.

Allow me to restate Dr. Couch's answer more accurately: "Abraham believed what YHWH had told him." YHWH's grace through Abraham's faith in YHWH's historically current testimony accessed Christ's propitiatory merit by believing on YHWH: not faith in a coming redeemer, but faith in the ever-present Redeemer YHWH. Not faith through Genesis 3:15, not faith through Isaiah 53, not faith in a coming redeemer-messiah-christ, but faith in YHWH the Redeemer, faith in YHWH's testimony, Genesis 15:4–5. YHWH was the object of saving faith, YHWH's immediate testimony the content of saving faith.

My next step was to search Dr. Couch's digital book for the word "promise." Couch wrote the following to support his Promise soteriology.

> From Genesis 3:15 and throughout the Old Testament, the central character is the Messiah. Unger [Dr. Merrill Unger] explains that He [the "seed" in Genesis 3:15] is seen as the promised Redeemer. Everywhere He is to be traced in type, symbol, promise and prophecy. His person and work form the warp and woof of the narrative from the "seed of the woman, the promised Redeemer," in the Genesis passage, to the "sun of righteousness," seed of David, Israel's King, in Malachi 4:2, returning in glory to dispel the darkness of Israel's unbelief and rejection, and as the "Prince of Peace" (Isa. 9:6) to usher in the resplendent Millennial day.

There is no messiah mentioned in Genesis 3:15, so how does Dr. Couch or Dr. Unger know Old Testament messianic testimony begins at Genesis 3:15? The first time in the Old Testament revelation a coming *mashiah* is mentioned is in Psalm 2:2, thousands of years after Genesis 3:15.

There are several hermeneutical problems with Dr. Unger's analysis. Let's look at them one by one.

Problem one: "He [the "seed" in Genesis 3:15] is to be traced in type." The problem is nothing in the Old Testament revelation may be legitimately recognized as an Old Testament type without a New Testament revelation antitype identifying the Old Testament type.

> Definition: A type in Scripture is "an illustration of some biblical truth whereby a person, place, thing, or idea in the Old Testament is identified in the New Testament as prefiguring a New Testament truth."

That is my definition, developed by consulting several sources, e.g., Virkler, Scofield, Fairbairn, Kaiser & Silva. From the definition, a hermeneutical rule.

> Until revealed in the New Testament revelation, nothing in the Old Testament is a type, nothing in the Old Testament may be recognized or understood as a type, nothing in the Old Testament exists as a type, until so identified in the New Testament revelation by a corresponding antitype.

Anything other than identification of a type-antitype relationship by the New Testament revelation may be valid spiritual perception, or may be imagination run amok—no one can know which. Isn't it the rule that our doctrine is formed by Scripture? Yes. No scripture identifies a type of Christ in Genesis 3:15. Imagination? Yes. Eisegesis? Yes. A biblical hermeneutic? No.

The *zera'* (aka: "seed") in Genesis 3:15 was not a type of a coming redeemer-messiah-christ to Adam, to the Woman, to their children, or to any other Old Testament descendant of Adam and Eve. Nor is *zera'* in Genesis 3:15 a type of a redeemer-messiah-christ to any of Adam's New Testament descendants. Why? Because the New Testament revelation does not identify the Genesis 3:15 *zera'* as a type of a coming redeemer-messiah-christ. Nor does the Old Testament explain the Genesis 3:15 seed as the coming Messiah.

Allow me to emphasize: no human being from Genesis 2:7 to Revelation 22:21, is able to say with Scripture authority, that the *zera'* in Genesis 3:15 is able to be traced in Scripture of a coming redeemer-messiah-christ. Either we believe the Scripture, or we use imagination as our hermeneutic.

Don't believe me? Be a Berean, search the Scripture to see if these things are so. Prove me right or wrong. Nothing in the Old or New Testament Scripture identifies the *zera'* of Genesis 3:15 as a type of a coming redeemer-messiah-christ. No Scripture, in no Hebrew, Aramaic, or Greek text, in no book, no chapter, no verse, no word in the Scripture, in no way, ever identifies the *zera'* of Genesis 3:15 as a yet-future-yet-to-come redeemer-messiah-christ. How then can the *zera'* be "traced in type" to Christ? Not through the Literal hermeneutic. But imagination takes us wherever we want to go.

The problem with types is not the definition but the recognition. What makes a person, place, thing, or idea in the Old Testament a type? Answer: identified in the New Testament.

Some make just about anything a type. The other day I read a comment on social media that when Moses' hands were held up in Israel's battle with Amalek, Exodus 17, that was a type of the cross of Christ; which is why Israel had the victory. Many make the Old Testament Joseph a type of Christ, and while there are some similarities—but more differences—the New Testament never mentions Joseph in connection with the Christ. This type of personal perception is subject to great abuses. For example, Joseph in prison is not a type of Christ in the tomb, and Joseph's elevation to Prime Minister is not a type of Christ's return as king; or whatever.

As both a student and user of the Literal hermeneutic, and believing in its consistent application, I recognize a person, place, thing, or idea in the Old Testament as a type when it is identified in the New Testament by the antitype. John Baptist said, John 1:29, "Behold God's lamb, he who takes away the sin of the world!" No one before John knew that type-antitype relationship, nor could know the type-antitype relationship between the sacrificial lambs and Jesus the Christ, until John said it and it was recorded in Scripture for all to hear.

Unger's second hermeneutical problem: "He is to be traced in symbol." Dr. Unger mentions symbols for the coming promised redeemer. Symbols depend on accumulated testimony to understand. It would be helpful to know what symbols Dr. Unger had in mind, but unfortunately Dr. Couch does not give a source in Unger's works for this information.

A symbol is a metaphorical representation of some biblical truth. Nothing can be positively declared a symbol without some basis (usually multiple occurrences) to develop a metaphorical explanation. Symbols originating in the Old Testament should be understood as defined by their Old Testament use and then appropriately applied to their New Testament context. The Holy Spirit is consistent in his use of symbols over the 1500 years or so the Scripture was written. Two examples.

In the Old Testament the word "fire" has a literal meaning and two symbolic meanings developed from that literal meaning. The literal meaning is fire consumes its object; things are burned up. The figurative meanings are fire represents judgment, or fire represents cleansing. Figurative meanings are always derived from the literal meaning. Fire consumes: judgment. The refiner's fire is used to remove impurities: cleansing. Our God is a consuming fire, Hebrews 12:29. Symbolic meaning: God judges the unsaved for their sin and purifies the saved from their sins. The metaphorical use of fire throughout both Testaments supports the use of fire as a symbol of judgment or cleansing.

Second example. In the New Testament revelation, a literal "sword" is used as a metaphor to represent the written Scripture, Hebrews 4:12, or to represent the word of God in the mouth of God doing the will of God, Revelation 1:16. The sword is used multiple times in the New Testament to represent the written Scripture. That association with written scripture is how we know a sword is used as a symbol of written scripture.

On the other hand, the burning bush in Exodus 3 is not a symbol of YHWH or Christ. The bush that burned but was not consumed is YHWH manifesting his presence. How do we know the burning bush was not a symbol but a manifestation? We read the scriptures and understand them in their plain and normal sense. Wherever God is present, the place he is present becomes holy while he is present. Moses was told to take off his sandals because the ground was holy. Shoes are used to protect the feet from defilement. When God is present there is no defilement. In Exodus 3 God was really present.

The burning bush was not a symbol and is never used as a symbol. Nor it is a type.

For an Old Testament word, phrase, event to become a New Testament symbol of Messiah-Christ, it must be identified by consistent use as representing something other than the literal meaning, a metaphorical use that may be legitimately connected to the literal Messiah-Christ. What Old Testament words, phrases, or incidents did Dr. Unger have in mind?

Perhaps the "symbol" Dr. Unger had in mind was the *zera'* in Genesis 3:15? That Hebrew word is never used metaphorically in its 230 occurrences in the Old Testament revelation. It always means human male semen, literal plant seed, or offspring as the result of procreation—which is why the serpent's offspring cannot be from Satan.

In the New Testament revelation, in some of the forty-five occurrences, the Greek equivalent of the Hebrew *zera'*, which is *spérma*, is symbolic of written Scripture, of believers, of the kingdom, of the Good News of salvation (e.g., the four soils parable, where Christ states the *spérma* is a symbol). But in every New Testament reference to the Old Testament, *spérma* is used literally of procreated individuals, not metaphorically of a redeemer-messiah-christ. That is even true in Galatians 3:16, where a literal descendant of Abraham is in view—a *spérma*, Isaac of Abraham and Sarah, and Jesus of Mariam and God.

Abraham knew Isaac was his *spérma* (Genesis 15:4) but could not know Jesus was his *spérma* without extrabiblical revelation or illumination, which he did not have and was not given. How do I know? No such information is in the written Scripture indicating Abraham had received revelation or illumination that his *spérma* would be a coming redeemer-messiah-christ. Therefore, any claim he did know is imagination, not exegesis.

Dr. Couch wrote that Dr. Unger said Christ is also "to be traced in promise." Many things are promised in the Old Testament; which promises are about a future coming redeemer? I can point to a coming Messiah-King, e.g., Genesis 49:10 with 2 Samuel 7:13–16; Psalm 2. But a "promised Redeemer" in Genesis 3:15? That is assuming what must be proved, that the *zera'* in Genesis 3:15 points to Christ; and as I have shown in a previous chapter, it does not, when that scripture is understand in the plain and normal meaning of the Hebrew language and words.

Dr. Couch also reports Dr. Unger saying the "promised redeemer" may be "traced in prophecy." Is there prophecy of a coming Messiah-Redeemer in the Old Testament revelation? Yes many, but only when understood in the light given by the New Testament revelation. But without that New Testament revelation? No.

A perfect example is Daniel 9:26, ca. 540 BC, which no one understood. This prophecy can be known as a prophecy of a coming Messiah, because it uses the word *māshîah*, and earlier revelation said the *māshîah* was a king. But the Daniel 9:26 prophecy says the king will die. A king cannot die and be king, which is why this prophecy is never found in the four gospels, not even as a comment made by the Matthew, Mark, Luke, or John. No one understood Daniel 9:26 was about a coming Messiah-Redeemer. In fact, there is no Old or New Testament reference to Daniel 9:26. That prophecy stands alone in the Scripture.

No one in the Old Testament saw a coming Messiah-Redeemer in Daniel 9:26. If they did, no one, including the Holy Spirit, has told us they did—not in any Old or New Testament scripture, nor in any Jewish intertestamental literature. How can that be if the Old Testament peoples were previously informed by Genesis 3:15 that there was a coming Redeemer whom Satan would kill, and by his death this promised Redeemer would save sinners from their sin? Answer: Genesis 3:15 says nothing about a coming redeemer.

(Why do I believe Daniel 9:26 is about Messiah-Redeemer? New Testament revelation. I have made a connection between "cut off but not for himself" and Christ's vicarious act of propitiation on the cross. That is spiritual perception driven by New Testament revelation, e.g., 2 Corinthians 5:21; 1 John 2:2; Romans 3:25. There is no New Testament revelation for spiritual perception to connect anything in Genesis 3:15 with a coming redeemer. Spiritual perception does not work in the fictional world of imagination where anything might happen. Valid spiritual perception works through the written revelation.)

Genesis 12:3 is another one of those Old Testament scriptures of a coming redeemer that is only understood of Messiah-Redeemer when the light of New Testament revelation shines on it, to wit, Galatians 3:8. Abraham did not have Galatians 3:8. No one in the Old Testament had Galatians 3:8. No one in the Old Testament knew there was a coming redeemer. As I have stated before, the Old Testament people believed in and were saved by the ever-present Redeemer YHWH.

Looking again at the declaration in Daniel 9:26, was that understood by the Old Testament peoples as a promise of a coming Redeemer? Compare Matthew 16:21–22. Peter understood Jesus of Nazareth was YHWH's Messiah of Psalm 2:2, 7. Obviously he did not understand Jesus was the Messiah-Redeemer of Daniel 9:26. Let us remember Peter's knowledge of Messiah was from the synagogue, so what he said accurately reflects what the Jewish teachers of his time believed. The Messiah-King could not die and be king.

Therefore, at no time after the prophecy was given, ca. 540 BC, did the Jews believe Daniel 9:26 referred to a Messiah-King, and they did not recognize it as referring to a Messiah-Redeemer. The word was there, *mashîah*, but that "anointed" one was not understood by the Old Testament peoples as the coming anointed who would reign as their king.

Reformed and Promise soteriology will always point to Isaiah 53, as a prophecy of a coming redeemer. But as I have pointed out previously in this book, the Hebrew word for YHWH's coming anointed, *mashîah*, is not in Isaiah 53; nor in any of the suffering servant songs. There was no way for the Hebrews to connect Daniel 9:26, 200 years after Isaiah, with Isaiah 53; nor Isaiah 53 with 2 Samuel 7:13–16; Psalm 2:2, 300 years before Isaiah. If you need proof of that assertion, read the four gospels. No contemporary of Jesus of Nazareth connected him to Isaiah 53 during the times of his public ministry on earth; Acts 8:31–35, about three years *after* the resurrection, is additional proof.

The misuse of *mashîah* by Reformed and Promise soteriology is a good example of how not to interpret Scripture. The word occurs thirty-nine times in the Old Testament. The word means "anoint." Literally to put oil or ointment on a person in a ritual that recognized their appointment to some office or duty. From that ritual the word gains its primary meaning of appoint or ordain.

The first use of *mashîah* is Leviticus 4:3. Priests are anointed to their duties. So too kings, 1 Samuel 16:1 with 16:12–13. Some are anointed to a specific duty, such as the gentile Cyrus, Isaiah 45:1. So also the coming king, Psalm 2:2. In Daniel 9:25–26 (where it is unaccountably transliterated as messiah) the anointed is appointed to die but not for himself—which to the Old Testament peoples reading that scripture was not an understandable reference to a substitutionary atonement by a Messiah-Redeemer as a propitiation of God for human sin. How do I know *māshîah* in Daniel 9:26 is about a substitutionary atonement? The New Testament revelation gave me sufficient information to connect "cut off but not for himself" with Christ's propitiation of God for human sin.

Psalm 2:2; Daniel 9:25, 26 are the only Old Testament scriptures where *māshîah* refers to one who is coming to be king and redeemer. Redemption of the nation through the Messiah-King line of prophecy was understandable within its Old Testament context. Individual redemption from the penalty due sin through the Messiah-Redeemer line of prophecy was not understandable within its Old Testament context. It is simply a biblical fact Old Testament redemption from sin was through faith in the ever-present YHWH, not in someone supposed to be coming at some unknown time in an unknown future.

Those two unique uses of *māshîah*, Psalm 2:2; Daniel 9:26 present two separate lines of prophecy. The coming *māshîah* will not come at the same time as both king and redeemer, but will come once to rule, Psalm 2, and once to redeem, Daniel 9:26. How do I know that? The New Testament revelation of two advents. With the New Testament revelation we are able to trace out each line from beginning to conclusion. Without the New Testament revelation the Hebrews saw the coming king but not the coming redeemer. The Old Testament Hebrews, as Schurer reported, saw only the king.

I said Promise and Reformed soteriology misuse *māshîah*. In what way? By finding the word where it does not exist, such as in Genesis 3:15, or Isaiah 53. The first line of prophecy recognized as of a coming *māshîah*, i.e., anointed king, begins ca. 1000 BC, 2 Samuel 7:13–16; Psalm 2. When did Israel become a nation? About 1445 BC. What is the first Old Testament prophecy we can connect to the Messiah-King prophecy? Genesis 49:10, ca. 1640 BC, a scepter and lawgiver out of the tribe of Judah; but there is no *māshîah* mentioned in that scripture, so no one in Old Testament times knew Genesis 49:10 was about the

Messiah until the Holy Spirit through the prophet Nathan, and the Holy Spirit through the King and prophet David, revealed a Messiah-King out of Judah in 2 Samuel 7:13–16; Psalm 2. Only by later revelation are any able to make the connection between Genesis 49:10 and a Messiah-King. That is the way progressive revelation and the Literal hermeneutic are used to interpret Scripture.

The same is true of Messiah-Redeemer. With the later New Testament revelation, the association of certain Old Testament scriptures with Messiah-Redeemer is apparent. Without that later revelation the association cannot be known.

Is the Hebrew word *māshîah* is used in Psalm 22? No. In Isaiah 53? No. There was no way to connect the dots until the New Testament revelation. Dr. Couch allows his theology to sidestep these simple facts. Perhaps you can understand why I am saying Promise and Reformed soteriology misuse *māshîah*.

Here is another problem. Dr. Couch approvingly cited Dr. Unger as saying, "He [the promised seed] is seen as the promised Redeemer … His person and work form the warp and woof of the narrative from the 'seed of the woman, the promised Redeemer,' in the Genesis passage."

The problem with Dr. Unger's theology is simple: no scripture, no passage, no verse, no word in the Old Testament revelation mentions the *zera'* of Genesis 3:15 as "the promised redeemer" from sin. No scripture, passage, verse, or word in the New Testament either. The entire house of Promise soteriology is built on sand and of sand, washed away by the facts of Scripture. Is there a promised redeemer from gentile oppression? Yes, certainly, the Messiah-King, but that is not in Genesis 3:15, but thousands of years later in Psalm 2. Compare Luke 1:51–52; 70–71.

Genesis 3:15 says nothing about a promised redeemer from sin. There is not a whisper, not the merest breath, of redemption from sin in the Hebrew text of Genesis 3:15; nor in any accurate translation or interpretation. I challenge you, anyone, to set aside the New Testament revelation and find "the promised Redeemer" in Genesis 3:15, using the principles and rules of the Literal hermeneutic.

To find a "promised redeemer" from sin in the Old Testament revelation one must import the idea from the New Testament. Do I exaggerate? Let's ask the Ethiopian eunuch, Acts 8:31–35. Let us search the New Testament scriptures for any reference to Isaiah 53 from any historical contemporary—parent, relative, friend, foe, disciple, apostle—of Jesus during his three years of public ministry; and No, we cannot count passages such as John 12:38–42, which is John's comment from his AD 95 perspective—60 years after the events in his gospel.

I can agree with Dr. Couch in one place. "One of the fundamental tenets of Judaism, coming from the Old Testament, is the belief in the promised Messiah, who is to come, redeems the people of Israel from their suffering in exile." Yes; Judaism developed during the intertestamental period, after the Old Testament revelation was completed. Yes, absolutely; that Old Testament revelation clearly reveals a King to redeem the nation from gentile oppression. A Messiah-King rescuing the nation Israel from gentile oppression is plain and clear in the Old Testament revelation. Mariam and Zecharias understood the Messiah to be a king, not a redeemer of souls, Luke 1:51–52, 71–74. When Miriam speaks of her Savior, Luke 1:47, she is speaking of the ever-present Redeemer YHWH.

Dr. Couch never makes his case from the written Old Testament revelation that the Old Testament sinner believed in a promised seed as redeemer from sin. And he proves that very clearly, albeit not intentionally. He wrote.

> The great and respected [Hebrew] scholars, Michael Avi-Yonah and Zvi Baras have documented what the Jewish people were teaching during the time of Jesus. They were looking for the Messianic reign to begin.

They were looking for a Messiah-King. No one was looking for a promised seed who would be Messiah-Redeemer. No one understood Genesis 3:15 was about a future coming promised redeemer. No one understood two lines of messianic prophecy met in the person Jesus the Christ.

Dr. Couch has vividly demonstrated a Promise soteriology beginning in Genesis 3:15 is not scriptural soteriology.

Theologian Lewis Sperry Chafer (1871–1952)

Because Dr. Couch used Dr. Chafer as a resource, I will take a brief look at Dr. Chafer's soteriology, having already made some pertinent comments. I am using his work, *Systematic Theology*.

In general terms Dr. Chafer, a Dispensationalist, is orthodox in his soteriology. But he begins his examination of soteriology like a Reformed theologian, with the "preincarnate Christ." That term assumes the Christ was present and knowable during Old Testament times. Dr. Chafer speaks [*Systematic*, 3:12] of "Christ's preincarnate existence as one of the triune Godhead." I previously discussed that the *christós* was an office of God the Son that began at the incarnation. A "preincarnate Christ" is an oxymoron, a contradiction in terms. If we are going to speak of an appearance of God prior to the incarnation, then let us speak of the preincarnate God the Son, whose normal manifestation was as the angel of YHWH.

Dr. Chafer devotes chapter 5 of his soteriology volume to "The Sufferings and Death of Christ in Types." I will mention only a few, then move on to other theologians.

"Genesis 3:15 is a preview of the death of Christ ... it is intimated" [*Systematic*, 3:125]. That seems unlikely as there is no mention of Christ in Genesis 3:15. And in fact, the Analogy of faith proves my response, because the only mentions of Genesis 3:15 in the entire Bible are Genesis 4:25; Romans 16:20; Revelation 12:9, and none say anything about Christ. Dr. Chafer says "intimated" which means "imply or hint." "Imply" means not stated; "hint" means to suggest indirectly. Both require reading into the words and sentences of others what we think they mean, or what we want them to mean. In terms of Scripture revelation, "intimated" means it is not really there.

Dr. Chafer points to Psalm 22:1–21; 40:6–7 as predictions on the death of Christ [*Systematic*, 3:126]. How does he know that? Because those Psalms are quoted in the New Testament revelation. These are Psalms the four gospels use to describe the crucifixion.

Psalm 16:10 — John 20:9

Psalm 22:1 — Matthew 27:46; Mark 15:34

Psalm 22:7; 109:25 — Matthew 27:39; Mark 15:29; Luke 23:35

Psalm 22:8 — Matthew 27:43

Psalm 22:18 — Matthew 27:35; Mark 15:24; Luke 23:34; John 19:24

Psalm 25:19 —John 15:25

Psalm 31:5 — Luke 23:14

Psalm 34:20 — John 19:36

Psalm 38:11; 88:8 — Luke 23:49

Psalm 41:9; 109:8 — John 13:18; 17:12

Psalm 42:5 — Matthew 26:38; Mark 14:34

Psalm 69:21 — Matt 27:34, 48; Mark 15:36; Luke 23:36; John 19:28

Psalm 110:1, 2 — Matthew 26:64; Mark 14:62; 16:19

Without the New Testament revelation, no one in the Old Testament could know these Psalms were about the death of Messiah-Redeemer to bring redemption from the penalty of sin. (Psalm 40:6–7 is used in Hebrews 10.)

In vol. 3, chapter 11, "The Convicting work of the Spirit," Dr. Chafer does not deal separately with Old Testament salvation. He wrote, "the Spirit, exerts an influence upon the unsaved by which they may make an intelligent acceptance of Christ as Savior" [*Systematic*, 3:210]. In the previous section Dr. Couch quoted Dr. Unger as saying, "From Genesis 3:15 and throughout the Old Testament, the central character is the Messiah. Unger explains that [the *zera'*] is seen as the promised Redeemer." Apparently Dr. Chafer believed the Reformed teaching that the object of saving faith in Old Testament times was Christ, and the content of saving faith in Old Testament times was Christ coming. That is not Dispensational soteriology.

Theologian Floyd H. Barackman (1923–2007)

Mr. Barackman was an instructor in systematic theology at Practical Bible Training School, Bible School Park, New York. I am using his book, *Practical Christian Theology* for this review. I recommend this book as good instruction in biblical theology and the practice of the Christian life. My complaint is with his Promise soteriology, which occupies one paragraph [bottom of p. 296] and one page [365] in the 576 page book.

As unlikely as it sounds, Mr. Barackman begins his promise soteriology in the chapter "Hamartiology," the doctrine of sin [p. 296]. He defines *zera'* in a way the Literal hermeneutic would avoid. For grammatical reasons explained in my exegesis of Genesis 3:15 in a previous chapter, the *zera'* of the serpent and the *zera'* of the Woman both refer to the Woman's natural descendants. The *zera'* of the serpent are human beings with the serpent's characteristic of no faith. The zera' of the Woman are human beings with her characteristic of faith. Compare Gensis 4:25, Able and Seth, not Cain, are the Woman's *zera'*. Cain is confirmed as the serpent's *zera'* in the later revelation of 1 John 3:12.

Mr. Barackman's hermeneutic gives *zera'* two meanings.

Meaning One. A 'spiritual product' rather than 'natural offspring.'

This allows "the *zera'* of the serpent to be fallen angels and unsaved humans" and the *zera'* of the Woman to be "saved humans, redeemed through the atoning work of her descendant, the Lord Jesus Christ." One can agree the limitless merit of Christ powers any, every, and all salvations. However, his interpretation of *zera'* is more imaginative than biblical.

Mr. Barackman knows Satan does not procreate, and resolves the "serpent's offspring" problem by using a metaphorical view of offspring for the serpent, i.e., for Satan. But as I explained in the chapter "Genesis 3:15," one cannot (or at least should not) switch interpretive horses in mid-interpretation of a passage. Both the serpent's offspring and the Woman's offspring must be literal offspring or both must be metaphorical offspring. Grammatically the coordinating "and" makes both of the same kind. No one, of whom I am aware, gives a metaphorical interpretation to the Woman's offspring. No one should give a metaphorical interpretation to the serpent's offspring.

Mr. Barackman's second meaning of "offspring is this.

In a prophetic sense, *the seed of the woman* [emphasis Barackman] was a veiled reference to Jesus, the son of the virgin Mary [296–297].

I will discuss the "veiled reference" below. But first, Dr. Barackman adds a new twist to *zera'*. He wrote, "In this case, the woman represented the nation of Israel, through which God the Son entered the human family (Romans 1:3; Revelation 12:4)." No Old Testament or New Testament scripture validates the interpretation Eve represented national ethnic Israel. Indeed, Adam used his authority to name her "the mother of all living," Genesis 3:20. If, as is the case, Eve was the mother of all living, then her *zera'* is every human being, not just one human being or a nation of human beings.

If, as proposed, the *zera'* of the Woman was a veiled reference to Jesus son of Mariam, how did Mr. Barackman remove the veil? Not by an Old Testament reference, but by misusing two New Testament scriptures, Romans 1:3; Revelation 12:4.

> Romans 1:3, concerning his Son, who was born out of the offspring of David according to flesh.

> Revelation 12:4, And his tail draws a third of the stars of heaven; and he threw them to the earth. And the dragon is standing before the woman who is about to give birth, so that when she gives birth he might eat her child.

One of the most notable things about Genesis 3:15—I know I am repeating and ask the reader's indulgence—is Genesis 3:15 is *never* used anywhere in the entire Bible to refer to Jesus the Christ. Never. It is biblically, scripturally, exegetically impossible to find Jesus Christ in Genesis 3:15 using the Literal hermeneutic. Using the Christocentric hermeneutic or an allegorical interpretation? Yes, certainly, you can put into Genesis 3:15 anything or anyone you might imagine by abandoning the Literal hermeneutic. (For example, Dr. Fruchtenbaum, see below, puts the Antichrist of the Tribulation into Genesis 3:15.)

Romans 1:3 says God's Son was born "out of the offspring of David." Yes, ultimately Eve was the ancestor, but Scripture only indirectly makes that connection, e.g., 1 Corinthians 15:22. I could just as easily, using Mr. Barackman's *modus operandi,* say, "In this case, Noah represented the nation of Israel, through which God the Son entered the human family (Genesis 8:17)." The genealogy is sound, but Romans 1:3 speaks of the Christ as out of the offspring of David, according to the flesh. In the New Testament revelation the writers make the connection between Messiah-King and Messiah-Redeemer.

To connect Revelation 12:4 to Genesis 3:15 is just as preposterous; it is a silly notion. I have a complete exegesis of Revelation chapter 12 in vol. 2 of my commentary on the Revelation (Revelation 8–16). The following is from the introduction to chapter 12.

> Revelation 12 is a difficult chapter because of the many symbols. A synopsis may be helpful.

> 12:1–2, national ethnic Israel and its future under the Abrahamic and Davidic covenants: to birth the people of YHWH and to birth an ultimate heir, in order to fulfill both

covenants.

12:3–4, national ethnic Israel persecuted in Old Testament by Satan and his fellow messengers, who are trying to break the covenants.

12:5, (first advent) national ethnic Israel birthing the heir that will fulfill the covenants; the heir's ascension to heaven to wait until the time to inherit the (second advent) kingdom.

12:6, the persecution of national ethnic Israel in the future Tribulation, during the latter 1,260 days.

12:7–9, the dragon and his messengers thrown down to the earth, or why national ethnic Israel will be persecuted in the latter 1,260 days of Tribulation.

12:10–12a, proleptic view of Christ's coming kingdom and the believer's victory over Satan.

12:12b, the reason for the appearance of the beast (chapter 13) at the mid-way point of the Tribulation period.

12:13–17, God's protection of national ethnic Israel and gentile believers during the persecution of the latter 1,260 days of Tribulation.

Everything in the chapter concerns national ethnic Israel, the Abrahamic and Davidic covenants, and those particular events of the Day of the Lord known as the Tribulation.

The Revelation, from chapters 5–20, is the outworking of the Old Testament Day of the Lord, which is specifically defined in the Old Testament as the time of Jacob's (national ethnic Israel's) trouble, Jeremiah 30:7. The Tribulation is all about national ethnic Israel in the Day of the Lord (see the Old Testament book of Joel). The Messiah-Redeemer is at work during the Day of the Lord, e.g., Revelation 7:9–10, but the Day of the Lord ends in the fulfillment of the Psalm 2 line of Messiah-King prophecy, Revelation 19–20.

The only way to connect any Scripture concerning the Christ to Genesis 3:15 is to do what the Holy Spirit never does: attach other scriptures with no contextual connection. The Holy Spirit makes three and only three references to Genesis 3:15 in the entirety of Scripture, and those are Genesis 4:25; Romans 16:20; Revelation 12:9. Romans 16:20 says, "Now the God of peace will crush Satan under your feet shortly." The crucifixion is not in view, because verb tense is future. Christ is not mentioned, but the God of peace. What is in view? In terms of Genesis 3:15, victory in the continuing conflict between the offspring of the serpent, those of no faith, and the offspring of the Woman, those of faith.

Let us move to Mr. Barackman's chapter "Soteriology." Again, the only issue I have is with his Promise Soteriology.

One notable fact, as he works through his doctrine, everything he says is supported by the New Testament revelation. Mr. Barackman's soteriology finds no differences between Old Testament and New Testament salvation, including the object and content of faith. In the essential doctrine of salvation that is how it should be. But like others, just like Reformed soteriology, when Mr. Barackman says "gospel," he means the object and content of faith for sinners in both testaments is a coming redeemer-messiah-christ.

About forty pages into his doctrine of soteriology [on pp. 364–365], Mr. Barackman turns to "The Method Of Salvation In Other Ages." Many opinions are given about many subjects. I will focus on the statement pertinent to Genesis 3:15.

> Both Adam and Eve believed God's promise of the coming Seed, who would eventually destroy Satan (Gen. 3:15).

In no place in the entire Bible does the Holy Spirit show a coming seed destroying Satan. The only coming seed-offspring is "the seed-offspring of David," John 7:42; Romans 1:3; 2 Timothy 2:8. Those scriptures say nothing about destroying Satan.

In fact Jesus, prior to his crucifixion, states that by his crucifixion, "the ruler of this world will be cast out," John 12:31, not destroyed. Satan is, in fact, never destroyed. His fate is to be imprisoned endlessly in the lake of fire, Revelation 20:10, a place prepared for him when he sinned, Matthew 25:41. From the beginning Satan has been a defeated enemy, with judgment deferred but inevitable.

Jesus is speaking proleptically in John 12:31, because both then and now Satan was, and is, and will continue to be active in this world, not cast out, until the end of this present universe. Is Satan somehow cast out in this present world? Yes, the same way he has been cast out from the beginning, by removing some of his victims through salvation, Hebrews 2:14–17.

In the continuing struggle between faith and no faith predicted by Genesis 3:15, victory is gained when those of no faith become those of faith through salvation. Then, even though they will continue to experience that struggle, they already stand in the place of victory. And how were the Old Testament sinners saved? Not through faith in a coming redeemer-messiah-christ. I will address their faith, and the faith required in every dispensation, in the next chapter. But let me say here that from the side of man's responsibility, salvation is always by faith in God and God's current historic testimony given during their times.

The essential question is this. If as proposed by Dr. Barackman and others, Adam and Eve believed God's supposed promise of a coming redeemer-messiah-christ who would eventually destroy Satan, what is the scriptural basis for identifying that belief. What prior Old Testament revelation did they receive, the Analogy of Scripture, from Genesis 1:13–3:14, that allowed them to interpret Genesis 3:15 as Christ destroying Satan? Where is a *māshîah-christós* mentioned in Genesis 3:15, or earlier revelation? Where is *śātān* mentioned in Genesis or earlier revelation? "Oh," you say, "in Genesis 3:1, 4–5." How do you know that? Revelation 12:9, the only Scripture connecting Satan with the serpent in Genesis 3. Congratulations, you have abandoned the Literal hermeneutic by giving Adam and the Woman New Testament revelation written many thousands of years *after* their experiences in Genesis.

No one knew with any certainty that the serpent in Genesis 3 was Satan until the New Testament revelation given in the Book of Revelation, 12:9. As an Old Testament believer one might assume Satan empowered the serpent, by using Ezekiel 28:13; or that Satan was the evil power behind the serpent, by using Isaiah 14:12–14, or perhaps using Job 1–2, or Zechariah 3:1–2, or 1 Chronicles 21:1. But certainty came with the New Testament revelation in Revelation 12:9.

As to "seed," in relation to human beings, *zera'* always means human semen or human offspring through natural procreation. Did Adam and Eve really believe they would procreate *māshîah-christós?* And if they did, how would we know? (Some propose Genesis 4:1; I will address that in a later section.) No written Scripture, Old or New Testament, gives that information. Only by reading the New Testament revelation into Genesis 3:15 are Mr. Barackman and others able to transcend the original meaning of Genesis 3:15 in its original context.

What Mr. Barackman then wrote requires a long and complicated refutation. I will respond to each part.

> Other people of faith who believed God's salvational revelation were Enoch (Genesis 5:22; Hebrews 11:5–6), Noah (Genesis 6:8; Hebrews 11:7) and Abraham (Genesis 15:5–6), Abraham's faith in the coming Seed (Savior) was divinely credited to him for righteousness," It appears that he had earlier believed the salvational revelation (Genesis 12:3; Galatians 3:8–9).

> How much detail was known about the Redeemer before written divine revelation was given to mankind is not certain. It was probably more than the Old Testament record indicates (John 8:56; Hebrews 11:10, 13, 14). In any case it was sufficient for salvational faith in him.

Let me begin with the second part, about unknown revelation. Mr. Barackman does not know what it was, but he is sure it was given. He does not know what it was, but he is sure it was sufficient. What Mr. Barackman *is* sure of is the unknown revelation received as "sufficient for salvational faith in" Christ, *was not Scripture.* He wrote, "It" the unknown revelation, "was probably more than the Old Testament record indicates." This is unknown verbal tradition, and because it is unknown, it may be anything our imagination might imagine it to be.

But we do know what it was, and we do know it was sufficient, because God had Moses write it out in the book of Genesis. What God revealed to anyone prior to the written word that Moses penned is in the written word that Moses penned. If we say otherwise we have committed the error of extrabiblical revelation, as does Mr. Barackman.

The Holy Spirit gave us through Moses an accurate written record of what was said and done (inspiration). In no place in that written Old Testament record is there a salvational message about a promised yet future, yet-to-come, seed-redeemer-messiah-christ, or Jesus, until the New Testament revelation made that salvational message clear—and not by referring to Genesis 3:15. The Old Testament sinner was saved by the salvational message that was revealed and was understandable in the Old Testament revelation alone, as each received that message in the progressive revelation of truth. YHWH was the Savior; what need was there for a yet future, yet-to-come redeemer-messiah-christ?

Mr. Barackman's reference to the book of Hebrews does not prove his case. Hebrews 11 says those people had faith, but does not describe the content of that faith as a promised redeemer-messiah-christ. The object of their faith was YHWH. The object of Abraham's faith was YHWH, the content of Abraham's faith was YHWH's promise of a permanent dwelling in the land, 11:9–10, through an heir conceived by him and Sarah, 11:11–12.

Not that the heir of the permanent dwelling had to be Isaac, but Genesis 17:21, "my covenant is established in Isaac" and Genesis 21:12, "in Isaac your offspring will be named." Galatians 3:16 makes that clear: one offspring, Isaac, through whom came the one offspring, Jesus of Nazareth, who would inherit all the promises. We know because the New Testament revelation tells us, a revelation the Old Testament peoples *did not have*.

And how were the Old Testament peoples assured of the promises? See Hebrews 11:13. Look at Hebrews 6:13–15, "For God having promised to Abraham, because there was no one greater to whom to swear, he swore by himself, 14 saying, "Truly if assuredly blessing I will bless you and multiplying I will multiply you." 15 And so waiting patiently, he obtained the promise." Not by faith in a promised redeemer-messiah-christ from Genesis 3:15, but by faith in YHWH and YHWH's historically current promise of an inheritance through an heir, Isaac.

Then Mr. Barackman points to Galatians 3:8–9 as proof Abraham knew the Woman's *zera'* would be Jesus Christ, What saith the Scripture?

> Having foreseen, then, the Scripture that justifies the gentiles by faith, God foretold the Good News to Abraham: "In you all the peoples will be blessed." 9 So then those of faith are blessed together with the believing Abraham.

In a different version (HCSB).

> Now the Scripture foresaw that God would justify the Gentiles by faith and foretold the Good News to Abraham, saying, All the nations will be blessed in you.

I doubt the Scripture, being an immaterial, impersonal object, foresaw anything. The HCSB and other versions, influenced by Reformed soteriology, present an interpretive translation that within the Genesis 12:3 promise was a foreseeable fulfillment in Christ, which Abraham having been informed, saw and understood. No.

Abraham did not foresee Christ. God foresaw, "the Scripture that justifies the gentiles by faith." Of course God foresaw because God knew within himself what he would have all the Scripture's human authors write. Knowing that yet future Scripture, Galatians 3:8–9, God told Abraham that in him, in Abraham himself, "all the peoples will be blessed." Not blessed in a coming redeemer-messiah-christ not yet revealed, but blessed in Abraham himself through Abraham's (and Sarah's) faith to procreate an heir. Abraham through his faith would become the blessing.

Let me repeat that: Abraham himself, not some unknown, yet future, promised redeemer-messiah-christ, but Abraham himself, by his faith in the promise of Genesis 12:3, as fulfilled in the promise of 15:4–6, Abraham himself became the prophesied blessing of Genesis 12:3. Isn't that what Galatians 3:7–9 states?

> Know then that those of faith, these are sons of Abraham. 8 Having foreseen, then, the Scripture that justifies the gentiles by faith, God foretold the Good News to Abraham: "in you all the peoples will be blessed." 9 So then those of faith are blessed together with the believing Abraham.

The Good News, the "gospel," God told to Abraham was exactly that: in you, Abraham, all the peoples of the earth will be blessed.

God gave the promise to Abraham, Galatians 3:18, to be fulfilled in his heir, which ultimately is the Christ, Galatians 3:16, through the promised offspring, Isaac, in whom God established his covenant with Abraham. So the blessing is by Abraham's faith. If Abraham and Sarah had not by faith procreated Isaac, there would not be a blessing.

Abraham had faith in the promises God was giving to him then and there, in his lifetime: a land, an heir from his own body, other blessings. Was Abraham not only the father of Isaac, but also all Isaac's heirs, including Jesus? Yes, for it is a peculiarity of the Hebrew language that there is no word for grandfather. The father of the primary offspring is the father of all the offspring's descendants. Say this of myself, or does the scripture say this also? Luke 1:32, "And the Lord God will give him [Jesus of Mariam] the throne of David, his father."

Abraham did not know of a coming redeemer-messiah-christ, but he did know his heir Isaac, and he did believe God's promise an heir from his own body would inherit the promises. Through that heir, Isaac, who began the line of descent to Jesus, "those of faith are blessed together with the believing Abraham," Galatians 3:9. But Abraham only saw Isaac, and by faith believed that Isaac, or one of Isaac's descendants, would inherit the promises (which explains John 8:56). Abraham did not know, he could not know, that the heir who would receive all the promises was Jesus of Nazareth; and there is no mention of Genesis 3:15 or a coming redeemer-messiah-christ.

Abraham's faith in the promises is why "those of faith are blessed together with the believing Abraham." Abraham's faith led him (Hebrews 11:12), and Sarah (Hebrews 11:11), to have sexual intercourse at a time in their lives when conception of a child was physically impossible, by faith trusting God would bring conception. Because of that faith there was an heir, Isaac, to inherit the promises, and an heir, Jesus of Nazareth, Luke 3:23–34; Mathew 1:2–16; Galatians 3:16, to receive the inheritance.

Mr. Barackman also points to John 8:56, "Abraham your father rejoiced in that he should see my day, and he saw and rejoiced." I discussed this scripture in a previous chapter. Like so many, Mr. Barackman reads the verse as though Abraham saw Jesus Christ. But that is not what Jesus said. From my commentary on John's gospel, vol. 1 (John 1–12).

> God gave Abraham certain promises concerning his posterity, and it was Abraham's faith in these promises to which Jesus referred. Abraham need not understand messianic fulfillment to have faith in and rejoice in the promises which later revelation said would be fulfilled by the Messiah.

Abraham did not see Jesus. Abraham by faith believed in a yet-future time, a "day," when one of heirs, if not Isaac then through Isaac, would receive all the things God had promised. All Abraham knew when he died is Isaac might not be the heir who would receive the promises; but Abraham did not lose faith that his heir Isaac or some descendant of his heir Isaac would receive the promises. Even so, the Christian does not lose faith in the promises, seeing their fulfillment by faith.

What of Enoch and Noah? Mr. Barackman again overstates his case when referring to Hebrews 11. The object of Enoch's faith was YHWH,

11:5. The content of his faith was not in a promised seed, but that he "pleased God." How did Enoch please God? Genesis 5:24, Enoch "walked with God."

How does one walk with God? Not physically, but spiritually, exactly the same way one walks with God in these New Testament times. The word "walk" is being used figuratively as manner of life, how one behaves in his or her life. Enoch had faith in YHWH, so he ordered his behavior according to YHWH's values, he worshiped YHWH according to YHWH's instructions. So simple; so biblical; so in line with the entire teaching of the Scripture.

Mr. Barackman goes on in the same manner. He says the Old Testament people "anticipated the fulfillment of God's promises." But to "prove" that assertion he must appeal to the New Testament revelation. He has no Old Testament scriptures to identify that supposed anticipation to prove his assumption.

Mr. Barackman simply cannot prove his case for Promise soteriology using only the Old Testament revelation.

Promise soteriology depends on the same hermeneutic as does Reformed soteriology: transcend the Old Testament revelation and the Old Testament author's intent by reinterpreting the original meaning of the Old Testament revelation with the New Testament revelation. That means Promise soteriology has abandoned the plain and normal meaning of the Scripture to develop an Old Testament doctrine of God's testimony concerning salvation that is not supported by the Scripture.

Theologian Michael Rydelnik (1957–)

Dr. Rydelnik is professor of Jewish studies at the Moody Bible Institute in Chicago, Illinois. His book is *The Messianic Hope*, subtitle, *Is the Hebrew Bible Really Messianic?* His answer is "Yes." The same as the other books I am examining, Dr. Rydelnik's book is also worthy reading. As also with the other books, my research focused on Promise soteriology.

One of Dr. Rydelnik's themes is "Jesus of Nazareth fulfilled messianic prophecies." To this I agree without reservation. As I have previously mentioned there are two distinct lines of Old Testament messianic prophecy. These two lines may be summarized in the only two Old Testament scriptures identifiable as speaking of a coming messiah, i.e., the only scriptures that actually use the word *māshîah* in reference to a coming *māshîah*. From Psalm 2 there is the Messiah-King line of prophecy. From Daniel 9:26 there is the Messiah-Redeemer line of prophecy.

The New Testament revelation tells what the Old Testament revelation does not: both lines were to be fulfilled at two different times in two very different ways. Both lines meet in Jesus of Nazareth, i.e., in the incarnate person Jesus Christ. The Daniel 9:26 Messiah-Redeemer line of messianic prophecy was fulfilled in the first advent. The Psalm 2 Messiah-King line of messianic prophecy will fulfilled in the second advent.

The Messiah-King prophecy begins at Genesis 49:10, but it was not then understandable of a coming messiah. With later Old Testament revelation it is understandable of the Messiah-King. I have explained these things before. Both Reformed and Promise soteriology conflate Messiah-King with Messiah-Redeemer, and reinterpret Old Testament scriptures with New Testament revelation.

Dr. Rydelnik And Promise Soteriology

Dr. Rydelnik does not directly address Dispensational Promise Soteriology. That was not his purpose in writing, and I am not sure why he was recommended as a proponent of Promise soteriology. Regardless, in chapter 9, "An Example From the Law: Interpreting Genesis 3:15 As a Messianic Prophecy," he does promote a Reformed and Promise soteriology view of this scripture as a prediction of a future coming redeemer-messiah-christ.

Dr. Rydelnik does view Genesis 3:15 as "the protoevangelium, or the 'first gospel.'" I have responded to that view in the previous chapter, showing its origin as in the 1600s, and then as an allegorical view of that scripture. Dr. Rydelnik views any non-messianic interpretation of Genesis 3:15 as an error. His hermeneutic is "the Old Testament should be read as a messianic text, designed by its author to promote a messianic hope" [129]. That hermeneutical presupposition determines his exegesis before he reads a single Scripture. Of course, this is the Christocentric hermeneutic dressed in new clothes (see discussion, chapter "The Literal Hermeneutic") with the same faults. The interpreter using the Christocentric hermeneutic tends to become a hermeneutical hammer that beats every Scripture until reshaped to be about Christ. The blessing of the Literal hermeneutic is it sees each scripture within its own particular context: not everything is about Christ.

Dr. Rydelnik explains four interpretive views of Genesis 3:15. Significantly, the Literal hermeneutic is not among them. The view he names "Symbolic" may seem like the Literal hermeneutic, but it is not. Naturally only the "Messianic View" meets with Dr. Rydelnik's approval, and given the other three views he discusses, I can see why, I would also reject those views as Liberal theology in whole or in part.

The Messianic view. "The essential *messianic* view [emphasis Rydelnik] is that Genesis 3:15 ultimately predicts the coming of a future individual (a 'seed') who will have victory over the serpent through his own death" [134]. (He rightly rejects the "virgin birth" interpretation.)

Dr. Rydelnik reveals the basis for his Messianic View [135].

> The author of the Torah offered a hint of a coming redeemer in Gen. 3:15, then used the rest of the Pentateuch to identify Him as the future Messiah.

My question is, how does Dr. Rydelnik know the author of the Torah wrote Genesis 3:15 as a "hint" of a coming redeemer? I thought Moses was reporting history as it actually happened. Isn't that inspiration; that what happened, what was actually said and done, is accurately reported? As I read Genesis 3:15, the words are from God as the source, not the Torah writer. Nor am I able to see an authorial intent to reveal a redeemer-messiah-christ. The right words are not in the verse.

The word "hint" tells the story. Dr. Rydelnik sees what he wants to find. I searched the next twelve pages of text looking to validate Dr. Rydelnik's claim Moses somewhere in the Torah offered an interpretive hint for Genesis 3:15, and that the Torah writer "used the rest of the Pentateuch to identify Him [the supposed 'coming redeemer' in Genesis 3:15] as the future Messiah." Only Numbers 24:5–9; 17–19 were proposed. Apparently the evidence supporting the Torah writer's "hint" is sparse.

The Book of Numbers passages are the report of Balaam's prophecies concerning Israel. Again we have the issues of source and accuracy in reporting. Are these Balaam's words, or the Torah's writer's words? Balaam spoke the words but they were God's words, Numbers 22:35. "The messenger of YHWH" said "Go with these men, but only say what I tell you to say." So what Balaam said in his prophetic utterances is what YHWH said.

Under the supra-natural influence of the Holy Spirit, Moses gave an accurate report of what God had Balaam say. God's prophecies through Balaam are messianic. But which Messiah is in view, the King, or the Redeemer? Without doubt Messiah-King is in view.

> Numbers 24:17–19 (LXX), I will point to him, but not now; I bless him, but he draws not near: a star shall rise out of Jacob, a man shall spring out of Israel; and shall crush the princes of Moab, and shall spoil all the sons of Seth. And Edom shall be an inheritance, and Esau his enemy shall be an inheritance of Israel, and Israel wrought valiantly. And one shall arise out of Jacob, and destroy out of the city him that escapes.

None of Balaam's prophecies are about a coming redeemer from sin. None of Balaam's prophecies reference Genesis 3:15.

Contrary to Dr. Rydelnik's conclusions, the "author of the Torah" *did not* "offer a hint of a coming redeemer in Genesis 3:15," and *did not* "use the rest of the Pentateuch to identify Him as the future Messiah" Redeemer. Only a determined, single-minded Christocentric hermeneutic is able to force, find, insert, or import Christ into Genesis 3:15 or the rest or the Pentateuch. Only the New Testament revelation justifies seeing Christ in some places in the Pentateuch, e.g., 1 Corinthians 10:4.

In citing Numbers 24:5–9; 17–19 as his only Pentateuchal validation that Genesis 3:15 is messianic, Dr. Rydelnik has unintentionally set up a conflict with his earlier statements. To summarize.

> Dr. Rydelnik states Genesis 3:15 is the "first gospel," and speaks of the coming of a future individual (a 'seed') who will have victory over the serpent through his own death.

> But the scriptures Dr. Rydelnik presents as proof of his assertion, Numbers 24:5–9; 17–19, speak of a coming king, not a coming redeemer.

In addition to Dr. Rydelnik's hermeneutical presuppositions, his other problem is the usual problem: conflating two lines of messianic prophecy into one. He believes Genesis 3:15 speaks of a coming messiah, identifying him as both king and redeemer. But in fact, there is no messiah in Genesis 3:15, when using the Literal hermeneutic, which does not presuppose authorial intent, but depends on contextual, lexical, syntactical and other methods of analysis to find authorial intent and thereby interpret scripture.

To its credit, Dispensational Promise soteriology does not usually conflate Messiah-King with Messiah-Redeemer. But I have previously interpreted their key scripture as not messianic in any sense. Therefore I also disagree with Dr. Rydelnik's conclusion, "It seems appropriate to understand Genesis 3:15 as the first specific messianic prophecy of the Bible. . . . this text . . . does promise that Messiah will descend from humanity and he will destroy the evil force that tempted Eve" [145].

Again, show me a coming redeemer-messiah-christ in Genesis 3:15 without injecting any later revelation, Old or New, into the passage— isn't that the Literal hermeneutic? To find the primary meaning of the passage in the passage? The only Old Testament revelation the Holy Spirit connects with Genesis 3:15 is Genesis 4:25; the only New Testament revelation is Romans 16:20; Revelation 12:9. I realize it is a big challenge to read the entire Bible looking for a contextual connection with Genesis 3:15, but I present that challenge to you. Some of you, who have read the Bible "cover to cover" many times, know what I am saying is true.

Dr. Rydelnik does offer a light exegesis of Genesis 3:15. His key point is a "kind of oscillation" [140] between the collective meaning of *zera'* in other scriptures and the individual meaning in Genesis 3:15. Detecting this "kind of oscillation" in other scriptures can be objective through the immediate literary context of any passage using *zera'*, but in Genesis 3:15 it is wholly subjective; Rydelnik is not paying attention to the lexical-syntactical parameters of the verse. Citing another's work [140, n. 40], Dr. Rydelnik argues the singular pronoun and singular verb in the last clause means a single individual.

> "he [singular] shall strike your [singular] head and you [singular] shall strike his [singular] heel."

Certainly the noun *zera'* is always singular, so it is not grammatically surprising pronouns referring to *zera'* are singular. (See the chapter, "Genesis 3:15," for an exegesis.)

Regardless of how we view Dr. Rydelnik's interpretation, it does not and cannot answer the primary issue. How do Dr. Rydelnik, or the other Promise soteriology Dispensationalists, know the personal identity of the person or persons represented by the singular pronouns "he" and "your?" To identify the singular pronoun as "a future individual who will have victory over the serpent through his own death," blatantly assumes what is not in evidence in the text; it is eisegesis.

Eisegesis is the consequence of any hermeneutic that assumes rather than prove. Dr. Rydelnik's "Messianic" hermeneutic begins with the presupposition all the Old Testament is about the Messiah. Dr. Rydelnik opens his Bible having already thrown an objective exegesis out the window. How much better if he had sought to prove his point to the reader with an objective exegesis, rather than assume his point must be true, and dogmatically declare Genesis 3:15 must be about a coming redeemer, and interpret the words and grammar according to his presupposition?

What does the Scripture say? I do not need more than the plain and normal meaning of the words to know the Woman, Eve, identified three individuals that fit the prophecy, her offspring Cain, Abel, and Seth. I have pointed out before that in Genesis 4:25, Eve identifies Abel and Seth as her offspring (so not one individual), implying Cain was the serpent's offspring; later revelation, 1 John 3:12, re: the Analogy of Faith, confirms that identity. If Eve was looking for a fulfillment in one individual, there it was, Cain murdered Abel. But Eve also identified Seth as her offspring. There is no reason to think she thought the prophecy completely fulfilled in the death of Abel, because there were other offspring to interact with the prophecy: Seth Genesis 4:25, and "sons and daughters," Genesis 5:4.

Certainly Adam and Eve, the people who received the prophecy, and were directly affected by the prophecy, could not and did not identify the singular pronoun as one specific yet future individual "who will have victory over the serpent through his own death"—unless we want to inject extrabiblical revelation or illumination, or interpretive presuppositions. How may I be so confident? The Analogy of Scripture and the Analogy of Faith. Nothing God revealed prior to this moment or after this moment gave them or anyone else during Old Testament times the necessary information to identify "he" as "a future individual who will have victory over the serpent through his own death."

Let us reason together. As I explained in chapter "Genesis 3:15," the Hebrew word *shûp* can be translated bruise, strike at, or crush. Only one of those, crush, implies death. If, as proposed by both Dr. Rydelnik and "coming redeemer" soteriologies, the serpent causes the offspring's physical death by crushing the heel, then the offspring crushing the serpent's head must cause some kind of significant physical injury to the serpent. "He [Woman's offspring] shall crush your [serpent's offspring] head and you [serpent's offspring] shall crush his [Woman's offspring] heel." That is the contextual, lexical-syntactical reading required by the Literal hermeneutic.

Both Dr. Rydelnik and the "coming redeemer" soteriologies identify the prophecy as directed at an evil power hidden behind the serpent, aka: Satan. But no one knew the serpent was Satan until Revelation 12:9. Christ was physically killed. Was Satan physically injured? No, he suffered no harm to his person.

To use a metaphor, you cannot switch horses midstream in an interpretation. Grammatically, the coordinating "and" means *shûp* applies in a similar way to both sets of offspring: if used on one in a physical manner, then it must be used of the other in a physical manner. Christ was killed; Satan was not. Christ is not in Genesis 3:15, unless we bring him to the interpretation. Satan is not in Genesis 3:15 unless we bring later revelation to the interpretation. Neither one of those options is the Literal hermeneutic.

The "coming redeemer" interpreters want it both ways: Christ was physically killed but Satan was spiritually or metaphorically injured. Hermeneutically that is not possible. Grammatically that is not possible, the conjunction "and" connects two subjects that are performing the same kind of action.

The word *shûp* is used of the actions of both the offspring of the Woman and the offspring of the serpent. Either both physically harm each other, or neither physically harms the other. If both do not physically harm each other, then the individual who is proposed as the promised seed-redeemer cannot be the Christ.

However, there is absolutely nothing in Genesis 3:15 that promotes the idea of a promised future coming redeemer-messiah-christ. There is literally no mention of a coming anyone, let alone some yet future coming individual. There is no mention of a need for redemption from the penalty of sin that would require a coming redeemer. God had already forgiven their sin, he had restored them to fellowship. He gives rules to confirm his earlier rules concerning their relationship, and to manage the sin now part of their lives. God gives a rule concerning the interaction between the Woman's offspring, i.e., those of faith and those of no faith. We see that rule at work in Genesis 4:25; Romans 16:20.

Seeing a coming redeemer-messiah-christ in Genesis 3:15 is purely eisegesis created by throwing out the Literal interpretation and overwriting Genesis 3:15 with the New Testament revelation; or as with Dr, Rydelnik by using a presupposition all Old Testament Scripture must be interpreted as messianic. That concept originated in the desire of Reformed soteriology to have the one way of salvation be man-centered, faith in Christ, rather than God-centered in the unlimited efficacy of the propitiation made by Christ. That desire created the "first gospel" view of Genesis 3:15, after 1600 years of a Christian soteriology that did not interpret Genesis 3:15 as the first proclamation of the gospel.

In fact, no person, no scripture verse, no scripture book, chapter, paragraph, sentence, phrase, clause, word, syllable, or alphabet character in the entire Old Testament and New Testament can be demonstrated as understanding Genesis 3:15 as the "first gospel."

Reformed and Dispensational Promise soteriologies transcend—they go beyond—the meaning of Genesis 3:15 by shifting that scripture from the Old Testament into the New Testament. It is like making Malachi 3:10 the most popular New Testament scripture on tithing (the New Testament does not teach tithing for the New Testament church). Or like making Exodus 20:8 the most popular New Testament scripture on Sunday worship (the New Testament scripture does not teach a mandatory and particular day of rest, let alone a mandatory and particular day of worship). The Reformed faith has a long history of transcending the meaning of the Old Testament. Too many Dispensationalists are in lock-step with them.

The Promise soteriology view is not different in substance than Reformed soteriology. Reformed soteriology teaches the content of Old Testament faith was a coming Christ-King-Redeemer, beginning with Genesis 3:15. Dispensational Promise soteriology teaches the content of Old Testament faith was a coming Redeemer-Messiah-Christ beginning with Genesis 3:15. I cannot see a meaningful difference.

An interpretation following the rules of the Literal hermeneutic does recognize what happens to one must happen to the other. The better translation of *shûp* is "strike," which incorporates injury or death. The Literal interpretation understands both kinds of offspring are the Woman's, one kind is of faith the other kind is of no faith. In the continuing conflict between those of faith and those of no faith, some will be hurt, some will die. That has been the experience of those of faith for millennia. The Analogy of Faith supports that interpretation in Genesis 4:25; Romans 16:20.

A reminder seems appropriate. The issue is not, did Jesus Christ propitiate God for human sin by dying on the cross? He did die for your sin, he did resurrect for your justification. The point of these discussions is you can't get there from Genesis 3:15, at least not by using the Literal hermeneutic.

Theologian Walter C. Kaiser Jr. (1933–)

Dr. Kaiser's book is *The Promise-Plan of God*. This book is a "thoroughly revised and expanded edition" of his previous book, *Toward an Old Testament Theology*. The theme of the book is summed in the title of the introductory chapter, "God's Promise-Plan in Both Testaments." The book is solid and informative Bible study, but as with other Promise Dispensationalists, his view of Genesis 3:15 is in error. As with others in this review, I will focus on Genesis 3:15.

Dr. Kaiser defined the "Promise-plan" in this way (emphasis Kaiser) [19].

> The promise-plan is God's word of declaration, beginning with Eve and continuing on through history, especially in the patriarchs and the Davidic line, that God would continually *be* in his person and *do* in his deeds and works (in and through Israel and later the church) his redemptive plan as his *means* of keeping that promised word alive to Israel, and thereby for all who subsequently believed. All in that promised seed were called to act as a light for all nations so that all the families of the earth might come to faith and to new life in the Messiah.

The first hermeneutical problem is the first promised offspring (seed) in the Old Testament Scripture is not a coming redeemer-messiah-christ, but Abraham's offspring Isaac, and through Isaac and his descendants to Christ, as we know from later revelation.

The second hermeneutical problem is Dr. Kaiser does what others do. He conflates two distinct lines of messianic prophecy that meet in the person Jesus Christ, but are fulfilled at two different times in two distinct ways. In that way he thinks to connect Genesis 3:15 to the crucifixion and resurrection of the Christ, even though there is no mention of a messiah in Genesis 3:15, and no Old or New Testament scripture speaks of a messiah in Genesis 3:15. Dr. Kaiser's Promise Plan begins by injecting his presupposition into Genesis 3:15.

As I have explained before—I keep saying it because the error keeps repeating—the Messiah-Redeemer line was fulfilled at the first advent through the crucifixion and resurrection. That was the fulfillment of the Abrahamic promise, Genesis 12:3, Galatians 3:8, blessing to all families of the earth, through Abraham's heir Isaac, Genesis 21:12, "in Isaac your seed will be named," cf. Romans 9:7; Galatians 3:6–16; Hebrews 11:18.

The Messiah-King line will be fulfilled at the second advent through the Davidic-Messianic Kingdom. This line of prophecy began at Genesis 49:10, and was further revealed in the promise to David, 2 Samuel 7:13–16; and David's inspired interpretation of that promise in Psalm 2.

Those lines of prophecy meet in Jesus Christ, which means they are distinct in the Old Testament revelation. They do not directly include Genesis 3:15. Which is to say, the Messiah-Redeemer line of prophecy does not begin in Genesis 3:15 but in Genesis 12:3, a fact we know only because of Galatians 3:8.

The only way Jesus Christ is connected to Genesis 3:15 is he is one of the believing offspring of the Woman who suffers from the unbelieving offspring of the Woman. His crucifixion and resurrection to be the Messiah-Redeemer is fulfillment of the messianic prophecy at Daniel 9:25–26,

> Know and understand, from the issue of the word to restore and rebuild Jerusalem until the Anointed Prince, there shall be seven sevens and sixty-two sevens; the marketplace will be built again, and the wall, even in times of distress. After sixty-two sevens the Anointed will be cut off and have nothing for

himself.

Again, how do I know? Among other scriptures, Acts 8:32–35; Romans 3:25; Hebrews 2:17; 1 John 2:2; 2 Corinthians 5:21.

Was the Messiah to be a redeemer as king? Yes, national redemption from gentile oppression. The Holy Spirit makes that clear in Luke 1:51–52, 70–74. Jesus made that clear also, beginning his public ministry with the proclamation of himself as the king, and then changing the message when the nation rejected him as king. Matthew 16:15–21 examples the change.

> He says to them, "But you, who do you say me to be?" 16 Now Simon Peter answering said, "You are the Christ, the son of the living God." 17 And Jesus in reply said to him, "Blessed are you, Simon son of Jonah. Because flesh and blood revealed this not to you, but my Father who is in the heavens. 18 Now I also say to you, that you are Peter, and on this the rock I will build my church, and the gates of hades will not prevail against it. 19 And I will give you the keys of the kingdom of the heavens; and whatever if you might bind on earth will be bound in the heavens, and whatever if you might loose on earth will be loosed in the heavens." 20 Then he commanded the disciples that to no one should they say that he is the Christ.
>
> 21 From that time Jesus began to show to his disciples that it is necessary for him to go away to Jerusalem, and to suffer many things from the elders and chief priests and scribes, and to be killed, and on the third day to be raised.

Jesus told them no one was to "say that he is the Christ," because all in Israel during that time understood the "Christ" as the Messiah-King. That line of messianic prophecy would not be fulfilled in the first advent. In the first advent the Messiah-Redeemer will build his New Testament church, beginning with his death to propitiate God for human sin, and his resurrection to be the redeemer.

Returning to Dr. Kaiser's book.

Dr. Kaiser interacts with Genesis 3:15 on page 43.

> In the midst of the dirge of gloom and rebuke came God's surprising word of prophetic hope (Gen. 3:15) ... is climaxed with triumphant appearance of a "he"—no doubt a

representative person of the woman's seed. He would deliver a lethal blow to the head of the serpent, while the best the serpent would be able or even permitted to do would be to nip the heel of this male descendant.

As I recall the details of the crucifixion, it was God, not Satan, that delivered a lethal blow to the Messiah-Redeemer. For it was God that made the Savior die spiritually, "My God, my God. Why have you forsaken me?" That is the spiritual separation required by the penalty due sin. And it was God who caused the penalty of physical death, "bowing his head, he [Jesus the Christ] yielded up his spirit." God allowed Satan to arrange the circumstances, Acts 2:23, but redemption is all from God, from beginning to end, not from Satan at all.

How was Satan injured by the death of Christ? Satan's goal is to be worshiped and to deny God glory. God kept on saving sinners, and keeps on giving them the means, spiritual regeneration, to deny temptation. From the moment of his first act of sin Satan has always been a defeated enemy, his doom assured, Matthew 25:41.

Contrary to Dr. Kaiser's view of Genesis 3:15, Satan was not injured by Christ's crucifixion. Nor was Satan destroyed by Christ's crucifixion. And certainly Satan was not prevented by Christ's crucifixion from continuing to do evil.

I previously discussed the grammatical requirements of "He [Woman's offspring] shall crush your [serpent's] head and you [serpent] shall crush his [Woman's offspring] heel." The coordinating conjunction "and" between the two actions requires both subjects and both actions be equal in some manner.

If the serpent causes the offspring's physical death by "nipping the heel" then grammatically, by reason of the coordinating "and," we should expect something similar from the Woman's offspring toward the serpent. What does Dr. Kaiser propose of the Woman's offspring? "He would deliver a lethal blow to the head of the serpent." The way I read the New Testament, that did not happen happened. The serpent motivated Jesus' enemies to have him crucified, God punished Jesus for the sins of others (loss of fellowship = spiritual death), and Jesus deliberately and voluntarily separated his soul from his body—the act of physical death to complete the penalty due sin.

Did Dr Kaiser forget Jesus really and truly and actually died physically? Did Dr Kaiser forget Satan continued to live and do what he has always done. Christ did not kill Satan; Satan only indirectly inflicted injury to Christ. We must get over this presupposition Satan killed Christ. Yes, "the rulers of this age" crucified the Lord of glory, 1 Corinthians 2:8, providing the means of physical death, but Jesus suffered under God's hands, Matthew 27:46, and Jesus caused his own physical death, Matthew 27:50; Mark 15:37; Luke 23:46; John 19:30.

Dr. Kaiser's conclusion is incorrect: "God's surprising word of prophetic hope (Gen. 3:15) … is climaxed with triumphant appearance of a 'he'—no doubt a representative person of the woman's seed."

No. There is no one representative person of the woman's seed in view in Genesis 3:15. Was The Woman not named by Adam, who has just heard the prophecy, as the mother of *all* living, Genesis 3:23? If, as proposed by Dr. Kaiser, as proposed by others, Adam and the Woman understood the Woman's seed specifically as one particular person of the yet future, then why did not Adam say "she is the mother of the coming Seed who will deliver human beings from sin"?

I have discussed too many times that the person to whom the prophecy was addressed, the Woman, interpreted *zera'* in a collective sense: Abel and Seth. Did you think the Holy Spirit gave us Eve's word in Genesis 4:25 just for some kind of historical filler? "God has given me another *zera'*, Seth, to replace my first *zera'* Abel, whom another of my literal *zera'*, Cain, murdered." What could be plainer than the Woman understood the *zera'* in a collective sense, a seeds of faith and seeds of no faith?

There is no one representative individual in the Genesis 3:15 prophecy, that will "deliver a lethal blow to the head of the serpent." To say so is the typical Reformed eisegesis that comes from using the New Testament revelation to transcend and change the authorial intent of the Old Testament writer: Moses and the Holy Spirit. Eisegesis that ignores the New Testament revelation's testimony that Christ died and the serpent lived. Eisegesis that ignores the biblical testimony that God put Christ on the cross through the sins of Satan and other sinners, Acts 2:23, that God inflicted spiritual death on Christ by withdrawing fellowship when Christ became "sin for us," 2 Corinthians 5:21; Matthew 27:46, and that Christ caused his own death, John 19:30.

The Bible student will always be repaid by seeking out the whole teaching of Scripture on any subject. Christ's crucifixion did not "deliver a lethal blow" to Satan. Satan is alive and well, always tempting humanity, always seeking to rob God of his glory, always seeking human worship. Do we not find him after the end of the New Testament church age, during the Tribulation period? Yes. And again after the Davidic-Messianic millennium ends, Revelation 20:7–10.

What did deliver a lethal blow to Satan, and his fallen angels? His sin as Lucifer, for it is then he was cast out of heaven, it is then he became a defeated enemy, it is then his endless destiny was sealed by "the everlasting fire prepared for the devil and his angels," Matthew 25:41, compare Revelation 20:10. The execution of that sentence waits in the timing of God, but today, after the crucifixion, he is uninjured and continuously working evil. Dr. Kaiser's "lethal blow to Satan," is nothing less than reworking the non-literal Reformed interpretation of Revelation 20:3, that Satan is right now, during the New Testament church age, imprisoned.

To his credit, Dr. Kaiser says the one, individual "male descendant" [43] of the Woman's offspring, is "not immediately revealed." But then he follows with the normal and usual Reformed interpretation: the Woman "expected that God would supply a person who would care for their sin that had occasioned the fall." And he practically, if not explicitly, identifies that one person as Christ. As I have pointed out, God had already taken care of Adam and Eve's sin, he had forgiven them and restored them to his fellowship. But God had left the sin attribute in their human nature, and Genesis 3:15–19 addresses that new fact of life.

For support Dr. Kaiser looks to "the enigmatic phrase" (Kaiser's description) of Genesis 4:1, interpreting it favorably to his doctrine, "gotten a man, even the Lord." But the most natural translation of the preposition '$\bar{e}t$ is "from," not "even" [Harris et al., s. v. 187], "gotten a man from the Lord." Indeed, throughout the Old Testament revelation the conception and birth of a child is attributed to YHWH, e.g., Genesis 30:2, Jacob was angry at Rachel, and said, "Do I stand in the place of God, who has withheld from you the fruit of the womb?" Compare 1 Samuel 1:11. Where did godly men and women get that idea, that a child is "from the Lord"? From the Scripture, beginning with Genesis 4:1.

On the whole, Dr. Kaiser has done good service to the Christian community through his book. He illuminates certain Old Testament scriptures with New Testament revelation as messianic in their fulfillment. However, his "illumination" of Genesis 3:15 is dogmatic (giving opinion as fact), not exegetical, because there is no Old Testament or New Testament revelation identifying Genesis 3:15 as messianic.

Pastor W. A. Criswell (1909–2002)

Pastor Criswell was a highly respected figure in the Southern Baptist denomination. In 1971 Pastor Criswell published a series of sermons in one book under the title *the Scarlet Thread Through The Bible*. The book had a welcome reception and a significant influence.

Pastor Criswell's book was recommended to me as supporting Dispensational Promise soteriology. The edition of the book I purchased has no publication data, so I cannot refer you to a page number and assume it will be the same in all editions.

In the chapter titled, "Part Two The Struggle Between Evil and Good," Pastor Criswell explains in Genesis 3:15 YHWH was speaking to Satan.

> In the Garden of Eden ... the Lord ... turned to the devil, he turned to Satan, he turned to Lucifer ... He said, "In this woman whom you have deceived ... I will create out of her, I will create that one who will crush your head" ... as all of us know, "seed" is masculine. Seed belongs to the man. A woman doesn't have seed. It belongs to the man.

The first hermeneutical problem is importing Revelation 12:9 into Genesis 3:15. A Literal exegesis would identify the serpent as an unnamed symbol of evil or no faith.

The second hermeneutical problem is implying a virgin birth from Genesis 3:15. I am reasonably confident Pastor Criswell knew *zera'* means offspring, not semen, in Genesis 3:15. That interpretation is simply inexcusable.

The third hermeneutical problem is assuming a "coming redeemer," which leads to the improper interpretation the prophecy is directed solely against the serpent, not his offspring. Pastor Criswell chooses to identify the serpent as Satan, something Adam and Eve could not do. In fact, no one knew the serpent was Satan until Revelation 12:9. Genesis 3:15 is the first metaphorical use of a serpent in the Old Testament revelation, identifying offspring, not one individual. The second metaphorical use is Numbers 21:8, as a symbol for the sin of the people and deliverance through confession of that sin. A "serpent" as a symbol of sin in Numbers fits the Genesis 3 testimony concerning the tempting serpent, and the evil his offspring will do. Jesus, the one who was "made sin for us," agrees with that interpretation, John 3:14.

Satan is never connected to Genesis 3:15 in the eighteen uses of the word *śātān* in the Old Testament revelation. Nor in the thirty-four uses of the word *satanás* in the New Testament, except Romans 16:20; Revelation 12:9.

Pastor Criswell chooses to use the English translation "seed," although undoubtedly he knew the Hebrew *zera'* means "semen, plant seed, procreated offspring." In doing so he creates a fulfillment of the prophecy as between one person, Satan, and another person, the "seed," whom he identifies as Christ: "the age-long conflict and struggle between the hatred of Lucifer" (he means Satan) "and the love of God in Jesus Christ." A dogmatic interpretation of Genesis 3:15 from an English translation has been the bane of Christian understanding for centuries.

The next time in Pastor Criswell's book that Genesis 3:15 is the subject is chapter "Part Six From the Prophets to the Christ to the Preaching of Paul."

... and the great promise of God almighty to Eve the woman, that great prophecy comes to pass .... In the seed as of one.

Pastor Criswell understands Genesis 3:15 as a prophecy of the death of Christ by the hand of Satan.

Those two widely separated passages are all Pastor Criswell had to say about Genesis 3:15 in his book. I have addressed that interpretation in depth in this and other chapters in this book. As a review of Old Testament history Pastor Criswell's book is informative and useful. As an interpretation of Genesis 3:15 it is not.

Theologian Arnold Fruchtenbaum (1943–)

Dr. Fruchtenbaum is considered an important figure in modern

Christianity and Dispensationalism. The book I used for research was *Messianic Christology*, published by Dr. Fruchtenbaum's Ariel Ministries in 1988.

The subtitle of the book is *A Study of Old Testament Prophecy Concerning the First Coming of the Messiah*. I recommend this book to any believer with an interest in how the New Testament revelation reveals Old Testament messianic prophecy in fulfillment. The book is less useful as an exegesis of how Old Testament prophecy is to be interpreted using the Literal hermeneutic. Dr. Fruchtenbaum consistently breaks the Analogy of Scripture and the Vlach rule [*Dispensationalism*, 31] based on that hermeneutical principle, against transcending Old Testament meaning with New Testament revelation. And he knows better.

Dr. Fruchtenbaum strikes the right note in the Introduction, p. 11. He wrote, "We have a tendency to read back into the Old Testament a level of New Testament understanding which did not exist in those days." He immediately ignores that warning.

Dr. Fruchtenbaum opens his messianic arguments with this line [14]. "The seed of the Woman refers to Christ, the Messiah, and the seed of the serpent will be the Antichrist." Pertinent questions come to mind.

> 1. How does Dr. Fruchtenbaum know Genesis 3:15 is about the Messiah?

There is no use of the word *māshîah* in the written Scripture prior to Genesis 3:15 or in Genesis 3:15. I remind the reader that the Analogy of Scripture, which I am sure Dr. Fruchtenbaum knows, asks, "How does a passage fit into the total pattern of God's revelation that was revealed *prior* to its writing?" Prior to Gensis 3:15 the word *māshîah* is not used; no Hebrew word with even the remotest connection to the messiah can be found in Genesis 1:1–3:15. How does Dr. Fruchtenbaum know Genesis 3:15 is about the Messiah? He imports the word from its first use of a coming messiah in Psalm 2:2. Why does Dr. Fruchtenbaum believe Genesis 3:15 is about the Messiah? Because he imports the New Testament revelation into Genesis 3:15.

> 2. How does Dr. Fruchtenbaum know Genesis 3:15 is about the Antichrist? ("… the seed of the serpent will be the Antichrist.")

This claim is even more astounding. The first time a recognizable concept of a person identified in the Revelation as the Tribulation beast, aka: Antichrist, appears in the Scripture at 2 Thessalonians 2:3–4. One might point to Christ's statement in John 5:43, "I have come in the name of my Father, and you do not receive me. If another should come in his own name, him you will receive." But that scripture is without a context or precedent to define "another coming in his own name" as the specific person Antichrist of the Tribulation. Jesus left that identification for later revelation by Paul and John.

The only time the word "antichrist" appears in Scripture is the New Testament revelation, in 1 John 2:18, 22; 4:3; 2 John 2. To identify in Genesis 3:15 the specific end times person Antichrist-beast is clearly eisegesis by Dr. Fruchtenbaum. Satan is not mentioned by name in any place in the Book of Genesis, let alone his end times minion the Antichrist-beast. At the beginning of his book Dr. Fruchtenbaum has proven himself an untrustworthy guide to the Old Testament Scripture.

Dr. Fruchtenbaum's next error appears on p. 15. "Eve clearly understood from God's words in Genesis 3:15 that the serpent will be defeated by a God-man." This is the old, and long discredited, interpretation the "woman's seed" speaks of the virgin birth, because (in that interpretation) "women do not have seed." All I have said of *zera'* prior to this point should easily dispel that notion (which is based on an inaccurate English translation of *zera'*).

The word "God-man" does not appear in any scripture in the Bible. The concept of a God-man, which is to say the incarnation of God the Son with Jesus of Nazareth, is a New Testament revelation. For example, Colossians 2:9; Philippians 2:5–8. Only by using the New Testament revelation does a New Testament believer know Psalm 2:7 speaks of the incarnation. But take away that New Testament revelation and no one, not any man or any fallen angel, knew the Messiah would be deity incarnate. Because this issue is important to understand, I have included an appendix on the subject, "Who Knew Jesus was God Incarnate?"

What did Eve understand from Genesis 3:15? Dr. Fruchtenbaum also ignores the Analogy of Faith, which asks, "How does a passage fit into the total pattern of God's revelation that has been revealed at any time?" I have mentioned several times the only scriptures that reference Genesis 3:15 are Genesis 4:25; Romans 16:20; Revelation

12:9. Genesis 4:25 is Eve's own commentary on her understanding of Genesis 3:15.

> Genesis 4:25 (ESV), And Adam knew his wife again, and she bore a son and called his name Seth, for she said, "God has appointed for me another offspring instead of Abel, for Cain killed him."

Eve clearly names Abel and Seth as her *zera'*, offspring, using the exact same word and concept she heard God say in Genesis 3:15. Not a God-man, not a Messiah, not a redeemer, but two normal children born the normal way. Should we not take Eve at her word? Does not the Literal hermeneutic counsel us to take Eve at her word? Isn't taking Eve at her word authorial intent? Yes, yes, and yes.

Dr. Fruchtenbaum also ignores that neither Eve, nor Moses, nor the Holy Spirit, nor any other biblical writer, Old or New Testament, names Cain as her offspring. He was her physical offspring, but no scripture identifies Cain as "the Woman's offspring" of Genesis 3:15, as she does for Abel and Seth. You can validate this for yourself. All the biblical mentions of Cain are in Genesis 4; Hebrews 11; 1 John 3; and Jude. The implication is that Cain, one of her physical offspring, is one of the serpent's offspring, because Cain was a man of no faith. By using the Analogy of Faith we are able to validate that interpretation with this inspired information.

> 1 John 3:12, Not as Cain, who was out of the evildoer.

With Eve's interpretation of Genesis 3:15 in 4:25, the meaning of 3:15 becomes clearer—that is the way the Literal hermeneutic works. All the offspring in Genesis 3:15 are the Woman's offspring, but some are of faith, like Abel and Seth, and some are of no faith, like Cain, and there will be conflict between the two kinds of offspring. Again using the Analogy of Faith, Genesis 4:25 and Romans 16:20 validates the conflict view of Genesis 3:15, as does 1 John 3:12.

Dr. Fruchtenbaum [15] tries to shore up his messianic interpretation of Genesis 3:15 by translating Genesis 4:1 in this manner.

> And the man knew Eve his wife, she conceived and bare Cain and said, "I have gotten a man: Jehovah."

I very briefly addressed this scripture in the section for Dr. Kaiser.

Between the Hebrew word for man and the Hebrew word *YHWH* is the preposition *'ēt*. The proper translation of *'ēt* is "from" [Harris et al., s. v. 187]. Dr. Fruchtenbaum ignores this preposition in his translation, even though he knows it is there, because he has reproduced the Hebrew text in the book. Genesis 4:1 should be translated.

> And the man knew Eve his wife, she conceived and bare Cain and said, "I have gotten a man from YHWH."

But once one starts down the dark path ignoring the Literal hermeneutic, and interprets the Old Testament revelation apart from its context, any kind of interpretation is possible. For example, the serpent's seed is the Tribulation Antichrist.

Dr. Fruchtenbaum cannot make his case that Genesis 3:15 is messianic by using the Old Testament revelation.

Though not directly related to the subject of this book, Dr. Fruchtenbaum makes another error I must address. He gives Satan foreknowledge of future events. On p. 17, he wrote,

> In order to try to corrupt the Seed of the Woman at Satan's command, fallen evil angels, "the Sons of God," intermarry with human women, foreshadowing the supernatural conception of the Antichrist also indicated in Genesis 3:15.

> [Dr. Fruchtenbaum, an Old Testament scholar and Hebrew language linguist, knows *zera'* does not mean "seed' when speaking of human beings.]

First, in no Scripture in the entire Bible, from Genesis 1:1 to Revelation 22:21, is the Antichrist said to be supernaturally conceived. I have thoroughly studied all Scripture has to say about the end times Antichrist-beast. What Dr. Fruchtenbaum states is pure fiction, a child of imagination not Scripture. See my book *Antichrist, His Genealogy, Kingdom, and Religion*, where every possible Scripture reference to the Antichrist is examined. The man who becomes the Antichrist-beast is just another human being brought by Satan to a position of power, as Satan's visible and worshiped surrogate during the Tribulation.

The main issue in the quote is Dr. Fruchtenbaum has given Satan knowledge of the future. Satan is a created being. He has no clue what God has planned for the future. Satan has zero spiritual perception. He is intelligent, and can calculate many possibilities and prepare many contingency plans. But he receives no grace from God, and he absolutely lacks all spiritual perception. There is nothing in Genesis 3:15 pointing to a future Messiah or a future Antichrist. Satan knew YHWH was talking about him in Genesis 3:14–15, which we know from Revelation 12:9, but he did not and could not and does not know the future. His response to Genesis 3:15 was to act normally—a completely corrupt sinner totally lacking the influence of God's grace—and tempt humankind to commit the very conflict among human beings God prophesied.

A secondary issue is how Dr. Fruchtenbaum has influenced other Dispensationalists concerning Genesis 6:2. Satan did not command fallen evil angels to intermarry with human women. This is a Jewish interpretation originating in intertestamental times, reflected in the translation of *nᵉpîlîm* as "giants" in the LXX, ca. 250 BC.

Because Dr. Fruchtenbaum's interpretation predominates the modern interpretation of Genesis 6:2. I feel I must completely refute that false interpretation through an explanation of Genesis 6:2 using the Literal hermeneutic. I have placed that refutation in an appendix, "Adam's Unbelieving Descendants."

Charles C. Ryrie (1925–2016)

Dr, Ryrie was a leader in modern Dispensationalism, and his book *Dispensationalism*, in any of its three editions, is must reading. So is his book *Basic Theology*. In that book Dr. Ryrie addresses Genesis 3:15, on pp. 234–235. His comments under heading "C. On Satan (Gen. 3:15)," are pertinent to this discussion. Emphasis is Ryrie's.

> 1. *Satan's seed and the Woman's seed*. Enmity will exist between Satan's seed (all the lost, John 8:44; Eph. 2:2) and the Woman's seed (all the family of God).

Dr. Ryrie is right in identifying Satan's offspring as all the lost, and the Woman's offspring as all the saved, but it is regrettable he was not able to identify the scripture that makes that identification plain, Genesis 4:25. His Ephesians 2:2 reference is not contextually close to Genesis 3:15.

Dr. Ryrie has a second point.

> 2. *Death for Satan; bruise for Christ*. An individual from the woman's seed (Jesus Christ) will deal a death blow to Satan's

head at the cross (Hebrews 2:14; 1 John 3:8) while Satan will cause Christ to suffer ("bruise his heel, KJV). Pre-Christian Jews showed a "veiled acceptance of messianic idea in Genesis 3:15."

Dr. Ryrie references the quote ("veiled acceptance of messianic idea in Genesis 3:15") to David Baron, *Rays of Messiah's Glory.* Let me begin with the actual words of David Baron. I will give the quote in its context. I have italicized the part Ryrie says he quoted, but actually paraphrased, to support his theology. Mr. Baron wrote.

> The prophets teach two advents of the same Messiah—not two Messiahs, a theory in which the Rabbins have taken refuge from their perplexity in not being able to reconcile the prophecies which speak of Messiah's suffering and humiliation with those which speak of His kingdom and glory, and under the cloke [*sic*] of which we detect a *partial acknowledgement of the claims of Jesus of Nazareth*.

When Mr. Baron wrote, "the Rabbins," he is not speaking of the Old Testament revelation. What Dr. Ryrie does not tell the reader is Mr. Baron is not reporting what the Old Testament saints thought, but what Jews thought after the Old Testament canon was competed. Ryrie's "pre-Christian Jews" are not Old Testament biblical sources from the Hebrews in the Old Testament, but Jewish literature that began about 200 years after the last book in the Old Testament was written, and continuing throughout the intertestamental period.

Moreover, Mr. Baron is not saying the Rabbins gave a "partial acknowledgment" of "the claims of Jesus of Nazareth," but that he, Mr. Baron, thought he detected a "partial acknowledgement" in his opinion of their writings. As to Dr. Ryrie, having read many quotes given by many theologians and exegetes, I have learned to follow that best of policies, go read the source.

As to the Old Testament saints, all we have to do is read the Old Testament Scripture, and understand it in its plain and normal meaning, to discover the Old Testament saints *did not* have a veiled or seminal type of messianic idea from Genesis 3:15. To give the Old Testament saints that understanding, one must supplement their Old Testament scriptures with information from the New Testament.

Dr. Ryrie makes the same unwarranted assumption as others: "Death for Satan; bruise for Christ." As I have previously discussed, just the opposite happened. Contrary to Ryrie, Satan arranged the murder of Jesus, not his bruising. Contrary to Ryrie, Satan is not dead but is alive and well after the crucifixion that led to Jesus' death.

In previous discussions I said the coordinating conjunction "and" in "he [woman's seed] will *shûp* your [serpent's seed] head and you [serpent's seed] will *shûp* his [woman's seed] heel, requires the action performed by each subject to be equivalent. I did not create that grammatical rule, but actually learned it from Ryrie, in his book *The Basis of Premillennial Faith*, 68–69, commenting on Galatians 6:16.

> The apostle is singling out believing Jews in this benediction pronounced upon the entire body of Christ, which, of course, includes these Jews . . . It is another indication that Gentile and Jewish believers are on the same level since the conjunction [and] links coordinate parts of the sentence.

Ryrie learned from Ellicott, the biblical Greek scholar: "the simple copulative [and] meaning seems more probable" [Ryrie, *Premillennial*, 68–69].

Why did Ryrie not apply that same understanding to the simple copulative in Genesis 3:15? Because of the influence Reformed soteriology has had on Dispensationalists.

Ryrie references two scriptures, "An individual from the woman's seed (Jesus Christ) will deal a death blow to Satan's head at the cross (Hebrews 2:14; 1 John 3:8) while Satan will cause Christ to suffer ("bruise his heel, KJV)."

Hebrews 2:14 is one of those scriptures where good exegetes seem to forget their theology.

> Since, therefore, the children have partaken of blood and of flesh also, he in like manner shared in the same things, so that through death he might render ineffective the one holding the power of death, that is, the Devil

Only God has the authority and power of life and death. How then did Christ by his death "render ineffective" the Devil, and what was the "power of death" held by the Devil? The word I have translated "might render ineffective," is *katargéō* [Zodhiates, s. v. 2673] in the aorist tense subjunctive mood. Zodhiates gives this definition: "to render inactive, idle, useless, ineffective," and states this about its use in

Hebrews 2:14, "the *kata* gives to the intransitive *argéō* the transitive meaning of to make to cease," Notice, not to make to cease existing, not to destroy, but "cessation from outward activity." Satan was not destroyed, he was rendered ineffective. The salvation of a sinner renders Satan's power of temptation ineffective in the born-again believer.

What, then, was the "power of death" held by the Devil? The explanation requires a longish quote from my commentary on Hebrews.

> Through his death, Christ destroyed him who was holding the power of death. The word choice by the Writer is deliberate. The devil (Satan) does not "have" the power of death (many versions) as though death originated with him. Only God has the power of death. The Devil in some fashion holds the power of death, meaning in some way he uses death. Through his work on the cross Jesus Christ rendered the use of death ineffective for those whom he has saved.

> What is in view in 2:14 is spiritual death that continues into physical death. The power of physical death is that it permanently separates the lost unsaved soul from God. There is no salvation beyond physical death; salvation is to be gained only in this present physical life. The unsaved are spiritually dead—separated from God, and at physical death that state continues for all eternity. Hence the need to be saved now, today, because physical death may come in any form at any moment, sealing the soul into its spiritual state for all eternity.

> The Savior experienced both a spiritual and a physical death in order that the power of death is rendered ineffective for those who are his brethren. Jesus used his death as a means of destroying the maliciousness of death.

> The devil is said to hold the power of death for two reasons. One, his self-origination of sin into God's creation caused the penalty of death to be applied. God did not create death because the devil sinned. God's moral law is an expression of his righteous character. Before the universe came into existence his law required death as the consequence for sin.

> The Devil is not the one who directly brings either spiritual or physical death to individual sinners—he is not the angel of

death. Death is the consequence of breaking God's moral law, God applies the penalty, not Satan. But Satan has the power of temptation to sin—it really is his only power—and through temptation human beings commit acts of sinning. This is the second reason Satan is said to hold the power of death, his power of temptation.

Jesus render ineffective the power of both spiritual and physical death. The word translated "rendered ineffective" is *katargéō*, a word meaning "to render inactive, or ineffective." Jesus did not immediately eliminate death in all its aspects. He immediately rendered inactive the power of spiritual death for those who have faith in God's plan of salvation. Physical death still exists for the believer, but that is because the material body is not redeemed (but Ephesians 1:14); the body remains corrupted by sin, therefore still subject to the physical penalty of sin.

But sin's power to separate the soul from God has been rendered inactive toward the believer. And physical death has become the believer's entrance into God's immediate presence in heaven, and it is the way in which God removes the sin resident in the believer's human nature.

Was the devil himself "rendered ineffective" when Jesus propitiated the guilt of sin through his death? In the immediate sense, only partially. Satan exercises the power of death in that he is actively working in the world to persuade men to rebel against God. He is actively working to hide the truth of the Gospel (2 Corinthians 4:3–4). He is actively working to cause the physical death of unsaved men, because physical death will confirm their state of spiritual death. In this we see that death is not a power Satan possesses, but is a spiritual and physical condition that he tirelessly tries to apply to all mankind through his power of temptation.

Since the power of death was rendered ineffective by Christ's crucifixion and resurrection (for those who are saved), in that sense it may be said that the Devil, whose act of sinning and subsequent acts of temptation caused the law of death to be applied, has been rendered ineffective. Satan continues to tempt to sin, but he is ineffective, because 1) the believer's born-again human nature has been spiritually empowered to say "No," to temptation, and enforce the decision, and 2) spiritual death can no longer separate the believer from God, and 3) the power of physical death to lock the person into an unsaved state cannot affect the believer.

The meaning of Hebrews 2:14 is Jesus delivers believers from the penalty of sin and the power of sin. See *A Private Commentary on the Book of Hebrews* for additional commentary.

Ryrie also uses 1 John 3:8 to support his contention "the woman's seed (Jesus Christ) will deal a death blow to Satan's head at the cross."

1 John 3:8, The person habitually practicing sin is from the Devil, because from the beginning the Devil has been sinning. For this purpose the Son of God was revealed: that he might destroy the works of the Devil.

Again we see the English word "destroy," and again it does not mean "a death blow," as Ryrie wants to interpret the word. The word here is *lúō* [Zodhiates, s. v. 3089]. The word means "to loose, loosen what is fast, bound, meaning to unbind, untie." In 1 John 3:8 *lúō* is used in a figurative sense, to loosen the power of sin on the believer, so that the believer is not "habitually practicing sin," even as 1 John 3:9 says, "Every person who had been born from God does not habitually practice sin, because his [God's] seed abides in him." (See my commentary on John's Epistles for further discussion.)

Ryrie says, "Satan will cause Christ to suffer ("bruise his heel KJV)." Is that what God meant in Genesis 3:15. Did God say in Genesis 3:15 that Satan would cause Christ to suffer? No, that is not said in Genesis 3:15—at least when seeking authorial intent through the Literal hermeneutic, a hermeneutic which Ryrie said is one of the three "without which nothing" (*sine qua non*) essentials of Dispensationalism.

Who really caused Christ to suffer?

Isaiah 53:4 (ESV), Surely he has borne our griefs and carried our sorrows; yet we esteemed him stricken, smitten by God, and afflicted.

Isaiah 53:10 (ESV), Yet it was the will of the Lord to crush him; he has put him to grief; when his soul makes an offering for sin, he shall see his offspring; he shall prolong his days; the will of the Lord shall prosper in his hand.

Matthew 27:46, Now about midafternoon Jesus cried out with a loud voice, saying, "Eli, Eli, lama sabachthani?" that is, "My God, my God, why have You forsaken me?"

Acts 2:23, Him [Jesus], by the determinate counsel and foreknowledge of God, delivered by lawless hands, having crucified, you [the lawless hands of men] put to death.

2 Corinthians 5:21, The one not having known sin [Jesus Christ], God made to be sin for us [human beings], so that we might become the righteousness of God in him [Christ].

The correct doctrine is God caused Christ to suffer.

Ryrie's Genesis 3:15 interpretation and theology is seen to be the same Reformed soteriology as others holding to Promise soteriology.

Conclusion And Summary

There can be little doubt God promised a Messiah-King to national ethnic Israel, e.g., Genesis 49:10; 2 Samuel 7:13–16; Psalm 2. There is also little doubt God promised a Messiah-Redeemer, Genesis 12:3; 21:12; Daniel 9:26, which no one understood. The two lines of prophecy seemed contradictory; how could the king die? Genesis 12:3; 21:12 were interpreted by the Old Testament peoples and their descendants during the intertestamental period as belonging to the Messiah-King. Daniel 9:26 was not understood.

I have mentioned there is no Old Testament or New Testament reference to Daniel 9:26. The LXX translates Daniel 9:26 in this way [Brenton, 1044], "And after the sixty-two weeks, the anointed one shall be destroyed, and there is no judgment in him." The passage is not in the recovered manuscripts forming the *Dead Sea Scrolls* (Daniel 9 ends at 9:17). The Apocrypha also have nothing to say about the biblical Daniel. There are no scriptures from the Book of Daniel in the Mishnah. There is no mention of Daniel 9:26 in the Babylonian Talmud. My resources are limited, but as much I am able to determine, no Jewish literature comments on Daniel 9:26.

The resolution of all the messianic prophecies, which is the two advents, was not apparent to the Old Testament peoples, because two advents is a New Testament revelation. As Schurer said, they were looking for a king to redeem them from oppression, not a redeemer for the penalty of sin. Every time a Dispensationalist believer in Promise soteriology attempts to prove the Old Testament people understood a promised Messiah-Redeemer from sin, he must turn to the New Testament revelation for support. When they do turn to the Old Testament revelation, the meaning is expanded beyond the plain and normal sense of the language and words. In the Old Testament YHWH was the Savior, not a coming redeemer.

For example, in the Abrahamic covenant, YHWH states, "In you" i.e., in Abraham, not in a yet future redeemer from sin, "all the families of earth shall be blessed." In Genesis 12:3, YHWH's blessing is in an unstated and therefore unknown manner, through Abraham, not through someone yet to come. In later revelation Abraham is blessed through an heir from his own body, whom we later discover to be Isaac, in whom the covenant is established, and through whom we know from New Testament revelation is the heir receiving all the promises, Jesus of Nazareth, Galatians 3:16.

The New Testament teaches us the blessing was through Abraham's faith. Promise soteriology is only too happy use the New Testament revelation to define the cause of that blessing as Jesus Christ, and then loudly proclaim, "See, right there in the Old Testament revelation we find the promise of a redeemer from sin," which is incorrect, because Genesis 12:3 *does not say* what that blessing is to be, nor how that blessing is to be achieved. We only know Genesis 12:3 is about Christ because of the New Testament revelation of Galatians 3:8.

When God gave Abraham Genesis 12:3, Abraham did not know how that promise would be fulfilled. Dare we give Abraham more knowledge than God gave him? Abraham did know later, Genesis 15:4-6, when God promised him an heir, and knew more a few years later, Genesis 17:19, when God affirmed that heir; the historical narrative reveals that heir was Isaac. When did God name the ultimate heir of Abraham who would receive all the promises and fulfill the all the prophecies? If Matthew's Gospel was the first written, then Matthew 1:1–16. Only then did anyone know Jesus of Nazareth was Abraham's heir. Dare we give Abraham that knowledge? Mariam knew, or could have worked it out, Luke 1:32–33, for she would have known her genealogy, Luke 3:34. Dare we be smarter than God and give Abraham that knowledge? Yet, some do.

In Genesis 3:15 God did not mention a redeemer or Satan. Eve confirms that in Genesis 4:25. So does the rest of the Old Testament revelation. Yet many discover a redeemer and Satan in Genesis 3:15 where absolutely no Old Testament Scripture, and only one New Testament Scripture, places only Satan, not also a redeemer. Then why give Adam and the Woman an understanding that transcends the written revelation? An understanding God did not give to them.

Dr. Fruchtenbaum, and others, have brilliantly revealed that with the New Testament revelation in hand many Old Testament scriptures may be understood as messianic. But they miss the key point—the point with which Dr. Fruchtenbaum begins his book. "We have a tendency to read back into the Old Testament a level of New Testament understanding which did not exist in those days." A wise warning that he and others have choosen to ignore.

Without the New Testament revelation, which Adam, Eve, Enoch, Noah, Abraham, and all their descendants did not have—which no one in Old Testament times possessed—without the New Testament revelation there is no redeemer or Satan in Genesis 3:15. No Old or New Testament revelation states, hints, alludes to, or implies there is a redeemer in Genesis 3:15. Satan in Genesis 3:15? Yes, as the power behind the serpent, Romans 16:20; Revelation 12:9, but *obviously* that information *was not available* to any person in the Old Testament. Why then do some give Adam and the Woman an understanding God did not give to them?

Adam and Eve are told there will be continuing conflict, and not many years later experienced the first act of the conflict. Abraham receives the first promise of a coming redeemer—we only know that from Galatians 3:8—but not how, and certainly not in whom, the blessing will come, not even that there will be a redeemer from sin, someday, in the very far future yet to come. Just that there will be a blessing through Abraham. Why then do some insist on giving Abraham more understanding that God gave him?

Were the Old Testament peoples given progressive revelation of a coming redeemer from sin? At Genesis 12:3 Abraham is told he himself will bless all the families of the earth, not a coming redeemer. At

Genesis 15:4–6, Abraham is told his heir would be "one who will come from his own body," later clarified as Isaac, Genesis 17:18, 21; but not a coming redeemer.

Isaac passes the promises to his son Jacob, but does not mention a coming redeemer. Jacob passes the promised inheritance in the land to his sons, and to Judah, Genesis 49:10, is given the first notice of a coming King. But absolutely nothing is said about a coming redeemer. And then talk of a coming king ceases, for about 650 years, until 2 Samuel 7:13–16, which also says nothing about a coming redeemer.

And so it goes until the New Testament revelation identifies Jesus of Nazareth as the Christ, and the apostles identify Jesus the Christ as the Redeemer of sinners. And one apostle, Paul, identifies the Christ as the fulfillment of the promises made to Abraham. Until then no one could understand Genesis 12:3 as the promise of a future redeemer from sin to bless all families of the earth. No one in the Old Testament saw a specific redeemer from sin in Genesis 3:15—I have read the written record cover to cover—because God the Holy Spirit did not put that information into that scripture, not in any scripture, in the Old and New Testaments.. One cannot get to Christ the Redeemer using Genesis 3:15—if one properly uses the Literal hermeneutic.

Therefore, after carefully reviewing the Old Testament Scripture (much more carefully than outlined here) I find it difficult in the extreme to validate the Promise soteriology claim that a coming redeemer from sin was revealed progressively, to Israel, through the Old Testament Scripture, beginning with Genesis 3:15. Once Genesis is invalidated as teaching a coming redeemer-messiah-christ, both Reformed and Dispensational Promise soteriology fall. That is why each group holds onto their presuppositions like a corpse in rigor mortis. My hope and prayer is some are reborn to understanding through this book. That is why I have tried to "explain the way of God more accurately."

Summarizing

Dispensational Promise soteriology is able to find their promise of a Redeemer from sin throughout the Old Testament by using the New Testament revelation to illuminate what the Old Testament peoples could not know. Did the Old Testament revelation have meaning for the Old Testament peoples within their historical-cultural contexts? Or does the Old Testament revelation only become meaningful with the addition of the New Testament revelation? The Literal hermeneutic says within their own historical-cultural contexts. Other hermeneutical methods say only meaningful with the addition of the New Testament revelation. Sadly, one must include Dispensational Promise soteriology in the latter camp.

We saw one Dispensationalist state Adam and Eve and all their descendants had to receive verbal revelation of a promised "seed" in Genesis 3:15 to redeem them from their sins, because the Old Testament revelation was not yet written. But was it not written by Moses, who told us what God said? If we see accurately and exactly what God said in what Moses wrote, is that not the inspired written record? Is it not written Scripture? When did verbal revelation become Scripture? Answer: unknown verbal revelation has by the alchemy of allegory and eisegesis become Scripture in Reformed and Promise soteriology.

The Promise soteriology Dispensationalists learned the hermeneutical method of transcending the Old Testament by the New Testament from Reformed hermeneutics. In other distinctive dispensational doctrines it is the Literal hermeneutic all the way, but when arriving at soteriology, the "Promise" Dispensationalists abandon their principles for Reformed hermeneutics. Those Dispensationalists should be honest and call their Promise soteriology what it really is: the Reformed soteriology that makes Jesus the Christ the Old Testament object and content of saving faith.

Final Discussion

To close this chapter, my Dispensational Promise soteriology friend, Dr. Keith A. Sherlin (to whom I have dedicated this book) asked me to properly represent Dispensational Promise soteriology. I assured him I had. But just to make sure, here (again) is Dr. Sherlin's description of Promise soteriology.

> Promise soteriology is "the view that the Old Testament believers believed a coming redeemer/deliverer that would crush the head of the serpent, a symbol of Satan, but did not have all of the details then & only understood as much as was revealed progressively through eras of history until the full picture was revealed in the New Testament."

Just as I have done with other Dispensational theologians, I will analyze Dr. Sherlin's Promise soteriology,

Dr. Keith A. Sherlin (1974–)

Dr. Sherlin is well educated in Scripture and theology, holding a ThD and two PhDs, one in theology and one in philosophy, with an emphasis on the history of Christian theology. He is a professor and also dean of students at Tyndale Theological Seminary. My communication with Dr. Sherlin is through his "Christicommunity" Facebook (FB) group, FB DM, video links, and personal email, and as copyeditor for a PhD dissertation and a book. We have had many discussions of theology, including the topic of this book.

Dr. Sherlin's description (above) identifies the essential problem with Dispensational Promise soteriology. The problem is hermeneutical: where does the Promise soteriology view of "a coming redeemer/deliverer that would crush the head of the serpent, a symbol of Satan" come from? Dr. Sherlin does as other advocates of Promise soteriology must do—as this chapter has made clear by quoting their works—he points to Genesis 3:15 as the beginning of the promise, without a shred of Old Testament proof. He transcends the Old Testament revelation with the New Testament revelation. He gives knowledge of a coming redeemer to Adam and Eve from Genesis 3:15.

Let us set aside for a moment "a coming redeemer/deliverer" and focus on the identification of "the serpent, a symbol of Satan." How does Dr. Sherlin know the serpent is a symbol of Satan? The Old Testament revelation told the Old Testament peoples a serpent was a symbol of evil. That much is clear from the Genesis 3:1–5 passage, and the Numbers 21:4–9 passage, and confirmed by later New Testament revelation, John 3:1–4.

However, no Old Testament revelation identifies the serpent in Genesis 3:15 as Satan. To the contrary, Eve identifies Abel and Seth as her offspring, but does not identify Cain as her offspring, leaving only one option, that Cain is the serpent's offspring. As a symbol of evil, the serpent's offspring in Genesis 3:15 represents Eve's descendants of no faith. That Literal hermeneutic, within context interpretation, conforms to both the Analogy of Scripture and the Analogy of Faith. That Literal hermeneutic, within context interpretation, eliminates the Reformed and Promise soteriology interpretation that the serpent in Genesis was known as a symbol of Satan by the Old Testament peoples; at least not known through the written Scripture they had received from YHWH. Later revelation confirms that analysis, 1 John 3:12, Cain is of the evil one. The serpent's offspring are the Woman's literal offspring who possess the serpent's spiritual characteristic of no faith.

Not until many thousands of years after Genesis 3:15 does God inform his saved people that Satan is the serpent of the beginning, Revelation 12:9. Dispensational Promise soteriology gives God's progressive revelation a new beginning, by moving Revelation 12:9 to Genesis 3:15 to inform Adam and Eve and all their Old Testament descendants that Satan is the serpent of the beginning.

Why is the above analysis important? Because Genesis 3:15 is not merely the cornerstone of the Old Testament salvific edifice built by Reformed soteriology. Genesis 3:15 is also the foundation on which Dispensational Promise soteriology has been built. Whatever later Old Testament revelation that Dispensational Promise soteriology proposes as informing the Old Testament peoples of a coming redeemer, that later revelation is said to be sensible of a coming redeemer, only because Promise soteriology says Adam and Eve, upon hearing God, were given the understanding, according to Dispensational Promise soteriology, that "the serpent [is] a symbol of Satan." No.

I have shown through a brief review of the passing of the promise to Abraham's heirs through Isaac, that Genesis 3:15 was not part of the promises God made to Abraham. Nor to Noah and his family before Abraham. They were the heirs and the transmitters of all prior revelation. Some may say, "They did it verbally," but if it isn't written, it isn't Scripture; we know what was Scripture for Noah and his family, because God through Moses told us.

I have shown the only way any Old Testament person could have known with certainty the serpent symbolized Satan, thousands before that information was revealed, is by extrabiblical revelation or illumination. Some in the Old Testament might have made a supposition, using scriptures in Job, Isaiah, 1 Chronicles, Ezekiel, and Zechariah, but no one could know with certainty that Satan was the evil power behind the serpent until Revelation 12:9.

I have shown the only way Reformed and Promise soteriology can find a coming redeemer-messiah-christ in Genesis 3:15 is to bring him with them, to transcend the primary meaning of that Old Testament scripture with New Testament revelation.

Of course, once the identification of Satan is confirmed, then the identification of the Woman's offspring as "a coming redeemer/deliverer" is an easy next step, because once again the answer is supplied by reading New Testament revelation into Genesis 3:15, and then "discovering" the salvific doctrine in the supposed first gospel proclamation.

Please, tell me again how Dispensational Promise soteriology is different from Reformed soteriology. I am not convinced by either their protestations or by the Scripture.

When Genesis 3:15 is read and interpreted within its own historical, lexical, syntactical, contextual, and literary context, there is no redeemer or Satan in Genesis 3:15. No Old Testament Scripture says otherwise. Everyone claiming differently knows this to be true, because they one and all appeal to the New Testament revelation to discover a coming redeemer and Satan in Genesis 3:15.

Dr. Sherlin describes Reformed Soteriology as "those who think the Old Testament believers had the same level of understanding about salvation as the New Testament believers." But by defining Promise soteriology as a promise in Genesis 3:15 that a redeemer is coming to crush the head of Satan, Dr. Sherlin has given his Old Testament believer an understanding of salvation based in New Testament revelation, not Old Testament revelation.

Both Dispensational Promise and Reformed soteriology begin at the same place: a coming redeemer-messiah-christ to crush the head of Satan and thereby redeem sinners from the penalty of sin. As I discussed in chapter "Genesis 3:15," this interpretation is not an exegesis of the verse using the Literal hermeneutic. All Dispensationalists affirm they must use the Literal hermeneutic to interpret Scripture. Why then abandon the Literal hermeneutic at Genesis 3:15?

I have also discussed that the Reformed-Promise interpretation disregards the fact that redemption from sin has nothing to do with Christ crushing Satan. Redemption from sin is Christ satisfying God's holiness and justice for the crime of sin. God crushes Christ—Christ dies for our sin—Christ does not crush Satan, who has nothing to do with our redemption. Satan was and is neither more nor less than an instrument, a tool, whom God allowed to act according to his sinful nature, thereby motivating human beings to crucify Christ, Acts 2:23, thereby placing the Christ exactly where God wanted him to be, so God could justly and publicly crush him as justice for the imputed crimes of human sin.

Dispensationalists claiming a Promised Seed soteriology think to distinguish their soteriology from Reformed soteriology by claiming their Old Testament believer knew a little less than Reformed Old Testament believers, and therefore their soteriology is different. It is not. For both soteriologies the foundation is a New Testament interpretation of Genesis 3:15. Both inject New Testament revelation into Old Testament revelation to give their believer understanding he could not have gained from the Old Testament revelation God delivered to the Old Testament believer. In a word, Dispensational Promise soteriology is as much extrabiblical revelation and illumination as Reformed soteriology. As I have labored to show throughout this book, that is not Dispensational soteriology.

Dr. Sherlin and I are good friends, bound together by the essentials of the Christian faith. We disagree on the means by which God informed the Old Testament sinner of the way of salvation. In all other aspects of soteriology we are in full agreement.

I intend to demonstrate in the next chapter, from Scripture and by reasonable argument, the genuine Dispensational soteriology.

Dispensational Soteriology

Introduction

Three propositions

Proposition one. The Holy Spirit knows more than he reveals.

Proposition two. The Holy Spirit chose to reveal to some less than he revealed to others.

Proposition Three. During the progress of time the Holy Spirit revealed all that needs revealing.

Those propositions support what is called the progressive revelation of truth. The omniscient God the Holy Spirit knows the end from the beginning, so from the beginning he knew all the revelation he intended to give to humankind. But from the beginning the Holy Spirit chose to give that revelation a little here and a little there, from time to time, through chosen men, until he had revealed all he chose to reveal. The result of that progressive revelation of truth in relation to soteriology is just this.

No one could know the entire story of redemption until all the revelation was given.

Throughout Old Testament times—the times before Christ's crucifixion-resurrection-ascension—God redeemed sinners through the revelation he had given from time to time, a little here and a little there.

What the Holy Spirit had revealed at any one time during Old Testament times was sufficient to redeem sinners at any time.

Dispensationalism, through the Literal hermeneutic—which is the solid foundation for all Dispensational theology—recognizes and works with those limitations intrinsic to God's Old Testament and New Testament revelation. If it is genuine Dispensationalism. That does not mean (as is sometimes falsely asserted) the Old Testament has no meaning for New Testament believers. It means the Old Testament is to be interpreted within its historical context at any one time. It means the Old Testament had meaning for the Old Testament peoples without the New Testament revelation. It means the primary meaning of any Bible passage is to be found in that passage.

The foundation of the New Testament revelation is the Old

Testament revelation, but the Old Testament revelation, being the foundation, exists without the structure built upon it, which is the New Testament revelation. Therefore, one is able to understand the Old Testament revelation without resorting to the New Testament revelation for understanding. An interpretation of the Old Testament revelation that consists of New Testament truths is eisegesis, not exegesis. An interpretation of the New Testament revelation that does not include Old Testament truth is incomplete exegesis.

Those simple, reasonable, rational principles stated above are the basis for an Old Testament soteriology that does not look to the New Testament to find "a coming redeemer/deliverer that would crush the head of the serpent, a symbol of Satan" in Genesis 3:15, but instead depends on what was actually revealed to the Old Testament peoples, without restoring to the eisegesis that inserts New Testament truths into the Old Testament revelation.

No one could know the entire story of redemption until all the revelation was given. Throughout Old Testament times—the times before Christ's crucifixion-resurrection-ascension—God redeemed sinners through the revelation he had given. Practical impact? Genesis 3:15, occurring at the beginning of the Old Testament revelation, was not intended to be the New Testament revelation of redemption from the penalty due sin.

No Old Testament person could discover a redeemer-messiah-christ in Genesis 3:15, because the Holy Spirit did not put that revelation into the Genesis 3:15 message. The New Testament must not be used to reinterpret or transcend Old Testament passages in a way that overrides or cancels the original authorial intent of the Old Testament writers.

Perhaps in simpler terms, we know now because we have the New Testament revelation; they did not know then because they did not have the New Testament revelation. To say they knew is to reinterpret their revelation with our revelation—the very definition of eisegesis: to read into the text what the interpreter wishes to find.

For the Dispensationalist the Literal hermeneutic is bedrock, a firm foundation on which to build. Except in soteriology, it seems, for some.

The Holy Spirit did not supplement his written Old Testament revelation with unwritten revelation or illumination. The Holy Spirit did not give the Old Testament sinner a New Testament understanding of the Old Testament Scripture.

What, then, is genuine Dispensational soteriology?

> In every dispensation, in every age of humankind, in the entire history of redemption, a sinner is always saved by God's grace and the merit of Christ's propitiation, through the sinner's faith in God and God's historically current testimony as to the means of salvation, as given by the Holy Spirit in the written progressive revelation of truth.

That is the definition of genuine Dispensational soteriology, a definition that correctly describes the way salvation has been accessed by any sinner saved from Genesis through Revelation.

What has God Revealed, and Why?

The question has never been what God knows, but "What has God chosen to reveal?" It is like the oft repeated mantra "God can do anything." Yes, of course, God is omniscient and omnipotent. But the genuine issue is not what God can do, but what does God chose to do?

To answer the question, "What has God chosen to reveal," we can use our imagination—eisegesis, an allegorical and spiritualizing method, a presuppositional Messianic hermeneutic, the Christocentric hermeneutic misapplied—or we can seek the plain and normal meaning of the Scripture using the Literal hermeneutic. Only the Literal hermeneutic leads the New Testament interpreter to discover the same "what does it mean" as the Old Testament person understood the scriptures given to him or her within their particular historical-cultural context.

In choosing a biblical hermeneutic by which to develop an Old Testament soteriology, you must answer this question. Did God by an unwritten revelation or illumination save some Old Testament sinners? Reformed and Promise soteriology yell out a resounding "Yes!" every time the advocates of those soteriologies discover a coming redeemer-messiah-christ in an Old Testament passage that says nothing about redemption from sin by a coming redeemer-messiah-christ.

I prefer to base my understanding on principles derived from the Scripture and then applied to the Scripture. So rather than try to meet individual scriptures some might use as proof of the Reformed and

Promise soteriology proposition, I will use general principles of interpretation that cover all Scripture—for if the principle is sound, then what one might think are exceptions to the principle, are not.

As I study the Scripture, I find two principles. The first is to seek the plain and normal meaning of the language and words of Scripture. In an earlier chapter I gave several examples: Moses understood the universe and the world he inhabited was literally created and formed in seven sunset-to-sunset days. Abraham literally understood God's command to sacrifice Isaac. Jesus chose to interpret the creation narrative and the Jonah narrative literally.

The second principle needs no more proof than everyday experience: no one can know what has not yet been revealed. Put another way, Scripture can never mean what it never meant. Therefore, another principle. If the interpretation is not sound, then all the fruit derived from that interpretation is unsound. Genesis 3:15 never meant a coming redeemer from sin, and therefore no one was saved in Old Testament times by faith in a coming redeemer from sin, but by faith in the ever-present Redeemer, YHWH.

I believe the quote below applies the principles stated above.

> We believe that according to the "eternal purpose" of God (Ephesians 3:11) salvation in the divine reckoning is always "by grace through faith," and rests upon the shed blood of Christ. We believe that God has always been gracious, regardless of the ruling dispensation, but that man has not at all times been under an administration or stewardship of grace as is true in the present dispensation .... We believe .... that the principle of faith was prevalent in the lives of all the Old Testament saints. However, we believe that it was historically impossible that they should have had as the conscious object of their faith the incarnate, crucified Son, the Lamb of God (John 1:29), and that it is evident that they did not comprehend as we do that the sacrifices depicted the person and work of Christ [Dallas Seminary doctrinal statement, Article V, quoted in Ryrie, *Dispensationalism,* 116].

The principles are simple: no one can know what has not yet been revealed; Scripture can never mean what it never meant.

I have previously shown a *coming, yet future* redeemer from the penalty due sin was not clearly revealed in the Old Testament. I have shown that the understanding of a coming Messiah-King did not include the understanding he would be a redeemer from the penalty due sin. I used a completely objective source not involved in the Reformed-Promise-Dispensational soteriology debate, Emil Schurer [division 2, 2:129–130].

> The older Messianic hope ... is nothing else than the hope of a better future for the *nation* .... it should be governed by a just, wise, and powerful king of the house of David.

And I used a source from Promise soteriology, Dr. Couch quoting a Jewish opinion.

> The great and respected [Hebrew] scholars, Michael Avi-Yonah and Zvi Baras have documented what the Jewish people were teaching during the time of Jesus. They were looking for the Messianic reign to begin.

And this opinion from the book, *What is Dispensationalism?*

> It would have been exceedingly difficult for someone to find the way of salvation [faith in the person Christ] in an unfinished Old Testament, since it is exceedingly difficult to find the way of salvation [faith in the person Christ] in the completed Old Testament, [Pastor Bob Bryant, in Miles, *What is Dispensationalism?*, 171].

And this opinion.

> There is no specific command to believe in a future Messiah for salvation, nor is there any mention of an Old Testament saint who put faith in a promised saviour [*sic*] for salvation. [James Meyers, quoted in Miles, *Current Issues in Soteriology*, 106.]

Others agree, and this is the reason Reformed and Promise soteriology give New Testament understanding to the Old Testament peoples. They know the limitations of the Old Testament revelation— what the Holy Spirit chose not to reveal or illuminate—and they have chosen to supplement that Holy Spirit designed limitation by giving the Old Testament people a New Testament understanding of redemption.

Not a complete New Testament understanding, at least not in Dispensational Promise soteriology, but a greater or lesser amount, depending on how each soteriology understands the consequences of the doctrine of progressive revelation. Reformed soteriology gives a nearly complete understanding to the Old Testament peoples in Genesis 3:15, from Christ the Redeemer seen in Genesis 3:15 to Christ the Redeemer seen in the sacrifices of the Mosaic Law. Dispensational Promise soteriology is more restrained, giving them a promised redeemer in Genesis 3:15 but requiring the Old Testament peoples to work it out through the progressive revelation.

Genuine Dispensational soteriology says the Holy Spirit worked with and within the amount of revelation and understanding of redemption from sin that he chose to give to each generation through his written revelation. That message did not begin with Genesis 3:15.

To put a modern twist on the Reformed and Promise explanations of Genesis 3:15, the Holy Spirit did not put a music band and flashing colored lights on the stage to help the message, he simply preached the simple message of redemption from the pulpit. Because he is the author of the message, he knows how to use it to bring sinners to salvation, as written, no help from verbal revelation or illumination needed. As a famous TV detective was wont to say, "Just the facts."

Dispensational Soteriology

Reasoning from the principle, if a coming Christ as the redeemer from the penalty due sin was not clearly revealed for their faith through the written Old Testament revelation given to the Old Testament peoples, then we are limited to two solutions.

1. Their faith and understanding resided in what the Holy Spirit revealed and illuminated through the plain and normal sense of the written Old Testament revelation.

Or,

2. Their faith resided in something the Holy Spirit revealed and illuminated apart from the written Old Testament revelation.

The first is genuine Dispensational soteriology based on the consistent application of the Literal hermeneutic. The second is Reformed and Promised soteriology based on a hermeneutic other than the Literal hermeneutic.

Throughout this book I have exampled solution one as the correct solution. Messianic prophecy supports my choice.

The Messiah-King, a line of prophecy clearly seen in 2 Samuel

7:13–16 and Psalm 2 (but actually beginning in Genesis 49:10).

The Messiah-Redeemer, a line of prophecy not clearly seen in the Old Testament revelation, but with the additional knowledge of the New Testament revelation seen in Genesis 12:3; Daniel 9:26, and other Old Testament scriptures that may be recognized as about the Messiah-Redeemer using illumination from the New Testament revelation.

The Vlach hermeneutic principle looms large: we do not—we should not—as Dispensational exegetes, change or transcend the authorial intent in the Old Testament message just because we have a New Testament understanding. We must understand the original message in the same sense as the human authors who wrote that message and the human beings who heard that message: through the inspiration (the authors) and illumination (all others) given by the Holy Spirit within the historical context of, and the progressive revelation given to, the writers and all the other Old Testament peoples. The Holy Spirit works through the written Scripture, not above, around, in spite of, or beyond the written Scripture. The Holy Spirit through Moses tells us exactly the scripture he (the Holy Spirit) gave to Adam and Eve.

Unlike those using Reformed or Promise soteriology, the Holy Spirit never confuses or conflates the two lines of messianic prophecy. The Holy Spirit keeps them distinct in the Old Testament revelation until they meet in Jesus the Christ in the completed New Testament revelation. The Holy Spirit waited until the New Testament revelation to reveal how those two lines of messianic prophecy would come to fruition.

The Old Testament peoples thought Messiah-King would come and redeem them from gentile oppression. The New Testament revelation revealed Messiah-Redeemer came at the first advent to deliver sinners from the penalty due sin. The New Testament revelation reveals Messiah-King will rule and redeem at the second advent. The Holy Spirit did not give the Old Testament peoples advance knowledge of his New Testament revelation.

When the common sense principles, "no one can know what has not yet been revealed," and "Scripture can never mean what it never meant" are consistently applied, the result will always be the consistent application of the Literal hermeneutic to the Old Testament Scriptures.

The faith and understanding of the Old Testament peoples resided in what the Holy Spirit revealed through his written Old Testament revelation, and illuminated through his interpretation of the plain and normal sense of his written Old Testament revelation. Illuminating the understanding with the plain and normal meaning of the written inspired scriptures is how the Holy Spirit works now, and that is how the Holy Spirit worked then.

That, I think, provides a reasonable and rational solution to every appeal to individual scriptures attempting to prove the Old Testament peoples understood more than had been revealed in the Old Testament Scripture. (In a previous chapter I examined some of those objections, to demonstrate the principles always apply.)

Old Testament Understanding

Did the Old Testament people have spiritual perception to understand the Scripture? Yes, in every saved person the soul's faculty of spiritual perception is alive and active, discerning spiritual things, 1 Corinthians 2:15–16. So also in those unsaved whom God has given his gift of grace-faith-salvation, the enlivened spiritual perception works in them efficaciously to inevitably bring them to faith and salvation, using the historically given revelation, and nothing else.

Here is the key thing, spiritual perception cannot perceive what is not there to perceive. To repeat, one of the simple but key rules of the Literal hermeneutic is "the Scripture cannot mean what it never meant." Of course, you say, so obvious, an axiom of interpretation. Then how do Reformed and Promise soteriology find a coming Jesus Christ, or a Promised Seed-Redeemer, in Genesis 3:15?

> And enmity I will put between you and the woman, and between your offspring and her offspring, he shall strike your head and you will strike his heel (my translation).

There is not a Hebrew *gōʾēl* (redeemer) or *māshîah* (messiah), not a Greek *sōtér* (redeemer), *messías* (messiah), or *christós* (christ), in that scripture. What is there? YHWH, a woman, a serpent, offspring, conflict. Those are the building blocks for an interpretation. The primary meaning of any Bible passage is found in that Bible passage.

Reformed and Promise soteriology make that scripture mean what it never meant by injecting New Testament revelation to force it to mean what it never meant.

The Holy Spirit works through his written testimony, the Scripture. The Berean Jews knew that simple axiom, "every day examining the Scriptures, if these things were so." They did not look at other Hebrew literature, only the written Scripture. The did not seek out theologians or preachers to confirm what they heard from Paul (cf. Acts 13:38–39), they searched the written Scripture. Would that all were like the Bereans.

The Holy Spirit works through the soul's faculty of spiritual perception to give understanding of the written Scripture. The Holy Spirit does not use verbal tradition, or extrabiblical revelation, or illumination apart from the written Scripture to explain his written Scripture. He works with what he has written, because what he has written, at any time during the history of redemption, is sufficient.

What did the Old Testament people understand about redemption. They knew it required faith. "Abraham believed in YHWH and it was reckoned to him for righteousness," Genesis 15:6, cf. Romans 4:3. Faith in what? What did Abraham believe? God's testimony: Genesis 12:1–3; 13:14–17; 15:4–5; 17:21; 21:12, confirmed to us by later revelation in Romans 9:7; Galatians 3:8, 16; Hebrews 11:18.

Strange the Holy Spirit never once says Abraham believed in a coming redeemer of Genesis 3:15, but that Abraham believed in YHWH (the word in the Genesis 15:6 Hebrew text), the ever-present Redeemer. The very Redeemer who did not speak of a different, yet-to-come redeemer in Genesis 3:15.

Indeed, in Genesis 3 YHWH the Redeemer was always and ever present, and had forgiven their sin and restored them to fellowship. So also in Genesis 4, 5, 6, 7, all the way throughout Old Testament times to the end of the Book of Malachi, YHWH is the ever-present Redeemer. Why would the ever-present Redeemer YHWH tell Old Testament sinners to believe in a not-yet-present, yet-to-come redeemer? The very notion is nonsensical and indefensible.

Both Reformed and Promise soteriology want to make the one way of salvation the proclamation of the Good News. No. The proclamation of the Good News is not the one way of a salvation. The one way of salvation is by Christ's propitiation. The work of the Good News is to define the proper object and content of the sinner's saving faith that accesses that one way of salvation.

What was the redemptive revelation—the sinner's content of saving faith—given within each historical era? In my book, *Covenants and Dispensations in the Scripture*, I have stated what I believe to be the content of faith for every dispensation. Contrary to Reformed and Promise soteriology, redemption was and always will be accessed by "mere faith or trust in God" (quoting Hodge, 2:371–372), which is to say, by responding in faith to what God revealed to them. How could they respond in faith to what God had not revealed to them in the written revelation? Here is what I wrote about the content of faith in *Covenants and Dispensations in the Scripture*.

The Content Of Faith In The History Of Redemption

Adam's Dispensation, which began post-sin.

> Faith in God the Creator and worship through obedience and sacrifice. Just prior to the Flood, God added to the content of faith: judgment is coming, get into the ark to be saved. (Noah was part of the Adamic Dispensation, and we see before the announcement of the flood, he had "found grace in YHWH's eyes.")

Noah's Dispensation, which began after the Flood.

> Faith in God the Judge and the conditions and promises of the Noahic covenant. Every gentile from Noah until Christ's crucifixion-resurrection was under the Noahic dispensation.

Abraham's Dispensation, which began Genesis 12:1–3.

> Faith in the God who gave the promises of the Abrahamic covenant. A specific people group, national ethnic Israel, beginning with Abraham, were the only people group under the Abrahamic dispensation (individual gentiles could proselytize into the covenant). (See my book, *Dispensational Eschatology*, for how the many promises to Abraham were distributed to his physical heirs and to other people groups.)

Moses' dispensation, which began Exodus 19:8.

> Faith in God and God's testimony that the proper sacrifice for sinning, offered with faith and repentance, resulted in the forgiveness of acts of sinning. (God by grace accepting their faith as it was expressed according to God's testimony in the Mosaic Law.) This content of faith was for the specific people

group national ethnic Israel during the times between 1445 BC to Christ's resurrection, and those gentiles who proselytized to YHWH-ism during those times. Salvation was by God's grace through the sinner's faith not by personal merit but by Christ's merit alone.

The New Testament church dispensation, which began with Christ's resurrection. Content of Faith.

Acts 2:38, Then Peter to them: "Convert, and be immersed, every one of you, in the name of Jesus Christ, for the forgiveness of your sins, and you will receive the gift of the Holy Spirit.

Acts 13:38–39, Therefore be it known to you, men, brethren, that through this one, to you forgiveness of sins is proclaimed. 39 And from all things from which you were not able in the Law of Moses to be justified, in him everyone believing is justified.

Acts 16:31–32, And they said, "Believe on the Lord Jesus, and you will be saved, you and your household." 32 And they spoke to him the word of the Lord, and with all those in his house.

Romans 10:12, 13, For there is no distinction between Jewish and Greek, for the same Lord of all is rich toward all those calling him. 13 For all that may call upon the Lord's name will be saved.

Tribulation Dispensation, which begins with the fulfillment of Daniel 9:27a; Revelation 6:2. Content of Faith.

Revelation 7:10, Salvation to our God, the one sitting on the throne, and to the Lamb!

Revlation14:7, Fear God, and give him glory, because the hour of his judgment has come, and worship the one having made heaven, and the earth, and sea, and springs of waters.

Davidic-Messianic-Millennial Kingdom Dispensation, which begins Revelation 20:1–6.

Believe on the King and Savior the Lord Jesus Christ and you will be saved.

See my book, *Covenants and Dispensations in the Scripture*, for extended discussion.

Summary

In previous chapters I quoted Emil Schurer that Old Testament national ethnic Israel was looking for a Messiah-King to redeem the nation from gentile oppression. I cited scriptures in Luke 1 showing that same hope in Mariam and Zecharias, as each was filled with the Holy Spirit and gave inspired testimony.

The Messiah-King line will be fulfilled at the second advent through the Davidic-Messianic Kingdom. This line of prophecy began at Genesis 49:10, and was further revealed in the promise to David, 2 Samuel 7:13–16; Psalm 2. I quoted Matthew 16:15–21 to show when Jesus Christ changed his message from Messiah-King to Messiah-Redeemer.

The Messiah-Redeemer line was fulfilled at the first advent through the crucifixion and resurrection. This is the Abrahamic promise, Genesis 12:3, blessing to all families of the earth, through Abraham's heir Isaac, Genesis 21:12, "in Isaac your seed will be named," cf. Romans 9:7; Galatians 3:6–16; Hebrews 11:18, culminating in Abraham's heir, Jesus of Nazareth, the Christ of God, who saves sinners out of every nation, tribe, people, and language.

The two lines of messianic prophecy meet in Jesus the Christ, which means they are distinct in the Old Testament revelation. They do not include Genesis 3:15. Which is to say, the Messiah-Redeemer line of prophecy does not begin in Genesis 3:15, but in Genesis 12:3 (as confirmed in Galatians 3:8).

The heart of genuine Dispensational soteriology for the Old Testament revelation is the principles and rules of the Literal hermeneutic applied correctly to the written Old Testament scripture. The Literal hermeneutic does not seek to find in a scripture or scripture passage what isn't there, but what is there.

The analyses methods of the Literal hermeneutic work with the written Scripture, not an unknown unwritten revelation or illumination, nor a misapplied New Testament revelation, to discover that the Old Testament peoples believed unto redemption. Any theological system or doctrine that seeks more than the plain and normal meaning of the Scripture in its historical-cultural, lexical-syntactical, literary context is seeking to put into the Scripture something the Holy Spirit did not put there. Reformed Old Testament soteriology and Dispensational Promise Old Testament soteriology are not biblical Old Testament soteriology.

The Dispensational soteriology I have proposed and defended in this book is the genuine Old Testament soteriology.

Election

The statements of doctrine in this and the following chapters are from my personal doctrinal statement, developed over many years from Scripture, historic orthodox creeds, and similar Reformed and Dispensational statements of doctrine. The explanations may be found in many of my other books. Out of those I recommend *Christian Living and Doctrine* or the more compact *Thirty-Six Essentials of the Christian Faith*, as validation that these are the doctrines believed and taught by me and other Dispensationalists. In relation to Dispensationalism I recommend my book *Understanding Dispensational Theology* or the abridge version, *A Primer on Dispensationalism*.

The purpose of the following chapters is to validate my credentials against the charge Dispensationalism and Dispensationalists are unorthodox in their doctrines and practices. My views on soteriology have already been explained.

Dispensationalism as a theology conforms to the historic orthodox faith of the New Testament church, which existed long before the Protestant Reformation. Objections by those of Reformed theology or others will need to prove my Dispensational beliefs and scripture support are not biblical.

Election: Statement of the doctrine.

> Election. The choice of a sovereign God (Ephesians 1:4), to give the gift of grace-faith-salvation to effect the salvation of some sinners (Ephesians 2:8), and to take no action, positive or negative, to either effect or deny salvation to other sinners (Romans 10:13; Revelation 22:17).

> The decree of election includes all means necessary to effectuate salvation in those elected. God's decree of election ensures the salvation of the elect, but does not prevent any non-elect sinner from coming or willing to be saved. God will act savingly toward any who choose to seek him and come to him for salvation (Rom. 10:13; Eph. 1:4; Rev. 22:17).

God would have all persons to be saved (1 Timothy 2:4), but he wills for certain persons to believe (Ephesians 1:4; 2 Thessalonians 2:13), thereby guaranteeing the elect will believe, without any kind of decree preventing any from believing.

What is election? Election is God's foreordaining choice to give to certain persons his gift of grace-faith-salvation (Ephesians 2:8), so that they will infallibly choose to believe.

Because God would have all persons to be saved (1 Timothy 2:4), God does not will any person to reprobation, but permits any person not elected to choose to believe, if they will. God does not prevent faith, that is what sin does.

All persons begin life as reprobate (Romans 3:23). All persons believing are saved from reprobation and have eternal life (John 3:15; 17:2). All persons not believing remain reprobate and will endlessly experience God's just wrath against their sins (Revelation 20:15).

God's wrath is his justice in action against the impenitent.

> God's wrath against the sinner who dies unforgiven and thus unsaved is expressed as endless punishment.

> God's wrath against the unrepentant believer who has committed an act of sinning is expressed as chastisement.

Jesus Christ on the cross suffered the wrath of God justly due the unsaved sinner, through the imputation of the sinner's judicial guilt to Christ, 2 Corinthians 5:21.

Discussion of Election

I previously discussed the doctrine of sin in the chapter "Soteriology." All persons are conceived as sinners and unless saved, die as sinners. This chapter will focus on the election of sinners to salvation. Because from the instant of conception all are sinners needing salvation, this chapter will also address election from the moment of conception. It is impossible to discuss election without some mention of the lapsarian orders of God's pre-creation decrees. However, an in depth discussion will not be done here but in the chapter on Propitiation.

I defined election above.

> The choice of a sovereign God (Ephesians 1:4), to give the gift of grace-faith-salvation to effect the salvation of some sinners (Ephesians 2:8), and to take no action, positive or negative, to either effect or deny salvation to other sinners (Romans 10:13; Revelation 22:17).

Election is the consequence of foreordination. Therefore a presentation of foreordination is required.

Foreordination is a very difficult subject. All opinions on foreordination, as may be expressed by any person, are theological constructs: logical and rational reasoning based on the Scripture to arrive at a conclusion not explicitly stated in the Scripture. The scriptures used to derive a doctrine of foreordination are those relevant to God's sovereignty, human nature, and the obvious fact some are saved, some are not.

I will not here discuss the merits of this or that particular view of foreordination, but my own conclusions only. I briefly discussed Arminian foresight (or prescient) election in the chapter "Arminian Soteriology." The consequence of foresight election is God took no foreordaining action resulting in election. Molinism is foresight election, simply on a larger scale.

In Arminian soteriology election is individual based on foreseen faith. In Molinism soteriology God chose worlds not individuals: God foresaw all possible universes he might create, and who would believe on each Earth in each universe. God then chose to create one universe where those believing suited his purpose in creating. Thus, foresight election.

Foreordination

For a complete discussion of foreordination see my book, *God's Choices, the Doctrines of Foreordination, Election, and Predestination.*

> Foreordination. The decree of God occurring between his decision to create and his act of creation as to which agents, events, and outcomes, out of all possible agents, events, and outcomes potential in the decision to create, would pass from possible to actual, in which the liberty or contingency of secondary causes is established, in which God is not the author of sin, and in which no violence is done to the free will of his creatures.

Prior to the act of creation, God omnisciently knew within himself whatever might or could come to pass upon all supposed conditions. This was not the knowing of foresight, but God omnisciently understanding all possible agents, events, and outcomes (which outcomes included all possible freely made choices that might be made by all beings he would create and all possible consequences resulting from their choices) that could develop from the act of creation. God did not decree anything because he foresaw it as future, but because he determined all that was possible, and then chose which of all possible agents, events, and outcomes he would foreordain as actual. That choice effectuating possible to actual included freely made choices.

In an illustration, we might say God omnisciently "calculated" that from cause A, events 1, 2, 3, a, b, c were possible, and then chose which possible events to make actual. Not because he foresaw the events, but because he omnisciently understood within himself all that might be possible from his decision to create, and then chose which possible things he would effect in the universe he would create. God then created the universe his choices effectuated.

Foreordination is not fate or determinism. Foreordination makes choices certain but not necessary. The choices we make during our lifetime are certain because foreordained, but not necessary because those choices are freely made, God having effectuated certain possible choices from possible to actual, as fit his purpose in creating the universe. Within the historic in-the-moment of decision, all sentient creatures freely decide in agreement with God's choices. That is foreordination through sovereignty not foreknowledge.

Several illustrations will be helpful. What your computer does upon turn-on was foreordained by the computer's programmer. When you drive to the grocery store in your vehicle, at every four-way intersection you have four choices: straight, left, right, U-turn. God chose which of those four possible choices to effect from possible to actual. During a chess game a grandmaster can see up to twenty possible moves ahead. Before the game begins God sees all possible moves from beginning to end and chooses which moves to effect from possible to actual.

How does foreordination interact with election? That depends on your lapsarian view of God's pre-creation decrees. The suffix -lapsarian refers to the "lapse" in man's holiness, i.e., Adam's act of sinning.

When God chose to create a universe, what did he do first, second, third, etc.? The lapsarian views of God's pre-creation decrees are opinions of God's decrees relevant to salvation. Of course, God's creation decree was one decree, but it is helpful to think of that act of creation as we might act, having several rational sequenced steps. For example, my first step in putting together my kid's tricycle for her birthday was to grab the directions, then sort the parts, then inventory the parts, then get the tools, etc., etc., until the tricycle was fully assembled. How did God assemble his universe? More to the point of this discussion, how did God decide whom to save and how to save them.

The supralapsarian view, initially proposed by Isidore of Seville (ca. 560-563), and revived by Thomas Beza (1519–1605) says God's first decision was to elect to salvation some of the human beings he would create, and elect to reprobation (damnation) all other human beings he would create. Then God decided to decree (not permit) Adam would commit an act of sinning, then God decided to send Christ to save those whom God had elected to salvation. I will discuss the ramifications of this view in the chapter on Propitiation.

The infralapsarian view adopted by the Synod of Dort (1618–1619) says God decided to permit Adam's fall into sin. That choice determined all of Adam's descendants would be sinners (see discussion of sin in chapter "Soteriology"). Then, seeing all human beings as sinners, God chose to elect some out of this fallen mass to be saved, and to leave the others as they were, and then chose to provide a redeemer for the elect.

In the sublapsarian view, after the Synod of Dort, God chose to permit the fall, to provide a redeemer, to elect some out of this fallen mass to be saved, and to leave the others as they were.

Those are the three views of God's foreordination to elect some to be saved. But those views do not give the process of election. What I am saying is election was a choice made by God, but how was that choice effectuated? How are those sinners who were to be elected identified as those who were elect? The answer is twofold.

First, God never tells us the basis on which one was elected and another was not. All we know is the choice was not based on foreseeable merit: all were sinners, none had merit. As I explained in an earlier chapter, in Arminian soteriology God looked outside himself into the history of the universe he would create, decided to give all prevenient grace, saw who would believe and who would not believe after receiving prevenient grace, and elected to salvation those he foresaw would believe. In Arminian soteriology God acted because of what he learned.

Reformed and Dispensational soteriology says God looked inside himself (omniscience), and thereby knowing all human beings he would create, decided which of those human beings he would give prevenient grace for salvation (Ephesians 2:8). Those individuals God decided to give prevenient grace are identified as elected to salvation, because of the infallible efficacy of the gift.

That brings us to the second answer: the process of electing is God foreordaining to give to certain sinners his prevenient grace; or as it is otherwise known, God's gift of grace-faith-salvation, Ephesians 2:8. God's decree that a particular person will receive God's gift, at some point during the course of that person's lifetime, is the foreordaining act of electing that person to salvation, an act that occurred before God created the universe.

Therefore election is "the choice of a sovereign God (Ephesians 1:4), to give the gift of grace-faith-salvation to effect the salvation of some sinners (Ephesians 2:8)."

What about those not elected? The traditional Reformed solution, to which many Dispensationalists will agree, is to propose God has a secret will and a revealed will. The revealed will calls all to believe, knowing the secret will says only some can believe because only those elected to believe can believe.

I disagree. None can know the secret will of God, Deuteronomy 29:29, but we can know that what has been revealed to us cannot contradict what has not been revealed to us. Therefore the salvific call of God to "whosoever will" cannot contradict an unknown "secret will." If all are called to believe, then all must have the same opportunity to believe. Therefore election cannot prevent belief in any of the all.

(The supralapsarian gets around this logical reasoning by redefining "all" as "only the elect.")

I believe election guarantees the salvation of those elected but says nothing about those not elected. Thus, in his decree to elect some, God took no action, positive or negative, to either effect or deny salvation to other sinners (Romans 10:13; Revelation 22:17). What stands in the way of salvation is sin—all are sinners—overcome in the elect by God's gift. God does not prevent salvation, that is what sin does.

I believe Scripture teaches salvation is conditioned upon faith in God and God's testimony as to the way of salvation. There are two consequences of that belief. The first is election guarantees some will believe, that is its purpose, and by election the condition of faith will be met by the elect.

The second consequence is election does not prevent any non-elect from believing. If a non-elect person would choose to repent of his or her sin and freely believe on God and God's testimony as to the way of salvation, God would act savingly toward that person, because the purpose of election is to guarantee salvation, election does not prevent salvation. Thus God's requirement that the proclamation is to be made to all for all to believe, because none are prevented by God from believing.

I have an illustration.

> The river of sinful humankind is justly racing toward the waterfall of death emptying into the lake of eternal fire; God reaches into the river and saves many; he prevents no one from swimming to the safety of the heavenly shore; he puts his saved people on the shore encouraging all to believe on God and his testimony of salvation and be saved; he saves all that come to him by faith in God and his testimony.

What prevents salvation is the freely made choice to rebel against God. All are infected with this spiritual condition, from birth. God chose to give some his gift of grace-faith-salvation to effect their salvation through his gift. God leaves the others as he found them, unsaved sinners, which also means he leaves them to their own choices. God never prevents the choice to believe and be saved, their own sinful nature makes the choice to reject God and his salvation the natural choice.

Yes, God foreordained every choice, but every choice is a freely made choice, freely made by the person during the course of his or her lifetime. The choice of disbelief is the natural choice of the sinner, there are no other possible choices, hence the gift of grace-faith-salvation. But if there were other possible choices, God has foreordained all are sinners, so the promise of salvation might be given to those who believe.

Even the choice of the elect to believe is a freely made choice, foreordained by God, through his gift, because the gift of God efficaciously changes the moral boundaries of human nature (see chapter "What is Free Will"), changing the unable and unwilling sinner to able and willing. But even the elect would not choose to believe if God had not foreordained to give them his gift. Therefore all are free to make the choice to believe, but the elect are guaranteed to make that choice, because God foreordained those he elected to receive his gift.

Election And The Morally Undeveloped

One of the more troubling issues—and highly charged emotionally–is the relationship God's election has toward those who either have not or never will develop the moral capacity to decide for faith or no faith. Usually these are defined as babies or infants. But the reality is as a group those with an undeveloped moral capacity include human beings from conception to birth; babies, infants, small children; adults who never develop the moral capacity to decide for faith or no faith.

From an observational point of view, we cannot know if the persons in that class of people—the morally undeveloped—have believed unto salvation. Let us be honest: we become aware of who we believe is among the elect through a credible profession of saving faith. That criteria is unavailable in the morally undeveloped group of persons. Because we cannot observe the choice for faith or no faith in that group, we are emotionally distressed that the "innocent" (none are innocent, all are sinful) may be unfairly condemned. The usual solution is to manipulate Scripture to say, "babies and infants are automatically saved," disregarding all others in that group.

Some, who understand that all are sinners from conception forward (the legal guilt of Adam's sin is imputed to every sinner), have a slightly different solution: the intrinsically sinful nature is not counted against the morally undeveloped until they commit an act of sinning. This solution manipulates Scripture to create a standard of moral accountability (an "age" of accountability) that begins with the moral choice to commit an act of sinning. This is similar to that aspect of Arminian soteriology that says inability absolves responsibility.

What says the Scripture? The following is drawn in part from my book, *Adam and Eve, A Biography and Theology.*

Culpability For Sin From Conception

If, as Scripture teaches, all persons are culpable for the moral guilt of sin from the moment of conception (see *Adam and Eve*, arguments under Hamartiology)—which we know is true because physical death, the observable consequence of sin's judicial guilt, may occur between conception and birth—then how are those persons who are morally undeveloped to make a faith-based decision—the unborn (a human being from conception to birth), infants, small children, adults who never became mentally or morally competent—how are they able to express saving faith and be saved from their sin?

The answer, as far as can be known by observation, is that they cannot. I am not saying that a person must verbalize his or her faith in order to be saved. The exercise of saving faith is not necessarily verbal. Saving faith is the positive response of the soul to God's gift of grace-faith-salvation. However, the way a person's saving faith can be known to others (other than God) is when it is verbalized or actualized.

The persons under discussion cannot verbalize faith and they cannot demonstrate their faith by their works. Therefore, we cannot know if this class of persons are saved, because they are not capable of making their salvation (or lack of salvation) known. Since they are culpable for their sin, but as much as we can observe are morally undeveloped to make a faith-based decision, can they be saved? Let me firmly answer that the question is not, "can these persons be saved," because they can, but "how can we know if these persons can be saved?"

The answer is in the efficient cause of salvation and the choices made by God. We will discuss the latter later. As to the former, the one and only basis of salvation is the propitiating death of Christ, decreed in eternity past, effective from eternity past through eternity future, and accomplished in historical space-time. The efficient cause of salvation is the remission of sin's guilt and penalty by the application of Christ's limitless merit.

In those who are mentally competent to make a choice between faith and no-faith, Christ's merit is applied by their receiving God's gift of grace-faith-salvation, and through the means of personal faith in God's revealed means (way) of salvation, they exercise saving faith. However, the unborn, infants, small children, and adults who never became mentally or morally competent cannot, as far as may be known, grasp or express saving faith. Nor does Scripture deal with their need for salvation. Scripture focuses on those who are able to make a decision for faith or no-faith. Scripture does not directly address the salvific needs of the unborn, infants, small children, and adults who never became mentally or morally competent.

Two Scriptures are often used to defend the salvation of infants and small children (neither of which addresses the unborn or the morally undeveloped adult.)

The first is 2 Samuel 12:15–23. The story is familiar to most Christians. David the king committed adultery with Bathsheba and she became pregnant. David recalled her husband from the battlefield so he could have sex with his wife and make it appear he was responsible for the pregnancy. He did not have sex with her, so David had him abandoned on the battlefield so he would die in conflict with the enemy; in God's eyes it was an act of murder. Then David married Bathsheba. The child was born. The child became ill and died.

During the illness, David prostrated himself in prayer and fasts. After the child died, David got up, washed and anointed himself, changed his clothes, went to the tabernacle, and worshiped YHWH. His servants were amazed he did not mourn. David replied,

> When the child was alive I fasted and wept. I said to myself, 'Who is able to know whether YHWH will be gracious to me that the child may live?' But now he is dead; should I continue to fast? Can I bring him back again? I shall go to him, but he shall not return to me.

Was David saying he also would die. Was David saying that when he died he would meet this infant in heaven, i.e., that this one infant had been saved prior to its physical death? (Salvation must occur prior to death, Hebrews 9:27.) To answer this question we must ask, who was speaking? Was it David the prophet or David the grieving father? We must ask, is what David said revelation from God? The words are inspired, which means that what David said was accurately recorded, but was what David said revelation from God the Holy Spirit regarding the spiritual state of all infants? Or even this one infant. David says his son cannot come back from death, but he, David, will go to him, the child, when he, David, dies.

If David was speaking as a prophet, and if David knew by divine revelation the eternal fate of this one infant, does that understanding apply to every other person dying in infancy from Adam forward to the end of the world? No. What David said was a singular statement, meaning that nothing like it, or corresponding to it, or parallel with it, or similar to it in thought or idea, appears anywhere else in Scripture. One of the rules of theology is, do not build a doctrine from a single verse. I will respect that rule in regard to this singular verse. In my view, this one verse only answers the question concerning the salvation of either this one infant or all infants if you bring the answer with you. (And what about all the other morally undeveloped persons?)

The second verse, rather, the incident recorded in Matthew 19, Mark 10, and Luke 18, is Jesus with little children. The passage says nothing conclusive about their salvation. Jesus was displeased that the disciples sought to prevent parents bringing their children to Jesus. However, it was culturally unusual, very unusual, that parents would bring their little children near to any "holy man," such as a rabbi, teacher, or prophet.

In the ancient world children were not prized as they are today. In modern times children are evaluated on their assumed adult potential. In the ancient world children were evaluated on what they might contribute to society or family as children. As a result, they were not valued at all (a high mortality rate for infants and children did not help the situation). Christianity is actually one of the impelling reasons the attitude toward children changed.

So, it was unusual in those times for parents to bring their children to a teacher, a holy man, a prophet. But they did bring their children to Jesus and he did receive them. He used them as an illustration to teach that saving faith is trusting faith, on the order of the naïve kind of trust expressed by little children: faith without suspicion; faith without doubt. The passage does not say if little children will be saved, but it leaves no doubt they can be saved—if they can express saving faith.

Neither the 2 Samuel passage nor the gospel passages answer the question concerning the salvation of the unborn, infants, small children, and mentally-morally undeveloped adults. To answer the question we must return to the basis of salvation, Christ's propitiation and its efficient application, and add in the final point, the choices made by God. What is required to save those who cannot express saving faith, who (as far as we can know) cannot make a choice between faith and no-faith, is the application of the merit of Christ to the sinful condition of their soul.

That is, in fact, the need of everyone. No one seeks after God, no one understands, all have gone the way of sin. If no person seeks God, if the inclination of the sinful nature is to rebel against God, then how is anyone saved? The answer is Ephesians 1:4, "he chose us in him before the beginning of the universe." Not every human being is chosen, but no human being is beyond the reach of God's electing choice, from the moment of conception to physical death.

All those whom God has elected will certainly be saved. Those persons *who are morally developed* will be saved by responding to the Good News of salvation with faith; Scripture gives no other way to salvation.

As to the unborn, infants, and others similarly so morally undeveloped that they are unable to make the moral choice between faith and no faith, if they are saved, "it cannot be on their own merits, or on the basis of their own righteousness or innocence, but must be entirely on the basis of Christ's redemptive work and regeneration by the work of the Holy Spirit within them" [Grudem, 500].

What I am saying is that if God has chosen any one of these morally undeveloped persons to salvation, then God will by grace give them the gift of grace-faith-salvation, and by grace they will positively respond to the gift by the exercise of saving faith, and by grace God will apply the merit of Christ to their soul. The manner of their positive response—how they might express saving faith—cannot be known, because they cannot tell us by word or deed.

Is the God who created human beings unable to effectively communicate with the human soul that he designed and created *ex nihilo?* At any stage of human development, beginning at conception? The omnipotent God in whom my faith rests is able.

God's electing choice is the primary condition affecting the salvation of every human being from Adam forward to the end of this present universe: God saves whom he has chosen; he prevents no one from coming to him to be saved. Beyond this no one can go with certainty. No one can say with scriptural certainty that all, some, or none of the unborn, infants, small children, or adults who never became morally developed are saved. Perhaps God has elected every single person who dies without having the moral development to decide for faith or no-faith. Perhaps some of these are saved and some not. Perhaps none are saved. Is God righteous, holy, and just only when I understand? Certainly not! For then how will God judge the world?

Whatever God has decided it is holy, it is righteous, it is just. As Abraham said, God does not execute the righteous with the wicked, Genesis 18:25. What are the options?

> If all the unborn, infants, small children, and morally undeveloped adults are saved, God is just, God is holy.

> If only some, or none, are saved God is just, God is holy.

Justice and holiness are essential characteristics of God. God has no sin and takes no action that would be unjust. There is an election according to grace—the blessing of God given to those with no merit. God does make a choice, "Jacob I have loved, but Esau have I hated," meaning God drew one into a covenant with himself but not the other, and "the children not yet being born, nor having done any good or evil, that the purpose of God according to election might stand, not of works, but of him who calls." God has chosen not to reveal the why or who of his electing choice. One must either accept that God is holy, righteous, and just in all his ways, or create a soteriology not based on Scripture.

What has been said about the unborn, infants, small children, and morally undeveloped adults cannot be applied to those who have developed the moral competence to make a decision for faith or no-faith. All morally developed people of any physical age, in all the millennia of humankind on this earth, are morally required to believe in God and God's testimony as to the means of salvation. All Christians are required to go and "disciple all the peoples," Matthew 28:19. How God deals with that one class of sinners without moral development is one of the secret things that belong to YHWH our God (Deuteronomy 29:29). This also is part of the doctrine of soteriology.

Propitiation

Introduction

Most Dispensationalists adopt one of the three Reformed views of Christ's propitiation—which Reformed theology names "atonement." The older Reformed thought an atonement was a "covering for sin" because Hebrew language experts of the times defined the biblical atonement by a similar Arabic word that meant to cover. But time, better linguistic studies, and paying attention to the Scripture has revealed the Hebrew word atonement means the same thing as its Greek equivalent propitiation.

There are two differences between the Old Testament atonement and the New Testament propitiation.

> The Old was through the believer offering an animal sacrifice, the New is through Jesus Christ's sacrifice of himself on the cross. Both satisfied God for the crime of sin.

> The Old satisfied God for the past act or acts of sinning sin for which it was offered, the New satisfied God for every act of sinning sin past, present, and future of the whole world.

Both atonement and propitiation mean God was fully satisfied and forgave the sinner. The difference is the extent of the satisfaction. The Old Testament atonement fully satisfied God's holiness and justice for the specific sin or sins for which it was offered. The propitiation of Christ fully satisfied God's holiness and justice for all sin.

Finally, an Old Testament sinner was saved by a sacrifice offered as an atonement, not because the "blood of bulls and goats" remitted the judicial guilt of sin, but because God by grace accepted the act of faith that offered the atoning sacrifice as the God-ordained means by which the limitless merit of Christ's propitiation was accessed, by grace through faith. The merit of Christ's propitiation, and the salvation principle (Ephesians 2:8–9) have always been in effect, from the beginning.

Three Views Of Christ's Propitiation

The three Reformed views are the supralapsarian, infralapsarian, and sublapsarian order of God's precreation decrees. Each focuses on the application of Christ's propitiation of God for human sin. I propose a fourth view of Christ's propitiation that focuses on the primary purpose and incorporates the application. My view is expressed in the "statement of the doctrine," below.

Statement Of The Doctrine.

> Propitiation. The satisfaction Christ made to God for sin by dying on the cross as the sin-bearer, 2 Corinthians 5:21; Romans 3:25; Hebrews 2:17; 1 John 2:2; 4:10, for the crime of sin committed by human beings, suffering in their place and on their behalf.

Christ alone propitiated God for the crime of sin. The purpose of Christ's propitiation was to fully satisfy (propitiate) God's holiness and justice for the crime of human sin. Christ's propitiation was of limitless merit, because his Person is of limitless worth.

The application of Christ's limitless merit to overcome the demerit of sin and save a soul, is through the election God decreed before he created the universe, and is personally applied by each sinner through the exercise of saving faith in response to God's gift of grace-faith-salvation (particular redemption), Ephesians 2:8. Christ's righteousness is imputed to the saved sinner so that he/she eternally stands uncondemned before a holy God, Romans 8:1, 31.

The merit of Christ's propitiation is also applied in a manner consistent with God's mercy to give temporal benefits to all humankind. What is mercy? The attribute of mercy has two aspects. Mercy delays deserved judgment; mercy relives suffering. God acts in mercy toward all human beings because of Christ's propitiation.

Christ's propitiation was of infinite merit, because his Person is of infinite worth. The application of that merit is personally made by each sinner to his or her sin through faith in God and God's testimony as to the proper object and content of saving faith. Christ accomplished the propitiation of God for sin by enduring spiritual and physical death on the cross. Christ endured spiritual death when he was separated from fellowship with God ("My God, my God, why have you forsaken me?"), and physical death when he separated his soul from his body ("[B]owing his head, he gave up his spirit.")

The Application Of The Merit

How is God is able to be merciful when confronted by human sin? God's holy character has an automatic reaction to sin: immediate judgment. "God is light and darkness is not in him, none at all," 1 John 1:5. If, as is true, "in him we live and move and exist," Acts 17:28, then how does God tolerate our darkness within his light? The answer is Christ propitiated God for our darkness, i.e., our sin.

Jesus Christ "is propitiation for our sins—but not for ours only but also for all the world," 1 John 2:2. Was Christ's propitiation for all? Today, Theodore Beza's supralapsarian order of God's pre-creation decrees is the most popular view of Christ's propitiation—the limited atonement view Christ died only for the elect. Most popular, but not most biblical.

What did the person whom Beza claimed as his mentor, John Calvin, say? From *Calvin's Commentary* on the gospels (emphasis Calvin).

> On Matthew 22:22, The word *many* is not put definitively for a fixed number; for he contrasts himself with all others. And in this sense it is used in Romans 5:15, where Paul does not speak of any part of men, but embraces the whole human race. [*Commentary*, vol. 16, *On A Harmony of the Evangelists*, 2:427].

Calvin argues in Romans 5:15 the "many" are all those who are in Adam, which is the entire human race, as descended from Adam, the original human being.

> But observe, that a larger number (*plures*) are not here contrasted with many (*multis*) for he speaks not of the number of men: but as the sin of Adam has destroyed many, he draws this conclusion,—that the righteousness of Christ will be no less efficacious to save many. [*Commentary*, vol. 19, *Romans*, 207.]

Christ in some sense propitiated God for all human beings. In his comments on Romans 5:15, Calvin rightly contrasts the many who are sinners in Adam with the many who are in Christ. The "many" in Christ, Romans 5:15, are those who receive eternal life from Christ. But as Christ died for the many who are in Adam, in what sense do those not in Christ receive benefits from his death?

In this way. God is able to justly have mercy toward all humankind—delaying just judgment and relieving misery—because Christ propitiated God for all human sin, 1 John 2:2; Romans 3:23–25; Hebrews 2:17. The temporal benefits of that propitiation, God's mercy and goodness, apply to all human beings: the rain falls on all, good and evil. The eternal benefits of the propitiation are applied to some human beings according to God's decrees concerning salvation from the penalty of sin.

This is not only my doctrine, but a doctrine shared by many past and present.

> Martin Luther: "He bears all the sins of the world from its inception; this implies that He also bears yours, and offers you grace... Christ was given . . . not for one or two sins, but for all sins . . . Christ has taken away not only the sins of some men but your sins and those of the whole world. The offering was for the sins of the whole world, even though the whole world does not believe. So do not permit your sins to be merely sins; let them be your very own sins. That is, believe that Christ was given not only for the sins of others but also for yours." [Quoted by C. Daniel, "Hyper-Calvinism and John Gill," Ph.D. diss., University of Edinburgh, 1983), 512–513.]

The Synod of Dort taught Christ's propitiation of God was sufficient for all, efficient to salvation for the elect.

> Canons of Dort, Second Head of Doctrine, Article 3, "The death of the Son of God is the only and most perfect sacrifice and satisfaction for sin, and is of infinite worth and value, abundantly sufficient to expiate the sins of the whole world."

There is room in that statement for temporal benefits toward all humankind.

> C. Hodge: "It does not follow from the assertion of Christ's atonement having a special reference to the elect that it had no reference to the non-elect. Augustinians readily admit that the death of Christ had a relation to man, to the whole human family, which it had not to fallen angels. It is the ground on which salvation is offered to every creature under heaven who hears the gospel . . . . moreover, it secures to the whole race at large, and to all classes of men, innumerable blessings, both providential and religious. It was, of course, designed to produce these effects; and, therefore, he died to secure them. . . . There is a sense, therefore, in which Christ died for all, and there is a sense in which he died for the elect alone." [Hodge,

Systematic Theology, 545–546]

C.H. Spurgeon: "Our older Calvinistic friends deal with 1 Timothy 2:6 and 'all men' [and] they say, 'That is, some men'; as if the Holy Ghost could not have said 'some men' if he had meant some men. 'All men,' they say ... is 'some of all sorts of men'; as if the Lord could not have said 'all sorts of men' if he had meant that. The Holy Ghost by the apostle has written 'all men,' and unquestionably he means all men ... I was reading just now the exposition of a very able doctor who explains the text so as to explain it away: he applies grammatical gunpowder to it." [quoted in Ian Murray, *Spurgeon v. Hyper-Calvinism*, 150.]

Dr. John MacArthur is a recent voice noting God's love is both temporal and eternal. Dr. Keith Sherlin kindly provided these quotes from Dr. John MacArthur.

I am troubled by the tendency of some—often young people newly infatuated with Reformed doctrine—who insist that God cannot possibly love those who never repent and believe .... Those who hold this view often go to great lengths to argue that John 3:16 cannot really mean God loves the whole world. Perhaps the best-known argument for this view is found in A.W. Pink who wrote, 'God loves whom he chooses. He does not love everybody' .... We must understand that that it is God's very nature to love. The reason our Lord commanded us to love our enemies is 'in order that you may be sons of your Father ... for he causes his sun to rise on the evil and the good (Matt. 5:45) .... Reformed theologians have always affirmed the love of God for all sinners. John Calvin himself wrote regarding John 3:16 ... 'the Father loves the human race, and wishes that they should not perish' ... Calvin points out ... that [God's love is] by no means limited to the elect alone. [MacArthur, *The Love of God*, 12–18.]

Christ's atonement is unlimited as to its sufficiency, but limited as to its application. Real benefits accrue for all because of Christ's all sufficient atoning work. The gospel may be preached to all ... moreover, in a temporal sense the entire race was spared from immediate destruction ... and individual sinners experience a delay in God's judgment on their sins. [MacArthur, *First Timothy, New Testament Commentary*, 72]

The supralapsarian view God's love extends only toward those he elected to salvation is simply not the testimony of the Scripture.

> Matthew 5:44–45, But I say to you, love your enemies, and pray for those persecuting you; bless those cursing you, do good to those misusing you and hating you, 45 so that you may be sons of your Father in the heavens. Because he makes his sun rise on evil and good, and sends rain on righteous and unrighteous.

> John 3:16, For God so loved the world that he gave the Son, the only begotten, that everyone believing in him should not perish but may have eternal life.

The "world" in the 3:16 context reasonably means the world of sinners.

The propitiation was and is sufficient for all: all are drawn.

> John 12:32, And I, when I am lifted up from the earth, will draw all persons to myself.

> Revelation 22:17, And the Spirit and the bride say, 'Come.' And the one hearing let him say 'Come.' And the one thirsting—the one desiring—let him come, let him take freely the water of life.

The propitiation is sufficient for all, efficient to salvation for the elect.

> 1 John 5:15, Whoever confesses that Jesus Christ is the Son of God, God in him abides, and he in God.

If God's love and Christ's propitiation was restricted to a certain group, the elect, then the Holy Spirit lies in the many "whoever" texts proclaiming salvation to whoever believes. As I discussed earlier (see chapter "Election"), the purpose of election is to guarantee salvation to the elect, not to prevent the salvation of the non-elect.

In relation to Dispensational, Reformed, and Arminian soteriology, all believe Christ's propitiation of God for human sin is efficient to completely save the believing sinner from the eternal penalty due sin. As I demonstrated in the chapter, "The Content of Faith Concept," from the earliest days of church history the orthodox doctrine has been Christ's propitiation fully and completely saves the sinner. More plainly, there is no such thing as a partial salvation, and 2 Corinthians 5:8

applies to every saved person, Old Testament and New Testament.

I mention this because there is an unorthodox view the Old Testament saved went to a "good side" of hades to wait for the historical event of Christ's propitiation so they could be fully saved and go to heaven. I addressed that view in chapter, "Soteriology."

Popular Reformed preachers have turned this unorthodox view [a "good side of hades," a sort of Protestant limbo] into a doctrine; a false doctrine some Dispensationalists have adopted. That doctrine first appeared in the "Apostle's Creed" in AD 390 and again in AD 650. There are twelve versions of the Apostle's Creed, appearing AD 200, 220, 250, 260, 341, 390 (two versions), 400, 450, 650, 750. Only the AD 390 and AD 650 have the "descended into hell" statement. Unfortunately, the AD 650 statement is the one adopted for popular use. You may investigate the development of the Apostle's Creed in Schaff, *Creeds*, 2:39–55. The Creed is part of the discussion in my book *Did Jesus Go To Hell?*

The Purpose Of Christ's Propitiation

There is controversy within the Reformed and Dispensational camps over the extent of Christ's propitiation of God for human sin (aka: the "extent of the atonement"). This controversy is based on the question, "For whom did Christ die," a misstatement of the biblical doctrine, "What was the purpose of Christ's propitiation?"

Arminian soteriology's prescient election has an easy answer: for everyone God saw who would believe. For Reformed and Dispensational believers there are three answers, depending on the person's lapsarian views, on the extent of Christ's propitiation (aka: atonement).

Christ's Propitiation was limited to the elect only

Christ's Propitiation was sufficient for all efficient for the elect

Christ's Propitiation has eternal benefits to the elect, temporal benefits to all.

The limited position is held by supralapsarians. The unlimited sufficient-efficient position is held by infralapsarians and sublapsarians. The temporal-eternal benefits position is an historic Reformed and dispensational view, as I demonstrated above through a few quotes.

In an earlier chapter I referred to the supralapsarian,

infralapsarian, and sublapsarian positions. Because all these positions are held by both Reformed and Dispensational, a discussion is warranted. The issues are not complex, but are detailed.

The word "lapsarian" refers to Adam's sin. The prefix "supra" means "before the lapse," the prefix "infra" means "below the lapse," and prefix "sub" means "after the lapse. These lapsarian views each propose an order of God's pre-creation decrees relevant to soteriology.

Before God created the universe, what kind of universe did he decide to create, and how did those decisions affect humankind? The question the lapsarian views answer is this: "Were the objects [humankind] of the divine decree [of election] contemplated as fallen creatures? Or were they contemplated merely as men whom God would create, all being equal" [Harrison, *Dictionary*, s. v. Predestination]?

Before proceeding further, it will be helpful to know how the Bible defines predestination, and how Reformed theology defined and continues to define "predestination" in the lapsarian debates.

> Bible: Predestination is God's decree to conform the believer to be like Christ according to certain aspects of Christ's spiritual character and physical form (Romans 8:29–30; 1 John 3:2), and to place the believer in the legal position of God's son and heir (adoption) (Ephesians 1:5, 11), so that the believer has an inheritance from God and is God's heritage.

Should the reader consult Reformed sources on this issue (and probably not a few Dispensational sources) knowing what Reformed theology means by "predestination will be helpful.

> Reformed: the word "predestination" mashes together four distinct biblical doctrines: foreordination + election + predestination + providence.

In this book I do not confuse foreordination, election, predestination, and providence. I will define each doctrine. (Quiggle, *Dictionary of Doctrinal Words*).

> Foreordination. The decree of God occurring between his decision to create and his act of creation as to which agents, events, and outcomes, out of all possible agents, events, and outcomes potential in the decision to create, would pass from possible to actual, in which the liberty or contingency of

252

secondary causes is established, in which God is not the author of sin, and in which no violence is done to the free will of his creatures.

Election. The choice of a sovereign God (Ephesians 1:4), (1) to give the gift of grace-faith-salvation to effect the salvation of some sinners (Ephesians 2:8), and (2) to take no action, positive or negative, to either effect or deny salvation to other sinners (Romans 10:13; Revelation 22:17). The decree of election includes all means necessary to effectuate salvation in those elected.

Predestination. God's decree to conform the believer to be like Christ according to certain aspects of Christ's spiritual character and physical form (Romans 8:29–30; 1 John 3:2), and to place the believer in the legal position of God's son and heir (adoption) (Ephesians 1:5, 11), so that the believer has an inheritance from God and is God's heritage.

Providence. That which God's foreordination effectuated in eternity-past, God's providence accomplishes in historical-present. Providence is a term used to describe God's unceasing works by which he maintains and preserves the universe and all his creatures, and governs its operations and their actions, so as to accomplish his plans and eternal purpose.

The Lapsarian Views

In this section I will present the lapsarian views and make a few comments. Some of this information comes from Thomas, *The Extent of the Atonement*, but I am solely responsible for its use.

Supralapsarian

The supralapsarian position, first proposed by Isidore of Seville (ca, AD 560-563) and revived by Theodore Beza (1519–1605), says God decided to elect some to salvation and elect others to reprobation. (Reprobation: to be disqualified from heaven and subject to judgment and eternal punishment.) This is also known as the "double predestination" view. In terms used above, the supralapsarian position says Christ died only for the elect. The supralapsarian order of God's pre-creation decrees:

To elect to life some of the persons who were to be created, and to condemn to reprobation all other persons who were to be created.

To create.

To decree the fall of humankind into sin.

To send Christ to redeem the elect.

To send the Holy Spirit to apply this redemption to the elect.

According to the supralapsarianism order, election precedes the decision to create and the decision to decree the fall into sin. (Only supralapsarian view says God decreed Adam must sin.)

Beza was a friend and student of John Calvin (1509–1564). As many have noted, Calvin's writings may be used to support both the supra and infra positions, because he himself was undecided. Beza drew from Calvin's writings to support the supralapsarian order. The student of church history will take note that unlike the infra- and sub-positions, the supralapsarian position was unknown in the New Testament church for over 500 years, and was rejected by every synod that considered it, including the Synod of Dort. Although the supralapsarian position is known as Calvinism, it is really Bezanism. Calvin died before Beza revived the supralapsarian order (although Beza and Calvin exchanged letters on the subject).

Beza's intent in reviving the supralapsarian order of God's pre-creation decrees was to prevent any possibility of synergistic salvation, which I defined as both God and the sinner make significant contributions to the sinner's salvation. Jacobus Arminius (1560–1609), whose followers developed Arminian soteriology after his death from his writings (the "Remonstrants" opposed by the Synod of Dort), was not a contemporary of Calvin, but was 45 years of age when Beza died. Synergistic concepts were present during (and before) Beza's time, and long discussed by the New Testament church. Synergistic soteriology had long before Beza been developed by the Roman Catholic Church, and was confirmed by the Council of Trent (1545–1563) before Beza's death.

Beza accomplished his objective (to prevent any possibility of synergism) by elevating God's sovereignty above all other attributes, even to the exclusion of some attributes. The problem with that approach is God's attributes cannot be divided. God is one essence. No one attribute operates apart from all other attributes. God's attributes are not joined; they are in a state of oneness: "the whole essence is in each attribute and the attribute is the essence" [Shedd, 1:254; see also Dolezal, 43]. Supralapsarianism created an unjust God, a God who is a monster, a God who exercises arbitrary sovereignty.

Supralapsarianism has several serious problems.

> Problem one, men who are not contemplated as sinners are ordained to eternal punishment.

Since, in this view, God decided the eternal fate of men before the decision to decree sin, then he specifically created some men to eternal damnation, without a just reason for their damnation.

Put bluntly, in the supralapsarian view, those whom God created to elect to eternal damnation were viewed as righteous when he damned them. That is arbitrary sovereignty, that is unjust, that is monstrous.

> Problem two, God decreed Adam must commit his act of disobedience.

In the supralapsarian doctrine, God did not permit or allow Adam's exercise of free will to choose to disobey. In the supralapsarian doctrine God took away Adam's free will, God decreed Adam must sin. The supralapsarian doctrine makes God the culpable (criminally responsible) author of sin. Put bluntly, God created sin by making Adam sin.

> Problem three, attributes like love and mercy are not extended to all humankind.

In the supralapsarian doctrine, God loves only the elect. One modern supralapsarian, Dr. David Engelsma, in *Common Grace Revisited*, wrote, "God is not kind . . . to all unthankful and evil people" and the idea of God loving all is "absurd, if not blasphemous." Supralapsarian doctrine rules out any act of the Lord to show and display grace or mercy to those who never believe.

In the supralapsarian doctrine, when Jesus gave us the exhortation in Matthew 5:44–45, he did not really mean it.

> Love your enemies, and pray for those persecuting you; bless those cursing you, do good to those misusing you and hating you, 45 so that you may be sons of your Father in the heavens.

Because he makes his sun rise on evil and good, and sends rain on righteous and unrighteous.

In the supralapsarian doctrine, God makes the sun rise and the rain fall only on the elect, and if those things happen to affect the non-elect, that is just an unhappy coincidence, because the benefits of Christ's propitiation are only for the elect.

The supralapsarian doctrine is opposed by scriptural concepts and teaching of God as just, e.g., Genesis 18:25, "Shall not the Judge of all the earth do right?" The supralapsarian doctrine sees God as electing righteous persons to eternal condemnation—righteous because not yet fallen in the order of God's decrees according to the supralapsarian doctrine. This view also contradicts scriptural ideas concerning the treatment of the innocent, and relieving misery (an aspect of mercy).

In the supralapsarian doctrine, when Christ said, "disciple all the peoples (Matthew 28:19), and "Go into all the world, proclaim the Good News to all the creation," (Mark 16:15), he meant only go to the elect. When Christ said, "the one thirsting, the one desiring—let him come, let him take freely the water of life" (Revelation 22:17), and Paul said, "all that may call upon the Lord's name will be saved," Jesus and the Holy Spirit meant only the elect.

The supralapsarian doctrine seems to be the dominant view today. It isn't, it is just the one with the loudest supporters. Many only superficially understand. The supras- gained the upper hand in the debate when the TULIP was invented in 1905 [Stewart, *Ten Myths,* appendix], and then popularized in 1934 by Boettner's book, *The Reformed Doctrine of Predestination.* Since then the supras- have been the loud and obnoxious voice in the room; many follow the loudest voice without examining the content.

Excursus: John Owen

One who did understand the supralapsarian doctrine was John Owen (1616–1683), its most well-known supporter. Owen was three years old when the Canons of Dort were published, and grew up with the continuing debate of lapsarian views.

Owen viewed the infra- and sublapsarian doctrine of "sufficient for all," as a form of universalism, conveniently ignoring the latter half of that statement, "efficient to salvation only for the elect." His argument against universalism is long and complex, and here I will only give his summary of six previous points. [*Works*, 10:264. Reprinted in *The Death of Death in the Death of Christ*, 152].

> This, I say, being that reconciliation which is the effect of the death and blood of Christ, it cannot be asserted in reference to any, nor Christ said to die for any other, but only those concerning whom, all the properties if it, and acts wherein it doth consist, may be truly affirmed; which, whether they may be of all men or not, let all men judge.

Owen made two errors. The first is he denies the efficacy of faith. The unlimited merit of Christ's propitiation of God for sin must be applied by faith to be efficacious unto salvation. No faith, no salvation. In a mundane illustration, electricity is always at the electrical outlet, but nothing happens until one plugs into the outlet. So faith must plug into Christ's merit for there to be salvation.

Owen's other error is he made Christ's propitiation man-centered instead of God-centered. His argument is Christ died only for the elect. No, Christ died to propitiate God for the crime of human sin, thereby fully satisfying God's justice and holiness. Owen assumes a propitiation of God for all human sin must mean all sinners must be forgiven of their sins. But throughout the Scripture, Old Testament and New Testament, the merit that forgives—the merit of Christ's propitiation—must be applied by God's grace through the sinner's faith, else there is no forgiveness. The limitless merit of the propitiation is applied only by God's grace through the sinner's faith. No faith = no salvation.

Therefore, the right premise is God applies the limitless merit of Christ's propitiation according to his eternal decrees: temporal benefits for all humankind, eternal benefits for the elect.

Returning to the discussion of lapsarian views.

Infralapsarian

The infralapsarian view understands the order of God's foreordaining decrees to be the following. God decided:

To create.

To permit the fall.

To elect some out of this fallen mass to be saved, and to leave the others as they were.

To provide a redeemer for the elect.

To send the Holy Spirit to apply this redemption to the elect.

According to the infralapsarian view, the decree of election

257

followed the decree permitting the fall. Sin was the background in which God viewed all human beings, and from which he chose to save some. None were innocent because the fall was permitted (not decreed) before the election.

In the infralapsarian doctrine, there is no election to reprobation. In deciding who to elect God contemplated all as sinners. God chose to rescue some from sin. He chose to take no action, pro or con, toward those not chosen. Election guarantees salvation, nothing more, nothing less.

In the supra- order, God took away Adam's free will and decreed Adam must sin. In the infra- and sub- orders, God permitted-allowed Adam's freely made choice to sin. Looking back to a previous discussion of foreordination, out of all Adam's possible choices concerning the forbidden fruit, God chose to effectuate from possible to actual Adam's freely made choice to disobey and eat the fruit. Whether or not there was a different possible choice is irrelevant. Adam's choice was freely made within the historic context of his life, not decreed, and therefore Adam is criminally responsible for human sin. (For a discussion as to why the sinless Adam could chose to commit an act of sinning [his mutability and his free will are involved], see my book, *Adam and Eve, A Biography and Theology*.)

In the infralapsarian order man is the author of his endless punishment, God the author of endless salvation. This view agrees with Scripture, e.g., those who are saved were chosen out of the world in which all are sinful. All men are viewed as they are in sinful Adam, made out of the same lump of sinful clay, Romans 9:21, out of which God took some clay and fashioned it into vessels of honor.

The debates in the Synod of Dort concerning the extent of the propitiation were long and difficult, infamously at one point resulting in a challenge to a dual over competing positions. All agreed salvation was monergistic. All the monergistic concepts of the extent of the propitiation had been present in the history of the New Testament church since at least the beginning of the Reformation; longer if we include Augustine and other church fathers.

Yet, in the end, a consensus was reached among the participants, which did not satisfy all, but was agreeable to most. Nor did that consensus agreement fully answer all the issues posed by each competing view. The majority of the Synod declared for the infralapsarian order of decrees as the official Reformed doctrine of soteriology: sufficient for all, efficient for the elect. The loud and obnoxious supralapsarian doctrine stands outside the official statement of Reformed doctrine.

Sublapsarian

The sublapsarian view is similar to the infralapsarian view. The difference is the order of "provide a redeemer" and "election" are reversed.

To create.

To permit the fall.

To provide a redeemer

To elect some out of this fallen mass to be saved, and to leave the others as they were.

To send the Holy Spirit to apply this redemption to the elect.

The sublapsarian doctrine reverses two of the items in the infralapsarian order.

Infralapsarian: to elect; to provide a redeemer for the elect

Sublapsarian: to provide a redeemer; to elect.

The difference is this. In the Infralapsarian order Christ is the redeemer only for the elect; This is the strictest interpretation of Dort's "sufficient for all, efficient for the elect" doctrine.

The sublapsarian order takes the "sufficient for all, efficient for the elect" doctrine to its logical conclusion: Christ is a redeemer for all upon the condition of faith. More plainly, God's foreordained gift of grace-faith-salvation guarantees the salvation of the elect, but a) there are also temporal benefits to the non-elect, and b) because Christ is a redeemer for all, then any non-elect may be saved if he meets the condition for salvation: faith in God and God's testimony as to the way of salvation. Election has only the elect in view, guaranteeing their salvation, saying nothing pro or con about the non-elect. I repeat myself, God does not prevent faith or salvation that is what sin does.

The True Nature Of Christ's Propitiation

My order of God's precreation decrees is close to the sublapsarian order, but with a significant difference.

To create.

To permit the fall.

To satisfy God's justice and holiness through a propitiation for sin.

To elect some out of the fallen mass of humanity to be saved, and to take no action toward the others to affect or effect their sinful state.

To send the Holy Spirit to apply the limitless merit of Christ's propitiation to the elect, thereby effecting their salvation.

What is the difference? The supra-, infra- and sub-lapsarian orders teach propitiation = redemption. Those views make the purpose of Christ's propitiation man-centered. I believe the Scripture teaches the purpose of Christ's propitiation was God-centered. "To satisfy God's justice through a propitiation for sin." Salvation is an application of the propitiation, not the primary purpose. If no one was elected, if God had decided to leave all sinners to their own choices and none believed, God would still need to be propitiated, because his justice and holiness must act to satisfy itself. Could God act to propitiate himself and save no one? He almost did, in the Noahic Flood, when only eight were saved. How wonderful God's love and grace and mercy fully satisfied his justice and holiness so sinners could be saved, and that God chose to act directly to save some, and chose to not act directly to prevent any.

Christ's propitiation was the full satisfaction of God's justice for the crime of sin through a suitable vicarious sacrifice suffering the judicial penalty against sin. The primary purpose of the propitiation was to fully satisfy God's justice for the crime committed against his holiness.

Romans 3:25, Whom God set forth publicly as a propitiation, through faith in his blood, for declaring his righteousness.

Hebrews 2:17, in order to make propitiation for the sins of the people.

1 John 2:2, Now he is propitiation for our sins—but not for ours only but also for all the world.

1 John 5:10, In this is the love: not that we have loved God, but that he loved us, and sent his Son, a propitiation concerning our sins.

In the interpretation of Scripture, every scripture relevant to a doctrine must be considered, and harmonized, which is to say, no contradictions allowed. The three lapsarian views discussed above, supra-, infra-, sub-, and in fact every Reformed theology discussion on the subject, focuses on "a propitiation for redemption." But the simple scriptural fact is the purpose of Christ's propitiation was to satisfy God for the crime of sin, "for declaring God's righteousness," and salvation is one of the applications of that merit.

Therefore, the biblical doctrine is this: Christ propitiated God's holiness and justice for every human sin from Adam to the end of the world, and the limitless merit of that propitiation is applied according to God's decrees. The correct doctrine is not "limited atonement" as in the egregious TULIP, but "unlimited propitiation and particular redemption."

What does the limitless merit of Christ's propitiation mean for all humankind? In the supra- doctrine, nothing. In the infra- doctrine, potentially something. In the sub- doctrine most likely something. In the doctrine of others, including me, something for everyone according to God's mercy.

My studies in the Scripture have led me to believe positively that "something for everyone" is both temporal and eternal benefits to all humankind from Christ's propitiation of God for all human sin. I have already described the eternal benefits: conditioned upon saving faith. That condition is positively met for those saved by God's foreordaining choice, election, to give some sinners his gift of grace-faith-salvation, Ephesians 2:8. Therefore salvation is never a matter of personal merit, but of God's choice.

(Some may wonder why I refer to God's gift as grace-faith-salvation. The reasons are grammatical and doctrinal. Doctrinally, there is no salvation apart from God's grace and the believer's faith. Both are required for salvation, that is the salvation principle. Grammatically, the neuter pronoun "that," [and that not of yourselves] refers to both the masculine participle "you are saved" and the feminine noun "faith." See my commentary on Ephesians for more detail.)

The reason I believe in temporal benefits from Christ's propitiation is judicial: God's justice against the crime of sin has been satisfied. This is where the supralapsarian camp will shout out the accusation "universal salvation," but that is because their doctrine must make propitiation = redemption rather than propitiation = judicial satisfaction. The result of propitiation = judicial satisfaction is there are eternal benefits for some human beings and temporal benefits toward all humankind, each kind according to God's character and decrees.

Christ's propitiation of God for human sin fully satisfied God's justice for the crime against his holiness. Therefore, God can justly act in mercy toward the unforgiven sinner. God can justly delay judgment and justly relieve misery, which are the two aspects of God's mercy toward all humankind. (The delay in Satan's judgment to Revelation 20:10 is not due to Christ's act of propitiation. Christ propitiated God for human sin only.)

Above I criticized the supralapsarian doctrine for limiting God's mercy to the elect only, so that in the supralapsarian doctrine sunshine and rain on the non-elect is just an unhappy accident, not God's intent. The doctrine that propitiation = judicial satisfaction fully explains how God may be merciful to sinners. As one example,

> God's justice requires sin be immediately judged and the sinner immediately punished, no delay.
>
> Why is God able to delay judgment, and thereby give the sinner a lifetime to repent, belief, and be saved? Because propitiation = judicial satisfaction.
>
> How is God able to give blessings to the unforgiven sinner, when just wrath is required? Because propitiation = judicial satisfaction.

If Christ's propitiation = redemption, then God is justly unable to give mercy and blessing to any but the elect. Because propitiation = judicial satisfaction, God is able 1) to give undeserved temporal benefits toward all human beings, saved or unsaved, elect or not elect and 2) gives eternal benefits to his elect.

My Lapsarian Doctrine

My soteriology relevant to the order of God's pre-creation decrees may be described thus. The decree of foreordination incorporates all the righteous and sinful choices each person will make during their lifetime, and sovereignly causes all choices, holy or sinful, to accomplish the purpose God had in mind when he created the universe.

The order of God's foreordaining and electing decrees (including the subsequent decree of predestination) is proposed to be:

The decision to manifest his glory.

The decision to manifest his glory in a particular manner by creating a universe populated with sentient creatures.

The exercise of his omniscient knowledge and wisdom to understand all possible agents, events, and outcomes in the proposed universe that *could* fulfill his purpose.

The decree of foreordination: to create a particular universe by choosing to effectuate from possible to actual certain agents, events, and outcomes (out of all possible) that *would* fulfill his purpose.

The decision to permit the fall of mankind into sin.

The decree to satisfy God's justice and holiness through a propitiation for sin.

The decree to elect some out of the fallen mass of humanity to be saved, and to take no action toward the others to affect or effect their sinful state

The decree to send the Holy Spirit to apply the limitless merit of Christ's propitiation to the elect, thereby effecting their salvation.

The decree of predestination to conform the saved person to the image of Christ, and to adopt him or her as a son of God and joint-heir with Christ.

The omnipotent and omniscient act of creating the universe.

No list, of course, can fully capture, nor accurately define, exactly what God thought and did in eternity-past. However, based on what God has recorded in Scripture about God's character and God's decisions, and looking at subsequent events, and applying reason and logic to what the Scripture says, the order I have proposed seems a rational view of God's decisions, decrees, and actions concerning foreordination, election, and predestination.

The TULIP

The original points of the Canons of Dort are not accurately reflected in the TULIP, which is not surprising as the TULIP is a child of the supralapsarian doctrine. The Canons of Dort may be summarized in these points.

Personal, Gratuitous Election to Everlasting life

Particular Redemption

Depravity, native and total

Effectual Calling, or Regeneration by the Holy Spirit

Certain Perseverance of Saints unto Eternal Life

My soteriology also has a list of points.

Free Will Dominated by Sin

Christ's All-sufficient Propitiation of God

Particular Redemption by God's Choice

Enlivened by God's Efficacious Grace

Faith that Receives Salvation and Eternal Life

Perseverance in the Faith by Faith to the End of Life.

A good friend (Dr. Keith A. Sherlin) has suggested this acronym.

"S" for Sacred Image

"A" for Abandoned Goodwill

"V" for Victorious Atonement

"I" for Immutable Election

"O" for Overwhelming Grace

"R" for Regenerated Forever

Summary

The propitiation of God made by Christ on the cross is the only limitless merit by which a sinner—any sinner living in Old or New Testament times—may be saved from the penalty due the crime of sin. That salvation always was, is, and always will be full and complete, never partial. All saved persons are effected by the principle expressed in 2 Corinthians 5:8.

Christ's propitiation is not synonymous with or equal to the redemption of sinners. Redemption is one of the applications God makes of the limitless merit of the propitiation. He applies that unlimited merit to redemption according to his foreordaining decree that accomplished the election of certain sinners, through giving those chosen sinners his gift of grace-faith-salvation.

God also makes use of and applies the limitless merit of the propitiation to justly act in mercy, goodness, and kindness toward all humankind, both delaying deserved justice for their unforgiven sin, and relieving the misery cause by sin.

Christ's propitiation was judicial in nature, legally satisfying God's justice for the crime of sin committed against his holiness. Because God's justice was satisfied (propitiated) God is justly able to act redemptively toward the elect, and temporally toward all human beings.

The TULIP acronym was developed in 1905 as a mnemonic for the supralapsarian doctrine (see Stewart, Appendix.) The original five points of the Synod of Dort do not form a cute acronym, but accurately reflect the official standard for the Reformed and Dispensational doctrine of soteriology.

My own lapsarian order reflects my understanding of God's precreation decisions in foreordination, election, and predestination. My six points of soteriology reflect a complete and biblical Dispensational soteriology.

Justification

Statement of the doctrine.

> Justification. A believer is permanently positionally declared "not guilty of the crime of sin" through saving faith in Christ: in his court of justice God declares those whom he has saved "not judicially guilty," of the crimes of their sins, Rom. 8:1.

Justification is purely a legal matter. Possessing the sin attribute in human nature, and committing acts of sinning, are crimes against the laws of God. The sinner is guilty of the crime of sin by nature and by action. Justification declares the sinner Not Guilty of the crimes of sin.

The reason a sinner may be declared "Not Guilty" for the crime of sin is someone else paid the penalty for the crime. That someone else was Jesus the Christ. The limitless merit of Christ's propitiation is applied by God to remit the judicial guilt of the person God is saving.

In salvation the believer is freed from the penalty of sin, the dominion (power) of sin, the desire for and pleasure of committing sin, and at death (or rapture) endlessly separated from the presence of sin in his or her human nature.

The Holy Spirit regenerates the saved person's human nature, reprioritizing the attributes to serve God not self. In these New Testament times, the Holy Spirit takes up permanent residence in the believer's soul, John 14:17; Acts 10:44–48; 1 Cor. 6:19. The righteousness of Christ is imputed to the now-believing sinner, and a new principle of life, holiness, is added to the believer, Eph. 4:24, becoming the dominating principle in his/her human nature, 1 Thess. 4:7; 1 Cor. 3:17b; Col. 3:12; 1 Pet. 1:15–16.

The believer has been empowered through his or her saved human nature to say "No," to temptation to sin, and enforce that choice, and thereby is empowered to live a life of habitual righteousness, 1 John 3:9.

Justification is dependent on propitiation. The following is from my book, *God Became Incarnate* (lightly edited to the present purpose)

Jesus the Offering for Sin Died Physically and Spiritually

Jesus Died Physically

An offering for sin must be made physically as well as spiritually.

The body as well as the soul must suffer the penalty, because the penalty for sin is physical and spiritual death. When Adam and Eve sinned they were separated from fellowship with God: a spiritual death. Physically, they continued their slow decline to an inevitable physical death, Genesis 3:19 (there is nothing to suggest they were created physically immortal). So too their children, as revealed in the repeated "and he died" in Genesis 5, and throughout Scripture as men, women, and children physically died.

> One of the soldiers, seeing that Jesus was dead, John 19:33 (compare Matthew 27:54; Mark 15:44–45; Luke 23:47), stabbed the body through the heart with a spear. Why did he do this if he knew Jesus was dead? In the Roman military the soldiers responsible for the execution would suffer the penalty of the condemned if they allowed the condemned to escape. The soldier wanted to make sure there was no mistake. Out of a strong sense of self-preservation he stabbed Jesus through the heart to make sure his initial evaluation was correct: Jesus was dead.

> Jesus' state of death was confirmed to Pilate by the Centurion in charge, Mark 15:44. Not merely that Jesus was dead, but that "he had been dead for some time."

> Jesus' enemies also knew he was dead. In the ancient world people died at home, in the streets, on the battlefield, and at places of execution. Everyone from childhood to old age knew and recognized the state of death, for they saw death face to face in their daily experiences. Jesus' enemies went to Pilate to ask for guards for the tomb, saying, Matthew 27:63, "we remember while he was still alive," indicating their knowledge that Jesus was dead. They had watched him die on the cross. They had seen the soldier stab Jesus through the heart.

> Nicodemus and Joseph knew Jesus was dead, John 19:38–42. Death was a constant presence in the ancient world. There were no hospices, no hospitals, no funeral homes, no cremation societies. Family, relatives, and friends buried their dead. They knew a dead body when they saw one. If Jesus had merely fainted, then the constant handling required to wash and wrap the body would have revived him. Jesus was physically dead.

The soldiers knew he was dead, his enemies knew he was dead, and his friends knew he was dead.

Scripture states the death of Jesus in the plainest terms. Matthew 27:50, Jesus yielded up his spirit. Mark 15:37, Jesus breathed his last. Luke 23:46, Jesus breathed his last. John 19:30, Jesus gave up his spirit. He died physically, fully satisfying the physical penalty for sin.

Jesus Died Spiritually

Jesus imputed to himself, and the Father and Spirit imputed to him the judicial guilt of the sins of the world to Jesus.

2 Corinthians 5:21, The one not having known sin, God made to be sin for us, so that we might become the righteousness of God in him.

1 John 2:2, Now he is propitiation for our sins—but not for ours only but also for all the world.

Jesus deliberately and voluntarily died to pay the penalty for sin.

Jesus is the offering and the offeror: in the Old Testament type the offeror killed the sin offering, Leviticus 4:4, 24, 29, 33. John 19:30 answers the question. "Jesus said, 'It is finished.' Then bowing his head he gave up his spirit."

Jesus completed the spiritual death for sin before he caused his physical death. Spiritual death is separation from God. Was Jesus spiritually separated from God while on the cross? Yes, seen at Mark 15:34 when he said, "*Eloi, eloi, lama sabachthani*," which being translated is, "My God, my God, why have you forsaken me?"

As his time of spiritual death was ending, and the time for his physical death drew near, he was thirsty. He knew every Scripture from his incarnation to this moment had been fulfilled, except one, Psalm 69:21, "for my thirst they gave me vinegar to drink." He said, "I thirst," John 19:28; and then he drank, John 19:30a; he gave his cry of victory, Mark 15:34; and then he bowed his head and separated his soul from his body, John 19:30b. Before he died physically Jesus knew he had accomplished the spiritual death required by the penalty for sin.

During his last moments of physical life on the cross, we can see that the sin-debt was fully paid. Earlier he had cried out that God had forsaken him. Now he said, Luke 23:46, "Father." This word from their familial and filial relationship indicated the spiritual penalty had been paid and his fellowship with God had been restored. He said, "Father, into your hands I commit [entrust] my spirit," knowing that he would be received in heaven. And then he breathed his last. With the physical and spiritual penalties of sin paid in full, with every necessary Scripture fulfilled, he caused his soul to separate from his body, and went to his Father, taking the saved thief with him.

Permanently Justified

A believer is permanently positionally justified in Christ. Positional justification is God seeing the believer as in Christ. Christ is the Just One, the believer is justified from the crime of sin in Christ, because a) Christ is the only person who has propitiated God for human sin, and b) he/she has placed their faith God and God's testimony as the means by which God's grace in salvation and Christ's merit is to be accessed.

Jesus Is The High Priest

Jesus was not only the offering for sin, and the offeror, and the altar where the offering was made, he was also the high priest of God who presented the offering.

"For God is one, and one mediator between God and men, the man Christ Jesus," 1 Timothy 2:5 (cf. Gal 3:20; Hebrews 8:6; 9:15; 12:24). In the Old Testament the priest took the sacrifice killed by the offeror and presented it to God on the altar. The priest was appointed by God to be a mediator effecting reconciliation between God and man by presenting the completed sacrifice to God. In his work he illustrated Christ as the one true mediator who in his Person and work (on the cross) effected eternal reconciliation between the sinner and God. Christ is the true mediator because he is related to God and man and is the equal of both, thus able to fully represent the interests of both God and man.

The scriptures specifically state Christ came as high priest to offer a sacrifice for the sins of his people.

> Hebrews 9:11–12, Christ came as high priest . . . with his own blood . . . having obtained eternal redemption.
>
> Hebrews 9:28, Christ appeared in the presence of God on our behalf.
>
> Hebrews 10:12, Jesus, offered one sacrifice for sins forever.

At Hebrews 9:14 the Writer stated, "Christ . . . through the eternal spirit offered himself unblemished to God."

Many versions capitalize the word "spirit" as a reference to the Holy Spirit. The latter part of the verse is clear: Jesus the Christ was the priest who made the offering to God: he offered himself. The first part means Christ's soul and the Holy Spirit were both necessary to the offering of Christ. "The acting of his human soul with his deity essence was required for the *efficacy and effect* of his offering; the acting of the Holy Spirit was required for the *manner* of his offering" [Owen, Works, 22:304]. The whole person, the God-man, accomplished his work as high priest; the whole Trinity—Father, Son, Spirit—made the offering efficient to salvation.

Jesus Is God Who Received The Sacrifice

Jesus is God who received and accepted the sacrifice as full payment for sin. Every member of the Trinity participates in the works of each member of the Trinity. In discussing Hebrews 9:14, I said Christ and the Holy Spirit participated together in the offering of Christ. To whom was the offering made? To the Father, Mark 15:34; John 19:30; Luke 23:46, who accepted the offering as the full and complete satisfaction for sin. The godhead—Father, Son, and Spirit—received the God-man's propitiation for sin.

Is the one who made the propitiation also the one who received the propitiation? The Scripture says, "In Christ dwells all the fullness of the Deity," Colossians 2:9. The two definite articles ("the") in the Greek text require a specific fullness and a specific deity. The Deity is the one true God Christians worship. The fullness is the person God: the Father, Son, and Spirit who are con-substantial and co-essential. In Jesus the Christ dwells God the Son who is con-substantial and co-essential with God the Father and God the Spirit.

Summary

The God-man was the complete and full satisfaction for sin. By his deity acting through his humanity, with the continuing work of the Holy Spirit on his behalf, Jesus the Christ fulfilled every part required for a complete propitiation of God's holiness and justice for the crime of human sin. Jesus Christ became the sinless vicarious offering for sin by imputing sin to himself. Through his human nature he represented the offeror making a sacrifice for sin. His human body and soul were the altar where the propitiation was made. God consecrated him the High Priest-Mediator of humanity to present the completed sin-offering to God. Through his deity nature Jesus was God who received and accepted the completed propitiation for sin. The believer is wholly justified—declared not guilty—for the crime of sin through Christ's unlimited merit.

Sanctification

Statement of the doctrine. Sanctification has three aspects.

Positional sanctification is God separating the believer from sin and dedicating the believer to himself.

Experiential sanctification is the believer dedicating himself to God and separating himself from sin.

Eternal Sanctification is God removing the sin attribute from the believer's human nature at physical death or rapture, and then at resurrection the believer's dead physical body is transformed so as to be immortal and incorruptible, and enlivened by being permanently rejoined with the soul.

The believer is permanently positionally sanctified in Christ at the moment of salvation. God declares the believer dedicated to God and separated from sin (declared holy) in Christ.

A believer is called to experiential sanctification: personal holiness and righteousness of life; to perform and maintain good works which God has prepared beforehand (Eph. 1:4; 2:10; 2:21; 5:26; Rom. 12:1; Titus 2:14; 3:8). The believer is empowered to resist sin's temptations, live a holy life, understand the Scripture, worship, obey, fellowship with, and serve God. God hears and answers his/her prayers, and he/she perseveres by faith in the faith to lead a holy life, looking toward resurrection and eternal life in God's presence.

The believer will be eternally sanctified, which is that transformation of soul and body that occurs in the soul at physical death and in the body at the resurrection, thereby eliminating the sin attribute in body and soul, 1 Corinthians 15:53.

Sanctification In Greater Detail

Sanctification has three aspects: positional, experiential, and eternal.

Positional Sanctification: A result of salvation that occurs at the moment of salvation. The judicial guilt of personal sin is forgiven. The soul is regenerated to spiritual life. God shares the communicable aspects of his eternal life. The righteousness of Christ is imputed to the believer. The term "born-again" succinctly expresses initial sanctification. Initial (positional) sanctification defines the believer as he or she stands before God in Christ: forgiven, regenerated, possessing eternal life, judged as holy and righteous, placed into an eternal relationship with God. This status never changes, because sanctification is secured for the believer by Christ.

Experiential Sanctification: The sanctified believer uses the means of grace to conform his manner of living (thoughts and actions) to be more like Christ. God has given the believer new and eternal life, but has left the old nature (the sin nature) resident in the flesh. The new life a believer has is a product of grace and is maintained by grace, but requires personal effort to apply that grace so as to overcome the temptation of sin. Experiential sanctification is the believer's state before God in the world. One lives his or her life in such a manner so as to conform one's lifestyle to be godly and Christ-like. The believer makes a conscious effort to bring his state in the world to the same level of godliness, holiness, and righteousness as his standing in Christ. This is a life-long process in which the believer should steadily progress. A stairway illustrates the believers' progress in experiential sanctification. We learn, we practice what we learned (standing on a step), we progress (going up a step), sometimes we go down a step, we learn, we practice, we progress, etc. throughout life.

Eternal (aka: final) sanctification is that transformation of soul and body that occurs in the soul at physical death and in the body at the resurrection. Eternal sanctification eliminates the sin attribute in body and soul. In eternal sanctification the believer's state is the same as his standing. In every aspect of his or her life, for all eternity, the believer possesses godliness, holiness, and righteousness in every desire, every thought, and every action, sustained by God's grace.

Summary

Reformed and Dispensational soteriology agree on sanctification.

Predestination

Statement of the doctrine

> Predestination. God's decree to conform the believer to be like Christ according to certain aspects of Christ's spiritual character and physical form (Rom. 8:29–30; 1 John 3:2), and to place the believer in the legal position of God's son and heir (Eph. 1:5, 11), so that the believer has an inheritance from God and is God's heritage.

In Reformed theology, the term "predestination" smashes together four distinct biblical doctrines: foreordination + election + predestination + providence. See the definitions for each of these words.

Few people in Reformed or Dispensational theology distinguish predestination from election. In that aspect both theologies have done believers a great disservice. Election is God's decree affecting the unsaved. Predestination is God's decree affecting the saved.

> Election. Romans 8:28, "Now we know that to those loving God, all things work together for good, to those being *called according to his purpose.*"

The part I have highlighted is election.

> Predestination. Romans 8:29, For those whom he foreknew, also *he decreed beforehand to conform to the image of his Son,* for him to be firstborn among many brethren.

The part I highlighted is predestination.

Summary

Although both Reformed and Dispensational misidentify predestination as election, yet both agree God predestined the believer to be conformed to the image of Jesus Christ.

Perseverance

Statement of the doctrine.

> Perseverance. To persevere in the faith is to continue in the faith by means of faith throughout life and through physical death into eternity.

Perseverance is a grace God gives the believer to overcome all spiritual and physical obstacles to faith. Persevering faith is the believer using the means of grace God has provided for him or her to continue in the faith by faith. God tells his saved people to persevere, and he gives his saved people every grace and spiritual power necessary to be able to persevere.

By means of the grace of perseverance every believer will persevere in the faith by faith all the way through life to the end of physical life and into eternity in heaven in the immediate presence of God (Revelation 3:5, 12). Believers are those persons who receive and use the God-given grace of perseverance. Those who do not persevere in the faith by faith were never saved. (Hebrews 10:12, 14; Ephesians 2:8–9; John 10:9, 27–29; Romans 4:22–25; 5:1, 10–11, 18–19; 8:1; Hebrews 10:17–18.)

The subject of perseverance is important as part of the assurance of the believer's salvation, and as a challenge to the believer to use the grace given by God to persevere in the faith. Of secondary importance is opposing those theologies that deny God maintains the believer's salvation. Although some Dispensationalists are Arminian in their theology, the majority are not. The discussion is taken from my book *Christian Living and Doctrine*, lightly edited to the present purpose. One may also find a similar argument in my commentary on Hebrews.

What Is Persevering Faith

Persevering faith is often confused with the security of salvation or the assurance of salvation. The security of a believer's salvation is a matter of the basis of salvation, which is Christ's propitiation of God for human sin. If, as is the case, the only merit sufficient to save the sinner from the penalty due sin is the limitless merit of Christ's propitiation, then it must also be the case the only merit sufficient to maintain the sinner's salvation from the penalty due sin is the limitless merit of Christ's propitiation. This is exactly the argument in 1 John 1:8–2:2.

The merit that forgives a believer's acts of sinning, and allows Jesus Christ to be the sinning believer's representative before God when he or she does sin, is Christ's propitiation of God for sin.

The assurance of salvation comes from the testimony of the Scripture, the testimony of regeneration, and the righteous acts of the saved person.

> Assurance of salvation from the testimony of the Scripture: John 10:27–30; Hebrews 13:5.

> Assurance of salvation from the testimony of regeneration: 2 Corinthians 5:17; 1 John 3:9.

> Assurance of salvation from the testimony of righteous works: Ephesians 2:10; Titus 2:14.

For greater detail of assurance of salvation, see my digital format tract *How do I Know I Am A Christian?*, or the same information in my book *Christian Living and Doctrine*, chapter "How Can I Know I Am Saved."

The Basis Of Persevering Faith

That believers will persevere in the faith by means of faith is assumed throughout the New Testament. But there is a passage, Hebrews 10:36–11:1, that states the need for perseverance and the basis for persevering faith.

> Hebrews 10:36, 39, For you have need of perseverance, so that, having done the will of God, you may receive the promise ... But we are not of those withdrawing to destruction, but of faith to preserving the soul.

The above verses form the introduction to Hebrews 11, often called the hall of faith, but actually examples persevering faith for the reader's edification and encouragement. The opening verses state the basis of persevering faith.

> Hebrews 11:1, Now faith is the title deed of the things of which we are assured, the objective evidence of the things not yet seen.

Objectively, persevering faith is the "title deed" (*hupóstasis*), or "substance" of things "hoped" for. The word "hope" in Scripture, *elpízō*, means to expect with assurance; the word "expect" is the key to understanding Bible-based hope. This is not the "I hope it does (or doesn't) ..." of common speech; that brand of hope indicates uncertainty, perhaps anxiety. The hope of Scripture is certain: "I hope [I know with absolute assurance] that Jesus is returning, because he who promised is faithful" (John 14:3).

The "things of which we are assured" in Hebrews 11:1 are the promises God has made to believers concerning the future, 10:36. How then is "faith" the *hupóstasis* (title deed; substance) of the promises? The Writer's point is that faith gives certainty to the promises. What is a promise? Things of which we are assured but have not seen. Faith is believing God who cannot lie. Faith is informed by God's word and acts on the reality described by that word. Faith, then, is the *hupóstasis* of the promises—their substance, their present reality, a title deed—that gives certainty to the hope—the assurance—of receiving those promises.

How is faith itself the *hupóstasis?* The word *hupóstasis* means the real presence.

> In general, [*hupóstasis* is] that which underlies the apparent, hence, reality, essence, substance; that which is the basis of something, hence, assurance, guarantee, confidence (with the objective sense). The ground of confidence, assurance, guarantee, or proof. [Zodhiates, s. v. 5287.]

> Moulton and Milligan [659–660], give secular examples of *hupóstasis* to describe real property, thus, faith may be seen as the "title deed" of things hoped for; a title deed is the objective proof of legal possession.

A photograph or a sculpture of a person is representation. When the person is literally, physically standing before you, that is *hupóstasis*, the real presence, as seen of Christ as the person God, Hebrews 1:3, cf. John 14:9. But in Hebrews 11:1, the Writer uses *hupóstasis* in the sense of title deed, i.e., real possession. If I have the title deed to my car, house, or any real property, I have real possession whether or not the property is literally, physically before me. So faith is the title deed, the objective reality, of the things promised but not yet seen.

A simple real-world example. After my parents died, as the executor of their estate I tried to sell their recreational vehicle. I could not sell it without a series of legal actions to transfer the title to me. Why? The title deed said the RV was my parent's possession, and it did not matter they were dead, because it was their name on the title deed, not mine. Objective Holy Spirit given faith and understanding in God and his testimony in the Scripture is the title deed that gives us the assurance of receiving God's promises. The believer's name is on the title deed, written there by God and maintained by God. This title deed cannot be transferred or otherwise destroyed, because kept in God's hands, John 8:28–30.

On the basis of the objective reality of the promises, the believer perseveres in the faith by means of faith knowing he will receive the promises. Persevering faith is therefore a grace God gives that the believer may possess an objective reality of the promises, and perseverance is the grace the believer uses to persevere in that faith by means of faith.

The concept of faith itself being the objective reality of the promises will be new to some readers. So I will continue with the explanation.

An example of how the Hebrews Writer intends his readers to understand *hupóstasis* is in Hebrews 1:3. There the Writer says that Jesus is the visible "exact reproduction" (*charaktér*) of the *hupóstasis* (person/essence/substance) of the invisible God. The word *hupóstasis* at 1:3 means the Person of God was literally present: to see Jesus was and is to see God. Jesus was not a sculpture of God, not a photograph, not a hologram, not an appearance or manifestation; he was God in person, face-to-face.

As Jesus said to Philip, "he who has seen me has seen the Father," a statement indicative of both mental and sensual perception; compare the heard, seen, and touched of 1 John 1:1. The literal, physical presence of the incarnate God-man, Jesus the Christ, revealed the transcendent reality of the Father. Jesus the Christ is the *hupóstasis* of God: the physical, visible, audible presence of the reality of God in our universe, 1 John 1:1; John 14:9. Returning to Hebrews 11:1, the presence of faith is itself the real presence (*hupóstasis*) of the things anticipated with the certainty of their appearing (hoped for).

Another example of the Writer's use of *hupóstasis* is Hebrews 3:14. The Writer exhorted the believer to "hold the beginning of our *hupóstasis* (confidence) steadfast to the end." The word in the context of 3:14 could be translated "title deed." A title deed describes real property, such as land, a home, a car, or in this case, God's promises. When one legitimately possesses the title deed, he/she holds physical proof of possession of the property. When a believer has faith in the promise, faith is itself the title deed providing proof of possession of the promise. This is because genuine faith—title-deed kind of faith—cannot exist without conviction from the Holy Spirit.

Therefore, in Hebrews 3:14, *hupóstasis* refers to that certain reality in which one's faith is resting confident and assured. As the messenger of the confession of faith, 3:1, Jesus is the real presence of the reality of God (1:3) in which believers share, 3:14 [Kittel, 8:587]. So just as Jesus is the real presence of the reality of God, 1:3, and the proclamation of saving faith in Jesus, 3:1, is a description of the reality on which faith rests "from the beginning unto the end," 3:14, even so faith in the promise, 11:1, is the reality of receiving the promise. Persevering faith is based on the objective reality of the promises and the objective certainty of receiving the promises.

In Hebrews 11:1 faith is the *hupóstasis*. This is the kind or quality of faith in which the believer perseveres. When a believer has genuine God-given faith in the promises, then the reality of those promises is always present with the believer—his faith is his title deed to the promises. Not promises wished for or wondered about, nor an anxious "I hope so," but the steadfast assurance that the promises are real, genuine, imminent. God knows the doubts sin injects into our confidence, weakening our resolve to believe and persevere. He has given us promises, and given us faith as the title deed to the promises, to encourage us to use his grace of perseverance and persevere. By faith I am absolutely and completely assured of the reality of the things God has promised, and do in fact by the hand of faith hold them in my soul as a present reality.

In Hebrews 11:1, the word "substance," *hupóstasis*, and the word "objective evidence," *élegchos* [Zodhiates, s. v. 1650], are parallel descriptions. Faith is the *hupóstasis*, the presence of the reality, of things of which we are assured, and faith is the *élegchos*, the objective evidence, of things not seen. The Greek word *élegchos* is used in one other place in the New Testament, 2 Timothy 3:16, "All Scripture . . . is profitable . . . for *élegchos*, where it is translated "conviction" a subjective use of the word. In Timothy *élegchos* bears the subjective meaning "means of proof with a view to refuting," thus translated "conviction," or in some versions "reproof" or "rebuke."

In 11:1, *élegchos* is used in an objective sense. In one interpretation of Hebrews 11:1, *hupóstasis* and *élegchos* are interpreted as subjective: faith is the means of proof and persuasion of the things hoped for, not seen. A subjective interpretation means that the more faith you have (the quantity of faith), the stronger your belief in the promises. In this view, a small or weak faith cannot hold onto the promises; a large or strong faith holds fast to the promises.

That subjective view places the burden of perseverance solely on the believer. But Scripture teaches that God gives grace to persevere, e.g., Hebrews 13:5; Romans 8:28–39, grace which the believer is to receive and put to use in his or her life. Moreover, the Bible never speaks of the quantity of faith, but its quality, e.g., Matthew 17:20, where a tiny amount of faith is able to resolve big problems. Jesus' point was that one has faith, or does not. Quality, not quantity, is how faith perseveres: one either has faith, or does not.

> What is faith? Faith is inwardly believing the testimony of God through the infallible conviction given by the Holy Spirit, and faith is outwardly acting through the power given by the Holy Spirit to conform one's thoughts and actions to that conviction.
>
> A person is not "enabled" to believe by the Spirit's convicting power, but rather as being convicted of the truth, and on the basis of that conviction, each person appropriates and applies the truth to his or her specific circumstance, whether the spiritual issue is salvation or discipleship. That phrase, "appropriates and applies the truth," is what the Bible names "faith."
>
> Because genuine faith is conviction given by the Holy Spirit, the faith to persevere in the faith by means of faith is maintained in the believer by the Holy Spirit.
>
> Therefore, faith, like salvation, cannot be lost by the person who is genuinely saved.

An objective interpretation of *élegchos* is more in keeping with the use the Hebrews Writer makes of *hupóstasis*. For example, at 1:3, Jesus is not the means of proof demonstrating there is a God. Jesus is the objective presence of God. Since in Hebrews 11:1 *hupóstasis* and *élegchos* are parallel descriptions of persevering faith, then both must bear an objective meaning: the presence of faith is the objective reality (*hupóstasis*) and the objective demonstration (*élegchos*) of things *elpízō* (assurance), possessed though not seen.

An objective interpretation means God gives a believer that quality of faith which results in the steadfast assurance that the promises are genuine and imminent. An objective faith places the burden of "proof" on God and emphasizes the believer's moral responsibility to receive and use the grace God gives for perseverance.

Another reason both *hupóstasis* and *élegchos* must bear an objective meaning is that the things promised and hoped for, but not seen, are present in the spirit domain, i.e., in heaven. If the faith described in Hebrew 11 is subjective, then man is trying to discern the reality of things in heaven through his sensual and rational faculties. This is not possible. Spiritual things are perceived through the spiritual perceptive faculty of the soul, not the sensual faculties by which man subjectively understands the material world.

The unsaved sinner cannot understand the things of God just because they are spiritually discerned (1 Corinthians 2:14), and the unsaved sinner's spiritual perception is dead (inoperative) because of sin. Nor can the saved sinner perceive spiritual things through his material senses, because those senses were designed and created to perceive the material world.

Faith is the means of perceiving the spirit domain because God the Holy Spirit is the source of spiritual perception (1 Corinthians 2:10–11). He reveals spiritual things to material man through the soul's faculty of spiritual perception employed by faith. Faith is the objective reality of things of which we are assured, the objective evidence of things not yet seen.

The Use Of Persevering Faith

What has been said above concerning the conviction required for saving faith is true for persevering faith. Persevering faith is based on the objective conviction that spiritual realities testified to in Scripture are certain to be received. Persevering faith is possible because the believer knows by conviction God keeps the promises he has made in the scriptures. This is not a matter of human perception, nor is it a matter of feeling persuaded. I objectively know God keeps his promises, because the spiritual reality of the matter has been revealed to me by God the Holy Spirit. Yes, a personal rational comprehension of Scripture is essential to perseverance, because God has created us to be rational beings whose choices are supported by reason.

There is a difference, however, between being certain because of experience and having experience validated by the certainty of faith. The certainty of faith—which must be based in spiritual understanding of Scripture—validates our experiences as genuine or false in relation to the promises of God. The certainty of faith causes us to make the choice to persevere and informs us when the practice of our faith, perseverance, is based upon spiritual reality. In Hebrews 11:1 the writer is not talking about the choice to persevere, he is addressing the basis for perseverance: the fact that Holy Spirit-given conviction of faith in God's promises is itself the real presence of things hoped for, the objective evidence of things not seen. The God-given conviction "faith" is the title deed God has given me for the promises I have been given but not received.

Persevering faith begins in Scripture and is supported by God-given conviction: I know God is keeping his promises because God has convicted me that he is faithful. One may read the Scripture and deny its veracity. Holy Spirit given conviction leads to faith that accepts the veracity of Scripture. That certainty is the basis of persevering faith.

Therefore, my *choice* to persevere in my Christian life *must* be based upon that Holy Spirit-revealed knowledge and conviction of the absolute, genuine spiritual reality given in the scriptures. Worldly circumstances can discourage, but not destroy. I can endure a great struggle with sufferings because I know, from the scriptures, by Spirit-given, Spirit-convicting absolute knowledge that God who cannot lie will be faithful to his promises to me. The presence of Holy Spirit-given faith is itself the objective reality of God's promises. We can say, then, that faith itself is the substance and title deed (*hupóstasis*) of God's promises (the things of which we are assured) in the same sense in which Jesus the Christ is the literal, physical reality of the presence of God. Faith is the reality of the promises of God.

Faith is also the objective evidence (*élegchos*) of the spiritual reality of the things not seen. I can't say this more plainly: objective faith is given by God, not created by man. Man's faith is more subjective: I know, I reason, I feel, therefore I act. The biblical truth is I persevere in faith, a subjective act, because I have an objective faith in the reality of the promises. Because the believer has God-given faith, the believer has assurance in the things not seen: the presence of faith is the objective evidence of the things not seen.

Because the believer is a sensual, rational creature, I will say this in a more familiar way: one's faith gives the perception of immediate presence to spiritual realities. Put another way, perseverance is knowing that "God said it, that settles it, I'm going to believe it and do it." The objective reality, *hupóstasis*, that God gives in the promises is itself the objective evidence the believer possesses the promises, and is the assurance the believer will receive the promises, because that (kind or quality of) faith comes only from God. If one has God-given faith, then one has the certainty needed to persevere and receive the promises.

Persevering Faith By Example

For by faith the elders obtained a good testimony (Hebrews 11:2). This is the announcement of the Writer's theme for chapter 11. I will not discuss these examples of persevering faith, except to say the Writer will concern himself with the fruits and consequences which follow faith. The examples in Hebrews 11 reveal the believer's part in perseverance.

Faith in the promises provides the basis for perseverance. I have received from God that grace of perseverance that gives certainty (conviction) concerning the goal or end result of perseverance: to receive the promises God has made to me in the scriptures. Faith is not, however, the efficient cause of perseverance. The act of persevering is a choice: I am persevering in the practice of my faith because I intend to receive the promises. If this were not true, if a decision need not be made to persevere, then the Writer would not have written 10:25–29, or 11:1–39; indeed, he could have ended his epistle at 10:25. The exhortation, "do not cast away your confidence," 10:35, has its counterpart in "you have need of endurance," v. 36. Both express the choice to be made. Having received God's grace of perseverance through faith, the believer must choose to act in perseverance by means of faith. That he will so choose (because convicted) does not lessen the necessity of making a choice. The grace of God doesn't work in spite of the believer, but always works through the believer's regenerated nature to accomplish God's will for the believer.

The exhortations in Hebrews 11, illustrated by the example of the elders, are intended to encourage the believer to make the right choice: to persevere in the faith by faith. Thomas Manton called this faith "sanctifying faith," a typically Puritan emphasis on separation from sin and dedication to God. The testimony of the elders illustrates the experiential sanctification required of believers: what one believes one must do. Because genuine biblical belief is gained though Holy Spirit given conviction, then what one believes one will do.

Faith must influence all the parts of the spiritual life. Without faith perseverance is noble morality (or ignoble stubbornness). Perseverance by means of faith is the self-motivated personal pursuit of that experiential sanctification which conforms the life to God's commandments. In the Hebrews 11 context, to persevere is to maintain unswerving confidence in the promises God has given in Scripture, through the conviction the Holy Spirit gives to the believer concerning the promises.

The choice to persevere includes the choice to use the means of grace to maintain one's faith. I am not speaking of certainty, which is conviction, but the use one makes of that certainty, which is choice: inner conviction should result in an appropriate outward action. The text in Hebrews 11:2 is *en taúta gár*, "for in this" kind of faith, which is to say, because of this kind of faith, the elders obtained, etc. What is intended is that through the exercise of their faith the elders obtained a good report or testimony concerning their perseverance in and by their faith. Their inner conviction—that grace received—was the basis for an appropriate choice. By the *exercise* of their faith the elders *maintained* their perseverance by using the grace of perseverance they had been given: Abel offered to God, Enoch pleased God, Noah prepared as directed by God, Abraham obeyed by faith in God, etc. The choice to persevere includes the choice to use the means of grace necessary to maintain one's faith.

We must always remember that in this mortal life, in all things spiritual, there is always a God-ward side and a man-ward side. God's responsibility is convicting his people of the certainty of spiritual reality (found in the scriptures) and empowering their soul to achieve the goal of successful perseverance, which is receiving the promises proclaimed in the scriptures. Man's responsibility is to choose to make appropriate use of the means of grace God provides to strengthen, mature, and encourage the believer in his or her faith, in order to continue to live according to faith, that he/she might persevere and receive the promises. If one's faith is genuine faith, then he or she will always make that choice to persevere.

What, then, are the means by which we are empowered to persevere? The persevering faith of the elders is demonstrated in that they took action based upon what God's Word said was true, and by the conviction of faith they held those things to be true. The Writer has not only presented the truths of the Christian faith in his epistle, he has also exhorted his readers to the practical expression of these truths.

The more immediate context is what I call the privileges and obligations, or duties, of the faith, 10:19–25. Faith is not some ambiguous feeling; faith—if it is genuine, God-given, soul-saving, persevering faith—looks toward the promised future as a solid and sure reality that demands appropriate action. The certainty of faith causes the believer to make the choice to persevere and informs the believer when the practice of faith, his or her perseverance, is based on the spiritual reality witnessed to by Scripture.

The choice and the practice are equally essential to the maintenance of faith. Although the conviction of truth is objective and absolute, the recognition and practical application of that conviction is subjective within the soul. One might liken faith to a spiritual "muscle" that requires constant exercise to maintain its tone and strength. Without constant exercise through practical application the subjective recognition of faith weakens. The result is that one comes less often into God's presence, uses prayer and devotion less frequently, becomes apathetic toward his believing brethren, and calloused toward their suffering in the world; ultimately, one abandons gathering together with his Christian brethren (thus the exhortations in Hebrews 10:19–25). As these wrong actions become habitual, perseverance is lessened and faith is weakened. If this describes you, return to the source. The faith that saved you from sin is the same kind of faith that preserves you from sinning.

We are, in this physical frame, creatures of subjective sense and rationality, whose faith must be practiced in practical expressions to be maintained all the way through the end of life to the promised reward. The certainty of faith causes us to make the choice to persevere, and informs us when the practice of our faith, perseverance, is based upon spiritual reality. No wonder, then, the Writer of Hebrews energetically exhorted his readers to press forward to spiritual maturity by putting their faith into practice, as did their spiritual ancestors. We too, in this modern day and age, as we wait for the soon-appearing of Christ, must persevere in the faith as they did, both spiritually and practically.

To persevere in the faith is to continue in the faith by means of faith all the way through life and death. Perseverance is a grace God gives the believer to overcome all spiritual and physical obstacles to faith and thereby continue in the faith, and persevering faith is the believer using the means of grace God has provided for him or her to continue in the faith. God tells his saved people to persevere, and he gives his saved people every grace and spiritual power necessary to be able to persevere. By means of the grace of perseverance every believer will persevere in the faith by faith all the way through life to the end of physical life and into eternity. Believers are overcomers; when they fall down they get up; they persevere.

Eschatology

Eschatology is the doctrine of last things. My views on eschatology are in the appendix "My Doctrine," and I will not repeat them here. However, eschatology and soteriology intersect with Reformed and Dispensational soteriology, and that is the subject I will address.

Technically, eschatology concerns any prophecy in the Old Testament and New Testament between its proclamation and its fulfilment. All prophecies of events future to the time of proclamation look forward to what is, at the time of proclamation, a last thing. Popularly eschatology is identified by the non-biblical term "end times" and focuses on what is identified in Old Testament prophecies as the "Day of YHWH," aka: Day of the Lord.

This chapter will limit its focus to the "end times" aspects of eschatology and soteriology.

The intersection between Dispensational and Reformed soteriology with eschatology is this: Reformed eschatology has no soteriology; Dispensational soteriology is alive and active in eschatology.

The following discussion is partly drawn from my books (lightly edited to the present purpose), *Dispensational Eschatology; A Private Commentary on the Bible: Revelation 1–7; A Private Commentary on the Bible: Revelation 8–16.*

Reformed Soteriology During The Tribulation

There is no Reformed soteriology during the Tribulation. Reformed eschatology does not believe in a literal Tribulation period and does not believe in a literal Davidic-Messianic Kingdom on earth following Christ's second advent. [Quotes from Boettner, 4.]

> Postmillennialism is the view that . . . the return of Christ will occur at the close of a long period of righteousness and peace [caused by the gospel and the saving work of the Holy Spirit] commonly called the *Millennium.*

> Amillennialism is the view that . . . there will be a parallel and contemporaneous development of good and evil—God's kingdom and Satan's kingdom . . . until the second coming of Christ . . . [then there will be] resurrection and judgment.

Reformed eschatology conflates Revelation 19:11–21, with 20:11–15, and 21:1–22:21, as one event. Christ returns, conducts final judgment, and the eternal kingdom begins.

Some postmillennialists believe "that just before the end [when the post-millennial Christ comes to receive the kingdom prepared by the Holy Spirit and the church and judge the world] God does permit a limited manifestation of evil" [Boettner, 69]. That view, however, is not the end of the Tribulation, Revelation 19:11–21, but corresponds with the final rebellion, Revelation 20:7–10, before the Great White Throne judgment, Revelation 20:11–15.

Dispensational Soteriology During The Tribulation

Dispensationalists argue for a literal Tribulation period and a literal Davidic-Messianic-Millennial reign of Jesus on the earth because the second advent is literal. The hermeneutical method which discovers a literal second advent in Revelation 19:11–16, should be consistently applied to the texts that teach the outcome of that advent, 19:17–20:10.

Because Dispensational eschatology includes a literal Tribulation and a literal Davidic-Messianic Kingdom, Dispensational eschatology includes soteriology.

During the Tribulation, i.e., at the beginning of the Tribulation, God will save 144,000 Hebrews to be his initial witnesses of the Good News during the Tribulation.

> Revelation 7:4, And I heard the number of them being sealed: one hundred forty four thousand, having been sealed out of every tribe of the sons of Israel.

Why Israel? Why not 144,000 gentiles? Jesus gave the most concise answer. "Salvation is from the Jews," John 4:22. The Tribulation period is part of the outworking of the Old Testament Day of the Lord (which is both the Tribulation and the Davidic-Messianic Kingdom). During the Day of the Lord-Tribulation, God interacts with gentiles through his saved people Israel—initially the 144,000 Hebrews.

What is the work of the 144,000? Proclaiming the Good News.

> Revelation 7:9–10, After these things I saw, and look, a great multitude, which no one was able to number it, out of every nation, and tribes, and peoples, and languages standing before

the throne and before the lamb, clothed with white robes, and in their hands palm branches. 10 And they were exclaiming in a loud voice, saying, "Salvation to our God, the one sitting on the throne, and to the lamb!"

Can we know all those were saved out of the Tribulation? Yes, Revelation 7:14, "These are the ones coming out of the great Tribulation. And they have washed their robes and made them white in the blood of the lamb."

All this Reformed soteriology could know, but they have abandoned the plain and normal meaning of the Scripture in their eschatology by keeping, not reforming, the Roman Catholic Church's eschatology. In Reformed eschatology everything is allegorical, a hermeneutic that depends on the interpreter's imagination. Nothing is real, it all means something else than what it plainly says.

What will be Good News proclaimed by the 144,000, and by those saved through their evangelistic work? The Christ who came before is coming again, repent, believe, be saved, because he is coming as a king to rule and judge in his promised kingdom.

During the Tribulation, the enemy of God will kill those who have faith in the coming Christ. Revelation 13:7, "And was given to it [the beast of 13:4–6] to make war against the saints, and to prevail over them." The loss of saved lives is so great, that the testimony of the saved is greatly limited. But God has prepared a solution, Revelation 14:6–7.

> And I saw another messenger, flying in mid-heaven, having the everlasting Good News to proclaim upon the earth dwellers, and upon every nation, and tribe, and language, and people. 7 He was saying in a loud voice, "Fear God, and give him glory, because the hour of his judgment has come, and worship the one having made heaven, and the earth, and sea, and springs of waters.

With so many believers killed during the Tribulation (7:9–14; 13:7), and all the 144,000 killed by the end of the Tribulation, and the two witnesses also killed at the end of the Tribulation (11:7), how does God ensure the message of redemption will continue until Christ returns?

Toward the end of the Tribulation days, the number of living believers available to proclaim the gospel is at its lowest than at any other time during the Tribulation. The Antichrist-beast appears to have won. He has not.

God is not deterred by the low number of living believers. According to Revelation 14:6, toward the end of the Tribulation, God will send one of his holy messengers "flying in mid-heaven, having the everlasting Good News to proclaim upon the earth dwellers, and upon every nation, and tribe, and language, and people."

This messenger proclaims the "everlasting Good News … in a loud voice." He is low enough and loud enough to be heard. He is heard (probably not seen) by "the earth dwellers … every nation, and tribe, and language, and people." There is no one on earth who does not hear the "everlasting Good News."

All hear, but how will each react? John's gospel 12:28–29 is informative.

> "Father, glorify your name." Therefore a voice came out of heaven: "I have both glorified it and will glorify it again." Therefore the crowd, the ones having stood and having heard, said "There has been thunder." Others said, "God's messenger has spoken to him."

Each will hear according to his or her capacity for spiritual perception, a capacity dependent on God's gift of grace-faith-salvation.

What is this "everlasting Good News?" We are told what the messenger says as he flies around the world—assuming the proclamation is not limited to the biblical world, for at this time toward the end of the Tribulation, there will be representatives of "every nation, and tribe, and language, and people" at the heart of the Antichrist-beast's kingdom.

Here is the "everlasting Good News": Fear God, and give him glory.

Why believe the everlasting Good News? Because the hour of God's judgment has come.

How does one fear God, and give him glory? Worship the one having made heaven, and the earth, and sea, and springs of waters.

God has simplified the Good News of salvation: "I am the one who created. Worship me." That is the most basic Good News.

> Psalm 19:1–3 (ESV), The Heavens declare the glory of God, and the sky above proclaims his handiwork. 2 Day to day pours out

speech, and night to night reveals knowledge. 3 There is no speech, nor are there words, whose voice is not heard.

Romans 1:19–20, Because the known of God is revealed in them, for God has revealed it to them. 20 For that which cannot be seen visibly of him are perceived being understood from the creation of the world by the things made, both his eternal power and deity, for them to be without excuse.

Revelation 14:7, Fear God, and give him glory, because the hour of his judgment has come, and worship the one having made heaven, and the earth, and sea, and springs of waters.

At this very late, at-the-last-minute moment as sinners are swiftly running out of time, at a time when most of the earth dwellers have condemned themselves by receiving the mark of the beast, God continues to proclaim salvation to those who have not received the mark, but also have not believed in God to be saved. All that is required will be to deny what you have always believed and turn to the Creator—your Creator—and believe in him unto salvation. God will save some.

Some reading the Revelation may be troubled that the "everlasting Good News" says nothing about repentance from personal sin and faith in Jesus Christ the risen Savior. That message has been proclaimed every day preceding this moment. There were 144,000 Israeli evangelists and a great multitude of saved. The two witness also proclaimed the Good News during the days preceding the messenger. The earth dwellers had heard the Good News of sin, of Christ the risen and returning Savior, and of salvation by God's grace through the sinner's faith. The "everlasting Good News" is built on that foundation. It is a final proclamation to believe and be saved before the end.

This is the only time God uses a holy messenger to proclaim the Good News. Messengers support the saved, Hebrews 1:14, but proclaiming the Good News is the work of the saved, not the messengers. However, God's purposes cannot be frustrated. The messenger is sent to fulfill Matthew 24:14, "And this Good News of the kingdom will be proclaimed in all the world for a testimony to all the nations; and then the end will come."

How is "Fear God, and give him glory" the "Good News of the kingdom?" Because God will reign in person over the earth he created, in the person of the God-man, Jesus the Christ. The Davidic-Messianic-

Millennial Kingdom is founded on the kingdom mandate expressed in Genesis 1:26–28. Humankind, beginning with Adam, was to rule the earth; we have failed to properly exercise the stewardship required by that kingdom mandate. Christ will not fail. The incarnate God-man will reign over the earth he created. "Fear God, and give him glory ... and worship the one having made heaven, and the earth, and sea, and springs of waters," for he is returning to reign.

Dispensational Soteriology During The Kingdom

As noted above, Reformed eschatology does not believe in the literal Davidic-Messianic Kingdom of Jesus Christ on the earth. What is this kingdom?

> The Davidic-Messianic-Millennial Kingdom. The kingdom promised in the Davidic covenant, 2 Samuel 7:11b–17; 1 Chronicles 17:10b–15, and described in Psalm 2. The ruler is Christ; the ruled are physically living mankind; the domain is the earth; the duration is one thousand years. The raptured and resurrected New Testament church will reign with Christ in this kingdom, 2 Timothy 2:12; Revelation 5:10, as will the resurrected Tribulation saints, 20:4–6.

Reformed eschatology acts like Revelation 20:4–6 is not Scripture. The Reformed ignore all the Old Testament scriptures concerning a literal kingdom. The concept of the Davidic-Messianic Kingdom was once considered too prominent in Scripture to deny. As Edersheim said [1:265, n. 3],

> A Kingdom of God without a King; a Theocracy without the rule of God; a perpetual Davidic Kingdom without a "Son of David"— these are *antinomies* (to borrow the term of *Kant*) of which neither the Old Testament, the Apocrypha, the Pseudepigraphic writings, nor Rabbinism were guilty.

Unfortunately, in the modern world, men have taught themselves to deny the kingdom. A literal Davidic Kingdom where the son of David—Jesus the Christ—rules on the earth is denied by many theologies of the modern age.

How does Reformed eschatology get around Scripture? By denying the future existence of national ethnic Israel in the plans of God through an allegorical hermeneutic that says the New Testament church is God's new Israel, or is God's continuation and fulfillment of Israel. Then, by allegorizing, spiritualizing, or ignoring every Scripture that speaks to a literal kingdom, Reformed eschatology makes the Davidic-Messianic Kingdom now in heaven, and later to be the eternal kingdom on a new heaven and earth, Revelation 21–22.

This is simply not the place for a lengthy discussion of the future reality of Christ's Davidic-Messianic Kingdom on earth. But I will address a few issues. One issue involves national ethnic Israel's rejection of the kingdom offered by Christ. Was the Davidic-Messianic Kingdom postponed to the future for the New Testament church? No, the Kingdom was not postponed, it is where it always was.

The point must be stressed that the Davidic-Messianic Kingdom required a crucified Savior. The salvation and kingdom in Isaiah 54–66 are the ordained consequence of the crucifixion-resurrection in Isaiah 52:13–53:12. The prophesied rejection of messiah in Psalm 118:22 is followed by prophesied salvation, prosperity, and blessing. The suffering in Psalm 22 is followed by the kingdom, 22:28. In Psalm 2:1–3 the Gentile nations conspire and plot against God's anointed. What would be the outcome? After the suffering comes the kingdom, 2:6–9. There was not and never would have been a Davidic-Messianic kingdom for national ethnic Israel without a suffering, crucified, resurrected, and ascended Savior.

Was the Davidic-Messianic Kingdom postponed by Israel's rejection? No. God's plan was always the crucifixion, then the church age, then the Davidic-Messianic-Millennial Kingdom. Just because God chose not to reveal the New Testament church age to the Old Testament prophets does not mean it was not always part of the plan. The church age was always part of the plan, as Paul reveals in Ephesians 2:11–3:13. Abraham's seed was always physical and spiritual—the sand of the sea; the stars in the heavens. Christ blessing all nations, tribes, peoples, and languages was always the plan, Genesis 12:3; Galatians 3:8. The Davidic-Messianic Kingdom promised to national ethnic Israel was proclaimed to be at hand, a genuine offer whose rejection was known and prophesied, and it is at present where it was always planned to be by the foreordaining choices of God: yet-future.

We are dealing with a sovereign God, are we not? Then let us think on these things like the sovereign God. Was God surprised when Israel rejected their Messiah? Did he have to postpone the kingdom? Did he need to create a church age to deal with an unexpected rejection? No, no, and no again. God knew all possible outcomes arising out of his decision to create the universe. Out of all possibilities he chose to effectuate the existing universe in which all created things, persons, agents, events, outcomes, and consequences exist by God's sovereign foreordaining choices. God's choices incorporate the decisions and actions freely made by sinful creatures. Therefore Israel's rejection of their Messiah was always known, and the Savior's crucifixion and resurrection was always the plan. These things God revealed in the Old Testament prophecies. Therefore the church age, though unrevealed to the prophets, was always part of the plan, and therefore the Davidic-Messianic-Millennial Kingdom was always purposed and planned to occur after the church age.

The plans and processes of God concerning the rejection of Messiah and the intervening church age may be seen in a subtle change in Matthew's Gospel. In Matthew 4:17 Jesus proclaimed the Davidic-Messianic Kingdom: "from that time" Jesus proclaimed the kingdom to be at hand. The phrase, "from that time" gives structure to Matthew's Gospel, and it reoccurs in Matthew 16:21, where it indicates a shift in the focus. The kingdom and its Messiah had been rejected. "From that time" forward Jesus focused on preparing the twelve for his death and resurrection. This does not mean he stopped evangelizing, healing, and confronting his enemies, but that the focus from Matthew 16:21 forward was the training of the twelve to assume the gospel proclamation after Jesus' death, resurrection, and ascension. When the Kingdom was rejected Jesus initiated the next step in God's plan: to prepare his apostles for the New Testament church.

A recent voice has also demonstrated the need for a literal earthly kingdom. In a convenient graphic, Dispensational author Michael Vlach [*Premillennialism*, 18] has presented some of the Scriptures to make the argument, that a Davidic-Messianic Kingdom is required to fulfill the kingdom mandate. The Davidic-Messianic-Millennial Kingdom is founded on the kingdom mandate expressed in Genesis 1:26–28. Humankind, beginning with Adam, was to rule the earth; we have failed to properly exercise the stewardship required by that kingdom mandate. Christ will not fail. The incarnate God-man will reign over the earth he created. "Fear God, and give him glory … and worship the one having made heaven, and the earth, and sea, and springs of waters," for he is returning to reign.

[Copied from Vlach's Facebook page. Used by permission.]

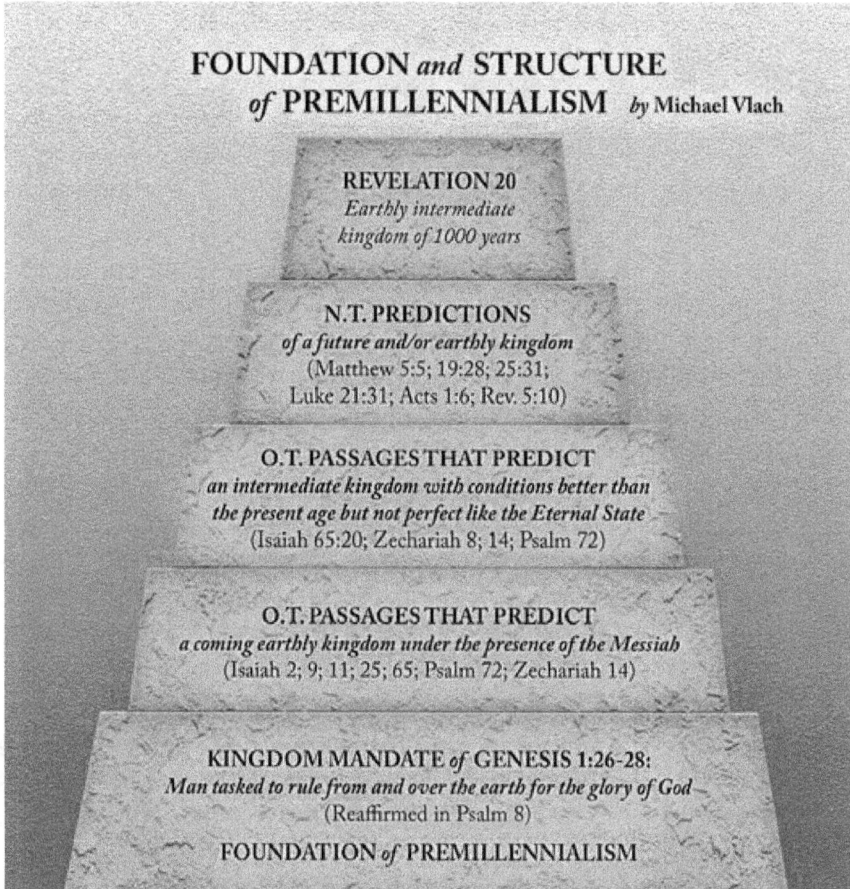

FOUNDATION and STRUCTURE of PREMILLENNIALISM by Michael Vlach

REVELATION 20
Earthly intermediate kingdom of 1000 years

N.T. PREDICTIONS
of a future and/or earthly kingdom
(Matthew 5:5; 19:28; 25:31;
Luke 21:31; Acts 1:6; Rev. 5:10)

O.T. PASSAGES THAT PREDICT
an intermediate kingdom with conditions better than the present age but not perfect like the Eternal State
(Isaiah 65:20; Zechariah 8; 14; Psalm 72)

O.T. PASSAGES THAT PREDICT
a coming earthly kingdom under the presence of the Messiah
(Isaiah 2; 9; 11; 25; 65; Psalm 72; Zechariah 14)

KINGDOM MANDATE of GENESIS 1:26-28:
Man tasked to rule from and over the earth for the glory of God
(Reaffirmed in Psalm 8)

FOUNDATION of PREMILLENNIALISM

God planned for the kingdom to be right where it is in God's "end times" scheme: on this present earth. Not created by the New Testament church (postmillennialism), not after final judgment, not on a new heaven and earth.

Let us now turn to soteriology during the kingdom.

The result of a literal Tribulation during which sinners are saved will result in all those not saved being executed for their sins, and only the saved entering the Davidic-Messianic Kingdom.

> Revelation 19:19–21, And I saw the beast, and the kings of the earth, and their armies, assembled to make war against the one sitting on the horse and with his army. 20 And the beast was captured, and with him the false prophet, the one who did signs in his presence, by which he deceived those who had received the mark of the beast and those worshiping its image. These two were thrown living into the lake of fire burning with sulfur. 21 And the rest were killed with the sword of the one sitting on the horse, going out of his mouth. And all of the birds were filled with their flesh.

> Matthew 25:41, 46, And then he will say to those on the left, "Depart from me, you cursed, into the eternal fire prepared for the devil and his messengers" ... And these will go away into eternal punishment, but the righteous into eternal life.

> Revelation 20:4–5, And I saw thrones, and they sat upon them. And judgment was given to them. And the souls of those who had been beheaded by reason of the testimony of Jesus, and by reason of the Word of God, and those not worshiping the beast, nor his image, and did not accept the mark upon the forehead, and upon their hand. And they lived and ruled with Christ a thousand years. 5 The rest of the dead lived not again until the thousand years should be completed. This is the first resurrection.

Only the saved surviving the Tribulation will enter into the Kingdom. These are living saints, not resurrected saints. Living saints like you and me, who will have children like you and me, children needing salvation. How do I know there will be those needing salvation during the kingdom?

> Revelation 20:7–9, And when the thousand years should be completed, Satan will be set free out of his prison, 8 and will go out to deceive the nations in the four corners of the earth, the Gog and Magog, to gather them to make war, of whom the number of them as the sand of the sea. 9 And they came up over the great expanses of the earth and encircled the camp of the saints and the beloved city. But fire came out of heaven and consumed them.

There will be people needing salvation during the Kingdom, therefore there will be Good News proclaimed so that sinners may be saved. The content of the proclamation is our next subject.

One of the facts of Scripture is it focuses more on the here and now of salvation than the future. Salvation is always by faith in God and God's testimony. The testimony in the millennial kingdom cannot be of a Christ who came, as it is during the New Testament church age, or a Christ who is coming as it will be during the Tribulation. Jesus Christ will be literally, visibly on the earth reigning. (Some believe David will be reigning as Christ's regent; perhaps, but Christ's return indicates he will be present.)

The Scripture does not give the content of faith for the kingdom. I believe the content of faith will something like repent of your sins, believe on Jesus Christ who is the ever-present Savior and King, and be saved. Who will deliver that message? Even as it has always been delivered: the living saved.

An Objection: The Temple During The Millennium

An objection is often made that a literal Davidic Kingdom requires the literal temple and literal offerings described in Ezekiel 40–48 and Zechariah 14. Since Christ is present, then what need is there for an Old Testament temple and Old Testament offerings? This objection does not negate the literal form of the Kingdom, nor the necessity for salvation during the kingdom. As with many things which seem contradictory, it is susceptible to satisfactory and rational interpretation.

A temple is a place where God meets with human beings. In the Davidic Millennial Kingdom, when Christ is present, there is a temple where human beings may meet with God for worship and salvation. Saved persons in the kingdom are not transformed and glorified. Therefore they require a place of worship. Undoubtedly the New Testament model of local places of worship will continue, but God has told us in Scripture that there will also be temple. There are also unsaved in the kingdom needing to be saved. A similar condition existed with Israel in the wilderness. God was present in the tabernacle—the pillar of cloud and fire—among a people saved but not transformed and glorified, and people not saved needing to be saved.

A temple serves two functions: a place to worship; a place to hear about and receive salvation. The temple in the Davidic Millennial Kingdom serves both purposes. The condition in the kingdom is confirmed by its opposite in the eternal state. God himself is the temple in the eternal state, Revelation 21:22, because everyone entering into the eternal state is saved, transformed, and glorified.

In this New Testament dispensation the saved are the temple. Individually or gathered together they worship God in their soul and body, which in this New Testament dispensation is the temple of the living God, 1 Corinthians 6:19. They also evangelize the lost: the temple of God preaching the Good News of God; and they disciple the saved: the temple of God receiving with joy those who believe and are saved. The saved also meet together in local assemblies for worship, evangelism, and discipleship. Their congregating is in essence a larger temple where God is present with his people. In the Kingdom it will be the living saved who worship, preach the gospel, and disciple in rebuilt temple building.

In the Kingdom, there will be living saved and living unsaved. There is a need, therefore, for a temple. The saved enter the temple to worship. The unsaved enter the temple to hear the word of salvation and receive the opportunity to believe and be saved.

What about the offerings? Zechariah says the living peoples of the Kingdom will come to the Kingdom temple to worship and keep the Feast of Tabernacles. From the beginning the purpose of this feast was as a memorial of deliverance. Israel kept the feast to remember that God delivered the nation from Egypt, Leviticus 23:43. This feast was also known as the Feast of Ingathering, Exodus 23:16; 34:22, to celebrate the end of the year's harvests. Both are appropriate to the Kingdom. Jesus delivered the living saved out of the Tribulation; he gathered the gentiles and national ethnic Israel into the Kingdom.

The propriety of a memorial to things past did not stop when Jesus ascended. He left the church a memorial, the Lord's Supper (Communion; Eucharist). Do this, he said, in remembrance of me, to proclaim my death, until I return, 1 Corinthians 11:23–26. That memorial will end at the rapture of the church.

In the kingdom dispensation, a memorial of his second advent and the deliverance made by his second advent seems appropriate. Moreover, a celebration of past deliverance speaks of a present salvation, available to any who will believe and be saved. Therefore, the Feast of Tabernacles and a temple in which to celebrate the feast seems appropriate to the Kingdom.

Ezekiel is very certain about the existence of the temple and offerings during the Kingdom. He describes offerings, a priesthood, and the necessary furniture (e.g., altar, tables, etc.) used in the tabernacle and temple structures. This seems like a return to the Old Testament practices. Is it?

At 43:1–7, Ezekiel sees the glory of the Lord return to the temple (the glory had left 10:4). At 43:7a God speaks and says the temple is the place of his throne and the place of the soles of his feet (in the Godhead only God the Son incarnate—Jesus the Christ—has feet), where he will abide in the midst of the people of Israel. God says in 43:7b–11 that the purpose of the temple (and by inference the offerings) is to encourage Israel to be ashamed of their sins and put their sins away from the Lord.

In Ezekiel's historical context these instructions would encourage those persons returning from the Babylonian captivity. There is no reason to think the eschatological view is different, because there are living people in the Kingdom. One purpose, then, of the Kingdom temple and sacrifices, will be to continually remind the people of the Kingdom to put away their sins. We should remember that the living saved in the kingdom have indwelling sin within their human nature, just as believers in the present time. The unsaved in the kingdom suffer the dominion of sin, just as they have the present times since Adam and Eve. Sin never stops tempting. The sacrifices are a reminder of that, as they were to ancient Old Testament Israel. The Law was the guardian of morality, an expression of faith, and the accuser of sin. Every sacrifice reminded the people of their sins. Where there is no sin there is no sacrifice, but when there is sin there must be a sacrifice, Hebrews 10:1–10. For the saved, the animal sacrifices would be types of Christ's redeeming death, which would provide them a form of worship, and point sinners to the Savior.

But (I hear the objection) if Jesus is present, then there is no sacrifice needed for sin, because Jesus paid it all. Yes, he did; but not everyone in the kingdom is saved. They could come to Jesus for salvation, but according to Revelation 20:7–8 many will not. Yet a faithful God and Savior continually reminds men and women of their sins; in which reminder there is a picture of the Savior and his salvation.

Will the saved in the kingdom sacrifice? Ezekiel's description is clear that they will. One cannot pick and choose when to apply the literal method of interpretation. There is no indication the temple and offerings/sacrifices are symbolic—and if they were, what would they be symbolizing? The better course is to accept a literal view of Ezekiel's description of temple and offerings-sacrifices. So, why do the saved in the Kingdom make offerings and sacrifices?

Ryrie [*Premillennial*, 152–153] offers a quote from another commentator on this subject. The opinion offers a good reason for animal sacrifices in the millennium. The quote is lengthy, but the entire quote is necessary to see the answer in its proper context.

> To answer this objection, let us step back and look at God's entire program from a distance. Throughout the Old Testament, the Jews were worshiping God in their tabernacle and temple through animal sacrifices. They were looking forward to a day of peace and prosperity, a kingdom over which their Messiah would be their king. Their Messiah came, but they refused to accept Him as such and continued with their sacrifices. In the meantime, He was crucified as the one great Sacrifice sufficient for all. Outside of the small circle of believers of that day, this meant nothing to the vast majority except that an imposter had been put to death.
>
> Now then, the Epistle to the Hebrews was written not to the Jewish people in general, but especially to them who had professed faith in Christ as the one great final Sacrifice but since then had either continued in or gone back to their animal sacrifices. . . . They were warned not to return to their sacrifices since Christ had set them free. The context is concerning animal sacrifices during the day of grace. The subject before us is that of animal sacrifices in the millennial day.
>
> The church will be taken out of the earth at the rapture, at which time God's program for the Jew will be resumed and continue from where it was at the time of Christ's death. . . . [The millennium] will simply be a continuation of the old order,

this time with Christ accepted as and reigning as King. The Jews will continue their animal sacrifices in worship as they did before Christ died. It is true that these sacrifices will be types and symbols of their faith in Christ's death, but that does not make them nonetheless real. There will probably be mingled sorrow and joy in these sacrifices as they recall how their fathers refused to accept this Christ as their Messiah and how now they have the privilege of seeing it all so clearly.

I conclude, then, as does Ryrie and the author of the quote, that animal sacrifices (and grain offerings, and whole burnt offerings, as Ezekiel has written) will be offered during the Davidic-Messianic-Millennial Kingdom.

The immediate purpose of the Kingdom is to fulfill God's promises made to national ethnic Israel through Abraham (Abrahamic covenant), Moses (Palestinian covenant), David (Davidic covenant) and Jeremiah (New covenant). The expectation of those men, their fellow countrymen, and of their descendants, was a literal fulfillment. For God to transfer those promises to a hitherto unknown people group, the New Testament church, and then give those promises a non-literal fulfillment, is for God to have lied to Old Testament Israel. I refuse to believe God tells lies.

A literal kingdom requires literal salvation of sinners living in the kingdom. Dispensationalism teaches both.

A Final Word

Those of the Reformed camp will oppose the arguments and conclusions of this book. So also those in the Dispensational Promise camp whose Old Testament soteriology mirrors Reformed Old Testament soteriology. Their Old Testament soteriology depends on the Holy Spirit giving the Old Testament peoples an understanding of salvation that the Holy Spirit did not give in the written Scripture of the Old Testament revelation. I have, they will say, attacked not them but Scripture, and they must defend Scripture.

Never mind that to enforce their Old Testament soteriology they must look beyond the written Scripture to an unknown verbal revelation, or an unknown, because unwritten, illumination that perceives Christ where the plain and normal sense of the scriptures cannot find him. Then they will say, "It may not be in the Old Testament revelation, but it is in the New Testament revelation," and then they will say, "It is Scripture you are attacking."

No, it is scripture that I am defending. Eve gave an interpretation of Genesis 3:15 in 4:25; it is ignored. Moses did not leave behind a commentary on the Pentateuch that explained Adam and Eve saw a coming seed-redeemer-messiah-christ in Genesis 3:15, or that Abraham saw Christ as his heir, or that he himself (Moses) saw Christ in the Law. Such a commentary is imagined as verbal revelation. David did not write a commentary on the Psalms showing he saw a Messiah-Christ being crucified. Isaiah did not write a commentary to teach future generations that he saw a crucified Christ in chapter 53. Daniel did not write a commentary explaining why the messiah would die; nor did the angel Gabriel explain it to Daniel. Reformed and Promise Old Testament soteriology fill in all these blank spaces with New Testament revelation, and then give Eve, and Abraham, and Moses, and David, and Isaiah, and Daniel, and anyone else saved in the Old Testament, a New Testament understanding of their Old Testament scriptures.

Reformed soteriology imagines Old Testament sinners were saved by faith in a promised redeemer-messiah-christ yet-to-come, because in their soteriological system, the one way to be saved is faith in the person Christ. Yet, in the Old Testament revelation there is an ever-present Redeemer, YHWH. Dispensational Promise soteriology believes the same as Reformed soteriology, except believing in the yet-to-come person Christ has been changed to believing in a promise of a yet-to-come person they name "Seed" or "Redeemer." All this from Genesis 3:15, which never speaks of sin, or redemption, or Christ, and speaks of Satan under a symbol not recognized or known as Satan until Revelation 12:9.

Scripture tells us the one and only way to be saved is by God's grace through the sinner's faith apart from personal merit by the sinner but only by Christ's merit.

> The means by which Christ's merit is accessed by the sinner is God's grace and the sinner's faith in God and God's testimony as to the way of redemption, as given by the Holy Spirit in the historical progressive revelation of truth.

> The object and content of Old Testament saving faith was not a coming redeemer-messiah-christ.

> The object of Old Testament saving faith was the ever-present YHWH.

> The content of Old Testament saving faith was God's historically current testimony, as given in the progressive revelation of truth, illuminated by the Holy Spirit through the plain and normal meaning of the words of written Scripture.

Old Testament salvation is not the Reformed manta, "by grace alone by faith alone *in* Christ alone," but "by grace alone by faith alone *by* Christ alone." The Reformed want to apply their statement to Old and New Testament sinners alike, but it only works for those having received the New Testament revelation. The second statement actually does apply to both Old and New Testament sinners.

Only Christ's propitiation of God for human sin is effective to remit the endless penalty due sin. That is the one way to salvation. The content of saving faith, which changes in the dispensations, is discovered in God's revelation as progressively given during the history of redemption.

The historic orthodox doctrine of the New Testament church is that scripture is written, not verbal. All verbal tradition and all unwritten illumination is not scripture, it is extrabiblical. Reformed theology, and those of Dispensational Promise soteriology claim to believe scripture is written, not verbal, and condemn the Roman Catholic Church as a cult for its "Deposit of Faith" with its verbal traditions handed down from Christ. Yet Reformed theology, and those of Dispensational Promise soteriology, abandoned that truth when it created an Old Testament soteriology that depends on verbal tradition and unwritten illumination, that says the Old Testament peoples saw a coming Redeemer from sin in their scriptures. I have shown that Christ as redeemer is not in the key verse Genesis 3:15, nor in other Old Testament revelation claimed by Reformed and Promise soteriology. The reader must decide for him or herself.

The imaginary conversation in chapter "Reformed Soteriology" is not fiction. After I explained Christ crushing Satan is not in Genesis 3:15, that in fact God crushed Christ on the cross, I watched two friends, one Reformed, one Dispensational have this conversation.

> Dispensational friend. The way I understand it is that the promise [in Genesis 3:15] to crush the serpent (who symbolized Satan at that moment & often is the symbol for him) did occur at the cross.

> Reformed friend: Me too.

The hold this allegorical interpretation of Genesis 3:15 has on the Christian mind is profound.

Sadly, many Dispensationalists slip into the Reformed camp and join with them in validating verbal tradition and unwritten illumination as the source of Old Testament redemption. I am not sure why. Is the Literal hermeneutic only useful when convenient? Perhaps peer approval is more important than a biblical soteriology? Perhaps fear of the same old Reformed accusations of a different gospel? I do not know. Many past Dispensationalists of renown, including Ryrie, found a "promised redeemer" in Genesis 3:15 as the content of Old Testament faith for redemption.

Right doctrine is not decided by popular vote, but by the written scripture. Yet, none of the seven church counsels in the history of the New Testament church addressed Genesis 3:15. No one thought of Genesis 3:15 as a first gospel, as a protevangelium, until more than a century after the Reformation began; and then it was initially recognized as an allegorical interpretation of Genesis 3:15. When did it become the accepted and only interpretation?

No theology decided today by popular vote will move me one jot or tittle away from what I have taught in this book. I reject as a means to salvation all good works, a neutral free will, and any doctrine added to the Good News. I reject synergism. I reject extrabiblical revelation and illumination. I believe the Holy Spirit has taught me so that I may teach others also, 2 Timothy 2:2.

I do not stand alone.

> I do not agree with others respecting their *meaning*; for other interpreters take the seed for *Christ*, without controversy; as if it were said, that someone would arise from the seed of the woman who should wound the serpent's head. [Calvin, *Commentaries*, 170.]

> It would have been exceedingly difficult for someone to find the way of salvation [faith in the person Christ] ... in the completed Old Testament, [Pastor Bob Bryant, in Miles, *What is Dispensationalism?*, 171].

> What does the Old Testament itself say about salvation from sin? How were people saved in the Old Testament before Jesus Christ came in the flesh? It has often been said that people in the Old Testament were saved by looking forward to the cross by faith while people after Christ are saved by looking back to the cross. But is this true? Remarkable as it may seem, there is no explicit gospel message to be found in the Old Testament. There is no specific command to believe in a future Messiah for salvation, nor is there any mention of an Old Testament saint who put faith in a promised saviour [*sic*] for salvation. There are no clear salvation verses like John 3:16 or Acts 16:31 to be found in the Old Testament. [James Meyers, quoted in Miles, *Current Issues in Soteriology*, 106.]

> People who lived before the time of Christ did not have the same information that we have today. There are many things we know about the person and the work of Christ that simply were not revealed in the Old Testament. They could not understand the Saviour as we do today because they simply didn't have all of the revelation that we have. So, there are obvious differences between the content of the gospel in the Old Testament and the New Testament. The content of faith depends on the

particular revelation from God at any given time. [James Meyers, quoted in Miles, *Current Issues in Soteriology*, 108.]

Paul Enns [522], another dispensational theologian, said this: God's revelation to man differs in different dispensations, but man's responsibility is to respond to God in faith according to the manner in which God has revealed Himself. Thus, when God revealed Himself to Abraham and promised him a great posterity, Abraham believed God, and the Lord imputed righteousness to the patriarch (Gen. 15:6). Abraham would have known little about Christ, but he responded in faith to the revelation of God and was saved. Similarly, under the law God promised life through faith. Whereas the Israelite under the law knew about the importance of the blood sacrifice, his knowledge of a suffering Messiah was still limited—but he was saved by faith (Hab. 2:4). Dispensationalists thus emphasize that in every dispensation salvation is by God's grace through faith according to His revelation. [Quoted by James Meyers, quoted in Miles, *Current Issues in Soteriology*, 109.]

Others understand the Literal hermeneutic and the necessity of a rigorous application to every scripture, every doctrine, even as I do.

Think on this. Genesis 3:15, is never mentioned in the entire Bible in any kind of relationship whatsoever to Jesus Christ: not his birth, not the cross, not the crucifixion, not the resurrection, not anything related to Christ. Here are the only scriptures related to Genesis 3:15 in the Bible.

Genesis 4:25 (ESV), And Adam knew his wife again, and she bore a son and called his name Seth, for she said, "God has appointed for me another offspring instead of Abel, for Cain killed him."

Romans 16:20, Now the God of peace will crush Satan under your feet shortly. The grace of our Lord Jesus Christ be with you.

Revelation 12:9, And the great dragon was thrown out, the serpent of the beginning, who is called "Devil," and "Satan," deceiving the whole inhabited earth. He was thrown down to the earth; and his messengers were thrown down with him.

Read the scriptures, think and decide for yourself, does the Bible say anywhere that Genesis 3:15 speaks of Christ crushing Satan's head on the cross? Imagination can be a good tool when constrained by the Scripture, but if allowed to run amok, imagination can make anything seem reasonable. Are we people of the Word, or of imagination?

Reformed people. Dispensational Promise people. You need to ask yourselves a question. Why would the Holy Spirit teach sinners to place their faith in a coming redeemer-messiah-christ, when there was an ever-present Redeemer, YHWH, on the scene, saving sinners?

I will close with the words of Luther at the Diet of Worms (not that I am his peer, I merely borrow his declaration.)

> If, then, I am not convinced by proof from Holy Scripture, or by cogent reasons, if I am not satisfied by the very text I have cited, and if my judgment is not in this way brought into subjection to God's word, I neither can nor will retract anything; for it cannot be right for a Christian to speak against his conscience. Here I stand; I cannot do otherwise. God help me. Amen.

I trust and pray this Bible study has been helpful to you. You must believe what your conscience and convictions tell you to believe. I urge you to allow your conscience and convictions to be informed by a Literal hermeneutic exegesis of the Scripture.

Appendix: Strengths of Dispensationalism

Dispensationalism builds its theology from a consistent use of the literal grammatical historical [Literal] hermeneutic. A ground-up approach is used starting with hermeneutics, then exegesis, then biblical theology. The Literal hermeneutic is axiomatic and is the starting place for interpretation.

Dispensationalism relies on an Inductive approach to studying the Scriptures. Looks at the who, what, where, why, when, how of each book and draws conclusions from the context and grammar.

Dispensationalism places a strong emphasis on the singular meaning, and the authorial intent of the author.

Dispensationalism exegetes the Old Testament without reliance on a New Testament priority presupposition which obscures the Old Testament.

Dispensationalism builds a cohesive Biblical theology that brings together God's Kingdom, Covenant, and Dispensational program without elevating redemptive history as the lens by which we read scripture, ignoring other overarching themes.

Dispensationalism encompasses Israelology into their Systematic, whereas other positions tend to ignore the importance of God's people.

Dispensationalism distinguishes Israel from the Church, which leads to a proper understanding of both Israelology and Ecclesiology.

Dispensationalism incorporates a proper doxological philosophy of history.

Dispensationalism interprets the Old Testament prophecies literally, and doesn't spiritualize them to fit the church unnecessarily.

Dispensationalism doesn't replace Israel with the Church, honors God's faithful to his people Israel.

Dispensationalism utilizes a Christotelic approach, not Christocentric.

> A Christotelic view makes the distinction that, even though God (YYHW) is noted throughout the Old Testament, and even though Jesus is God, many of the Old Testament passages often

referred to as Messianic do not directly point to Jesus.

A Christocentric reading of Scripture views the Old Testament from a Christian viewpoint, seeing the Christ or Messiah on "every page" or at least regularly throughout the Old Testament writings.

[Christotelic definition: https://www.gotquestions.org]

Dispensationalism emphasizes redemption of not only the individual, but of nations, the cosmos, etc.

Dispensationalism incorporates typology, but doesn't overemphasize it.

Dispensationalism has the ability to adapt to criticism, because it is not tied to a creed or confession. It has undergone numerous changes as it attempts to align itself more with scripture.

Appendix: Principles and Precepts of the Literal Hermeneutic

An extract from James D. Quiggle, *The Literal Hermeneutic, Explained and Illustrated*, appendix.

Why A Literal Hermeneutic

A literal interpretation of the Bible is nonsense if the Scriptures are not inspired and inerrant (the Scriptures are authentic, accurate, and credible as God's revelation).

God intended Scripture be understandable (the doctrine of the perspicuity of Scripture).

People in the Bible can only know what God has revealed to them in the Scripture given to them in their historical circumstances, about himself, his requirements for his creatures, and his purpose, plans, and processes (the principle of special revelation).

Seven General Principles

One, God's values never change. His moral values arise from his immutable holy character, and therefore like his character his values cannot change. He has established moral standards and requires everyone to conform.

Two, God regulating sin is not God approving of sin. God has always regulated acts of sinning for the protection of the human race in general and his saved people in particular.

Three, God does not have to say a sin is wrong every time a sin happens. Sometimes God does states his disapproval concurrent with the sin, but not always.

Four, just because a believer commits an act of sinning does not mean God changes his moral values to approve that act of sinning.

Five, just because Scripture only says it once does not mean God later changed his values. Bestiality is condemned one time in Scripture—mentioned only that one time—but God's moral values never change.

Six, just because the Bible reports somebody thought it, said it, did it, or believed it doesn't mean God approved it. Just because the Bible reports the facts does not mean God accepted the wrong.

Seven, "Jesus said nothing" is the worst hermeneutic ever! Jesus always agrees with God's moral values because he is the God-man, whether he said anything, or not. Inspiration from the Holy Spirit gives all Scripture the same accuracy, credibility, and authority as "Jesus said."

Discovering Meaning

The purpose of the literal hermeneutic is to discover the meaning of Scripture and explain its significance.

Authorial intent defines meaning.

The literal hermeneutic determines the biblical author's intended meaning (his truth-intention) through the normal and plain sense of the words and language he used.

The biblical author's intended meaning is discovered through a six-fold analysis of Scripture: historical-cultural, contextual, lexical-syntactical, theological, literary (genre), and doctrine.

After the six analyses are performed, one should compare his or her tentative interpretation with the work of other interpreters.

Novel or new interpretations should be examined and validated by careful exegesis and comparison with historically relevant interpretations of the same passage or doctrine.

An interpretation should fit into the total pattern of God's revelation that was revealed *prior* to the writing of the passage being interpreted (the Analogy of Scripture).

An interpretation should not contradict the total pattern of God's revelation that has been revealed at any time (the Analogy of faith).

Scripture does not contradict itself.

The Scriptures explain themselves.

A text cannot mean what it never meant.

Do not reinterpret a clear Scripture with a difficult Scripture.

Understand the several contexts of the passage being interpreted. An interpretation of a Bible text must conform to the immediate historical, cultural, social, literary, and theological situation context of the Scripture text, the context established by the human author's other writings, the context of the Testament in which the text is located, and the context created by the completed revelation of the Scriptures.

The interpretation available for every biblical text ranges from what is possible, to what is plausible, to what is probable, to what is certain.

Understanding Words And Grammar

The natural meaning of words as understood by the original author and readers is the usual meaning.

The literal hermeneutic understands the plain and normal sense of words does not mean a word must mean the same thing in all contexts, does not refer to the same thing in all contexts, and may not be used to interpret a passage with a different context.

> The expositor must be careful not associate the same word in different contexts as the basis for an interpretation, but to only associate words in the same or similar context as the basis for an interpretation.

> If there is not a contextual connection, then there is not an exegetical basis to use one passage to inform the interpretation of another. Using the mere coincidence of words as the basis for interpretation is useless and deceitful (like the majority of "center column" references in most Bibles), and by it we may prove anything.

"Plain sense" is the basic, customary, social designation of a word, a description that by necessity includes the context in which a word is used.

Etymology is not a particularly useful Bible study tool. The meaning of a word is based in its use, not its history.

The interpretation of any passage of Scripture is not every sense which the words will bear, nor is it every sense which is true in itself, but that sense which is intended by the inspired writers and the Holy Spirit

Grammar affects meaning but should not be the sole factor in interpretation. Grammar contributes to the meaning clearly expressed in the context, it does not establish meaning by itself. Meaning is established by contextual evidence, not solely on the basis of possibilities in the grammar-syntax-vocabulary.

Don't misuse or overemphasize Greek verb tenses. Understand how grammar is used in the language, not how it is used in English equivalents.

Synonyms can be important. However, synonyms are often used for literary diversity to avoid repetition. What is important is how the writer uses a word and how he combines words.

Figures Of Speech

The original languages in which the Scriptures were written were not a divine language, but the common language of the cultures in which they were written.

The Bible was written in the every-day language of the people, which includes figures of speech, symbols, etc.

A figure of speech is a comparison (by example or analogy) of one thing with another that clarifies some aspect of the thing being illustrated by the figure of speech.

A figure of speech does not teach doctrine. A figure of speech clarifies what is being taught for the purpose of helping the understanding.

(Exception, the Parable. A parable is an illustration told in a word story in order to teach a single point.)

A figure of speech clarifies one aspect, not all aspects, of the thing being illustrated.

A figure of speech, symbol, etc., is not in and of itself literal.

A biblical symbol or figure is based on something literal and is intended to communicate something literal.

A symbol is not intended to communicate the literal thing on which it is based.

A symbol always communicates a literal meaning. A symbol always has a literal interpretive value.

Symbols originating in the Old Testament should be understood as defined by their Old Testament use and then appropriately applied to their New Testament context.

The author did not intend his words to be understood literally when:

> The author makes an explicit statement to that end.
>
> A literal interpretation is impossible.
>
> A low degree of correspondence exists.
>
> The imagery is highly developed.
>
> The author piles up multiple images.
>
> The author uses original imagery.
>
> The immediate context indicates the author's intent was not literal.
>
> The use of certain words throughout Scripture establishes a pattern of use which can help identify non-literal language.

Consistency in interpretation is necessary. One cannot mix methods and results of interpretation in a passage or passages of Scripture. The principle of consistency in interpretation resolves a great many interpretive difficulties.

A "type" is an illustration of some biblical truth whereby a person, place, or thing in the Old Testament is identified in the New Testament as prefiguring that New Testament truth.

> A type must never be used to teach a doctrine, but only to illustrate a doctrine elsewhere explicitly taught.
>
> It cannot be positively affirmed that anyone or anything is a type that is not somewhere in Scripture treated as such.
>
> Old Testament types should be defined and used according to their New Testament antitype.
>
> Types are interpreted by their use in the New Testament and

by their analogy with clearly revealed doctrines.

An illustration does not teach, it helps the understanding.

A parable is a story with a point. A parable is always based in something literal and teaches something literal.

A parable is neither figure, idiom, slang, symbol, or type, but may use one or more of these things.

A parable is like an arrow: it is aimed at one point. The details are the horse and cart that carry the one point the parable is intended to teach.

Prophecy

Prophecy, the same as any other biblical text, is the result of the author's intent to communicate something literal to the reader.

The literal hermeneutic interprets prophecy using the same methodology used to interpret every other kind of literature in the Bible.

Prophecy is intended to communicate an adequate understanding of the future. The writer intended to communicate with his original audience, and the Holy Spirit intended to communicate with believers in present and future generations. Therefore, the plain and normal sense of the words is the means by which prophecy may be understood.

Some parts of prophecy can be fully understood only by those who will live the prophecies, i.e., the completed sense of a prophecy is seen in its fulfillment. However, whether or not every jot and tittle is understood fully, a literal interpretation discovers the meaning and intent of prophecy.

Understanding the meaning and intent of an unfulfilled prophecy is not the same as knowing the date, time, or manner of its fulfillment. Nor does this mean every aspect or detail of unfulfilled prophecy can be discerned. An adequate understanding means we may discern some or all of what is to be accomplished in the prediction, although how it is to be accomplished may remain hidden.

Predictive prophecy conforms to the same laws of progressive revelation as does all Scripture: the initial germ of an idea is further developed by later revelations on the same subject.

There are three types of prophetic fulfillment: conditional; unconditional; sequential.

Some prophecies are stated complete in one utterance and fulfilled in one action. Some prophecies have multiple fulfillments. Some prophecies have a "now-yet future" component, where the fulfillment of some, but not all, aspects is applied to current and subsequent generations, until fulfilled in the ultimate generation in the far future.

The Old Testament prophets saw the near and far fulfillments of their predictions from the perspective of one sense and one meaning, without seeing the time between the near and far fulfillments.

Biblical apocalyptic literature is prophecy, neither more nor less, presented in more symbolic terms, versus the plainer language of other predictive prophecy.

The normative means by which to interpret apocalyptic biblical literature is the same means used to interpret any biblical symbol or type.

The distinguishing factor in interpreting apocalyptic literature versus other predictive texts is to consider its dependence on previous revelation. (The Scriptures explain themselves.)

Significance

There is one interpretation (meaning) of any biblical text. There may be many applications (significance, relevance) of an interpretation because God saves people out of every nation, tribe, peoples, and tongue. Culture varies throughout time and throughout the world.

The significance (relevance; application) of Scripture is dependent on the sense (meaning; interpretation) of Scripture. Significance is how the interpretation of a particular Bible text applies to the modern reader in the context of his/her historical and cultural circumstances.

Pay Attention

Pay attention to the different kinds of biblical literature.

Pay attention to the facts of chronology, geography, and history.

Pay attention to the biography of the biblical characters. God doesn't teach by treatise, but through lives and events, here a little and there a little.

Know what you should bring to the interpretive process. Objectivity in interpretation is possible if presuppositions concerning the Scripture are grounded in, verified by, and defensible by the Scripture.

Be aware the interpreter always brings his or her culture, experiences, beliefs, dogmatism, biases, and prejudices to Scripture; in a word, presuppositions. Watch out for them.

Not all presuppositions are bad; they are bad only when they lead to a wrong understanding of Scripture.

Don't personalize Scriptures intended by the biblical authors to be applied corporately.

Don't overlay the present on the past, which is known as "anachronism." The text and the interpreter stand in separate historical contexts and traditions. The interpretation of the text, no less than the original formation of the text, is influenced by historical contexts and traditions.

The antiquity of a belief does not make that belief true. The only criterion for truth is Scripture.

SUMMARY

The literal hermeneutic, when properly used, discovers what the Bible has to say to the sinner and the saved.

Appendix: My Doctrine

The Bible presents the following propositional truths.

Bibliology (the doctrine of the Scriptures). The Bible is inspired, inerrant, infallible, sufficient, and authoritative. In the original writings every word was inspired (verbal inspiration), every word was equally inspired (plenary inspiration), and every word accurately presents the authentic words (inerrancy) of God, holy and fallen angels, men and women. The Bible is therefore God's credible revelation to humanity concerning himself and his purpose, plans, and processes for the things and beings of the spirit and material domains (the Universe) which he created. God preserved his Word such that the accumulated copies descended from the original writings provide translations that are completely sufficient and authoritative as the rule and guide of personal faith and practice. In every respect the Bible Christians possess today is authentic, accurate, and credible on any and every subject it addresses. (John 15:26–27; 16:13–15; 2 Tim. 3:16; 2 Pet. 1:20–21; 1 Pet. 1:10–12; Heb. 1:1; Eph. 2:20; 3:5).

Theology Proper (the doctrine of God). The tri-unity (Trinity) of the One God, whose personal name was revealed in the Old Testament as YHWH, and in the New Testament as Father, Son, Holy Spirit. The Godhead is one essence/substance with three personal subsistences/persons: God the Father, God the Son, God the Holy Spirit. The Trinity is a unity, not a union, meaning each Person in the Godhead is consubstantial, coequal, and coeternal with the other Persons, being the same one substance or essence: God. (Matt. 28:19; 3:16–17; John 10:30; 16:16–18, 26; 2 Cor. 13:14). The one God is Father-Son-Spirit. The demonstration of the one essence of the Trinity is seen in that each person of the Trinity participates in the acts of the other persons. For example, at the creation, Gen. 1:1; Col. 1:16; Gen. 1:2; the incarnation, Heb. 10:5; Php. 2:7; Luke 1:35; the baptism, Matt. 3:16–17; Mark 1:9–11; Luke 3:21–22; the propitiation, Isa. 53:6, 10; Eph. 5:2; Heb. 9:14; the resurrection, Rom. 6:4; John 10:17; Rom. 8:11.

Christology (the doctrine of Christ). God the Son is a genuine Person in unity with God the Father and God the Holy Spirit, being of the same one essence/substance with them, consubstantial, coequal, and coeternal with God the Father and God the Holy Spirit.

God the Son became the Christ, Psalm 2:2, when he joined in union with himself a human nature and a human body—the incarnation—by a super-natural, non-sexual act which procreated a genuine male human being—Jesus of Nazareth—through the virgin Mariam, in whom Jesus was conceived by the omnipotent power of God and from whom he was birthed, Psalm 2:7; Luke 1:35.

Jesus the Christ is one Person with two natures: genuine deity and a genuine rational sinless human soul. He is immaterial deity essence and immaterial sinless human soul united with a genuine material sinless human body. In the Person Jesus the Christ, the attributes of deity were communicated to the humanity in such a way that, without adding to the humanity or subtracting from the deity, the humanity became an instrument through which the deity could exercise its power. The deity perfected the humanity, without elevating it to deity, so that his humanity possessed all things perfectly.

Jesus the Christ in his first advent was the messianic-redeemer of Daniel 9:26, as further explained in Isaiah 52:13–53:12 (Acts 8:35).

Jesus the Christ willingly took upon himself the sins of the world (2 Corinthians 5:21) and propitiated God (Isaiah 53:6, 10; Ephesians 5:2; Hebrews 9:14) for the crime of human sin (1 John 2:2; 4:10; Romans 3:25; Hebrews 2:17), dying spiritually (Matthew 27:46) and physically (Luke 23:46) to satisfy the judicial penalty for human sin.

Jesus the Christ was buried (John 19:40–42), was conscious and in heaven during his death (2 Corinthians 5:8), and three days later was resurrected by the power of God (Romans 6:4; John 10:17; Romans 8:11), being seen on the day of his resurrection (Luke 24:13–21; John 20:11–29), and for forty days after (John 21:4 ff.; Acts 1:3), by 500 persons (1 Corinthians 15:6).

Jesus the Christ ascended into heaven (Acts 1:9) and is

returning to earth at a yet-future date (Acts 1:11; Revelation 19:11–16), to judge his enemies (Revelation 19:17–21) and rule the world as the messianic-king (2 Sam 7:13, 16; Psalm 2; Zechariah 14:16–21; Revelation 20:4–6), after which he will judged the unsaved (Revelation 20:11–15), and reign on a new heaven and earth (Revelation 20:11; 21:1, 22–23).

Jesus the Christ is, therefore, the God-man, who will for eternity be Jesus the Christ, the Son of God, God the Son. (John 1:1; 1 John 5:20; Hebrews 2:14, 16–17; Luke 1:27, 31, 35.)

Pneumatology (the doctrine of the Holy Spirit). God the Holy Spirit is a genuine Person, being of the same one essence/substance with God the Father and God the Son, consubstantial, coequal, and coeternal with God the Father and God the Son. His work in the world is to testify of salvation in Christ, effect saving faith according to God's sovereign will, and restrain the works of sinners. His work in the Church is: seal the believer in salvation; indwell the believer as his temple; empower the believer to worship, fellowship with, obey, and serve Christ; join believers together spiritually into one body; administer the Church to evangelize sinners, disciple believers; and in all its ways and works glorify Christ. (John 14:26; 15:26; Rom. 8:16; Psalm 139:7; Gal. 5:22; Gen. 1:2; Titus 3:5; Eph. 1:13–14; 1 Cor. 12:1–11, 13; Eph. 2:22; 4:3; John 16:8–11). The Holy Spirit does not testify about himself, he testifies about Christ; he does not glorify himself he glorifies Christ (John 15:26; 16:13–15).

Anthropology is the doctrine of humankind. Adam was created sinless, but afterward self-originated a sinful desire to rebel against God, thereby adding the principle of rebellion, sin, to his otherwise perfect human nature. The addition of the sin attribute reprioritized all the attributes of human nature to serve self not God. Adam procreated his sinful human nature, Gen. 5:3 in his sinful likeness and image. God's Law of Biological Reproduction is "each kind of being reproduces its own kind of being and no other kind of being" (Gen, 1:11-12, 21, 24, 28), and so all of Adam's descendants possess the sin attribute in their human nature, 1 Cor. 15:22. As a result, all human beings are conceived and born in a sinful state, Gen. 5:3, Rom. 5:12–14, and remain in that unsaved sinful state unless saved from the penalty of sin (spiritual death) during the time of their mortal life by God's grace alone, through faith alone, in Jesus alone, Rom. 6:23a; Heb. 9:27. A person dying unsaved is eternally unsaved because the power of physical death is to seal the unsaved person's spiritual state for eternity, Heb. 9:27. Unsaved human beings are morally guilty of failure to be in God's image and legally guilty of failure to believe and live according to God's commandments.

Hamartiology (the doctrine of sin). Sin is the evil principle of rebellion against God resulting in rejection of God's will and disobedience to God's commandments. Sin is the moral violation of God's holiness by failure to conform to the image and likeness in which he created human nature, and sin is the legal violation of God's laws by disobedience. Sin is any thought or action that does not conform to the essence, personality, character, attributes, or purpose of God. Scripture uses the word "sin" to indicate both the evil life principle sin (the sin attribute) and acts of human nature as influenced by the sin attribute.

> When Adam committed his act of sinning, he added the principle of rebellion, sin, to his human nature: a sin attribute. The sin attribute interacts with all the other attributes of human nature, exerting such a dominating influence that the person chooses to self-determine his or her course in the world in opposition to God's holy character and revealed will, whether that will of God is discovered in Scripture, or in that revelation of himself God has made in human conscience. Sin is accomplished in acts of rebellion against God and disobedience to his commandments.

> Sin has authority (dominion, rule) over the sinner, Rom. 6:14, not as some invincible overlord, but as an innate part of human nature constructively working with all the other attributes of human nature to persuasively incline the will to choose an act of sinning. The evil attribute sin influences every other attribute with the inclination to sin, and in that sense sin can be said to dominate the will. The sinner freely chooses sinning because his will is of itself always inclined to choose sinning, and as being rebellious and disobedient toward God never desires to change its inclination to choose sinning to rebel against God, disobey his commandments, and seek a path in life apart from God.

The judicial guilt of Adam's sin is imputed to all human beings and Adam's sinful human nature is procreated in all human beings, Gen. 5:3; Rom. 5:12–14. Unsaved persons are personally guilty of being in a spiritual state of sin, personally culpable for their acts of sinning, and liable to God's judgments against sin both in this life and endlessly in the life to come. Sin affects every aspect of the unsaved person's human nature, resulting in the inability to comprehend spiritual issues, 1 Cor. 2:14. Unsaved persons are inclined to sin and unwilling to change that inclination, choosing to be in rebellion against God and act in disobedience toward God.

Soteriology (the doctrine of salvation). For human beings to be saved God must convict the sinner of his/her sin and give the sinner his gift of grace-faith-salvation, Eph. 2:8. For a person to be saved he/she must respond to God-given conviction of sin and believe God and God's testimony as the means by which God's grace in salvation is to be accessed. Every salvation is by grace through faith, without personal merit (works) but by Christ's merit alone, Eph. 2:8–9.

Election. The choice of a sovereign God (Ephesians 1:4), to give the gift of grace-faith-salvation to effect the salvation of some sinners (Ephesians 2:8), and to take no action, positive or negative, to either effect or deny salvation to other sinners (Romans 10:13; Revelation 22:17). The decree of election includes all means necessary to effectuate salvation in those elected. God's decree of election ensures the salvation of the elect, but does not prevent any non-elect sinner from coming or willing to be saved. God will act savingly toward any who choose to seek him and come to him for salvation (Rom. 10:13; Eph. 1:4; Rev. 22:17).

Propitiation. Christ alone propitiated God for the crime of sin. Propitiation is the satisfaction Christ made to God for sin by dying on the cross as the sin-bearer, 2 Cor. 5:21; Rom. 3:25; Heb. 2:17; 1 John 2:2; 4:10, for the crime of sin committed by human beings, suffering in their place and on their behalf. Christ's propitiation fully satisfied God's holiness and justice for the crime of sin. Christ's propitiation was of limitless merit, because his Person is of limitless worth (unlimited atonement-propitiation). The application of Christ's merit to overcome the demerit of sin and save a soul is applied through the election God decreed before he created the universe, and is personally applied by each sinner through saving faith in Christ in response to God's gift of grace-faith-salvation (limited redemption), Eph. 2:8. Christ's righteousness is imputed to the saved sinner so that he/she eternally stands uncondemned before a holy God, Rom. 8:1, 31.

Salvation: the remission of sin's penalty by the application of the merit of Christ's propitiation of God on the cross to the sinner's spiritual need. Salvation is when God rescues a sinner out of the state of spiritual death and delivers him or her into a permanent state of spiritual life. Salvation is the remission of sin's guilt and penalty by the application of Christ's limitless merit, through the means of God's grace and the sinner's personal faith in God and God's testimony, as revealed through God's historically current testimony as given in the progressive revelation of truth. Salvation is gained through Christ's limitless merit and salvation is maintain by Christ's limitless merit. In this New Testament age salvation occurs when a sinner repents of his or her sins and believes on Christ as their Savior: Acts 2:38; 3:19–20; 11:18; Rom. 3:22–26; 10:9–10, 13; Gal. 3:22; 1 Pet. 1:21; 1 John 3:23.

Justification. A believer is permanently positionally justified in Christ: God declares the believer "not guilty" of the crime of sin, Rom. 8:1. In salvation the believer is freed from the penalty of sin, the dominion (power) of sin, the desire for and pleasure of committing sin, and at death (or rapture) from the presence of sin, for eternity. At the moment of salvation the Holy Spirit regenerates the believer's soul; in New Testament times the Holy Spirit takes up permanent residence in the believer's soul, John 14:17; Acts 10:44–48; 1 Cor. 6:19, regenerating human nature. The righteousness of Christ is imputed to the now-believing sinner, and a new principle of life, holiness, is added to the believer, Eph. 4:24, becoming the dominating principle in his/her human nature, 1 Thess. 4:7; 1 Cor. 3:17b; Col. 3:12; 1 Pet. 1:15–16. The believer has been empowered to say "No," to temptation to sin, and enforce that choice, and thereby is empowered to live a life of habitual righteousness, 1 John 3:9.

Sanctification. Sanctification is the right standing before God resulting from the salvific experience. The believer is permanently positionally sanctified in Christ: God declares the believer dedicated to God and separated from sin (declared holy) in Christ. A believer is called to experiential sanctification: personal holiness and righteousness of life; to perform and maintain good works which God has prepared beforehand (Eph. 1:4; 2:10; 2:21; 5:26; Rom. 12:1; Titus 2:14; 3:8). The believer is empowered to resist sin's temptations, live a holy life, understand the Scripture, worship, obey, fellowship with, and serve God. God hears and answers his/her prayers, and he/she perseveres by faith in the faith to lead a holy life, looking toward resurrection and eternal life in God's presence. The believer will be eternally sanctified, which is that transformation of soul and body that occurs in the soul at physical death and in the body at the resurrection, thereby eliminating the sin attribute in body and soul, 1 Corinthians 15:53.

Predestination. God's decree to conform the believer to be like Christ according to certain aspects of Christ's spiritual character and physical form (Rom. 8:29–30; 1 John 3:2), and to place the believer in the legal position of God's son and heir (Eph. 1:5, 11), so that the believer has an inheritance from God and is God's heritage.

Perseverance. To persevere in the faith is to continue in the faith by means of faith throughout life and through physical death into eternity. Perseverance is a grace God gives the believer to overcome all spiritual and physical obstacles to faith. Persevering faith is the believer using the means of grace God has provided for him or her to continue in the faith by faith. God tells his saved people to persevere, and he gives his saved people every grace and spiritual power necessary to be able to persevere. By means of the grace of perseverance every believer will persevere in the faith by faith all the way through life to the end of physical life and into eternity. Believers are those persons who receive and use the God-given grace of perseverance. Those who do not persevere in the faith by faith were never saved. (Heb. 10:12, 14; Eph. 2:8–9; John 10:9, 27–29; Rom. 4:22–25; 5:1, 10–11, 18–19; 8:1; Heb. 10:17–18.)

The unsaved. Sinners who reject God's salvation throughout their mortal life are eternally lost. (Rom. 5:12–21; 1 Cor. 2:14; Rev 20:15). Their location after physical death is hades (Luke 16:23), there to wait in constant torment until the Great White Throne judgment of their works, (Rev. 20:11–13), and subsequent endless imprisonment in the lake of fire, consciously enduring the judgment of God's wrath (Rev. 20:14–15).

Ecclesiology (the doctrine of the New Testament church). The local church is an organism composed of individuals joined together so that each can make vital contributions to the work and welfare of the whole body, a community of persons who strive to please God in celebrating his worship.

In greater detail. A local church is a body of baptized believers, joined together upon a credible profession of saved by grace through faith in Christ the only Savior, regularly meeting together under the leadership of elders and deacons, participating together in a common purpose to worship God, to propagate the Gospel locally and worldwide, to make disciples, to observe the ordinances of baptism and the Lord's supper, to present a common witness of faith and doctrine centered on the Word of God, and to encourage one another in the daily practice of the principles, precepts, and values of God as expressed in his Word.

The proper order in the local church are the ordinances of baptism and the Lord's Supper; the offices of elder and deacon; the works of evangelism and discipling; and ecclesiastical separation from those teaching false doctrines. (Matt. 28:19; 1 Cor. 11:23–26; 1 Tim. 3:1–13; Titus 1:6–9; 2 Tim. 4:5; Acts 8:4; 10:42; 2 Tim. 2:2; 1 Cor. 6:14–18; 1 John 4:1–3; Jude 3, 16–23).

The New Testament church has not replaced, superseded, or become the continuation of national ethnic Israel in the proposes, plans and processes of God. God will fulfill his promises to the New Testament church (e.g., John 17:24) and his covenants with national ethnic Israel (e.g., Gen. 12:2–3; 15:4–16; 17:2–8).

Eschatology (the doctrine of last things). Technically, eschatology concerns any prophecy in the Old Testament and New Testament between its proclamation and its fulfilment. All prophecies of events future to the time of proclamation look forward to what is, at the time of proclamation, a last thing. Popularly eschatology is identified by the non-biblical term "end times" and focuses on what is identified in Old Testament prophecies as the Day of the Lord. The focus of this doctrinal statement is prophetic proclamations concerning or related to the "end times."

> The entire New Testament church age between the AD 33 Pentecost and the Rapture of the New Testament church is the last time before the end times, 1 John 2:18; 1 Peter 1:5; Jude 18. In biblical terms, the "last hour" or "last time" is the period of time immediately preceding the latter days, last days. The New Testament church dispensation is the last time/last hour before the Day of the Lord.

> Rapture. The "catching away," or Rapture (from the Latin translation, *raptuare*, of the Greek *harpagmós*) is the imminent, pretribulational, premillennial, bodily return of Christ for his church to resurrect the dead in Christ, transform the living and the resurrected to be fit for God's presence, 1 Cor. 15:51–52, call the transformed church up to himself in the air, and take the church to heaven, John 14:2–3; 1 Thess. 4:13–18. Christ's return for his church is not preceded by any signs but may occur at any moment, 1 John 3:2–3.

> Latter days. In eschatology the period of time immediately following the last hour/last time and immediately preceding the second advent of Messiah; it is the Tribulation period of the Day of the Lord. Sometimes incorporates the second advent and its immediate consequences. Examples: Isaiah 2:2; Jeremiah 30:24; Ezekiel 38:16; Daniel 2:28; 10:14; Micah 4:1–5.

> Day of the Lord: the entire period of time beginning with the Tribulation and ending with the Eternal state. The Day of the

Lord follows the "last time," during which God moves in judgment and salvation. Scripture discussions of the day of the Lord usually incorporate the second advent. Two Peter 3:10–13 looks to the end of the current heavens and earth, Revelation 20:11; 21:1, as part of the Day of the Lord. Examples: Isaiah 2:12; 13:6, 9; Ezekiel 30:3; Joel 3:14; Obadiah 15; Zephaniah 1:7, 8, 14, 18; Malachi 4:5; Acts 2:20; 1 Thessalonians 5:2; 2 Peter 3:10. Sometimes referred to as "that day," e.g., Isaiah 19; 52:6; Ezekiel 38:19; Zechariah 14:9. Once referred to as "the time of Jacob's trouble," Jeremiah 30:7.

Second Advent. Christ will return bodily to the earth at the end of the Tribulation, bringing the New Testament church, the Old Testament saints, and the angelic host of heaven with him, to destroy his enemies and reign over the earth on the throne of David for 1,000 years in the Davidic-Messianic Kingdom. After this he will conduct the judgment of the lost and effect their eternal punishment. (1 Thess. 4:13–18; 5:1–5; 2 Thess. 2:3; 1 Thess. 1:10; 5:9; Rom. 5:9; Rev. 20:4–6, 11–15).

The Davidic-Messianic Kingdom: based on the Davidic covenant (2 Samuel 7:11b-17; 1 Chronicles 17:10b-15) promised to national ethnic Israel through King David's heir, who is Christ. The ruler is Christ through national ethnic Israel. The ruled will be all the inhabitants of the earth, Psalm 2:8–12. The church will reign with Christ in this kingdom (2 Timothy 2:12; Revelation 5:10; 20:6). The Davidic-Messianic Kingdom ends with the destruction of the current heavens and earth, Revelation 20:11; 2 Peter 3:10, and the Great White Throne Judgment, Revelation 20:11–15. The Eternal Kingdom, Revelation 21–22, follows the Davidic-Messianic Kingdom.

Eternity. There is an eternal judgment, eternal heaven, and eternal hell. The saved will be judged and rewarded for their works done as believers and then will enjoy eternal happiness in heaven in the presence of Christ (2 Cor. 5:10; 1 Cor. 3:11–15; Rom. 14:10–12). The lost will be judged for their works as unbelievers at the Great White Throne judgment and be cast into the lake of fire (hell) to suffer eternal punishment from the presence of God.

These three judgments are separate events: the church age saved are judged for rewards (not salvation) at the Bema Seat at the rapture (2 Corinthians 5:10; Romans 14:10; 1 Corinthians 3:11–15); the Tribulation saved are judged at Christ's return to the earth for rewards (not salvation) to reign (Rev. 20:4–6) ; all the lost from Adam to the end of the Millennial Kingdom are judged for endless punishment (not salvation) after the Davidic-Messianic Kingdom (Rev. 20:11–15; 21:8, 27; 22:3–5).

Angelology is the doctrine of the immaterial spirit beings known in Scripture as *ma'lāk* (Hebrew) and *ággelos* (Greek). Both words translate to "messenger." God's messengers are created, sentient, immaterial spirit-beings. They were created before Adam was created. They live in the second heaven, an immaterial domain God created as a habitation for immaterial spirit-beings. God's messengers are divided into two groups: the holy messengers who never sinned against God; the fallen messengers who did sin against God. The holy messengers have access into the third heaven, where God has a permanent manifestation of his presence, and where saved human beings go after death into the presence of God. The fallen messengers cannot enter into the third heaven. Scripture does not give an argument or origin for God's messengers. They simply appear in the Bible to serve God (the holy messengers) or oppose God and humankind (the fallen messengers). (Job 38:7; 1:6–7; Isaiah 14:12–14; Ezekiel 28:13–18; Revelation 4:6–8; 5:11–12; 12:7, and many other scriptures).

Appendix: Adam's Unbelieving Descendants

When discussing Dr. Fruchtenbaum's views on Dispensational Promise soteriology (see chapter "Promise Soteriology"), Dr. Fruchtenbaum makes reference to the "angel-human sex" interpretation of Genesis 6:2. Because that interpretation cannot be derived from the Literal hermeneutic, I indicated I would discuss the "angel-human sex" view of Genesis 6:2 in an appendix. The following is taken from my book, *Adam and Eve, A Biography and Theology*.

Genesis 6:1–7 is a simple explanation as to why God destroyed the world he had made and started over with eight believers and an ark full of "all food that is eaten" and "of every living thing of all flesh" (6:18–21). Chapter 6:5–6 is superbly clear: man was evil, making God sorry he had made man.

> 5 Then the Lord saw that the wickedness of man was great in the earth, and that every intent of the thoughts of his heart was only evil continually. 6 And the Lord was sorry that He had made man on the earth, and He was grieved in His heart.

It would be wrong to think of every person (Noah and his family excepted) being as evil as humanly possible. Jesus describes a very normal and mundane quality of life in Noah's time. The spiritual problem in Noah's day is described at Matthew 24:38–39 and 1 Peter 3:18–20: humankind did not know judgment was coming, despite Noah's preaching that judgment was coming. To express the spiritual conditions of Noah's times in a modern context, humankind was divided into three camps: the exclusively secular; those devoted to false religions; a dwindling number of believers in YHWH. Intermarriage between believers and unbelievers is given as a symptom of these conditions, the big example that describes what was wrong.

We should not think Noah was the only believer during these times. He found wives for his sons. Enosh, Cainan, Mahalaleel, Jared, Methuselah, and Lamech lived out the remainder of their lives in the time between Noah's birth and the flood. Methuselah and Lamech died just before the flood. YHWH maintained a righteous witness all the way to judgment day, but he removed his holy people from the earth—all but the remnant of Noah and his family—before the day of judgment.

The cause of the flood is stated at 6:5. It was a spiritual problem:

a persistent and continuously indulged inclination to sin, whose outworking was wicked thoughts and deeds in all aspects of life. A critical symptom of man's spiritual problem is stated at 6:1–2. It was a critical symptom because intermarriage between those of faith and those of no-faith revealed that religious formality had replaced genuine faith (which is the soul's whole-hearted dedication to engage persistently and continuously in worship, fellowship, obedience, and service to YHWH). This symptom, 6:1–2, of man's spiritual problem has often wrongly been interpreted (with 6:4 usually attached) as the cause of the flood. Genesis 6:1–2, 4, reads,

> 1 Now it came to pass, when men began to multiply on the face of the earth, and daughters were born to them, 2 that the sons of God saw the daughters of men, that they were beautiful; and they took wives for themselves of all whom they chose .... 4 There were giants on the earth in those days, and also afterward, when the sons of God came in to the daughters of men and they bore children to them. Those were the mighty men who were of old, men of renown.

There are three competing interpretations of these verses. Some improbably hold the "sons" as lineal male descendants of Seth and the "daughters" as lineal female descendants of Cain.

Another interpretation is that the "sons of God" are "Sethites," i.e., the lineal descendants of Seth, and the "daughters of men" are "Cainites," i.e., the lineal descendants of Cain. In this view all of Seth's descendants are believers and all of Cain's descendants are unbelievers. To think that all of Cain's descendants were sinners and all of Seth's descendants were saved is too simplistic; it does not conform to any Scripture or historical example. If a "Sethite line" was viewed figuratively as representing believers, and a "Cainite line" correspondingly viewed as representing unbelievers, then this view would be closer to the truth, which is that believers, the sons of God, married unbelievers, the daughters of men.

The second, and older, interpretation is that the "sons of God" are fallen angels and the "daughters of men" are human beings. These two races had sexual intercourse, the women conceived, giants were born. The flood cleansed the earth of these wicked people who mated with fallen angels. Modern adherents of the angel-human sex view rely on a misinterpretation of the term "sons of God," on an interpretation of Jude 6–7 and 2 Peter 2:4 that reads Genesis 6:2 into the texts, and on the antiquity of the interpretation, i.e., it was anciently the Jewish interpretation of the passage, and has been in and out of vogue throughout New Testament church history. Scripture interprets itself, and there are five scriptural reasons why the angel-human sex interpretation is wrong.

The **first reason** is the meaning of the terms "sons of" and "daughters of." When used symbolically neither is a gender specific term. The term "sons of" means a person possesses the characteristics of the person or thing he or she is a "son of." The "sons of rebellion," at 2 Samuel 23:6 were the rebellious. The "sons of the prophets," 2 Kings 2:3, were those men who were faithful to God and preached his Word. The sons of fools, and the sons of vile men, Job 30:8, were fools and vile. This same figurative use applies to the "sons of God" (*benê 'ĕlōhîm*). This term is used in Genesis 6:2, 4; Job 1:6; 2:1; 38:7; Matthew 5:9; Luke 20:36; Romans 8:14, 19; Galatians 3:26. In every use it refers to persons who are like God because they are in a faith-based relationship with God.

Genesis 6:2 is the first use of *benê 'ĕlōhîm* in Scripture. As the first use its interpretation should be guided by the fact that the only "sons of God" prior to the verse are human beings: Adam and Eve by virtue of God as parent. Additionally, no angels are mentioned in Genesis 1:1–6:2. Therefore, in its immediate historical-cultural and theological contexts, the term must refer to human beings. Some define the term strictly by Job 1:6; 2:1, which in their view applies specifically to angels. However, that interpretation is not certain, as it is reasonable to view man at worship and Satan appearing disguised among them. Moreover no fallen angel is ever named as a son of God (Satan in Job comes among the sons, not as one of the sons). When every occurrence is considered, the term in Genesis 6:2, 4 and Job 1:6; 2:1 must mean those of humankind who are in a faith-based relationship with God.

No fallen angel and no unsaved human being are ever characterized as a son of God. This at once eliminates the option that the sons of God in Genesis 6:2, 4 are fallen angels. Nor can the "sons of God" in Genesis 6 be holy angels. Holy angels would not commit sexual immorality with human beings, and (see below) angels do not have human sexual gender, and God's Law of Biological Reproduction prevents such a union (if it were possible) from bearing fruit.

Based on consistent Scripture use, the "sons of God" in Genesis 6 must be human beings who are men and women of faith. The term "daughters of men" occurs only in Genesis 6:2, 4.

The term "daughters of" occurs in many places, usually indicating a literal birth relationship. The term is used symbolically in Ezekiel 16 to describe the idolatry committed by both men and women.

"Daughters of men" occurs here because both biological reproduction and religious infidelity are in view. The sense is *not* that only males are sons of God and only women are daughters of men. Just as the term "sons of God" indicates persons who are in a faith-based relationship with God, the term "daughters of men" indicates persons who are not in a faith-based relationship with God. Man is by nature a sinful creature. The "daughters of men," by analogy with the term "sons of God," must possess the characteristics of man.

The true interpretation of the passage is that the sons of God were believers: those persons who were in a faith-based relationship with God, whether they were male or female, whether they were of the line of Seth or Cain. Those believers made a wrong decision and married persons who were not in a faith-based relationship with God: the daughters of men, whether they were male or female, whether they were of the line of Seth or Cain. More simply, believers were marrying unbelievers. The result was that wickedness was great on the earth because men and women of faith had compromised their faith.

The **second reason** the angel-human sex view is wrong is God's Law of Biological Reproduction: each kind of being reproduces its own kind of being and no other kind of being. Each reproduces according to its kind, Genesis 1:11–12, 21–22, 24–25, 28; 5:3. When God created material beings he established a commandment of biological reproduction that cannot be broken. Material beings reproduce each according to its kind. A physical sexual liaison between angels and mankind, if such a thing could occur, could not result in conception, because humans and angels are different kinds of created beings.

Angels are beings made of an immaterial (spirit) substance and humans are composite beings of material (body) and immaterial (soul) substances. Human beings reproduce both body and soul through their physical substance—through physical sexual intercourse. How could an immaterial being, an angel, engage in physical sexual intercourse with a material being? Even if they could physically have sex, how could an angel, a being of a different kind than human beings, cause human conception? Human beings mate with and produce offspring with other humans.

God's Law of Biological Reproduction is in action every day: birds only mate with and reproduce more birds; monkeys only reproduce more monkeys; cats, whether lions, tigers, civets, or house cats, each produces its own kind, an animal recognizable as a cat. This rule of biological reproduction is at the very heart of the Christian argument against evolution.

Christians can agree that there are changes within various "kinds" of creatures. But although there may be ever so many species of birds, yet they are all recognizable as a different kind from other animals: they are all birds. Christians cannot agree to changes from one kind into another kind, for example that dinosaurs evolved into birds, given enough time, mutation, and natural selection. If the evolutionists are correct, then there is no God-set limit to biological reproduction.

However, there is a limit. That limit also applies to human beings. A human being cannot mate successfully (cannot conceive or produce viable offspring) with any other kind of living being in the spirit or material domains. God has set limits to biological reproduction. God's limits apply to imagined sex between humans and angels. Each is of a different "kind" in God's biological economy.

Angels have a "body" that is suited for life in the spirit domain, not a material form like that of mankind. Angels are finite beings, which means they have a defined location in time and space. "Body" is a useful and usable name for that defined location. When angels appear in the material world (as versus the spirit domain which is their natural domain), there is no hint in Scripture that their now-visible form functions as a material human body. Angels were created as spirit beings, are not of material form, and therefore cannot mate successfully with human beings.

The **third reason** angels cannot mate with human beings is that angels do not have a sexual gender similar in kind to man's sexual genders. Jesus, who created the angels, declared that he made them neither sexually male nor sexually female. In Mark 12:25 Jesus says the resurrected saints are like the angels in that they neither marry, nor are given in marriage. The context of the passage indicates sexual intercourse is the subject. The Sadducees did not believe in the resurrection, and used as one of their arguments against it the supposed sexual abilities of those resurrected to a heavenly paradise. If a woman had multiple husbands in this life, then whose wife would she be in the next: wife in the sense of sexual mate as well as eternal companion?

Jesus exposed their error: the resurrected are like the angels; the angels neither marry nor are given in marriage. This specific language might seem redundant today, but in that culture men married and women were given in marriage. Thus, the resurrected saints and the angels neither marry, i.e., are not sexually male, nor are they given in marriage, i.e., they are not sexually female. Angels do not have sexual gender corresponding to human sexual gender (see also 1 Corinthians 15:39, 40). Angels did not mate with humans at Genesis 6:1–2.

The **fourth reason** is a proper exegesis of the Genesis 6:1–2, 4, passage. I have shown that 6:1–2 means believers married unbelievers. Those who believe in the angel-human sexual interpretation try to link 6:4 with 6:1–2, so they can make the so-called "giants" the fruit of the marriages between the sons of God and the daughters of men. Verse 4, however, does not follow 6:2, and 6:4 does not begin with a conjunction, which, if present, would indicate the continuation of the subject. Because 6:4 does not begin with a conjunction the writer was not trying to show the result of 6:1–2. More simply, the "giants" were not the result of the sexual relationship in 6:1–2. Moses states in 6:4 that there were "giants" *before* believers married unbelievers, and there were "giants" after believers married unbelievers. Therefore, marriage between the sons of God and the daughters of men was not the cause of the "giants."

The word translated "giants" is $n^e p\hat{\imath}l\hat{\imath}m$, used only in Genesis 6:4 and Numbers 13:33. The etymology of $n^e p\hat{\imath}l\hat{\imath}m$, and thus its meaning, is obscure. The most likely meaning is "heroes" or "fierce warriors" [Harris et al., s. v. 1393a]. Hamilton [*Genesis*, 270], disagrees. "A literal translation of *Nephilim* is 'fallen ones.'" The opinion of Harris et al., seems more consistent with Scripture. Regardless, "giants" is an improper translation.

Nephilim could refer to a tribe, race, or nation. The translation "giants" was first used in the LXX as an interpretation (not translation) to conform to Jewish views that 6:1–4 spoke of angel-human sex. According to the Jewish view the people in Numbers 13:33 were just like those Genesis "giants." If the Israelites were faced with giants, then they had an excuse for not entering into and conquering the land. The interpretation is self-serving—it tends to mitigate their sin. In Numbers 13:33 the ten spies said, "There we saw the *n⁰pîlîm*," then Moses interrupted the narrative with a parenthetical comment, "the descendants of Anak came from the *n⁰pîlîm*," and then the spies' statement continued, "and we were like grasshoppers in our own sight, and so we were in their sight."

The word *anak* means "men with long necks." "*Anak* is not the proper name of a man in these passages, but the name of a family or tribe ... *Anak* is supposed to signify long-necked; but this does not preclude the possibility of the founder of the tribe having born this name." [Keil and Delitzsch, 1:710.] The word "*anak*" occurs (all occurrences) at Numbers 13:22, 28, 33; Deuteronomy 9:2; Joshua 15:13, 14 (x2); 21:11; Judges 1:20.

The *n⁰pîlîm* in Genesis 6:4 are not the same as the *n⁰pîlîm* who were the ancestors of *anak*, nor the same as the *n⁰pîlîm* the spies saw in Palestine. The only people who survived the flood were in the ark. Neither Noah, his wife, their sons, nor their wives are described as *n⁰pîlîm*. Whatever the *n⁰pîlîm-anak* people were in Numbers, they were not the same as the *n⁰pîlîm* in Genesis.

What is more likely in Numbers is that the ancestors and children of *anak* were a tribe, race, or nation of "fierce warriors" rather than giants. However, to argue the opposing view (that the children of *anak* were indeed giants), how tall would someone have to be in order for the Israelites to consider them a giant? The average height in those ancient times was between 5'3"–5'6" (verified by archaeology). Saul stood out because "from his shoulders upward he was taller than any of the people," 1 Samuel 9:2, i.e., he was between 6'3"–6'6". Saul was not a giant, so a giant would have to be someone who was taller than Saul.

Goliath was nine feet tall. Was Goliath a giant? He is not called a giant and is not said to have been of the children of *anak* (all of whom were apparently killed by Caleb 375 years earlier, Joshua 15:14; Judges 1:20). Goliath is identified as a Philistine, a Gittite, a man of the city of Gath, 1 Samuel 17:23, but not as *anak* or *nᵉpîlîm*. So a giant would have to be taller than Goliath. In several translations three men are said to have been "born of the giant," at 2 Samuel 21:16, 18, 20, but the word mistranslated "giant" is a name, Rapha. These three men are not said to be *nᵉpîlîm* or *anak*. The report of one of these sons of Rapha states he was "a man of great stature, who had six fingers on each hand and six toes on each foot, twenty-four in number." These three sons of Rapha would seem to have been exceptions to the norm, perhaps suffering from a disease known in modern times as acromegaly, or giantism (gigantism). Perhaps Goliath and one or more of his brothers suffered from the same disease. One of Goliath's brothers wielded a spear whose shaft was "like a weaver's beam," 2 Samuel 21:19, but he is not said to be a giant.

There is a certain romanticism to "giants" in literature, but while there is no doubt these five men (Goliath, his brother, the sons of Rapha) were physically large, strong men, they were not *nᵉpîlîm*. Is it likely there was a tribe of people in Joshua's time who were taller than Goliath, his brothers, and the sons of Rapha, but of whom there is no archaeological or literary record? The more likely view is that "the *nᵉpîlîm*" the spies saw were a tribe of fierce warriors. The spies saw themselves as "grasshoppers" when viewed beside these "fierce warriors," not because "the *nᵉpîlîm*" were giants, but because they were warriors who were taller and stronger compared to the wandering Israelite shepherds and herdsman. The spies' problem was no-faith, not giants.

Genesis 6:4 reads (HCSB), "The Nephilim were on the earth both in those days and afterwards, when the sons of God came to the daughters of man, who bore children to them. They were the powerful men of old, the famous men." Compare the actual word order, "the *nᵉpîlîm* were on the earth days those and also after that when came the sons of God to the daughters of men bore [them]. Those were the mighty who old men of renown."

The pronoun "they/those" in the second sentence could refer to the *nᵉpîlîm*. The verse would then read, "The Nephilim (fierce warriors, heroes) were on the earth in those days; and afterwards, when the sons of God came to the daughters of man, who bore children to them. In this reading the Nephilim (fierce warriors, heroes) were the powerful men of old, the famous men."

To what period of history does the term "those days" refer? To 6:1, "when men began to multiply on the face of the earth, and daughters were born to them. What days were those? They were the days when Adam, Cain, Seth, Enoch, Enosh, Irad, Cainan, Mehujael, Mahalaleel, Methushael, Jared, Lamech, Enoch, Methuselah, Lamech, and Noah fathered sons and daughters. More simply, as the population grew to millions of people, some of those people became famous heroes, or fierce warriors, men with a reputation as being powerful.

On the other hand, the $n^e p\hat{\imath}l\hat{\imath}m$ are probably not the same as the "mighty men," the "men of renown." Based on his translation of $n^e p\hat{\imath}l\hat{\imath}m$ as "fallen ones" Hamilton, [*Genesis*, 270], says, "the Nephilim [are] distinct from the *mighty men*, who alone are the offspring of the union between the sons of god and the daughters of men." However, as I have shown, the $n^e p\hat{\imath}l\hat{\imath}m$ were not the offspring of the sons and daughters.

Grammatically it is more likely the pronoun "they" refers to the closer referent: those born from the sons and daughters. The word "children" is not in the text but is properly supplied in the translation because the daughters of men "gave birth," *yālad*, after the sons of God went in to them. The 6:4 text word order literally reads [Biblehub.com], "the $n^e p\hat{\imath}l\hat{\imath}m$ were on the earth days those and also after that when came the sons of God to the daughters of men bore [them]. Those were the mighty who old men of renown."

Moreover, the $n^e p\hat{\imath}l\hat{\imath}m$ existed before and after "the sons of God came into the daughters of men," but the "mighty men" (*gibbôr*) who were "men of renown" (*shem*) were born *afterward*, i.e., after "the sons of God came into the daughters of men." The Hebrew word *gibbôr* is used 156 times in the Old Testament, and is translated mighty, strong, valiant, mighty man, warrior (RSV), referring to "the heroes or champions among the armed forces" [Harris et al., s. v. 310b]. The Hebrew word *shēm*, translated renown, means "name," and is used 864 times. Here it has the meaning of reputation [Harris et al., s. v. 2405]. The children born as a result of the union between the sons of

God and daughters of men may have been *nᵉpîlîm,* but they were certainly "men who were the heroes and champions of the age, men of reputation." The *nᵉpîlîm,* when separated from any reference to the children of the sons and daughters, could be any physically large creature, man or animal. They were not the result of angel-human sex.

The **fifth reason** the angel-human sex view is wrong is the misguided assumption that the angels of Jude 6 (and 2 Peter 2:4) are the angels of Genesis 6. However, "as for Jude 6, there is no mention of Noah in Jude 5–8. The only way to derive the notion is by analogy from the sin of Sodom and Gomorrah (v. 7) and an argument that since the sin of Genesis 6 was a sexual sin involving angels and the sin of Jude 7 was a sexual sin, then if what happened in the case of the angels mentioned in Jude 6 is like what happened in Sodom and Gomorrah, Jude 6 must refer to angels in the days of Noah. It should be evident that such a line of argument grossly begs the question by importing Genesis 6 into the passage in Jude. Even if Genesis 6 does refer to angels, that still would be no proof that the angels mentioned in Jude 6 are the same angels—after all, there are more angels than just those which supposedly were active in the days of Noah. Thus, appeals to either 2 Peter 2:4 or Jude 6 initially beg the question, since neither passage indicates that the angels referred to are from the days of Noah" [Feinberg, *Westminster,* vol. 48, # 2].

To recap, there are many reasons Genesis 6:1–2, 4 cannot refer to angel-human sex.

1. The term "sons of" when used figuratively, is a non-gender-specific term which means a person possesses the characteristics of who or what he or she is a "son of." "Sons of God" identifies a person (angel or human) who is in a faith-based relationship with God: God's character is reproduced in that person.

2. No evil angel is ever characterized as a son of God. No unsaved human being is ever characterized as a son of God (all uses: Genesis 6:2, 4; Job 1:6; 2:1; 38:7; Matthew 5:9; Luke 20:36; Romans 8:14, 19; Galatians 3:26.)

3. The term "daughters of men" is a figurative term that means the person possesses the characteristics of mankind, which in the context—after Adam's sin—must mean sinful man.

4. The term "daughters of men" occurs only in Genesis 6:2, 4. It

occurs there because biological reproduction and religious infidelity was occurring between men and women. The sense is not that only males are sons of God and only women are daughters of men, but that those who were in a faith-based relationship with God married those who were not in a faith-based relationship with God. More simply, believers were marrying unbelievers. The result was that wickedness was great on the earth because men and women had compromised their faith.

5. God's law of biological reproduction prevents human beings from conceiving if angel-human sex was possible: each kind reproduces according to its kind. Genesis 1:11–12, 21–22, 24–25, 28; 5:3. Angels and humans are different kinds in God's biological economy.

6. Human beings are immaterial soul and material body; angels are immaterial, spirit beings without a material body. Humans reproduce sexually. The kind of physical contact required for sexual intercourse is not possible between immaterial and material beings. (While some angels have appeared in a human-like form, no angel ever demonstrated he was a material being, contrast Luke 24:40–43).

7. Angels do not have a sexual gender similar in kind to man's sexual genders, Mark 12:25 (men marry, women are given in marriage, the angels do neither). The implication of "angels do not marry" is that angels do not reproduce.

8. Believers, the sons of God, married unbelievers, the daughters of men, vv. 1–2.

9. Genesis 6:4 does not follow v. 2 and does not begin with a conjunction. Because it does not begin with a conjunction it is not trying to show the result of vv. 1-2.

10. Genesis 6:4, there were "giants" *before* believers married unbelievers, and there were "giants" after believers married unbelievers. Therefore, marriage between the sons of God and the daughters of men was not the cause for the "giants."

11. The word translated "giants" is *nᵉpîlîm*. This word is used only here and Numbers 13:33. The derivation and thus the meaning of the word is obscure. The most likely meaning is "heroes" or "fierce warriors." It could refer to a race or nation. The translation "giants" came from the LXX.

12. In v. 4 "the mighty men who were of old, men of renown" probably refers to the children born to the sons of God and daughters of men. The word translated "mighty men" means "the heroes or champions among the armed forces." The word translated "renown" has the meaning of "reputation."

13. Jude 6 and 2 Peter 2:4 do not mention Genesis 6:2, 4 as the cause of, or related to, the angels' sin. To find Genesis 6:2, 4 in Jude 6 (or 2 Peter) one must bring it to the verse.

14. The Genesis 6 passage does not require angels.

Based on five arguments from Scripture, one can confidently conclude that Genesis 6:1–2, 4, is not about angel-human sex. There was no angelic involvement in Genesis 6.

The events recorded in Genesis 6:1–5 reveal the slow decline of faith in the breakdown of godliness. Godliness is when the believer's thought, will, and action conform to the moral, holy, and righteous standard set by God's own character. God takes delight in those whose character and actions reflect his character and actions. Godliness is not naturally generated by the believing soul, but depends on the work of the Holy Spirit through the grace he gives to all believers to live a godly life pleasing to God. While it is true a life of faith is the product of God's grace, it is also true that a lot of personal effort must be expended in order to live a godly and righteous life. There is a cost to living a life of faith: denying the temptations of sin in the mind and flesh; alienation from the world and worldly practices; separation from sinning and sinners engaged in sin; caution in one's relationships with sinners. As the apostle said, "what communion has light with darkness . . . what fellowship has righteousness with lawlessness . . . what part has a believer with an unbeliever (2 Corinthians 6:14–15)?" The answer is, none, except a witness of faith and the testimony of righteous living. That is why he adds, "do not be unequally yoked together with unbelievers." These are the things Adam's believing posterity slowly abandoned in the centuries before the flood.

Appendix: Who Knew Jesus was God Incarnate?

In the chapter on Promise Soteriology, when addressing Dr. Fruchtenbaum's views, I made this comment.

> The concept of a God-man, which is to say the incarnation of God the Son with Jesus of Nazareth, is a New Testament revelation. For example, Colossians 2:9; Philippians 2:5–8. By using the New Testament revelation the New Testament believer knows Psalm 2:7 speaks of the incarnation. But take away that New Testament revelation and no one, not any man or any fallen angel, knew the Messiah would be deity incarnate.

This appendix is a discussion of that proposition. [First published in Quiggle, *Biblical Essays IV*, 269–290, lightly edited to the present purpose.]

Introduction

One of the issues in biblical interpretation is the relationship of the Old Testament revelation to the New Testament revelation. This appendix examines one aspect of that issue. Specifically, the tendency to interpret the Old Testament revelation with information available only in the New Testament revelation.

The question this article asks and will answer is this. Did the apostles, and others, know, from the day they met Jesus, up to the day they met with Jesus after his resurrection, did they know Jesus was God incarnate? The purpose of this article is to show from Scripture they did not know—that no one—the apostles, his disciples, those Jesus healed, those opposing Jesus, and the fallen angels—no one believed Jesus of Nazareth was God incarnate during the time of his earthly ministry, whether or not they believed him to be the Messiah.

The reason most believers today do believe the apostles believed Jesus the Christ was God the Son incarnate, is due to the traditions of Reformed theology, particularly preaching traditions based on English translations. Traditions are wonderful servants but terrible masters. They become terrible masters when "God's word is made of no effect on account of your tradition," Matthew 15:6.

Let me pause for a moment and assure the reader I believe Jesus the Christ was and is God the Son incarnate in Jesus of Nazareth. At the moment the human being Jesus was conceived in Mary's womb, God the Son joined himself to that newly conceived and still rudimentary human body and human soul. From that moment both the human being and the deity were inseparably the God-man. [Quiggle, *God Became Incarnate.*]

The hermeneutic used by Reformed theology is to blame for the belief the apostles and other disciples supposedly knew (during the time of his earthly ministry) Jesus was God incarnate. The basis for the Reformed hermeneutic is interpreting the Old Testament revelation by the New Testament revelation. In that hermeneutic, the Old Testament revelation is not allowed to speak for itself; original authorial intent is made subordinate to New Testament revelation. But as Vlach has said,

> The primary meaning of any Bible passage is found in that passage. The New Testament does not reinterpret or transcend Old Testament passages in a way that overrides or cancels the original authorial intent of the Old Testament writers. [Vlach, *Dispensationalism*, 31.]

The issue, then, is Dispensational: the proper use and application of the Literal hermeneutic. Too many Dispensationalists follow Reformed traditions. This article is part of an ongoing effort to correct that error.

To close this introduction, there are many side paths we might take during this discussion—for example, the Old Testament difference between Messiah as King and Messiah as Redeemer. To keep this article to a manageable length, I will avoid as many of those "rabbit trails" as possible.

Old Testament Revelation

Let us, then, begin with what the Hebrews of Jesus' time knew about the Messiah. The first necessary action is to set aside all we know about the deity of Jesus Christ from the New Testament revelation. That revelation was not available when Jesus walked the earth. The New Testament revelation can play only a limited part in answering the question, "Did the apostles know Jesus was God incarnate?" Our only sources of information are the Old Testament revelation, and what is recorded in the four gospels as spoken by angels, Jesus, the apostles, other disciples, those healed, and the enemies of Jesus. We may not use any explanatory comments the gospel writers may have made, only what was spoken, because that alone reveals what everyone thought and knew.

The Hebrew word *māshîah*, transliterated in the English "messiah," means "anointed" to an office or function. (The equivalent Greek word is *christós*.) The word *māshîah* occurs thirty-nine times in the Old Testament. However, only three times in those thirty-nine occurrences does *māshîah* refer to the person who would be Jesus the Messiah. Those three times are Psalm 2:2, Daniel 9:25, 26.

We may immediately dismiss Daniel 9:25, 26 from this discussion. The words "messiah the prince" in 9:25 do not communicate any revelation the messiah will be God incarnate. Daniel 9:26, messiah cut off" is understandable only through the New Testament revelation, and also does not communicate any revelation the messiah will be God incarnate. Those scriptures are never directly referenced in the gospels. The Jews did not connect 9:25 to the Triumphal Entry (to which it almost certainly refers, Luke 19:42), and the apostles did not connect 9:26, "Messiah cut off," to Jesus' several declarations of his impending crucifixion. No one in gospel times connected Jesus with Daniel 9:25–26. [Beale and Carson, *NT use of the OT*, index.]

Psalm 2

The key Old Testament scripture for understanding how the Hebrews understood the person and office of Messiah is Psalm 2. I have highlighted the key words. In the ESV:

> 1 Why do the nations rage and the peoples plot in vain? 2 The kings of the earth set themselves, and the rulers take counsel together, against the Lord and against his *anointed*, saying,
>
> 3 "Let us burst their bonds apart and cast away their cords from us." 4 He who sits in the heavens laughs; the Lord holds them in derision. 5 Then he will speak to them in his wrath, and terrify them in his fury, saying, 6 "As for me, I have set my King on Zion, my holy hill."
>
> 7 I will tell of the decree: The Lord said to me, "*You are my Son; today I have begotten you.*
>
> 8 Ask of me, and I will make the nations your heritage, and the ends of the earth your possession. 9 You shall break them with a rod of iron and dash them in pieces like a potter's vessel." 10

Now therefore, O kings, be wise; be warned, O rulers of the earth. 11 Serve the Lord with fear, and rejoice with trembling. 12 Kiss the Son, lest he be angry, and you perish in the way, for his wrath is quickly kindled. Blessed are all who take refuge in him.

This is the psalm of Messiah the King, not Messiah the Redeemer of souls from sin. YHWH would anoint a man to conquer and rule the gentiles. Without the New Testament revelation, that is what the Psalm says. A man would be anointed, 2:2, by YHWH to hold the offices or functions of king, 2:6, be YHWH's son, 2:7, conquer the rulers of the earth, 2:9, and rule as YHWH"s representative, 2:10–12.

Every Bible-believing Hebrew believed he or she was a son of YHWH, Hosea 11:1. Every believer is a "son of God," Genesis 6:2, Job 1:6; 38:7; Romans 8:14; Gal 3:26.

> The biblical "sons of" is a description of character. The biblical terms "seed of," "offspring of" "sons of," or "daughters of," are, when speaking metaphorically, those persons whose characteristics are like the person of whom they are a "seed of," "offspring of," "son of," or "daughter of."
>
> When used symbolically neither "sons of" nor "daughters of" is a gender specific term. The term "sons of" means a person possesses the characteristics of the person or thing he or she is a "son of." The "sons of rebellion," at 2 Samuel 23:6 were the rebellious. The "sons of the prophets," 2 Kings 2:3, were those men who were faithful to God and preached his Word. The sons of fools, and the sons of vile men, Job 30:8, were fools and vile.
>
> The term "sons of God" (Hebrew: *benê 'ĕlōhîm;* Greek: *huiós theós*) is used in Genesis 6:2, 4; Job 1:6; 2:1; 38:7; Matthew 5:9; Luke 20:36; Romans 8:14, 19; Galatians 3:26. In every use it refers to persons who are like God because they are in a faith-based relationship with God. No fallen angel and no unsaved human being are ever characterized as a son of God. [Quiggle, *Dictionary*, s. v. Sons of.]

Those Hebrews hearing Jesus had no issue with being identified as "sons of God." For example, no Hebrew objected to this saying by Jesus, "Blessed the peacemakers, because they will be called sons of God," Matthew 5:9. Compare Matthew 5:45, "So that you may be sons of your father in the heavens." Those in the resurrection—which every devout Hebrew expected to achieve—were "sons of God," Luke 20:36. So also Jesus was accepted when he said he was the son of God. Today, through the New Testament revelation, we know "Son of God" means "God the Son incarnate in Jesus of Nazareth. The phrase in the New Testament revelation always refers to the incarnate person. But those in gospel times *did not* have the New Testament revelation.

Do not be misled by translations. Every Bible version capitalizes "son" when referring to Jesus the Christ. In the mouth of Jesus such capitalization may be appropriate because he knew who he was (but did Jesus speak of himself in terms of English grammar; did he speak of himself in capital words?). In the mouth of his enemies it is highly inappropriate. In the mouth of disciples and apostles and others following him it is an assumption not born of Scripture.

In the absence of New Testament revelation, Psalm 2 meant to its Hebrew readers that the Messiah would be a devout Hebrew (devout because he would be a son of God), anointed by YHWH to conquer the gentiles and rule over them. In the absence of New Testament revelation, Psalm 2:7 does not teach an incarnation of God in human flesh, but a consequence of God anointing a human being to be messiah-king and God's son.

Nor could the Hebrews imagine or accept God becoming incarnate. The idea was repulsive, being too similar to the pagan concept of demigod: a human being as the offspring of one of the male gods and a human female, such as Hercules (1264 BC) or Perseus (700 BC). (Psalm 2 was written ca. 1000 BC.) No right thinking Hebrew would commit such blasphemy. Every time Jesus declared himself to be God he was accused of blasphemy.

Isaiah 9:6

Someone will say, "Surely Isaiah 9:6 taught the Hebrews the Messiah was God incarnate?" And so it would seem, "his name will be . . . mighty God . . . everlasting father." The first thing to note is the word *māshîah* occurs only once in Isaiah, at 45:1, where it refers to the Persian king Cyrus. There is a reference made to King David at 9:7. The child to be born will sit on David's throne, "even forever." What did this mean to Isaiah and subsequent Hebrew readers? One thing it mean is a child to be born would be the messianic-king (as the *Targum Isaiah* states [Beale and Carson, 19.]), thereby confirming 2 Samuel 7:13, 16 and Psalm 2. Second, this would be a human child, again confirming both 2 Samuel and Psalm 2. At this point it is difficult to see how any Hebrew would believe this child would be God-in-the-flesh, God incarnate. That was a pagan belief.

Again, we cannot allow ourselves to be misled by a translation. The only word in 9:6 that needs to be capitalized is *'ēl*, the most basic Hebrew word for God or god. For certain, this verse, seen apart from the New Testament revelation, does not teach the Messiah will be YHWH incarnate. However, in a later chapter, Isaiah uses the same words, mighty God (*'ēl*) to refer to YHWH. So Isaiah 9:6, in conjunction with other scriptures, does teach the messiah-king is God; the child to be born must in some way be God—a way not yet disclosed; Isaiah 7:14 had no obvious connection with Psalm 2:2, 7. (The angel Gabriel did not make that connection of Isaiah 7:14 with 9:6 or Psalm 2, see Matthew 1:23–23; Luke 1:31–33.)

What use did the people in gospel times make of Isaiah 9:6? Nothing. Not an angel, not Jesus, not his mother or Joseph, not his disciples or apostles, not his enemies. Nothing. Isaiah 9:6 is not quoted, not referred to, not alluded to in the four gospels [Beale and Carson, index]. No one, except perhaps Isaiah, learned from this verse that the messiah-king would be God incarnate. But let us remember Isaiah has said he is quoting God, 8:11, writing direct revelation word for word, "YHWH spoke thus to me." So Isaiah might not have understood; there is no indication one way or the other. What is certain is no one during Jesus' time on earth applied Isaiah 9:6 to messianic prophecy or to Jesus. With the application of New Testament revelation we can see it; but without that New Testament revelation no Hebrew understood it.

New Testament Revelation in the Four Gospels

What do the four gospels say about the beliefs of the Hebrew people concerning Jesus? What were they told, what did they understand, what did they believe? I will examine only a few scriptures.

Matthew's Gospel

Let us begin in Matthew.

> Matthew 1:23, Behold, the virgin shall be with child, and bear a son, and they shall call his name Immanuel, which is translated, "God with us."

350

The Hebrew words *immānū 'ēl* occur at Isaiah 7:14; 8:8, 10. The Greek equivalent, *emmanouēl*, occurs at Matthew 1:23.

The angel makes sure Joseph knew what the Greek word *emmanouēl* meant: God with us. The angel quotes from Isaiah 7:14 (ESV), "Therefore the Lord himself will give you a sign. Behold, the virgin shall conceive and bear a son, and shall call his name Immanuel [*immānū 'ēl*]."

Again, subtracting all subsequent New Testament revelation from our interpretation, we must look only at the uses Joseph knew. Did *emmanouēl* indicate to Joseph that this child born of a (the Hebrew word) `almâ (a young unmarried girl—thus, a virgin) would be God-in-the-flesh? No. As New Testament believers, having the benefit of all the New Testament revelation, we interpret "God with us" as "God incarnate." But all *immānū 'ēl / emmanouēl* really means is God would be with Israel, without specifying how God would be with Israel. A plain example is Isaiah 8:10 (ESV), "Take counsel together, but it will come to nothing; speak a word, but it will not stand, for God [*'ēl*] is with us [*immānū*]." God is with us to help us. No more can be known from the name, *emmanouēl*, in Matthew 1:23, within the historical context and the scriptures given up to that time, the Old Testament revelation.

Earlier prophecies might have shown Isaiah this "Immanuel" will be of the Davidic line, thus heir to the Davidic-Messianic throne (2 Samuel 7:13, 16; Psalm 2). Isaiah 8:8 refers to "your land, Immanuel." Isaiah and others probably made the connection between Immanuel and the coming messiah who was to be the heir of David. But, again, this is not the understanding of an incarnation. Nothing in the promise of an heir to David, as interpreted without adding in the New Testament revelation, indicates any one of those many heirs of David will be God incarnate.

For example, how could David's house and throne and kingdom be "established forever?" Through the natural generation of offspring continuing the Davidic line and inheriting the kingdom and throne. When we subtract the New Testament revelation from the interpretation of Nathan's prophecy, as we must, then another reasonable interpretation immediately presents itself. I know I am repeating, but the point of view must be remembered: the people in gospel times *did not have* the New Testament revelation by which to interpret or apply the Old Testament revelation.

That last statement unavoidably requires us to take a small side path away from the main discussion. At 2 Samuel 7:13, 16, the prophet says Davids' rule (his "throne) will be established "forever." How does the Bible use the term "forever?" A small excursus.

Excursus: Forever, Everlasting, Perpetual

(Source: Quiggle, *Life*, 37–38.]

Words such as forever (or "for ever," depending on the Bible version), everlasting, and perpetual are similar to the word "all" in that the meaning is determined by context. Sometimes "all" means "everything without exclusion," but more often the content of "all" is circumscribed (limited) by the context.

For example, Genesis 6:12, "God looked on the earth, and truly it was corrupt; because all flesh had corrupted their way on the earth." But if "all" in 6:12 means every person without exclusion, then the verse contradicts 6:8, "But Noah found grace in the Lord," and 6:9, "Noah was a just man, perfect among his generations." In 6:12 the word "all" means everyone except those who, like Noah, and his wife, his sons, and their wives, were righteous before the Lord.

So also the words forever, everlasting, and perpetual. For example, at Exodus 29:26–28, certain portions of meat from the offerings were to be for "Aaron and his sons by a statute forever." Here "forever" means as long as the levitical priesthood and the sacrifices and offerings of the Mosaic Law are in effect.

Another example is Genesis 13:15, "all the land you [Abraham] see I give to you and your descendants, forever." How long is this forever? At the least until this present earth is destroyed and a new earth created, 2 Peter 3:10; Revelation 20:11; 21:1, and perhaps longer, Revelation 21:12. On the other hand, Exodus 15:18, "YHWH shall reign forever," means YHWH will reign without end, because YHWH is eternal, and Scripture reveals nothing that will change the essence of God. Revelation 20:10 means the fallen angels, the Antichrist, and the false prophet will suffer in the Lake of Fire without end, because 1) angels are immortal, and 2) Scripture does not reveal a change or end to their sinful condition or to the Lake of Fire.

The mountains are "everlasting" and the hills are "perpetual," Habakkuk 3:6, until God scatters the mountains and bows the hills, same verse, compare Revelation 16:18, 20. The "everlasting" covenant of the rainbow endures until this present earth is replaced, because it was declared to be a sign this present earth would not ever again be destroyed with a flood, Genesis 9:11.

YHWH is the "everlasting God," Genesis 21:33, meaning his existence is without beginning and without end. God made with David an "everlasting," covenant, 2 Samuel 23:5, a reference to the "forever" son and throne of 2 Samuel 7:13, 16, which we know from New Testament revelation is a reference to David's greater heir Christ. But the prophecy itself does not teach the Christ will be God incarnate. The New Testament revelation teaches us the incarnate Christ will reign as King of kings and Lord of lords in his Davidic-Messianic-Millennial Kingdom commencing at his second advent, Revelation 20:4, and then without end in the new heaven and earth, Revelation 21:1, 22–23.

The person who savingly believes in Christ will have everlasting life, John 3:16, which is not merely immortality of body and soul, but a significant quality of life. Compare John 5:24. Because everlasting life comes from God, and God himself is everlasting, the everlasting life God gives his saved people is without end.

The word perpetual is to be treated the same, i.e., understood in context. Jeremiah 5:22 says God has "made the sand as the boundary of the sea, by a perpetual decree, the sea cannot pass beyond it." This perpetual decree will endure until the new heavens and earth, Revelation 21:1, which has no sea.

To sum up. Words relating to God's essential being are understood to mean without beginning and without end. Words relating to the promise of life to those whom God has saved are understood to mean a quality of life without end. Words relating to the punishment of the unsaved are understood to mean punishment without end. Words relating to conditions that do change, such as the Levitical priesthood, or the present earth, are "forever, everlasting, perpetual" until the condition upon which those things were predicated changes, such as the perpetual decree of the sea, or the forever covenant of the rainbow.

Returning to the discussion, within the Old Testament context, without adding in New Testament revelation, what the Davidic covenant meant to David and his fellow Hebrews, was just this: as long as there is a kingdom of Israel, so there will be a descendant of David on the throne. With the New Testament revelation added in, it is a prophecy of the Davidic-Messianic Kingdom, which as Dispensationalists we believe exists for a millennium. So even in the Dispensational point of view, the "forever" of the Davidic-Messianic Kingdom has an end, which is the end of this present earth, 2 Peter 3:10; Revelation 20:11; 21:1.

Luke 1:32, 41; 2:11.

Although there are more verses to consider in Matthew's Gospel, the angel Gabriel's conversation with Joseph calls to mind Gabriel's conversation with Mary of Nazareth months earlier (about three months, Luke 1:56). The pertinent verse is Luke 1:32, "He will be great and will be called 'son of the Most High.' And the Lord God will give him the throne of David, his father." Neither Mary then, nor Luke later, could hear a capital letter in the angel's voice, except the reverence given to "Most High" and "Lord God," which were recognized titles of YHWH. Mary would not have thought of a capital "Son" of the Most High, because a human being as God was blasphemous.

Everything in the angel's announcement conforms to 2 Samuel 7:13, 16; Psalm 2:2, 7. Indeed, it conforms to Isaiah 7:14, although Mary was not told of that connection, as Joseph was later. Nor in any recorded words of Mary throughout the four gospels do we see her making a connection with Isaiah 7:14. Nothing Mary says in the four gospels indicates she thought of her son Jesus as God incarnate. Nothing in Mary's song to Elizabeth infers or implies or alludes to an incarnation. No recorded word of Mary in the four gospels infers or implies or alludes to an incarnation.

Nor is an incarnation to be found Elizabeth's comment. Through the Holy Spirit Elizabeth recognized Mary as the mother of the messiah-king, not of God incarnate. That is what Elizabeth knew: her son would be the Messiah's herald, Luke 1:17. Nor did the shepherds know the Messiah was God incarnate. The angel told them the *māshîah* prophesied in Micah 5:2 had come to Bethlehem just as prophesied (and to their barn, as prophesied, Micah 4:8).

Matthew 4, the Temptation of Jesus

Did the fallen angels know Jesus the Christ was God incarnate? If they did, then those human beings they influenced against Jesus might know the same from them. But the fallen angels did not know.

One proof they did not know is the actions of their leader, Satan. In his third temptation Satan said to Jesus, Matthew 4:9, "These things [the kingdoms of the world and their glory], to you I will give all, if falling down you will worship me." If Satan had understood Jesus Christ was God the Son incarnate, he would not have made the offer. Satan knew God is "Holy, Holy, Holy," Isaiah 6:3, or as the later revelation of James 1:13 states, "God cannot be tempted by evil." God who created will never worship one of his creation.

354

Why, then, did Satan say, Matthew 4:3, "If you are the son of God," as though assuming Jesus' deity? I will show this statement by Satan did not refer to Jesus' deity. Satan was demanding Jesus prove God was right when God had said, "This is my son," at Jesus' baptism. We will see this by examining two issues. First, what does the "if" mean? Then, what does the term "son of God" mean?

The "if" in the phrase, "if you are the son of God," performs a certain grammatical function (in the Koine Greek dialect in which the New Testament was written) known as a condition of the first class. This is a "simple conditional assumption with emphasis on the reality of the assumption (not of what is being assumed); the condition is considered a real case" [Morris, *Matthew*, 73, n. 11].

Satan is stating a condition that was presented as reality (God had said, "This is my son"), but Satan is questioning whether the condition is factual by demanding Jesus furnish proof that God was right. Satan could be viewed as saying, "I assume as true that you are the son of God, so prove it by commanding these stones to become bread." Or, he could be viewed as saying, "In view of the fact that you are the son of God, command these stones to become bread." Satan's "if" meant, "Prove what God said about you is true. Prove you are a son of God."

(Side issue: why did Satan ask Jesus to "command" the stones to become bread, if he did not believe Jesus was God? Because Satan doesn't know much more than anyone else. Because Satan also reads commentaries and listens to preachers and Bible teachers. The Rabbis taught that the Messiah, as a prophet like Moses, Deuteronomy 18:15, would give them bread like Moses—their belief, John 6:31.)

Satan said, "if you are the son of God." The term "son of" in Scripture, when not used of literal physical descent, indicates a person has the characteristics of the person or thing of which he (or she) is a "son of." Sons of men are sinners, Psalm 4:2; 58:1–2. Sons of the sorceress are offspring of the adulterer and the harlot, Isaiah 57:3. The sons of the prophets (1 and 2 Kings) were preachers and keepers of God's Word, like the prophets. Adam was a son of God, Luke 3:38, a human being in a faith-based relationship with God. The phrase "sons of God" in the Old Testament identified human beings (Genesis 6:2, 4; Job 1:6; 2:1) and holy angels (Job 38:7). The completed revelation of scripture (Matthew 5:9; Luke 20:36; Romans 8:14, 19; Galatians 3:26) supports the earlier revelation. The "sons of God" are holy angels and human believers who are in a faith-based relationship with God. No fallen angel and no unsaved human being is ever identified as one of the sons of God. The sons of God possess the moral character of God, obey God's commandments, and glorify God in their words and deeds.

Satan tried to accomplish with Jesus what he did with Eve: he used God's words to suggest rebellion against God. Could this "son of God" prove he was a son of God? Jesus did, but not the way Satan proposed. Satan's temptations provided Jesus son of God the opportunity to act independent of God's will. Adam son of God self-originated sin when tempted to act independent of God's will (Genesis 2:17; 3:6). Will Jesus seek his own way, like Adam, or will he honor God? Put another way, the claim Jesus was a "son of" God was to be tested. Because Satan did not understand Jesus was God the Son incarnate, he presented temptations that would test the faith of a wholly human son of God. Jesus chose to endure the trial through the natural limitations of his humanity, because as a genuine human being the baptismal designation "This is my son" defined the character of his humanity, not his deity.

Satan did understand Jesus was the Christ. This was part of his motive for tempting Jesus. He had heard this Jesus would be given "the throne of his father David," Luke 1:32, and had heard this Jesus was "Christ the Lord," Luke 2:11. (The fallen angels are one-third, Revelation 12:4a, of an innumerable host, Revelation 5:11—thus present in sufficient numbers to know what is happening on the earth in both spirit and material domains.) Satan's understanding of the Christ was the same as the religious leaders: the Christ would be a human being, much like themselves, who had been specifically anointed (*māshîah*), Psalm 2:2, to be king, 2:6, be God's son, 2:7, to conquer the rulers of the earth, 2:9, and rule as God's representative, 2:10–12.

We must, therefore, wash away our presuppositions and interpretive traditions to place ourselves within the progressive revelation of biblical knowledge at that time, which was Genesis through Malachi. At this time in history, Satan did not use the term "son of God" to identify Jesus as the God-man (no one did). To Satan, Jesus was a human being in a faith-based relationship with God who had been *māshîah*, anointed, Psalm 2:2, by God, to fulfill the coming king and kingdom prophecy of Psalm 2. To Satan, Jesus of Nazareth was just another human being in a long-line of "sons of God" that he would defile, just as he had defiled the first son of God, Adam.

Like their leader, the fallen angels knew Jesus was the Christ, but did not know Jesus was God the Son incarnate.

> The divinity of Christ, or his identity with a divine person, does not seem to have been known to the spirit [Mark 1:24], but only that the man whom he addressed was one, to use his own expressions, whom the Father had sanctified and sent into the world (John 10:36), i.e., chosen and commissioned for an extraordinary service. [Alexander, *Mark*, 22.]

Why then did the fallen angels call Jesus, "the holy one of God"; "son of the Most High God"; "son of God"? These titles came from what they had heard: the angel Gabriel's announcement to Mary that this Jesus was "son of the Highest," Luke 1:32, the "holy one" and "son of God," Luke 1:35.

Conclusion. The fallen angels believed Jesus of Nazareth was the Christ, but none of them understood Jesus the Christ was God the Son incarnate.

Mark 1:23–25 is Jesus' first encounter with an angel inhabiting a human being.

> And shortly [after he had begun teaching] there came into their synagogue a man with an unclean spirit. And he cried out, saying, "What do you have to do with us, Jesus of Nazareth? Are you come to destroy us? I know who you are, the holy one of God."

The confrontation Mark reports here was the first such confrontation in Jesus' ministry, and it was the only time such a confrontation was initiated by a fallen angel. The angel who was cast out was undoubtedly surprised God had delegated this authority to a human being. The others, being warned by their comrade's experience, avoided Jesus as much as possible. In other such confrontations recorded in the New Testament, the fallen angels had not sought out Jesus but met him due to varied circumstances. See Mark 5:2, 8; 7:25, 30; 9:18, 25; Matthew 9:32–33; 12:22. The same is true during Jesus' preaching and healing tours, e.g., Luke 6:18. After this first encounter they knew he would cast them out.

The fallen angel asked, "Are you come to destroy us?" Various translations give "Did you come to destroy us?" or "Have you come to destroy us?" The angel wasn't questioning Jesus' origin, but purpose. If my analysis, above, is correct, then this purpose question must be seen in the light of the prophesied duties or works of the Messiah-Christ. One of those duties is expressed at Isaiah 61:1, "to proclaim liberty to the captives, and the opening of the prison to those who are bound." Jesus had quoted this verse at Nazareth a month or two earlier, Luke 4:18, "To proclaim deliverance to the captives . . . to send the oppressed into deliverance." The fallen angel's question was about himself and others like himself who were inhabiting human souls. Did "to destroy us" fit into the mission Isaiah had prophesied, and which Jesus had announced at Nazareth? Yes. Casting out demons wasn't all that prophecy meant, but casting them out was included.

The word translated "destroy" is *apóllumi*, to destroy, perish, deprive, ruin. Understanding *apóllumi* depends on how one views the fallen angels' understanding of Jesus.

If one believes the fallen angel in Mark 1:23–25 understood Jesus was God the Son incarnate, then *apóllumi* refers to eternal imprisonment in the lake of fire, Matthew 25:41, which verse was not yet spoken, but the demons knew from the beginning (of their original sin) that the "everlasting fire was prepared for the devil and his angels." The fallen angels are intelligent but have no grace or spiritual perception for understanding scripture. First Corinthians 2:14, the natural person does not understand spiritual matters, applies to them as it does to any unsaved human soul. They did not understand two advents, so they could have wondered—if they understood Jesus was God incarnate—whether the time had come for their eternal imprisonment.

If one believes, as I and others do, that the fallen angels did not understand Jesus was God the Son incarnate, then *apóllumi* refers to some other kind of ruin or loss. The most reasonable interpretation is fear of imprisonment in the abyss for the crime of habitation of a human being, Luke 8:31, "And they were begging him, that he would not command them to go away into the abyss.

The fallen angel, Mark 1:23–25, came on behalf of his comrades (the plural "us" in his questions) to find out who this Jesus was, and what this Jesus, "Christ," would do. He found out. Jesus cast into the abyss all fallen angels with whom he came into contact who were inhabiting a human being, thereby fulfilling (at least toward these particular angels) the messianic prophecy of Isaiah 61:1; Luke 4:18. Because Jesus did cast out every angel he met inhabiting a human soul, we may assume a law against habitation, and the punishment imprisonment in the abyss, there to join the large number of fallen angels already imprisoned, Jude 6, 2 Peter 2:4; Revelation 9:1–3. I believe every fallen angel Jesus cast out of a human being went into the abyss, per Luke 8:31. They knew the power to cast them into the abyss was from God. They may or may not have known, until that first confrontation, the Old Testament revelation gave the Messiah the authority to cast them out. The fallen angels, like their leader Satan, did not know Jesus of Nazareth was God-in-the-flesh.

Matthew 11:3, The Baptist Doubts

Did John the Baptist know his relative Jesus of Nazareth was God incarnate? Some think so from failure to consider all of John's testimony. When Jesus came to be baptized, on seeing him, the Baptist said, Matthew 3:14, "I have need to be baptized by you, and you come to me?" It would seem he knew. But the Baptist also testified, John 1:31, "I knew him not." He knew his relative Jesus. They had known each other for almost 35 years (their births ca. 5 BC to Jesus baptism late AD 29). They had seen each other every year at the three mandatory feasts, and probably at other times also, as the families visited one another over the years. The Baptist knew Jesus to be a righteous man. The Baptist was preaching the Messiah was coming, but he did not know who the Messiah would be, until he saw "the Spirit descending and abiding on him," John 1:33. No testimony of the Baptist states or implies he knew the Messiah would also be God incarnate.

If John Baptist knew Jesus was God incarnate, then why did he doubt he had baptized the right man? If you know the Messiah is God incarnate, then there is no doubt. John was informed by Old Testament revelation, neither more nor less. He knew the Messiah was coming to be king. He had not seen that expectation fulfilled. He did not understand Messiah as Redeemer of men from their sins. Jesus, Mathew 11:5, gave him the signs of Messiah the Redeemer, Isaiah

35:5–6; 61:1, which scriptures the Baptist knew. Jesus told him to have faith, 11:6.

Matthew 14:33

At Matthew 14:22–33, we have the incident when Jesus and Peter walk on water. When Peter and Jesus got into the boat, those in the boat, "bowed to him, saying, "Truly you are God's son." The issue here is not the Greek text, but the English translation. The common English translation says, they "worshiped him." Naturally, the reader assumes those in the boat believed Jesus the Christ was God incarnate. But the word English versions translate "worship" is *proskuneō*, to "do obeisance, show respect, fall or prostrate before, literally to throw a kiss in token of respect of homage" [Zodhiates, s. v. 4352]. To translate *proskuneō* as worship assumes what must be proved: that the apostles-disciples believed the man who had just walked on water was God-in-the-flesh.

Let us think clearly. If the twelve believed God was literally in their presence in the person of Jesus of Nazareth, then they would not have been able to function as his companions. They would have fallen flat on their faces and remained prostrate before him in reverent awe. They would have feared for their lives, because God had said to Moses, "No person shall see my face and live," Exodus 33:20 (NKJV). They were in awe of him, but not the worshiping, "you are God," kind of awe. No prophet had ever done what Jesus had just done. So they had continued to ask themselves, "Who is this man?" Here they come to a conclusion.

What, then, did they mean when they said, "Truly you are God's son"? Three meanings are available.

> One, they understood he was God incarnate in Jesus of Nazareth. This is unlikely. They were completely discouraged following the crucifixion, e.g., Luke 24:21, "we were hoping that it was he who was going to redeem Israel." They didn't understand he would resurrect, and didn't believe when they were told he had resurrected. The Holy Spirit withheld spiritual perception of Jesus as deity incarnate until after the ascension, compare Matthew 28:17 with Acts 3:33.

> Two, they could have been declaring him a true son of God. The

Hebrews believed they were sons of God. If this was the disciples' meaning, then they were giving respect to a prophet who had shown that he truly was a son of God, i.e., one to whom God had given great authority and power.

Three, they bowed to him and called him, "God's son" in the sense of Psalm 2:7, "I will declare the decree: YHWH has said to me, 'You are my son.'" If this was the case, it was a moment when they began to believe Jesus was the messiah-king—not merely a prophet in the Old Testament mold, but the deliverer and king promised by the prophets.

My view is that they saw him through the lens of options two and three.

Matthew 16:16, Peter Confesses Jesus is the Christ

Peter states Jesus, "is the Christ (of God, Luke 9:20), the son of the living God." Jesus says this understanding, that Jesus of Nazareth was the Christ of God, was given Peter by, "my Father who is in heaven." How did Peter know about the Christ of God? From schooling at the village synagogue, which every boy attended in his home village. From a lifetime of hearing about the Messiah when he attended the synagogue on Sabbath, what Peter knew about the Christ of God was what the Scriptures said and what the Rabbis taught. Everything Peter confessed fits into Psalm 2.

Peter: You are the Christ of God. Psalm 2:2, YHWH and his *māshîah*.

Peter: son of the living God. Psalm 2:7, You are my son, today I have begotten you.

Peter did not think of the Messiah as God incarnate. If he had he would have confessed, "You are God the Christ." If we doubt, and some will, let us look to the sequel, 16:22. Peter rebuked the Christ for revealing the Christ must die. If you believe the person in front of you is God incarnate, you do not correct him. You worship. You politely ask for an explanation of the thing you do not understand.

Matthew 26:63–64

The Bible scholars did not believe the Messiah was God incarnate.

> And the high priest said to him, "I adjure you by the living God, that you tell us if you are the Christ, the son of God." Jesus says to him, "You have said. Moreover, I say to you, from now you will see the Son of Man sitting at the right hand of the Power, and coming in the clouds of heaven."

Caiaphas needed legal justification in order to sentence Jesus to death and present the case to Pilate for Jesus to be executed. We see in 26:63 that Caiaphas obviously knew Jesus had performed miracles and that many people believed him to be the Christ. The question Caiaphas asks understands the terms "Christ" and "son of God" as indicating a relationship with God. But it is doubtful that Caiaphas used these terms in the same sense that Christians understand them today. Caiaphas was not a believer; he was not seeking faith in Jesus the Messiah.

The question Caiaphas asks, although not in these words, is whether or not Jesus will testify under oath that he himself is the Christ, the son of God. Jesus answers the question because 1) Caiaphas has asked in his official capacity as high priest, 2) the question is about Jesus' messianic claims, and 3) Caiaphas has called on Jesus to tell the truth with God as his witness.

Jesus' reply, "You have said," is an idiom meaning "You have stated the fact." This reply, in itself, was not sufficient to condemn Jesus to death. And Jesus knew this. The Christ was perceived by all as a man anointed by God to be king of Israel. We see this was the way the Sanhedrin understood the Christ by their accusation before Pilate—the accusation that caused Pilate to condemn Jesus.

> John 19:12, but Jews cried out, saying, "If this man you release, you are not a Friend of Caesar. Anyone making himself a king speaks against Caesar."

The accusation that made Pilate condemn Jesus was the claim he was a king. They had previously tried to get Jesus condemned for blasphemy, but that failed,

> John 19:7, The Jews answered Pilate, "We have a law, and according to the law he ought to die, because he made himself Son of God."

Notice here I capitalized the word "son." How had Jesus made himself, "Son of God." Not when Jesus had agreed with the high priest,

Matthew 26:63–64a, that he was, as the high priest had stated, "the Christ, the son of God." No one got excited over that claim. Claiming that Psalm 2 applied to you was not blasphemy.

The blasphemy was the next thing Jesus said. "I say to you, from now you will see the Son of Man sitting at the right hand of the Power, and coming in the clouds of heaven." To sit on the throne of God ("at the right hand of the Power") is to be equal with God. To come on the clouds of heaven is to command the angelic armies of heaven, which is authority possessed only by deity.

> Matthew 26:65–68, Then the high priest tears his clothes, saying, "He has blasphemed! Why have we any more need of witnesses? Look, now you have heard the blasphemy! What do you think?" Now answering they said, "He is deserving of death." Then they spit in his face, and struck him. Others slapped him, saying, "Prophesy to us, Christ, who is he having hit you?"

Obviously, they did not believe his claim to deity. No knowledgeable Hebrew believed a man could also be God. That was paganism, that was blasphemy.

After the Crucifixion and Resurrection

Did the apostles/disciples grasp Jesus was God incarnate after the crucifixion? Not until Jesus appeared to them. In the days between the crucifixion and resurrection the apostles and disciples went into hiding, not expecting Jesus would resurrect, John 20:19. What about when the empty tomb was reported by the women? No, their words seemed like idle tales, Luke 24:11. How about when Peter and John saw the empty tomb. No, Peter was amazed at what happened, Luke 24:12, and John believed a miracle had happened, but "they did not yet understand the Scripture, that Jesus must rise out from the dead," John 20:9.

Late on the resurrection day, about 8:00 p.m. [Westcott, 288], Jesus appeared to ten apostles, and others, Judas being dead and Thomas being absent, John 20:19. Did they then believe? They "rejoiced, having seen the Lord," but there is no positive indication they believed he was God incarnate. Eight days later Jesus again appeared to his apostles, and this time Thomas was present, John 20:26. Thomas sees Jesus and declares him to be, "My Lord and my God." All the events of the preceding three years suddenly added up for him to faith in Jesus the Christ as his God. Did the other apostles came to this same belief then, or perhaps eight days earlier? There is no positive indication they did, no indication they did not.

The same is true in John 21, when Jesus appeared to some of them at the lake in Galilee. Thomas was there, and Peter, John and James, and two who are not identified, so we know there was at least one person there, Thomas, who believed Jesus was God incarnate. Many days later Jesus appeared to the eleven in Galilee, at "the mountain which Jesus directed them. And having seen him, they worshiped; but some doubted," Matthew 28:16–17. Believing the man in front of you is deity is a difficult thing to grasp, even if he has resurrected from the dead.

At Matthew 28:19, prior to the ascension, Jesus gives the Trinitarian statement, but we do not have any comments about or from those who were present. Nor do we see any comments about or from the apostles and disciples at the ascension, as recorded in Mark 16:15–20; Luke 24:47–43; Acts 1:4–11.

At the Ascension, and on the Day of Pentecost

Did the apostles believe Jesus was deity at the ascension? Matthew's statement at 28:17 probably still applies, "they worshiped, but some doubted." They asked the Messiah about the kingdom, Acts 1:6, which supports the view some believed he was the Messiah, and some doubted he was God incarnate. But on the day of Pentecost, they were given understanding. Acts 2:33, "Therefore [the Christ] being exalted to the right hand of God." Acts 2:34, "God has made this Jesus, whom, you crucified, both Lord and Christ." Peter makes the same claim Jesus did at his trial, "you will see the Son of Man sitting at the right hand of the Power," Matthew 26:64. The Holy Spirit had come in power and given them understanding.

Jesus the Christ is the God-man

I have addressed selected scriptures to show that during Jesus' earthly ministry, the apostles did not understand this man, Jesus of Nazareth, whom they came to believe was the Christ, was also God incarnate. I have shown that the fallen angels did not realize Jesus the Christ was God the Son incarnate. Nor his family, nor his enemies.

We must be clear their disbelief was not because Jesus was reluctant or hesitant to reveal his deity (see below). But why did they not believe? There were those who naturally lacked the spiritual perception, 1 Corinthians 2:14, to comprehend God could and did become incarnate, because they lacked faith in Jesus as the Messiah. In those who did have faith Jesus was the Messiah, the Holy Spirit withheld their understanding of Jesus as the God-man.

I believe the Holy Spirit withheld understanding so Jesus the Christ could interact with his apostles and disciples as a normal human being. There is a holy fear when you believe God is standing in front of you, e.g., John 21:12. Although Jesus the Christ is clearly the God-man, and gave clear and sufficient evidence he was the God-man, it is just as clear he lived his life in complete dependence upon and submission to God. His life set the pattern for every believer. Believers are not to ask, "What would Jesus do?" because no believer has the same mission, nor the spiritual empowerment (every spiritual gift) that Jesus was given, to do what Jesus did. The believer is to walk with Jesus daily, in that same attitude of submission to and dependence upon God that characterized Jesus' life on the earth.

Jesus did reveal his deity. In every miracle Jesus revealed his deity; but they believed God had given great power and authority to a prophet, who might be (and some came to believe) was the Messiah.

In John 5, Jesus reveals his deity.

John 5:17, My Father is working up to the present moment, and I am working.

The Hebrew scholars had asked themselves, "If God keeps the universe running on the Sabbath, is God violating the Sabbath day by working on the Sabbath?" No. The Jews rationalized their law by recognizing the entire universe as God's domain. Therefore, in working on the Sabbath God did not break their Sabbath rules; but for anyone else work on the Sabbath was a religious and civil violation. Thus the enormity of Jesus' declaration: if Jesus had the authority to work when the Father worked, then Jesus was equal to the Father. But the Hebrews rejected Jesus' claim, "because he not only was breaking the Sabbath, but also he called God his own father, making himself equal with God."

Jesus claimed to be increate. John 5:26, "For as the Father has life in himself, so also to the Son he gave life, to have in himself." Only God is eternal (without beginning or ending), and only God has life-in-himself (self-existent, Exodus 3:14, "I exist because I exist"). The Father has granted the Son to have life-in-himself. Does this mean there was a time when the Son did not have life-in-himself, but now the Father has given him life-in-himself? Or perhaps Jesus meant that his incarnate self was granted life-in-himself by the Father. No. John clearly states that God the Son always had life-in-himself, John 1:4, "in him was life." When Jesus the Christ made this claim at John 5:26 he was claiming deity.

Jesus claimed, John 10:30, "I and my Father are one." The word translated "one" is the neuter *hen* not the masculine *heís*. Jesus and his Father are not one person, as the masculine would imply (else Jesus could not pray to the Father, or act in obedience to the Father, or be able to say, "I and my Father."). What is asserted is not identity but unity. Because of their essential deity unity they are one in the action of preserving the sheep. The neuter *hen* might lead some to believe the Father and Son are only one in purpose and action, a union of persons, not a unity of persons. But the Jews understood Jesus to be saying he and the Father were a unity of essence, 10:33, "You, being a man, make yourself God." They didn't believe him, but they understood his claim.

Application of this Doctrine

The views expressed in this article honor the scriptures as the accurate, authentic, and therefore credible record of all that was said and done—in a word, inspiration. One applies the inspiration of the Scripture by understanding the words in the plain and normal sense of their meaning—the Literal hermeneutic. Using the analyses methods of the Literal hermeneutic one arrives at an accurate interpretation—the historical-cultural, contextual, lexical-syntactical, theological, literary, and doctrinal analysis of the Scripture.

By properly using the Literal hermeneutic, performing all the required analysis, the interpreter avoids two errors. The first is the one mentioned at the beginning of this article: preaching Reformed traditions. The Reformed traditional interpretations that "discover" (meaning "insert") Christ into every Old Testament Scripture bleeds over into the New Testament interpretation that "discovers" the apostles and disciples knew the Christ was God incarnate. The conflict that view sets up is unbearable. If, as proposed, the apostles knew

Jesus was God incarnate, then why did Peter rebuke the God-man for announcing his death? Why did Judas betray the God-man? Why did all but John abandon the God-man at the crucifixion? Why did the eleven hide in fear after the crucifixion? Why did "some doubt," after the resurrection, Matthew 27:17? We come away believing the apostles were faithless men, not true to their convictions, and thereby justify our own lack of faith.

Better is the view expressed in this article. When we see the apostles as men of faith beset with the weaknesses that trouble every believer, our faith is encouraged and strengthened. They persevered. So too every believer is able to persevere.

The second error is even more pernicious: adding to the gospel of salvation. The gospel of salvation is simple volitional faith in God's testimony concerning ourselves as sinners and the risen Christ as Savior. Nothing else is required. But some want to add to the gospel, by making belief in Christ as deity necessary to saving faith. The apostles were saved without understanding Christ was deity.

We see their salvation in the spiritual perception given to them by the Holy Spirit. One sample should suffice, John 6:68–69, spoken by Peter after the feeding of the 5,000. Jesus had forced a crisis of faith. He had accused those who sought him after that event of seeking not him, but what he could give him—prizing the gift more than the giver. Some of those following Christ responded to this crisis negatively, they "turned back and no longer walked with him." Jesus asked the twelve, "Do you also desire to go away?" Peter gave the response of a saved man, "Master, to whom will we go? You have the words of eternal life. And we have believed and have known that you are the holy one of God." Not, "you are the holy God," but, "you are the holy one of God," exactly as the Scripture testifies: the *māshîah*, the *christós*, is the son of the living God, Psalm 2:7.

Conclusion

As Bible students, how we interpret Scripture is critical. The Literal hermeneutic requires a complete consistency in the interpretation of Old Testament and New Testament revelation: the primary meaning of a passage is in that passage. We dare not impose the knowledge given in the New Testament revelation onto the understanding of the Old Testament peoples. We dare not "reinterpret or transcend Old

Testament passages in a way that overrides or cancels the original authorial intent of the Old Testament writers" [Vlach, *Dispensational*, 31]. To even suggest the Old Testament peoples had the knowledge available only in the New Testament revelation is to teach extrabiblical revelation in Old Testament times—the four gospels are Old Testament times, being a form of Old Testament historical narrative. Surely as interpreters we want to avoid the hermeneutical error of putting New Testament revelation into the minds of the Old Testament peoples?

During the time of Jesus' earthly ministry, the apostles did not understand Jesus was God incarnate. Their daily interactions with him argue against that understanding. A simple example. In the last few months of their third year with him (between January–March, AD 32), Jesus will go to the tomb of Lazarus. Philip will say to his fellow disciples, "Let us also go, that we might die with him." Even after almost three years, after watching all the miracles, hearing all the discourses, they still did not believe Jesus was God incarnate. That would be paganism, that would be blasphemy—under the Law of Moses that would be idolatry, giving the invisible God a material image—and therefore the thought was never entertained. The Holy Spirit withheld their understanding, as suitable to the mission of the Christ. And even today, we avoid idolatry by understanding Jesus is not God, Jesus the Christ is the God-man, and so we worship the God-man, not the man.

The apostles interacted with Jesus as a man, not as the almighty God YHWH. The man born blind and healed by Jesus expresses the understanding of all who believed Jesus was the Christ. John 9:33 (highlighting added), "If this *man* were not *from* God, he would not be able to do anything." In their understanding Jesus was a man sent from God, not a man who was God.

Sources

Alexander, Joseph Addison. *Commentary on the Gospel of Mark*. 1864. Reprinted, Minneapolis, MN: Klock & Klock Christian Publishers, 1980.

Barackman, Floyd. *Practical Christian Theology*. Grand Rapids, MI: Kregel Publications, 1998.

Baron, David. *Rays of Messiah's Glory*. 1886. Reprinted, Eugene, OR: Wipf & Stock Publishers, 2001.

_____. *The Servant of Jehovah*. London: Marshall, Morgan, & Scott, n.d.

Beale, G.K. and D.A. Carson. ed. *Commentary on the New Testament Use of the Old Testament*. Grand Rapids, MI: Baker Academic, 2007.

Berkhoff, L. *Systematic Theology*. London: The Banner of Truth Trust, 1959.

Boettner, Loraine. *The Millennium*. Philadelphia, PA: The Presbyterian and Reformed Publishing Co., 1958.

Brenton, Sir Lancelot, C. L. *The Septuagint with Apocrypha: English*. London: Samuel Bagster & Sons, 1851. Reprinted http://ecmarsh.com, 2010.

Calvin, John, *Calvin's Commentaries* Grand Rapids, MI: Baker Book House, 1996.

Chafer, Lewis Sperry. *Systematic Theology*. Vol 3. Grand Rapids, MI: Kregel Publications, 1993.

Charnock, Stephen. *The Works of Stephen Charnock*. 1684. Reprinted 1865. Reprinted Carlisle, PA: Banner of Truth Trust, 1986.

Couch, Mal. *Messianic Systematic Theology of the Old Testament*. Clifton, TX: Scofield Ministries, 2010.

Criswell, W. A. *The Scarlet Thread Through the Bible*. No publication data.

Dolezal, James E. *All That Is In God*. Grand Rapids, MI: Reformation Heritage Books, 2017.

Edersheim, Alfred. *The Life and Times of Jesus the Messiah*. 1883. Reprinted, Grand Rapids, MI: Eerdmans Publishing, 1971.

Enns, Paul. *The Moody Handbook of Theology.* Chicago, IL: Moody Press, 1989.

Grudem, Wayne. *Systematic Theology.* Grand Rapids, MI: Zondervan, 1994.

Hamilton, Victor P. *The Book of Genesis, Chapters 1–17.* New International Commentary on the Old Testament. Grand Rapids, MI: Eerdmans Publishing, 1990.

Harris, R. Laird and Gleason L. Archer Jr., and Bruce K. Waltke. *Theological Wordbook of the Old Testament.* 2 vols. Chicago, IL: Moody Press, 1980.

Harris, Murray J. *Colossians and Philemon.* Exegetical Guide to the New Testament. Nashville, TN: B&H Publishing, 2010.

Harrison, Everett, F., ed. *Baker's Dictionary of Theology.* Grand Rapids, MI: Baker Book House, 1960.

Hodge, Charles. *Systematic Theology.* 1871–1873. Reprinted, Grand Rapids, MI: Eerdmans Publishing, 1981.

Kaiser, Walter C. Jr. *Is It The Case That Christ Is The Same Object Of Faith In The Old Testament? (Genesis 15:1–6).* Journal of the Evangelical Theological Society 55:2 (2012).

_____. *The Promise-Plan of God.* Grand Rapids, MI: Zondervan, 2008.

Kaiser, Walter C. and Moisés Silva. *An Introduction to Biblical Hermeneutics: The Search for Meaning.* Grand Rapids, MI: Zondervan, 1994.

Keach, Benjamin. *Preaching from the Types and Metaphors of the Bible.* Grand Rapids: MI: Kregel Publications, 1972.

Keil, C. F. and F. Delitzsch. *Commentary on the Old Testament.* Ten Volumes. 1866–91. Reprinted, Peabody, MA: Hendrickson Publishers, 1996.

Kelley, J.N.D. *Early Christian Doctrines.* 1960. Reprinted, Peabody, MA: Hendrickson Publishers, 2003

Kittel, Gerhard and Gerhard Friedrich. *Theological Dictionary of the New Testament.* 10 vols. Translated by Geoffrey W. Bromiley. Grand Rapids, MI: Eerdmans Publishing, 1967.

Marsh, Cory M., and James I. Fazio. *Discovering Dispensationalism, Tracing the Development of Dispensational Thought From the*

First to the Twenty-first Century. El Cajon, CA: SCS Press, 2023.

Miles, Paul. ed. *Current Issues in Soteriology: Papers Presented at a Symposium of The International Society for Biblical Hermeneutics.* International Society for Biblical Hermeneutics. Kindle ed. 2021.

_____. Ed. *What is Dispensationalism?* Wynnewood, OK: Grace Abroad Ministries, 2018.

Morris, Leon. *The Gospel According to Matthew.* The New International Commentary on the New Testament. Grand Rapids, MI: Eerdmans Publishing, 1992.

Moulton, J. H. and G. Milligan. *Vocabulary of the Greek Testament.* 1930. Reprinted, Peabody, MA: Hendrickson Publishers, 1997.

Quiggle, James D. *A Private Commentary on the Bible: Colossians,* Amazon/KDP, 2018.

_____. *A Private Commentary on the Book of Hebrews.* Amazon/KDP, 2012.

_____. *Adam and Eve, A Biography and Theology.* Amazon/KDP, 2011.

_____. *Biblical Essays IV.* Amazon/KDP, 2021.

_____. *Dictionary of Doctrinal Words.* Amazon/KDP, 2018.

_____. *Did Jesus Go To Hell?* Amazon/KDP, 2021.

_____. *God Became Incarnate.* Amazon/KDP, 2014.

_____. *Life, Death, Eternity.* Amazon/KDP, 2019.

_____. *The Literal Hermeneutic, Explained and Illustrated.* Amazon/KDP, 2018, 2020.

_____. *Understanding Dispensational Theology.* Amazon/KDP 2019.

Ramm, Bernard. *Protestant Biblical Interpretation.* Grand Rapids, MI: Baker Book House, 1970.

Roberts, Alexander and James Donaldson. *Ante-Nicene Fathers.* Vol. 1. *The Apostolic Fathers, Justin Martyr, Irenaeus.* 1885. Reprinted, Peabody, MA: Hendrickson Publishers, 1995.

Rydelnik, Michael. *The Messianic Hope: Is the Hebrew Bible Really Messianic?* ed. E. Ray Clendenen. Nashville, TN: B&H Publishing, 2010.

Ryrie, Charles C. *Basic Theology.* 1986, Reprinted, Chicago, IL: Moody

Publishers, 1999.

_____. *Dispensationalism*. Chicago, IL: Moody Press, 1995.

_____. *The Basis of Premillennial Faith*. Neptune, NJ: Loizeaux Brothers, 1953.

Schaff, Philip. *Nicene and Post-Nicene Fathers*. Second Series, Vol. 7. *Cyril of Jerusalem, Gregory Nazianzen*. 1894. Reprinted, Peabody, MA: Hendrickson, 1999.

_____. *Augustin: Expositions of the Book of Psalms*. *Nicene and Post-Nicene Fathers*. First Series, Vol. 8. 1888. Reprinted, Peabody, MA: Hendrickson, 1999.

_____. *The Creeds of Christendom*. 1931. Reprinted, Grand Rapids, MI: Baker Book House, 1983.

Schurer, Emil. *A History of the Jewish People in the Time Of Jesus Christ*. Division 2, vol. 2. 1890. Reprinted Peabody, MA: Hendrickson Publishers, 2020.

Shedd, W. G. T. *Dogmatic Theology*. 1863. 3 vols. Reprinted, Nashville, TN: Thomas Nelson Publishers, 1980.

_____. *The Doctrine of Endless Punishment*. 1885. Reprinted, Carlisle, PA; Banner of truth Trust, 1986.

Sherlin, Keith A. *The Calvinism of Dispensationalism*. Unpublished manuscript. 2023.

Smith, Kevin G. *The Christocentric Principle: Promise, Pitfalls, and Proposal*. Article published in pdf format by the South African Theological Seminary. Accessed via Google 6/9/2023. [https://sats.ac.za/wp-content/uploads/2020/02/].

Stewart, Kenneth J. *Ten Myths About Calvinism*. Downers Grove, IL: InterVarsity Press, 2011.

Thomas, G. Michael. *The Extent of the Atonement*. 1997. Reprinted Eugene, OR: Wipf and Stock Publishers, 2006.

Virkler, Henry A., *Hermeneutics, Principles and Processes of Biblical Interpretation*. Grand Rapids, MI: Baker Books, 1981.

Vlach, Michael J. *Dispensationalism, Essential Beliefs and Common Myths*. 2008. Rev. Reprinted, Los Angeles, CA: Theological Studies Press, 2017.

_____. *Premillennialism*. Los Angeles, CA: Theological Studies Press,

2015.

Wenham, Gordon J. *Genesis 1–15*. Word Biblical Commentary. Vol 1. Waco, TX: Word, 1987.

Westcott, B. F. *The Gospel According to St. John*. 1881. Reprinted, Grand Rapids, MI: William B. Eerdmans Publishing, 1978.

Zodhiates, Spiros. *The Complete Word Study Dictionary: New Testament*. Revised. Chattanooga, TN: AMG Publishers, 1993.